STUDY GUIDE
to accompany

GOVERNMENT IN AMERICA
Fifth Edition

STUDY GUIDE
to accompany

Lineberry • Edwards • Wattenberg

GOVERNMENT IN AMERICA
Fifth Edition

David M. Billeaux

Corpus Christi State University

HarperCollins*Publishers*

Study Guide to accompany GOVERNMENT IN AMERICA, 5/E
By David M. Billeaux

Copyright © 1991 by HarperCollins Publishers Inc.

ISBN: 0-673-52136-2
90 91 92 93 94 9 8 7 6 5 4 3 2 1

CONTENTS

INTRODUCTION

So, here you are about to take a course in American government.
If this is, for you, the first step in putting together a major in
political science, you will want to MAKE THE MOST OF IT!!! If, on
the other hand, to you this is just something the state
legislature says you have to take, or a part of a general
education social science requirement, you might as well make the
best of it (sigh). Of course, you may be taking the course simply
because you want to learn more about how the government works so
that you might be a better citizen. My experience suggests that
this is unlikely, but if so in your case it is most laudable
indeed! This study guide is intended to help you to make the most
(or best, if that be the case) of the course, and learn something
along the way. Thus, it should be useful to you regardless of the
source of your motivation.

The Guide is designed with a couple of general assumptions you
need to be aware of, and each chapter is divided into seven
sections that I will briefly describe below. First the general
assumptions. The most basic general assumption underlying the
Guide is that you want to get a good grade. I assume that is the
most important practical objective of most students. To do that,
however, you will have to learn something (a lot) about American
government - which is the most important practical objective of
the text, your instructor, and yours truly. That is the little
trick in our educational process and there is no way around it.
The deal is: you can meet your objective if you will help us meet
ours. The Guide is intended to help everybody get what they want.
For you, a good grade. For your instructor, authors, and myself,
a student who knows a lot about American government.

To that end, the Guide is designed to help you develop some
general learning skills useful in this course and throughout your
college career. Like it or not, most of us learn through
repetition. Thus the Guide is laid out in such a way that it
takes you over things several times. (It is not because I just
forgot that something was mentioned before, you see.) When you
begin to feel a little impatient with going over something - "This
again?" - or a question begins to seem "stupid" or "ridiculously
simple" - is when you know that you have really thoroughly learned
it.

You'll notice that this repetition is particularly prevalent in
the Guide's emphasis on Key Terms. The authors didn't go to the

trouble of identifying them, and the publisher didn't use all that extra ink to bold face them for no reason. If fact, introductory courses that "survey" a subject like this one are mostly about basic concepts. In order to be familiar with the concepts you must learn the subject matter's basic vocabulary which refers to the concepts. If understand the concepts well enough to use these terms yourself in original sentences, etc. - you are a long way toward success in the course. The guide will try hard to get you to work on these terms. (Course sounds easier already doesn't it?)

The Guide is also based on the assumption that you will learn better if you are "active" rather than "passive." Thus it provides an abundance of self testing materials, and tries to get you to read actively - looking for answers. The test items have the associated page listed with them for this purpose and two sections, Learning Objectives and Reading for Content, are intended to help you read with an objective or a question in mind. A reader who is looking for something is far more likely to find it, and remember it later, than one who is reading "passively" or with the only objective being to get to the end of the chapter.

I would also strongly recommend carrying over this bias toward "active" learning to the classroom. Think about your most successful (and probably most pleasurable) learning experiences. In all likelihood they involved doing something - trial and error, experimentation, and physical effort. In a very general sense, these things are transferable to studying and classroom learning. This sort of learning requires mental effort, trial and error with thoughts, and experimentation with ideas. Don't slip into the habit of acquiring information passively. Don't just sit in the classroom and take down every word the instructor says. Don't unquestioningly accept everything you read in the textbook. Question the information offered. Ask "what if" questions based on the information in the class lecture and text. Can you think of exceptions to generalizations made in the text and in class? Are their alternative explanations for some of the phenomena discussed? Try to polk holes in your text's arguments, your instructor's arguments, even your own arguments. Your mind needs "pegs" to hang information on if it is to remember - a structure of association -active learning helps you to build your structure - provide the "pegs." Besides, it makes the whole process a lot more fun. Don't be discouraged if this seems hard at first, or you are wrong a time or two, this is a skill that it takes time and practice to perfect, just like many others you have mastered in the past.

Now that I have you all pumped up and excited about active learning, let me introduce you to each of the sections of the Study Guide and briefly explain their function and use. Two of the sections, Learning Objectives and the Pretest, you should take a look at before you even start to read the chapter. They will give you an idea of what you can expect to learn from the chapter. One section, Reading for Content, should be used as you read the chapter so that you might better study it actively. The remainder of the sections are for review, special help, or just for fun.

LEARNING OBJECTIVES

Placed at the beginning of the chapter, the list of statements of what the student should be able to do after reading the text sometimes looks scary. Well, don't be frightened. These objectives can't hurt you. Don't let this imposing list discourage you either. When starting out, the list of objectives should serve only to alert you to key general points to look for as you read. I really think that they are more important function is _after_ you have studied the material. They provide a general guide to the information you should have mastered. Reviewing them before you take the Review Test, or leave for the next chapter, will give you an indication of how thoroughly you have the chapter's material down. Return to the Learning Objectives often, particularly before your exam.

PRETEST

The Pretest is sort of an "active learning" introduction to the chapter. It poses real questions (these also appear in your instructor's test bank) to get you thinking about the chapter's material and reading in order to find answers to specific questions. Don't be discouraged if you get most of these wrong - there no reason that you should know them! When you are through, go back and look up the answers. This will give you a good active learning overview of the chapter, the reward of some immediate practical knowledge, and prove to you that those learning objectives are "knowable." Doing the Pretest should also help to sensitize you to the form and style of the questions you will encounter on exams. Not a small aid in achieving your primary objective - a good grade.

READING FOR CONTENT

This is potentially the most important part of the Guide. It is important that you use it fully and use it correctly. In it you find a series of questions, each associated with a major section of the chapter. Here are my recommendations as to how best to use them:

1. Read all of the questions associated with a section and get familiar with them.
2. Then read the section with these questions in mind. As you read actively look for the answers to these questions.
3. As you find passages that provide answers underline or highlight these points.
4. When you reach the end of a major section, go back and try to answer each question associated with the section.
5. Check your answers for accuracy and inclusiveness with the passages you have highlighted or underlined. Fill out your responses to the questions after rereading these passages.

6. Now you are ready to go on to the next section of the chapter.

I know that this sounds like a lot. But this is what it takes to really actively study the material. Once you get practiced at this method of using the Reading For Content it will go fast, and you will be surprised at the increase in your level of comprehension and retention. It will make reviewing much easier, and your grades much higher. You will soon be able to provide you own little sets of question and apply the method to all your reading oriented courses. It is a bit more work than merely letting your eyes float across the words, but eventually it "pays to get As."

CHAPTER OVERVIEW

A rather thorough Chapter Overview is one of the unique features of this Study Guide. Often overviews are so sketchy as to be useful as neither an introduction or a review. This overview is thorough enough to be useful for either purpose, but its primary function should be for review. One good way to use it for review is to see how it matches up with the passages of the text you have highlighted or underlined. Much of it should be the same. Thus, it can help you review the questions in the Reading For Content section prior to exams. If it is more complete than your highlighting is some areas, use it to "fill out" your review. It can also be used for a quick, comprehensive review right before a test. The overviews are usually just 15 - 20 percent of the length of the chapter, so even a thorough reading won't take too long.

The drawback to such a complete Chapter Overview is the temptation they present as a substitute for reading the chapter itself. In short, like many good things, the Chapter Overview can be abused as well as used. Let me emphasize that it is not only not intended to take the place of a thorough reading of the chapter, it does not take the place of such a reading! They just aren't that thorough! If you need proof, try taking a Review Test armed only with a reading of the Chapter Overview. They don't, on their own, reach the level of detail necessary for taking an exam. As a review device, however, for one who has already carefully studied the full text, they will serve very well to refresh the memory of broader information. So, use them, don't abuse them. If you depend on them, the exam is likely to abuse you - and you can depend on that.

DOING RESEARCH

Students are often required to write a research paper in conjunction with an introductory American government course (as well they should be). These research and writing assignments give you an opportunity to enhance your learning by exploring some topic in much greater depth, and to practice your vital writing skills. Practice in organizing and expressing your thoughts on paper is of unsurpassed importance in your college education. The ability to do so will open many doors in the world that waits beyond the ivy. This section is included because many students have difficulty selecting a topic and getting started on their research. It is designed to provide some topical ideas associated with the subject matter of each chapter, and some direction on source material. If you have a paper assigned, get started early narrowing down your topic. Look ahead at this section in the guide for chapters to come. By the time we get to foreign and defense policy, for example, it will be too late to start a paper on SDI. Take your research and writing seriously and it will pay serious dividends.

REVIEW TEST

The Review Test should be taken after you have studied the text and reviewed the chapter's Learning Objectives and Reading For Content questions. Treat it like a real exam on the chapter's content. It will likely be more intensive and detailed than the real one, so doing well on it should be a good indication that you are ready. It is made up of items available to your instructor in his or her test bank, so it is a "real" test and useful in getting a "sense" for the style of questions.

It is intended to be used both for evaluation and as a learning device, however. If you miss some items, use the associated page number to read the passage in the text containing the answer. Knowing not only what is the correct answer, but why it is correct will help it stick in your mind.

Also, you will notice that there are not only a lot of practice questions included in the Guide (60 per chapter counting both the Pretest and the Review Test), but they are often rather long and fully stated. This is done to make the items themselves informational and useful as a review and refresher. Repeat the tests often until the information in the question, as well as the correct answer is second nature to you.

As with the Chapter Overview, there may be a temptation to abuse this extensive practice test set. Merely memorizing the answers to these items might help with the test, but it will not adequately prepare you. While the items are drawn from the instructor's test bank, the Study Guide does not have all the bank's questions in it. The instructor has more than enough to use only questions that do not appear here on the test. Not to mention those that come from his or her unique lecture material. Thus, the practice tests here are just that - good for practice. They are not, however, in and of themselves, a substitute for studying the material thoroughly.

BEFORE GOING ON

This sections simply provides you with the answers to the Review Test and, always and for every chapter, encourages you to be sure you know the Key Terms listed at the end of each chapter. Just for fun I pick one as the "word of the week," that is a particularly impressive "college" word you can spring on your friends, enemies, parents, dates, or pets - whatever.

Before you "go on" to the Guide, the text, the course, the semester, the rest of your college career (I'll stop with that), I'd like to encourage you generally to follow the common general practices that lead to success. These are simple and obvious, but often violated or thought to be "not all that important."

1. Try to go to class everyday. Don't drag yourself if you are about to pass away or an infectious hazard to others, but go in all other cases. Nothing is more important for success - not even the hours spent studying. Teachers stress what they think is important, and that is what shows up on tests. To know what is important to your instructor you need to be there.

2. Take an active part in class. Keep your mind active and ask questions about material you have read in the text and about points the instructor is making. Most instructors will welcome the challenge, it will make the lecture less of a "lecture" and more a "discussion," and it will help you learn what is being discussed. Besides, it will make the hour go faster.

3. Develop good note taking skills. Fundamentally, this means not trying to take down every word. That is not going to be possible unless the instructor talks very slowly - in which case all will likely be bored off their chairs. Instead, listen carefully to what is said. Jot down the point, and one example that illustrates it. Just enough to serve to remind you of what went on. It is good to go over the notes after class and fill in any needed details while still fresh in mind. If there are gaps or questions, stop by and ask your professor. After all, being there for you is why they are making that big money.

4. I know it is asking a lot, but try to schedule your study time so you have read the assignment before the class meeting on it. One reason to do this goes back to the importance of those vocabulary words again. A prior reading will familiarize you with terms that are likely to come up in class. It will also put you "a step ahead" - and thus more capable of understanding, raising questions, and challenging the text and the instructor.

In any case, make the most, or best, of the course. Learn a lot so you can get that good grade. Most of all - be an "active learner" so you can have some fun in the process.

                                        Dave Billeaux
                                        Corpus Christi State University

CHAPTER 1

INTRODUCING GOVERNMENT IN AMERICA

CHAPTER LEARNING OBJECTIVES

After reading Chapter 1, you should be able to:

1. Identify the basic themes of GOVERNMENT IN AMERICA.
2. Define and distinguish between government and politics.
3. Explain how government and politics are related to public policy.
4. Explain what governments do.
5. Identify the major actors in politics.
6. Explain the importance of linkage institutions.
7. Identify the major policy-making institutions.
8. Identify the principles of traditional democratic theory.
9. Distinguish the key differences in the three contemporary theories of American democracy.
10. Distinguish the key differences between liberals and conservatives.

PRETEST QUESTIONS

The pretest below will give you an idea of the state of your knowledge about Chapter 1. The questions should also help you learn what to look for while studying the text. Take the whole pretest, then check your answers against the key that follows (don't peek!). As you read the chapter, watch for where these questions are addressed (indicated after each question) so that you may learn why the answer is what it is.

1. _____ was replaced in office due to revolutionary upheaval in the twentieth century.
   (a) Czar Nicholas II
   (b) The Shah of Iran
   (c) Ferdinand Marcos
   (d) all of the above
   Page 6

2. An example of a public good is:
   (a) clean air.

1

      (b)   a loaf of bread.
      (c)   HUD housing.
      (d)   clothing.
Page 7

3.   Interest groups that are so narrow in their views that they
      examine a candidate's record on only one specific issue is
      called a:
      (a)   plurality group.
      (b)   participation group.
      (c)   single-issue group.
      (d)   none of the above
Page 9

4.   Almost no one thought about flag-burning until 1989 when:
      (a)   there was a sudden epidemic of flag-burning incidents
           around the country.
      (b)   a flag-burning incident set fire to the house of North
           Carolina Senator Jesse Helms.
      (c)   the Supreme Court ruled that flag-burning was punishable
           on the federal level.
      (d)   the Supreme Court ruled that the First Amendment
           protected flag-burning as free expression.
Page 10

5.   Today, the power of _____ is so great that most
      political scientists consider it a fourth policy-making
      institution.
      (a) the bureaucracy
      (b) the media
      (c) the Internal Revenue Service
      (d) the Central Intelligence Agency
Page 14

6.   Implementation of public policy is generally taken care of by:
      (a)   acts of Congress.
      (b)   the president.
      (c)   the courts.
      (d)   the bureaucracy.
Page 14

7.   The countries Czechoslovakia, Poland, East Germany,
      Romania, Bulgaria and Hungary were claimed by the Soviet Union
      after World War II and referred to as:
      (a)   the Soviet Bloc.
      (b)   the Iron Curtain.
      (c)   the Warsaw Pact.
      (d)   all of the above
Page 15

8.   In Romania, _____ and his wife tried to flee the
      country after ordering troops to fire upon demonstrators.

They were captured, put on trial and summarily executed.
- (a) Lech Walesa
- (b) Vladimir Tepesch Dracul
- (c) Nicolae Ceausescu
- (d) Deng Xiao-Ping

Page 15

9. _____, one of the delegates to the Constitutional Convention, said that "the evils we experience flow from the excesses of democracy."
- (a) Thomas Jefferson
- (b) Eldridge Gerry
- (c) Benjamin Franklin
- (d) John Jay

Page 16

10. Essential to enlightened understanding among the general citizenry is (are):
- (a) interest groups.
- (b) free speech and free press.
- (c) the right to property.
- (d) political parties.

Page 17

11. Although Americans believe in majority rule, they also feel it is vital to protect:
- (a) minority rights.
- (b) equality of condition.
- (c) single interest groups.
- (d) none of these.

Page 18

12. The _____ theory contends that our society is divided among class lines and that an upper-class elite rules regardless of the formal niceties of governmental organization.
- (a) elite
- (b) pluralist
- (c) hyperpluralist
- (d) all of these

Page 19

13. In the United States, about _____ of the nation's wealth is held by one percent of the population.
- (a) five percent
- (b) ten percent
- (c) twenty percent
- (d) a quarter

Page 19

14. _____ theory holds that ordinary citizens have the good sense to reach political judgments and that government has

the capacity to act upon those judgments.
(a)   Pluralist
(b)   Traditional democratic
(c)   Elite
(d)   Hyperpluralist
Page 19

15.   As human knowledge has expanded, it has become _____ to make
      knowledgeable decisions.
      (a)   easier
      (b)   much easier
      (c)   increasingly difficult
      (d)   impossible
Page 20

16.   Altogether, our government spends about one out of every
      _____ dollars of our gross national product.
      (a)   three
      (b)   five
      (c)   seven
      (d)   ten
Page 22

17.   In the United States, _____ support a more active
      role for government (in most spheres), together with higher
      spending and greater economic regulation.
      (a)   conservatives
      (b)   populists
      (c)   liberals
      (d)   libertarians
Page 25

18.   In 1987, _____ dropped his presidential ambitions
      after it was discovered that he had plagiarized one of his
      speeches from Neil Kinnock, head of Britain's Labour Party.
      (a)   Pat Robertson
      (b)   Gary Hart
      (c)   Joseph Biden
      (d)   Richard Gephardt
Page 30

19.   In the 1988 presidential campaign, George Bush and his
      campaign manager, Lee Atwater, succeeded in making a
      household name out of convicted rapist _____ to use against
      Michael Dukakis (who had been Governor of Massachusetts when
      the man was furloughed and committed the crime).
      (a)   Gerry Studds
      (b)   Barney Frank
      (c)   Willie Horton
      (d)   Donald "Buzz" Lukens
Page 31

20.   More and more, policy analysts and philosophers are
      warning that our society will need to _____ medical

care.
(a)   provide universal
(b)   ration
(c)   cut down on
(d)   end
Page 32

Pretest Answers:

1: d	11: d
2: a	12: a
3: c	13: d
4: d	14: b
5: a	15: c
6: d	16: a
7: d	17: c
8: c	18: c
9: b	19: c
10: b	20: b

READING FOR CONTENT

Listed below are sets of questions associated with the content of
each major section of Chapter 1. Carefully review the questions
associated with each section of the text before reading the
section. Have the questions in mind as you read the section and,
when you reach the end of each section, stop and see if you can
answer the questions well. If not, reread the relevant paragraphs
until you are sure of your response to each of the questions.

I.   Government, Politics, and Public Policy

      What is government?
      What do governments do?
      What is politics?
      Why do people get involved in politics?
      What is public policy?

II.   The Political System

      What is a political system?
      When does a political issue arise?
      What do linkage institutions do?
      What are three linkage institutions?
      Why are policy impacts important?

III. Democratic Government

      What are the principles of traditional democratic theory?
      What are the key views of pluralist theory?
      What are the key views of elite and class theory?

What are the key views of hyperpluralism?
What are the contemporary challenges to democracy?

IV. The Size of Government in America

How big is American Government?
What are the views of liberals on government's role?
What are the views of conservatives on government's role?
How does the U.S. government compare with other nation's?

V. Ethics and Politics: A Contradiction in Terms?

How is government involved with ethics?
What is political ethics?
Why is ethics in government and politics important?

CHAPTER OVERVIEW

I. Introduction (4-5)

Chapter 1 introduces three important concepts: government, politics and public policy. It also raises two questions that are themes of the text: "How should we be governed?" and "What should government do?" The first question gets at who holds power, while the second explores what the government does as a result of who holds power.

II. Government, Politics, and Public Policy (5-11)

Government, politics, and public policy are interrelated. Government makes decisions about public policy (what government does) through politics.

A. Government

Government is important to you because it fundamentally affects your standard of living, your freedoms, and your opportunities.

1. What Is Government? The institutions that make public policy for a society, such as our national Congress, the president, courts and bureaucracy, are known as GOVERNMENT. We also have similar institutions at the state and local level that are part of government in America.

2. What Governments Do. All governments, regardless of structure and form, share some functions in common. Among these functions are: 1) maintaining national defense; 2) providing public goods (things that everyone can share like clean air or public parks); 3) maintain public order (police powers to control crime or fight drug abuse, for example); 4) Providing public services (such as schools and hospitals); 5) socializing the young into the

political culture; 6) Collect taxes (to pay for services and defense).

Providing national defense and social services involves many questions about what government should do. Exactly how much defense is enough and how high social security taxes need to be, for example. We answer such questions through politics.

B. Politics

1. What Politics Is. One famous and useful definition of POLITICS is "Who gets what, when, and how" offered by Harold D. Lasswell. The "who" includes voters, candidates, political leaders, groups, and parties. The "how" involves bargaining, supporting, compromising and lobbying. The "what" refers to the public policies that come from government and distribute benefits (services) and burdens (taxes).

2. Political Involvement. People get involved in politics for many reasons and at many levels. In America most choose to limit their political participation to voting, and many do not participate in even this simplest and most fundamental political activity. Thousands of Americans, however, treat politics not as a casual civic duty (voting only), but as something critical to their interests. These people form or join interest groups. SINGLE-ISSUE GROUPS (those so single-minded that they base their vote on only one issue) have become a very significant factor in modern politics. Of course, for a very few politics is a vocation. These people make a living holding public office.

Individuals and organized groups get involved in politics because the public policy choices made by governments affect them in significant ways.

3. Public Policy

When people participate they are trying to influence the government's "policy agenda" - "the list of subjects or problems to which government officials...are paying serious attention at any given time." A government's policy agenda changes regularly in response to public demands, which are often a result of widely felt or perceived crises.

PUBLIC POLICY is a choice that government makes in response to some issue on its agenda. These choices include doing nothing - or doing nothing different - about a problem. Political debate often centers around the question of whether the government should act.

III. The Political System (11-14)

Chapter 1

A POLITICAL SYSTEM is set of institutions and activities that link together government, politics, and public policy.

A. Political Issues and Linkage Institutions

A political issue arises when people disagree about a problem or about public policy choices made to deal with a problem. Many issues arise, but government will act only on those that are high on its agenda. In a democratic society, parties, elections, interest groups, and the media are key LINKAGE INSTITUTIONS through which the preferences of citizens help set the government's policy agenda.

B. Making Public Policy: The Policy-making Institutions

The U.S. Constitution established three policy making institutions: Congress, the presidency, and the courts. Most political scientists consider the bureaucracy a fourth policymaking institution. Policymakers within these institutions can scan issues on the policy agenda, select some for attention, and make policies concerning them. Most policies are the product of policymakers in more than one policy-making institution.

C. Policies Have Impacts

POLICY IMPACTS are the effects policy has on people and society's problems. Having a policy implies a goal. Analyzing policy impacts involves the questions of how well a policy achieves its goal - and at what cost.

IV. Democratic Government (14-28)

Democracy is enjoying an unprecedented worldwide popularity. Since 1989 nations from eastern Europe to China to Latin America have experienced resounding demands for democracy. In eastern Europe these demands have resulted in stunning systemic changes.

What is meant by the term DEMOCRACY is not so clear, however. Democracy is often said to be "government by the people," but this definition is not very informative. There can be very different interpretations of who constitutes "the people." The definition used in this book is: Democracy is a means of selecting policymakers and of organizing government so that policy represents and responds to the people's preferences.

A. Traditional Democratic Theory

Robert Dahl suggests five principles for an what we call TRADITIONAL DEMOCRATIC THEORY:
1. Equality in voting (the principle of one person, one vote and an equal chance to express views.)

   2. Effective participation (people must participate in
      political institutions and such participation must be
      representative.)
   3. Enlightened understanding (a free press and speech to
      ensure civic understanding of issues.)
   4. Citizen control of the agenda (citizens can collectively
      make government address the issues they feel are most
      important.)
   5. Inclusion (government must extend rights to all those
      subject to its laws.)

In addition, democracies must practice MAJORITY RULE and preserve
MINORITY RIGHTS. Large societies must democratically select a few
to carry on the affairs of the many. The relationship between the
few leaders and the many followers is one of REPRESENTATION. The
closer the correspondence between representatives and their
electoral majority, the closer the approximation to democracy.

B. Three Contemporary Theories of American Democracy

Theories of American democracy are essentially theories about who
has power and influence.

1. Pluralism. PLURALIST THEORY contends that many groups compete
with one another for control over public policy, with no one group
or set of groups dominating. Bargaining and compromise among the
groups are essential ingredients in our democratic policy process.

2. Elite and Class Theory. ELITE AND CLASS THEORY contends that
our society - like all societies - is divided along class lines
according to wealth and property ownership. The upper class elite
rules regardless of the formal niceties of governmental
organization. Their wealth and property make it possible for them
to control key institutions and most policy decisions.

3. Hyperpluralism. Hyperpluralists claim that too many competing
interests groups cripple government's ability to govern.
HYPERPLURALISM claims that so many groups are so strong that
government is unable to act rationally or consistently. When
politicians try to placate every group, the result is confusing,
contradictory, and muddled policy - or no policy at all.

C. Challenges to Democracy

1. How Can The People Confront Complex Issues? As human knowledge
has expanded, it has become increasingly difficult for the
ordinary citizen to reach the informed judgments required of them
by traditional democratic theory. Instead, we live in a society
of experts, whose technical knowledge is likely to give them
inordinate influence in specific policy areas.

2. Are the People Doing Their Job? Citizens do not seem to take
their citizenship seriously, failing to be informed about who

their leaders are, what policy positions they are taking, or even to bother to vote for them in periodic elections. A lack of informed participation weakens democracy.

3. Is American Democracy Too Dependent On Money? If campaign contributions shape the voting patterns of representatives, they are representing money not people. When elections are bought, manipulated, sold, or sullied, democracy suffers.

D. Some Key Questions About Democracy

The text is designed to help you assess American democracy. Throughout it will be asking important questions about the current state of democracy in the United States.

E. How Big is American Government?

Government in America is a vast enterprize. Taken together, all levels of government (including some 83,237 governmental units) spent about 2 trillion dollars and employed about eighteen million people in 1990.

The national government alone spends about 1.2 trillion dollars, mostly for payments to individuals (like Social Security) and to state and local governments to help them provide their services. National defense and interest on the national debt are other major budget items.

Americans often complain about the cost of government, but there is little support to cut spending on most government programs. Resistance to taxes to cover the costs has resulted in budget deficits. Annual deficits have been very high during the last decade resulting in a national debt (all money owed by the national government) of more than 3 trillion dollars.

F. How Big is Too Big? The Great Debate

Ronald Reagan's election in 1980 signaled a national sense that government had grown too big. In practice, however, we continued to favor more spending for virtually every domestic program. Despite the anti-government rhetoric, government actually grew during the Reagan years.

1. Liberals and Conservatives. The question of the appropriate size of government most clearly divides liberals and conservatives. In most spheres LIBERALS support a more active role for government and conservatives a less active role. The exception is in noneconomic matters of public order and civil liberties. Here CONSERVATIVES favor using government to impose order (greater police powers) and enforce morality (prohibit abortions or promote prayer), while liberals oppose governmental interference with the individual freedoms such actions imply.

10

2. A Comparative Perspective. One way to evaluate such questions as the size of government is to compare the United States with other countries. For example, the United States has a comparatively large percentage of government devoted to national defense. Yet the overall size of government and tax burden is relatively small compared to other nations.

G. Questions about the Size of Government

Debate over the role and size of government is central to contemporary American politics. This is a theme the text will examine in each chapter that follows to help you explore the implications of the way politics, institutions, and policy work in America for the size of government.

V. Ethics And Politics: A Contradiction In Terms? (28-33)

Government is important because its decisions and actions touch our deepest values and most fundamental beliefs and morals. Politics in America has always been shaped by ethical debates. We think about politics partly in terms of right and wrong. POLITICAL ETHICS are matters of right and wrong with respect to government. Recent scandals and the rise of "negative campaigning" in elections have reinforced the belief in many Americans that most or all politicians are corrupt. The average American also suspects that government really serves the interests of the wealthy few.

Though held in relatively low ethical esteem, government and politicians are increasingly asked to face difficult ethical questions. Availability of advanced (and expensive) medical care for the poor is one such ethical issue. Will we have to ration medical care? Local governments will soon have to decide how much to spend to save a life.

DOING RESEARCH ON GOVERNMENT IN AMERICA

It is not too soon to start thinking about your research paper. Begin to select and narrow possible topics and see what your library has for resource material. You can begin to do these little chores some time soon in the time you have between classes.

Though it is an introductory chapter, Chapter 1 provides a wealth of possibilities for possible research topics. Look on page 21, for example, in the section entitled "Some Key Questions about Democracy." These questions all raise matters on which you might focus a lively paper. Moreover, a start can often be found on later pages of GOVERNMENT IN AMERICA! The same can be said for the questions raised in the section entitled "Questions about the Size of Government" on page 27. In addition, ethical questions provide an almost endless source of topics of contemporary relevance. The special "A Question of Ethics" box on page 33 provides one very good example.

So, now that you are all ready to head for the library to see what you can find on some topic, you need to know where to start, right? Well, before you leave for the library, check your copy of GOVERNMENT IN AMERICA. At the end of each chapter are those lists of books "For Further Reading." Check the titles in Chapter 1, or for any other chapter in the text that deals with a topic you are interested in. Also, your text is well documented. Pay attention to the footnotes. These sources could be important for you or could lead you to other sources that serve your purposes.

Armed with a list of whatever you found in the text, you are ready to stop by the library. The card catalogue (or its electronic equivalent) is a good place to begin to look for further books on your topic. Because the process of publishing a book takes a long time, they will not be the source of the most up-to-date information, however. Thus you will want to investigate the periodical literature, as well. At the index bar you will find two indexes that are excellent guides to periodical literature in political science. These are the Public Affairs Information Service (PAIS) and the Social Science Index (SSI). Articles are indexed by both subject and author in each of these resources. If you have any questions, don't hesitate to have your reference librarian help you.

REVIEW TEST

Before going on to the next chapter, reread the learning objectives listed at the beginning of the this chapter. Are you sure you have accomplished them? If not, reread the chapter overview with the "Reading for Content" questions in mind. When you feel prepared, take the review test below. Treat it like a real trial run for course exams and see how you do.

1.   As we approach the Twenty first century, there is a rush to establish _____ in many countries but not everyone agrees on what the word means.
     (a)   democracy
     (b)   socialism
     (c)   democratic socialism
     (d)   totalitarianism
Page 4

2.   Occasionally a society's form of government undergoes radical change. This occurred in America with the rebellion against British colonial rule in:

(a) 1066.
(b) 1492.
(c) 1776.
(d) 1865.
Page 5

3. The United States spends about _____ dollars a year
    on the national defense.
    (a) 2 billion
    (b) 10 billion
    (c) 100 billion
    (d) 300 billion
Page 6

4. In 1990, one of every three dollars earned by an American
    citizen was used to pay _____ taxes.
    (a) national
    (b) state
    (c) local
    (d) all of the above
Page 7

5. Presidential candidate George Bush claimed during the 1988
    campaign that _____ harbor was one of the dirtiest in
    the country.
    (a) San Francisco
    (b) Boston
    (c) New York
    (d) Miami
Page 8

6. When judging voter turnout, America has a _____
    turnout rate.
    (a) very low
    (b) slightly substandard
    (c) moderate
    (d) high
Page 9

7. The Supreme Court decision Webster v. Reproductive Health
    Services (1989) held that:
    (a) a person must have legal counsel when being questioned
         by the police.
    (b) each woman has a legal right to an abortion.
    (c) the state can restrict funds allocated to women who want
         to have an abortion but cannot afford one.
    (d) a person has the right to remain silent during police
         questioning and that anything they say can be used
         against them in a court of law.
 Page 10
8. The influence that single-issue groups have on voters and
    elected officials _____ efforts to seek the middle
    ground on various issues.

      (a)   complicate
      (b)   ease
      (c)   straighten out
      (d)   all of the above
Page 10

9.   Reporter Randy Shilts' book about the American government's response to _____, 'And the Band Played On,' told a sad tale of inaction in the face of this crisis.
      (a)   the Iran/Contra crisis
      (b)   the Watergate break-in
      (c)   the AIDS epidemic
      (d)   the homeless
Page 11

10.   _____ is a major forum through which potential agenda items receive public attention.
      (a)   A convention
      (b)   An election
      (c)   The media
      (d)   A caucus
Page 13

11.   Courts make decisions about what policies mean and whether or not they conflict with _____.
      (a)   the Constitution
      (b)   existing laws
      (c)   state laws already in effect
      (d)   federal laws already in effect
Page 14

12.   _____ policies are made by a single policy-making institution.
      (a)   All
      (b)   Many
      (c)   Very few
      (d)   No
Page 14

13.   _____ are the effects policy has on people and society's problems.
      (a)   Policy impacts
      (b)   Policy agendas
      (c)   Linkage institutions
      (d)   Political issues
Page 14

14.   '_____' began with these words: "A specter is haunting Europe. It is the specter of communism."
      (a)   The Magna Carta

    (b)   The Communist Manifesto
    (c)   What Is To Be Done
    (d)   Roosevelt's Four Freedoms Speech
Page 14

15. In 1990, _____ recommended that the Communist party's right to govern be eliminated from the Soviet Constitution.
    (a)   Soviet President Gorbachev
    (b)   U.S. President George Bush
    (c)   President of Russia Boris Yeltsin
    (d)   Czechoslovakian President Vaclav Havel
Page 14-15

16. In the fall of 1989, Solidarity, the trade union in _____ that had struggled for democracy for a decade, was legally elected to power.
    (a)   Turkey
    (b)   Iran
    (c)   Poland
    (d)   East Germany
Page 15

17. Certainly the most dramatic event in the fall of 1989 was:
    (a)   the tearing down of the Berlin Wall.
    (b)   the Challenger shuttle explosion.
    (c)   the election of George Bush as President of the United States.
    (d)   the release of Nelson Mandela from prison.
Page 15

18. The demonstrations in Tienneman Square in May and June of 1989 brought forth:
    (a)   new and startling reforms in China.
    (b)   the overthrow of the communist leadership in China.
    (c)   a promise for new reform in China.
    (d)   troops who crushed the protest using tanks and guns.
Page 15

19. _____, a delegate to the Constitutional Convention, said that the people "should have as little to do as may be with the government."
    (a)   Roger Sherman
    (b)   George Washington
    (c)   Alexander Hamilton
    (d)   James Madison
Page 16

20. The phrase "government of the people, by the people, and for the people" came from:
    (a)   the Declaration of Independence.

(b) Lincoln's Gettysburg Address.
(c) Marx and Engels' Communist Manifesto.
(d) King John I's Magna Carta.
Page 16

21. _____ is a means of selecting policymakers and of organizing government so that policy represents and responds to the people's preferences.
(a) Democracy
(b) Socialism
(c) Indoctrination
(d) none of the above
Page 16-17

22. According to Robert Dahl's theory, political participation need not be universal, but it must be
(a) majoritarian.
(b) representative.
(c) institutionalized.
(d) none of these.
Page 17

23. Nothing is more fundamental to democratic theory than:
(a) majority rule.
(b) minority rule.
(c) civil rights.
(d) political parties.
Page 18

24. Alexis de Tocqueville wrote that "the very essence of democratic government consists in the absolute sovereignty of _____."
(a) the minority
(b) the middle class
(c) the upper class
(d) the majority
Page 18

25. In America, the relationship between the few leaders and the many followers is one of:
(a) symbiosis.
(b) representation.
(c) distrust.
(d) "blind trust."
Page 18

26. According to _____, bargaining and compromise are essential ingredients in our democracy.
(a) elitists

     (b)   pluralists
     (c)   hyperpluralists
     (d)   socialists
Page 19

27. According to the _____, wealth is the basis of power.
     (a)   pluralist theory
     (b)   hyperpluralists
     (c)   elite theory
     (d)   anti-federalists
Page 19

28. The elite and hyperpluralist theories share the belief that
    _____ is rarely translated into public policy.
     (a)   power
     (b)   wealth
     (c)   the public interest
     (d)   group interest
Page 19

29. _____ is said to be the architect of the American
    economic system and was George Washington's secretary of the
    treasury.
     (a)   Aaron Burr
     (b)   Alexander Hamilton
     (c)   Benjamin Franklin
     (d)   James Madison
Page 20

30. Two pollsters found out that only _____ percent of the
    population knew how their representative in the House of
    Representatives voted on any issue.
     (a)   sixty five
     (b)   forty two
     (c)   twenty three
     (d)   seventeen
Page 20

31. It is up to public officials to actually make policy choices
    since American government is _____ rather than a pure
    democracy.
     (a)   majoritarian
     (b)   representative
     (c)   submissive
     (d)   authoritarian
Page 21

32. In 1990, expenditures for all American governments amounted
    to about _____ dollars.
     (a)   two billion

(b)   twenty billion
(c)   two hundred billion
(d)   two trillion
Page 22

33.   About _____ Americans work for either the state,
      local or federal government.
      (a)   ten million
      (b)   eighteen million
      (c)   five billion
      (d)   ten billion
Page 22

34.   Which of the following consumes the largest part of our
      national budget?
      (a)   payments to individuals
      (b)   the military
      (c)   interest in the national debt
      (d)   the space program (NASA)
Page 22

35.   _____ would typically favor using the power of
      government to restrict or prohibit abortions and to organize
      prayers in public schools.
      (a)   Liberals
      (b)   Conservatives
      (c)   Neoliberals
      (d)   Libertarians
Page 25

36.   Compared with the United States, only _____ among
      democratic nations devotes more of their economic resources
      to the military.
      (a)   Israel
      (b)   Greece
      (c)   neither of these
      (d)   both of these
Page 26

37.   _____ once said that "when a man assumes a public
      trust, he should consider himself public property."
      (a)   Thomas Jefferson
      (b)   Aaron Burr
      (c)   Lyndon B. Johnson
      (d)   Nicolo Machiavelli
Page 29

38.   In 1989, _____ became the first Speaker of the House of
      Representatives to resign in the face of a scandal.
      (a)   Newt Gingrich

(b) Tony Coelho
(c) Jim Wright
(d) Bob Michel
Page 30

39. The United States now spends ____ percent of its gross
national product on health care.
(a) twelve
(b) twenty five
(c) thirty
(d) thirty six
Page 32

40. In one of his first addresses to Congress, _____ said
that the government was too fat and promised to trim the
government (except for the military) every day he was
in office.
(a) Franklin D. Roosevelt
(b) Lyndon B. Johnson
(c) Jimmy Carter
(d) Ronald Reagan
Page 24

BEFORE GOING ON

Check your answers against the answer key below. If you did well
- congratulations! If you have missed some, go back and reread
the relevant passages on the page of the book indicated
immediately below those questions.

Review Test Answers:

1: a	11: a	21: a	31: b
2: c	12: c	22: b	32: d
3: d	13: a	23: a	33: b
4: d	14: b	24: d	34: a
5: b	15: a	25: b	35: b
6: a	16: c	26: b	36: d
7: c	17: a	27: c	37: a
8: a	18: d	28: c	38: d
9: c	19: a	29: b	39: a
10: c	20: b	30: d	40: d

Knowing not only what the correct answer is, but _why_ it is the
correct answer, will help you retain the information when it
really counts.

Finally, nothing is more important than having the terms down pat.
Look through the list of _Key Terms_ your text provides on page 34
and be sure all are familiar enough to comfortably and confidently
use in a sentence. Besides, an expanding vocabulary is the best

evidence to those important others in your life that you are actually learning something at college. For maximum effect, I suggest "hyperpluralism" as your "word of the week" to really impress your parents, friends, and others who need evidence of your education.

CHAPTER 2

THE CONSTITUTION

CHAPTER LEARNING OBJECTIVES

After reading Chapter 2, you should be able to:

1. Define the meaning and purpose of a constitution.
2. Identify the major events leading to the U.S. Constitution.
3. Identify the ideas of John Locke that contributed to the U.S. Declaration of independence and Constitution.
4. Identify the major philosophical views shared by the Framers.
5. Discuss the major equality, economic, and rights issues that shaped the debate at the Constitutional Convention.
6. Identify and discuss the elements of the Madisonian Model.
7. Identify and discuss the issues surrounding the Ratification of the Constitution.
8. Describe the steps and alternative routes of the formal amendment process.
9. Identify and discuss the various means of informal Constitutional change.
10. Explain how the Constitution is related to the democratic nature of the modern policy-making process

PRETEST

The pretest below will give you an idea of the state of your knowledge about the Constitution. The questions should also help you learn what to look for while studying the text. Take the whole pretest, then check your answers against the key that follows (don't peek!). As you read the chapter, watch for where these questions are addressed (indicated after each question) so that you may learn why the answer is what it is.

1. The book "Common Sense," written by _____, fueled anti-British, pro-revolution sentiment in the colonies.
    (a) Thomas Jefferson
    (b) Benjamin Franklin
    (c) Thomas Paine
    (d) Peyton Randolph
Page 46
2. John Locke built his treatise of civil government around the belief in:

21

    (a)   a natural monarchy.
    (b)   minority rights.
    (c)   democratic fervor.
    (d)   natural rights.
Page 46

3.   The Articles of Confederation were adopted in 1777 and went into effect:
    (a)   in 1781.
    (b)   in 1789.
    (c)   immediately.
    (d)   in 1779.
Page 51

4.   An abortive meeting in September, 1786, at _____, did succeed in issuing a call for all the states to meet in Philadelphia to form what would be called the Constitutional Congress.
    (a)   New York City, NY.
    (b)   Boston, MA.
    (c)   Annapolis, MD.
    (d)   Richmond, VA.
Page 53

5.   Most of the delegates to the Constitutional Convention were:
    (a)   coastal residents.
    (b)   urbanites.
    (c)   both (a) and (b) are correct
    (d)   residents of the expanding western frontiers.
Page 54

6.   The founders believed that governments run by factions were:
    (a)   prone to instability, tyranny and violence.
    (b)   necessary, to an extent.
    (c)   desirable when the alternative is a monarchy.
    (d)   none of the above
Page 55

7.   _____ was the head of the delegates that put forth the New Jersey Plan.
    (a)   William Paterson
    (b)   Patrick Henry
    (c)   Eldridge Gerry
    (d)   Gouverneur Morris
Page 56

8.   The most outspoken opponent of slavery in the Constitutional Convention was:

(a)   Thomas Jefferson.
(b)   Charles C. Pinckney.
(c)   Gouverneur Morris.
(d)   Eldridge Gerry.
Page 57-58

9.   On the question of equality and voting, the delegates decided to:
     (a)   leave the question of voting qualifications to the individual states.
     (b)   give every free, adult male universal manhood suffrage.
     (c)   put property qualifications on the right to vote.
     (d)   none of these.
Page 58

10. The proposed new Constitution gave Congress the power to obtain revenues through:
     (a)   taxation.
     (b)   borrowing.
     (c)   both of these.
     (d)   neither of these.
Page 59

11. _____ was the principal architect of the U.S. government's final structure.
     (a)   Thomas Jefferson
     (b)   John Rutledge
     (c)   James Madison
     (d)   George Washington
Page 63

12. Madison's plan placed only one element of government, _____, within direct control of the votes of the majority.
     (a)   the presidency
     (b)   the Senate
     (c)   the House of Representatives
     (d)   the bureaucracy
Page 63

13. In the original Constitution the president was to be elected by:
     (a)   special electors.
     (b)   a popular vote of the people in each state.
     (c)   state governors.
     (d)   none of these.
Page 63

14. In the original Constitution U.S. senators were given terms of ___SIX___ years.

(a) two
(b) four
(c) six
(d) eight

Page 63

15. In the case Marbury v. Madison, _____ asserted its power to check the other branches of government through judicial review.
    (a) The presidency
    (b) Congress
    (c) The Supreme Court
    (d) The House of Representatives

Page 64

16. Some of the members of the Constitutional Convention thought the Constitution so flawed that they refused to sign. One such delegate, _____, bluntly predicted that a "civil war may result from the present crisis of the United States."
    (a) Thomas Jefferson
    (b) Benjamin Franklin
    (c) Eldridge Gerry
    (d) Alexander Hamilton

Page 66

17. To allay fears that the Constitution did not protect individual liberties, _____ introduced twelve constitutional amendments (ten of which were ratified) into the First Congress in 1789.
    (a) Alexander Hamilton
    (b) James Madison
    (c) George Washington
    (d) John Adams

Page 69

18. _____ has the world's oldest two-party system.
    (a) The United States
    (b) Great Britain
    (c) Greece
    (d) France

Page 76

19. The _____ Amendment guarantees the right to bear arms.
    (a) Second
    (b) Fourth
    (c) Seventh
    (d) Ninth

Page 70

20. The _____ Amendment guarantees that no government can establish or prohibit the free exercise of any religion.
    (a) First
    (b) Third

24

(c)   Fourth
(d)   Sixth

Page 70

Pretest Answers:

1:	c	11:	c
2:	d	12:	c
3:	a	13:	a
4:	c	14:	c
5:	c	15:	c
6:	a	16:	c
7:	a	17:	b
8:	c	18:	a
9:	a	19:	a
10:	d	20:	a

READING FOR CONTENT

Listed below are sets of questions associated with the content of each major section of Chapter 2. Carefully review the questions associated with each section of the text before reading the section. Have the questions in mind as you read the section and, when you reach the end of each section, stop and see if you can answer the questions well. If not, reread the relevant paragraphs until you are sure of your response to each of the questions.

I.   The Origins of the Constitution

How did the ideas of John Locke contribute to the Declaration
   of Independence and Constitution?
What were the problems with which the Articles of
   Confederation proved inadequate to deal?

II.   Making a Constitution: The Philadelphia Convention

What were the common philosophical views shared by the
   Framers of the Constitution?

III. The Agenda in Philadelphia

What were the New Jersey and Virginia Plans?
How was the debate over equality of representation resolved?
How did the Framers handle the representation of slaves?
How did the Framers handle the question of suffrage?
What were the principal economic issues of concern to the
   Framers?
How did the Constitution resolve the economic issues of
   concern to the Framers?
What protections for individual rights are included in the
   Constitution?

25

Chapter 2

IV. The Madisonian Model

What are the three basic elements of the Madisonian Model?
What are some examples of constitutional provisions that
     reflect each of the elements of the Madisonian Model?

V.   Ratifying the Constitution

What were the major arguments of the Anti-federalists, who
     opposed ratification of the Constitution?
How did the Federalists attempt to respond to these
     arguments?

VI. Constitutional Change

How can a formal constitutional amendment be proposed?
How can a formal constitutional amendment be ratified?
In what ways does the Constitution change "informally."

VII. Understanding the Constitution

What does it mean that the Constitution created a republic
     not a democracy?
How has the Constitution been "democratized" over the years?
How has the Madisonian Model (and thus the Constitution)
     shaped the policy process?

CHAPTER OVERVIEW

I.   Introduction (44-45)

A CONSTITUTION is a nation's basic law. It creates political
institutions, assigns or divides powers in government, and often
provides certain guarantees to citizens. In setting the broad rules
for the game of politics, it necessarily gives some participants
advantages over others. That constitutions are not neutral is why
understanding them is important to understanding government. The
U.S. Constitution is regarded with a special reverence by Americans.

II. The Origins of the Constitution (45-53)

Compelling ideas drove our forefathers down the drastic and risky
path of revolt. It is important to understand these ideas to
understand the Constitution.

A. The Road to Revolution

Acceptable relations with the mother country began to deteriorate
after Britain acquired a massive new territory in North America
following the French and Indian War. Parliament felt that the cost
of defending this territory should be shared by the colonies and

unilaterally imposed a series of taxes to that end. Resentment over these taxes and their imposition without representation led to unrest and ultimately to the calling of the First Continental Congress in 1774.

B. Declaring Independence

During the ensuing two years talk of independence became more common and in May and June of 1776 the Continental Congress began debating resolutions about independence. On June 7, Richard Henry Lee moved "that these United States are and of rights ought to be free and independent states." On July 2, Lee's motion was formally approved, and the famous DECLARATION OF INDEPENDENCE, primarily written by Thomas Jefferson, was adopted on July 4th.

The Declaration was both a political and philosophical statement. Politically it was a polemic against the King intended to justify revolution. This was important at the time because the colonists needed foreign assistance to fight the most powerful nation in the world. Today, we study the Declaration more for its philosophical content. It is here that Jefferson succinctly sets forth the American democratic creed - as applicable today as it was in 1776.

C. The English Heritage: The Power of Ideas

The philosophical roots of the Declaration can be found in the writings of Englishman John Locke. Jefferson borrowed from and even paraphrased Locke's "Second Treatise of Civil Government." The foundation of Locke's influential philosophy is the notion of natural rights. Such natural rights, including life, liberty and property, are part of a natural law higher than human law. Thus, adherence to natural law could justify revolt against a king that violated natural rights. It also followed from these principles that government should be limited to protecting natural rights, and be based on the consent of those it so serves. Locke's philosophy thus provided the colonists with a philosophical justification for their "right to revolt," and with such basic governing principles as the CONSENT OF THE GOVERNED (popular participation) and LIMITED GOVERNMENT.

D. Jefferson's Handiwork: The American Creed

With these revolutionary ideas in mind, Jefferson claimed in the Declaration that people should have primacy over governments. Moreover, each person was important as an individual, "created equal" and endowed with "unalienable rights." Political power was made legitimate by the consent of the governed, rather than by tradition or the divine right of kings - the case in all previous governments.

E. Winning Independence

27

Chapter 2

The war that followed the Declaration of Independence was waged against an enemy of superior strength. It was won only at great cost.

F. The "Conservative" Revolution

The American Revolution, though bloody, did not involve great societal change or drastically alter the colonists' way of life. Its primary goal was to restore rights they felt already theirs as British subjects. The colonial leaders' belief that they needed the consent of the governed was a source of much needed stability for the new nation.

G. The Government that Failed: 1776-1787

The voluntary association of states called the Continental Congress appointed, in 1776, a committee to draw up a plan for a permanent union. That plan, our first constitution, was the ARTICLES OF CONFEDERATION.

1. The Articles of Confederation. The Articles established a very weak national government which left sovereignty with the states and most authority with the state legislatures. With limited functions, few powers, and no ability to tax, it was a largely ineffectual national government. Most notably, it was incapable of dealing with the hard times the nation experienced following the Revolutionary War.

2. Changes in the States. States were experiencing a dramatic increase in democracy and liberty. The expanded political participation brought a new middle class (largely small homesteaders) to power. Members of the old colonial elite found this development troublesome. Situations and activities that link together government, politics, and public policy.

3. Economic Turmoil. A post war depression brought economic issues to the top of the political agenda. Economic inequality played an important role in shaping public policy. Under the control of small homesteaders, legislatures listened to the demands of small farmers with large debts. Rhode Island particularly passed legislation favorable to debtors.

4. Shays' Rebellion. Policies favoring debtors did not please the economic elite. Moreover, they were frightened by a small band of farmers in western Massachusetts who rebelled against losing their land in 1786. Called SHAYS' REBELLION it was a series of armed attacks on courthouses intended to prevent foreclosures.
5. The Aborted Annapolis Meeting. In September 1786 a handful of leaders assembled in Annapolis to consider commercial conflicts that had arisen among the states under the Articles of Confederation. They accomplished little, but issued a call for a full-scale meeting of the states to consider reform of the Articles. The Continental Congress called such a meeting, and what we call today the

Constitutional Convention convened in May of 1787.

III.   Making A Constitution: The Philadelphia Convention (54-56)

Representatives from twelve state (all but Rhode Island) met "for the sole and express purpose of revision the Articles of Confederation." The delegates quickly went beyond this mandate, however, and began writing a new constitution.

A. Gentlemen in Philadelphia

An uncommon combination of philosophers and shrewd political architects, the fifty-five members of the convention had very different political views. They did have a common base, however. The group agreed on questions of human nature, the causes of political conflict, and the object and nature of republican government.

1. Views of Human Nature. The delegates shared the cynical view that people are self-interested and cannot be trusted with power. Thus they thought government must check and contain the natural self-interest of people.

2. Views of Political Conflict. The delegates agreed with James Madison: "The most common and durable source of factions has been the various and unequal distribution of property." Neither the majority faction (the propertyless) nor the minority faction (the wealthy) could be trusted with power. The effects of factions had, therefore, to be checked.

3. Views of the Objects of Government. Most delegates agreed (with John Locke before them) that the protection of property was, if not the only, then the most important object of government.

4. View of Government. Given the above beliefs, the founders felt that the secret of good government was balance. Human ambition set to counteract human ambition within government. A complex network of checks, balances, and separation of powers was, thus, required.

IV. The Agenda In Philadelphia (56-62)

Not only ideas and philosophy shaped the design, but also the need to address the difficult issues confronting the nation at the time.
A. The Equality Issues

1. Equality and Representation in the States. Whether the states would be equally represented in the new congress was a crucial issue. One plan for the new constitution, the NEW JERSEY PLAN provided for equal representation. Another, the VIRGINIA PLAN, called for each state to be represented in proportion to its share of the American population. The Connecticut Compromise, that created two houses of Congress, one employing equal representation

(Senate) the other proportional (House of Representatives) resolved this conflict.

Though it appears equitable, the plan advantages the people who live in small states. They enjoy greater representation in the branch that controls such key functions as the ratification of treaties, confirmation of presidential appointments, and hearing of impeachment trials.

2. Slavery. Though some delegates opposed slavery it could not be outlawed or severely restricted by the Constitution if the South was to be part of the union. They did agree to limit future importation of slaves, but also assured that slaves fleeing to free states would have to be returned.

How to count slaves for purposes of representation and taxation was also a difficult issue. It was resolved with the THREE-FIFTHS COMPROMISE, which in addition to the free persons, made three-fifths of "all other persons" (slaves) eligible to be counted for both representation and apportionment of taxation.

3. Political Equality. The delegates dodged the issue of who should be qualified to vote in national elections. They finally agreed to leave question of suffrage to the states, making anyone eligible to vote in state elections also eligible in national elections.

B. The Economic Issues

The delegates to the Constitutional Convention were deeply concerned about the state of the economy. Specifically, they felt the following problems needed to be addressed: 1) tariffs put up by states against products from other states; 2) paper money that was virtually worthless but forced on creditors for repayment of debts; and 3) the difficulty of the national congress in raising money, especially in hard times.

The delegates were members of the postcolonial economic elite. There interests would be served by greater economic stability. It is not surprising, then, that they sought to strengthen the economic powers of the new national government. Thus, the new Congress would have the power to tax and borrow and to appropriate funds. In addition, it was provided powers necessary for developing the nation's economic infrastructure, protecting property rights, and regulating interstate and foreign commerce.

The framers also prohibited practices in the states they viewed as inhibiting economic development, such as printing paper money, placing tariffs on interstate commercial traffic, and interfering with lawful debts.

The Constitution also obligated the new government to repay all the public debt incurred under the Articles. This ensured that money would flow into the economy and restored confidence of investors in the new nation.

C. The Individual Rights Issues

The founders desired a government that would not threaten individual rights. They felt that the limited government they had designed, with its dispersed powers and internal checks could not threaten personal freedoms. Also, they felt that the individual states were already adequately protecting individual rights. As a result the constitution provided only a few specific protections.
Among these are : 1) prohibition of suspension of the WRIT OF HABEAS CORPUS; 2) prohibition of Congress or states from passing ex post facto laws; 3) prohibition of religious qualifications for holding office in the national government; 4) a narrow definition and strict rules of evidence for conviction for treason; 5) the right to trial by jury in criminal cases. The absence of more specific protections became a source of great criticism and controversy during the struggle for ratification.

V. The Madisonian Model (62-67)

The framers believed that inequalities of wealth were the principal source of political conflict, but they had no desire to eliminate conflict by removing economic inequality. Government was to protect, not redistribute or eliminate private property. Too much democracy threatened tyranny of the majority, and the property of the wealthy minority. Thus they were faced with the problem of reconciling economic inequality with political freedom.

A. Separation of Powers and Checks and Balances.

James Madison was the principal architect of the government's final structure, and his work still shapes our policy-making process. He knew that both the minority and majority faction must be checked from tyrannizing the other. While the minority could simply be outvoted, the majority was more difficult to control. To prevent tyranny of the majority, Madison's plan included:
1) Place as much of the government as possible beyond the direct control of the majority.
2) Separate the powers of different institutions.
3) Construct a system of checks and balances.

Madison's plan placed only one element of government, the House of Representatives, within direct control of the votes of the majority. It provided for SEPARATION OF POWERS, placing the executive, legislative, and judicial functions in separate institutions of government. Powers were not separated absolutely, but shared so that each branch would require the consent of the others for many of its actions. This created a system of CHECKS AND BALANCES.

B. The Constitutional Republic

31

Democracy was, in the view of the framers, both undesirable and unworkable as a model for the new national government. Their solution was to establish a REPUBLIC: a system based on the consent of the governed in which power is exercised by representatives of the public. The complicated and delicately balanced decision-making system is not easy to maintain. It favors the status quo, making rapid change difficult if not impossible. While it encourages the virtues of moderation and compromise, critics argue that it is inefficient, preventing quick action on pressing problems.

C. The End of the Beginning

The Constitution reflected many compromises and perhaps none of the framers was completely happy with the finished product. Most found enough merit, or with Benjamin Franklin had "doubt a little of his own fallibility" enough to sign the document. Several, however, found it so wanting that they refused to sign. Such disagreement within the convention itself foreshadowed the struggle to come over ratification.

VI. Ratifying The Constitution (67-71)

The Constitution itself required that nine states approve the document before it could be implemented. We tend to forget that the opposition to the Constitution was substantial, and the process of ratification was the focus of a bitter political struggle.

A. Federalists and Anti-Federalists

A fierce battle erupted in the states between the FEDERALISTS, who supported the Constitution, and the ANTI-FEDERALISTS, who opposed it. Leaders of the Federalist cause, James Madison, Alexander Hamilton, and John Jay wrote a series of articles under the pseudonyms "Publius" that became known as the Federalist Papers. In defending the Constitution detail by detail, they provided an important statement of political philosophy.

The Anti-Federalists were not unpatriotic, but believed that the new government would be an enemy of the freedoms just won in the Revolutionary War. Their attacks were strong and sometimes brilliant critiques of the Constitution. Besides pointing out that the Constitution would weaken the states politically, the critics argued that the it was a class-based document, intended to ensure control of public policy by a particular economic elite.
Perhaps a more persuasive and even more influential argument was that, lacking specific protections for individual rights, the Constitution would erode fundamental liberties. To allay such fears the Federalists promised to add amendments to the document that would specifically protect individual liberties. Madison proposed 12 such amendments in the First Congress, the ten that were ratified became known as the Bill of Rights.

B. Ratification

The Federalists probably did not enjoy majority support. The founders had shrewdly specified that the Constitution be ratified by special conventions in each state, rather than by state legislatures likely to oppose its centralization of power. This, the arguments of the Federalists, and the promise of a Bill of Rights made it possible to get the Constitution ratified.

VII. Constitutional Change (71-79)

The U.S. Constitution is called a living document because it is constantly being tested and altered. Constitutional changes are made either by formal amendment or by informal processes. The informal processes, including unwritten tradition, practice and procedure sometimes called the UNWRITTEN CONSTITUTION, when altered may change the spirit and meaning of the Constitution.

A. The Formal Amending Process

Article V of the Constitution outlines procedures for formal amendment. There are two stages to the process - proposal and ratification - and each stage can be done in two ways. An amendment may be proposed either by a two-thirds vote in each house of Congress or by a national convention called by Congress at the request of two-thirds of the state legislatures. Ratification requires approval of either the state legislatures or special conventions called in three-fourths of the states. All but one have been proposed by Congress and ratified by state legislatures. The 21st, which repealed prohibition, was ratified in state conventions. All in all the formal amendments make the Constitution more egalitarian and democratic. They have ensured wider participation and forbidden various political and social inequalities based on sex, race, and age.

B. The Informal Process of Constitutional Change

1. Judicial Interpretation. Disputes often arise about the meaning of the Constitution requiring someone to decide how it should be interpreted. In MARBURY V. MADISON the Supreme Court claimed this role for itself, assuming the power of JUDICIAL REVIEW. Though not specifically granted in the Constitution, this power gives the courts the right to decide whether the actions of the legislative and executive branches of state and national governments are in accord with the Constitution. As a result, the Constitution ultimately means what the Supreme Court says it means.

2. Changing Political Practice. The rise of parties, unmentioned in the Constitution and undesired by the founders, profoundly affect the functioning of the institutions created by the document. The Congress is organized along partisan lines, for example, and the operation of the electoral college in presidential elections has

been fundamentally altered by the role of parties in the process.

3. Technology. The mass (especially electronic) media play a role unimaginable for the Framers. Such communication systems have given the president greater influence than expected in the system. Technology (such as computers) has also allowed a growth in governmental services (and bureaucracy) far beyond the Framers' wildest dreams. The atomic bomb has given the president's role as commander in chief a whole new meaning.

4. Increasing Demands on Policymakers. The people also have changed, making greater demands on government. Some of the increase in demands are due to the expanded role the United States plays in international affairs. This larger, more active role for government has also tended to increase the power of the president.

5. The Importance of Flexibility. The document the framers produced was clearly meant to be flexible rather than static. It was intended to create a system of government that could adapt to change. This flexibility has helped ensure the survival of both the Constitution and the nation.

C. The Elaboration of the Constitution

The Constitution is very short and does not prescribe the structure and functioning of the government in detail. Instead, it allows future generations to determine their governmental needs and create institutions to meet them.

VIII.   Understanding The Constitution

A. The Constitution and Democracy

The Constitution itself is rarely described as democratic. The writers were not supporters of "democracy," if by that was meant a government that attempted to directly translate the majority's preference into policy. On the other hand, the Constitution did not create a monarchy or a feudal aristocracy either. It created a republic, a representative form of democracy. Though anti-democratic in some ways, the Constitution established a government that was open to substantial movement toward democracy. Indeed, the gradual democratization of the Constitution is a central theme of American history. Five of the sixteen amendments since the Bill of Rights have expanded suffrage (15th, 19th, 23rd, 24th, and s26th). Another (the 17th) provided for the direct election of Senators. Parties have democratized the electoral college and the process of selecting presidential nominees. All in all, the American national government, despite the growth of the nation, has never been closer to those it serves.

B.   The Constitution and Policy-making.

The Constitution's separation of powers and checks and balances provide many avenues of access to the political system for groups to articulate demands. A group can usually find at least one sympathetic ear among the variety of policy relevant institutions. The system encourages a process of bargaining, compromise, and playing one institution against another in the making of policy. It also allows many opportunities to check or veto policy initiatives. Some argue that power is so fragmented with the Constitutionally designed policy process that effective government is almost impossible.

DOING RESEARCH ON THE CONSTITUTION

If you are of an historical bent or if you have a taste for fundamental issues, Chapter 2 offers a wealth of possible topics for further research. You may wish to investigate more fully the events and conditions leading up to the Declaration of Independence or the convening of the Constitutional Convention, for example. An interesting variation is to look at the pre-revolution period from the British point of view or the pre-Convention period from the viewpoint of the members of Shay's "Army." You might develop a paper explaining why the Crown took the actions it did, or that takes the form of a set of recommendations to the King on the handling of the crisis in the colonies. A paper defending Shay's Rebellion and its tactics prior to the calling of the Constitutional Convention would have similar possibilities.

Or you might prefer to select a particular delegate to the Constitutional Convention and explore the impact of their personality and ideas on the outcome of the convention. Delving more deeply into the events of an era and the lives of those that shaped it helps to bring it "alive," and often reveals that these people and events are far more interesting and colorful than they seem in more general accounts.

The Chapter also raises a number of general issues that can be interesting when analyzed from a modern perspective. For example, the Declaration's claim of a right to revolution certainly holds controversial possibilities. How might this right be operative today? Under what circumstances? How is it related to the legitimacy of civil disobedience, public demonstrations, and even the use of violence as forms of political participation today? Another possibility you might explore is the debate about "how democratic is the Constitution?" A look at the work of Charles Beard and his critics would provide mort than enough material.

Again, Government in America provides a good starting point for research into such questions. The works cited in the text, and listed under "For Further Reading" are excellent starting points. The Federalist Papers is an excellent guide to how the Constitution's supporters expected it to operate. Edited by Max Farrand, The Records of the Federal Convention of 1787 assembles the

35

minutes of the convention and the notes of many of the participants. It is an excellent base for understanding the convention itself.

The Constitution represents a unique event of political creation by an unusual collection of political talent. Its further investigation is always rewarding.

REVIEW TEST

Be sure to reread the learning objectives listed at the beginning of the this chapter and have them mastered. Reread the chapter overview and quiz yourself with the "Reading for Content" questions. When you feel ready, tackle the Review Test below.

1. The main reason for colonial discontent against the British government in the 1770's was:
    (a) that the British government wouldn't allow them to provide for their own defenses.
    (b) that in order to raise revenue for colonial administration and defense, taxes were imposed that the colonists found unfair.
    (c) that Britain did little in the area of foreign affairs and trade but liked to meddle in day to day domestic affairs.
    (d) all of the above
Page 45

2. Although a committee of five men worked on the Declaration of Independence in 1776, the finished product was largely the work of:
    (a) Thomas Jefferson.
    (b) James Madison.
    (c) Benjamin Franklin.
    (d) Robert Livingston.
Page 46

3. To John Locke, _____ was the primary goal of government.
    (a) the preservation of property.
    (b) the pursuit of happiness.
    (c) freedom of religion.
    (d) freedom of the press.
Page 48

4. At the beginning of the American Revolution, the colonists had 5,000 men at their disposal. They fought a British army of _____ men with _____ mercenaries on the British side.
    (a) 2,000; 5,000
    (b) 4,500; 10,000
    (c) 6,000; 20,000
    (d) 8,500; 30,000
Page 50

5. The colonial leaders' belief that they needed _____
    _____ gave the new nation a crucial element of stability.
    (a) the consent of the governed
    (b) a standing militia
    (c) a separate monetary system for each of the thirteen
         colonies
    (d) a president and a congress
Page 50

6. The Articles of Confederation established:
    (a) a government dominated by the states.
    (b) a national legislature with one house with each state
         having one vote.
    (c) a strictly limited (in terms of power) national
         legislature (i.e. the Continental Congress).
    (d) all of the above
Page 51

7. The last state to ratify the Articles of Confederation was: (a)
    New York.
    (b) Maryland.
    (c) Delaware.
    (d) Massachusetts.
Page 51

8. During the Revolutionary War, most authority rested with:
    (a) the military.
    (b) the Continental Congress.
    (c) state legislatures.
    (d) the Virginia legislature.
Page 51

9. The Continental Congress had the power to:
    (a) tax the states.
    (b) regulate commerce.
    (c) maintain the army and navy.
    (d) all of the above.
Page 51

10. By adopting bills of rights to protect freedoms and
    liberalizing voting requirements, the states:
    (a) brought a new middle class to power.
    (b) ended discriminatory practices for all men.
    (c) caused a decrease in political participation.
    (d) all of the above
Page 52

11. In 1786, _____ broke out when a small band of farmers
    in western Massachusetts rebelled at losing their land to
    creditors.

37

(a)   Shay's Rebellion
(b)   the Boston Massacre
(c)   Nat Turner's Massacre
(d)   the Battle of Lexington and Concord
Page 53

12. _____ feared centralization of power in national government and said he "smelled a rat" at the Constitutional Convention.
(a)   Patrick Henry
(b)   John Jay
(c)   George Washington
(d)   Thomas Jefferson
Page 54

13. There were _____ delegates to the Constitutional Convention in Philadelphia.
(a)   twenty six
(b)   fifty five
(c)   seventy six
(d)   ninety three
Page 54

14. Though poles apart philosophically, Alexander Hamilton and Benjamin Franklin could agree that:
(a)   people are generally other regarding.
(b)   that people are generally incapable of self government.
(c)   that people are generally self interested.
(d)   none of these.
Page 54

15. _____ said that giving "votes to people who have no property" would ensure that they would sell their votes to the rich who are able to buy them from the poor.
(a)   James Madison
(b)   Gouverneur Morris
(c)   Eldridge Gerry
(d)   George Washington
Page 55

16. _____ was the head of the delegates that put forth the Virginia Plan.
(a)   William Paterson
(b)   Edmund Randolph
(c)   Benjamin Franklin
(d)   John Jay
Page 56

17. Although the Connecticut Compromise was intended to maximize

equality between the states, it actually:
- (a) leaves more power to people who live in states with small populations.
- (b) leaves more power to people who live in states with larger populations.
- (c) makes little difference in the distribution of power.
- (d) none of these.

Page 56

18. At the time of the Constitutional Convention, slavery was legal in every state except:
- (a) New York.
- (b) Massachusetts.
- (c) Pennsylvania.
- (d) Rhode Island.

Page 57

19. On the question of slavery, the delegates to the Constitutional Convention did agree on:
- (a) limiting future importation of slaves.
- (b) outlawing the importation of slaves.
- (c) outlawing slavery eventually.
- (d) none of these.

Page 58

20. The idea that representation and taxation were to be based on the "number of free persons," plus three-fifths of the number of "all other persons" (meaning slaves) was called:
- (a) the Virginia Plan.
- (b) the Connecticut Compromise.
- (c) the three-fifths compromise.
- (d) the Emancipation Proclamation.

Page 58

21. A handful of delegates, led by _____, suggested that national elections should require universal manhood suffrage (or, a vote for all free, adult males).
- (a) Eldridge Gerry
- (b) Alexander Hamilton
- (c) Charles C. Pinckney
- (d) Benjamin Franklin

Page 58

22. Advocates of the proposed new Constitution who stressed the weakness of the economy were called:
- (a) the Democratic-Republicans.
- (b) the Anti-Federalists.
- (c) the Federalists.
- (d) the Whigs.

Page 59

23. To protect property rights, Congress was charged with all

of the following EXCEPT:
- (a) providing equal housing and opportunity for all U.S. citizens.
- (b) punishing counterfeiters and pirates.
- (c) ensuring patents and copyrights.
- (d) legislating rules for bankruptcy.

Page 60

24. _____, the first secretary of the treasury, stressed the link between a national debt and the emergence of capitalism.
- (a) Aaron Burr
- (b) Alexander Hamilton
- (c) John Adams
- (d) John C. Marshall

Page 61

25. The Constitution prohibits suspension of the writ of habeas corpus which:
- (a) enables persons detained by authorities to secure an immediate inquiry into the causes of their detention. prohibits questioning of a detained person until they have a lawyer present.
- (c) prohibits the practice of assessing a sum of money for the release of detained persons
- (d) all of the above

Page 62

26. The phrase "if men were angels, no government would be necessary" is found in:
- (a) Federalist no. 51.
- (b) the Declaration of Independence.
- (c) the Magna Carta.
- (d) the U.S. Constitution.

Page 63

27. In the original Constitution judges were to be:
- (a) elected by a popular vote of the people in each judicial district.
- (b) appointed by the president.
- (c) selected from the ranks of Congress.
- (d) appointed by the governor of each state.

Page 63

28. In the original Constitution U.S. congressmen in the House of Representatives were given terms of _____ years.
- (a) eight
- (b) six
- (c) four
- (d) two

Page 63

29. Madison's model for assuring that one branch could not control all of government's activities was called:

(a) the crucible.
(b) the art of realpolitik.
(c) checks and balances.
(d) the power triangle.
Page 64

30. The case Marbury v. Madison established the principle of:
(a) advise and consent.
(b) checks and balances.
(c) the separation of powers.
(d) judicial review.
Page 64

31. When asked what kind of government the delegates had produced, _____ said, "a republic, if you can keep it."
(a) Benjamin Franklin
(b) Charles C. Pinckney
(c) Roger Sherman
(d) John Adams
Page 66

32. The system of checks and balances and separation of powers: (a) does not favor the status quo.
(b) has a conservative bias.
(c) makes change easy to come by.
(d) does not encourage moderation or compromise.
Page 66

33. All of the following men were the authors of the Federalist Papers under the pen name Publius EXCEPT:
(a) James Madison
(b) Thomas Jefferson
(c) Alexander Hamilton
(d) John Jay
Page 68

34. _____ feared that the new U.S. Constitution would prove to be a class-based document intended to ensure that a particular economic elite controlled the public policies of the national government.
(a) The Anti-Federalists
(b) The Whigs
(c) The "Know-Nothings"
(d) The Federalists
Page 68

35. The most explicit means of changing the Constitution is through:
(a) a writ of certiorari.
(b) bill of attainder.
(c) a state convention.
(d) the formal process of amendment.
Page 71-72

36. _____ has the oldest functioning Constitution in the world.
    (a) Italy
    (b) The United States
    (c) Great Britain
    (d) Canada
Page 78

37. It is possible for a presidential candidate who receives the most popular votes to lose the election, although this has not happened since:
    (a) 1824 -- J.Q. Adams over Andrew Jackson.
    (b) 1876 -- Rutherford Hayes over Samuel Tilden.
    (c) 1888 -- Benjamin Harrison over President Cleveland.
    (d) 1960 -- John F. Kennedy over Richard Nixon.
Page 80

38. People did not elect their U.S. Senators directly until:
    (a) 1789.
    (b) 1833.
    (c) 1861.
    (d) 1913.
Page 80

39. The _____ Amendment protects individuals from having to testify against themselves in judicial proceedings.
    (a) First
    (b) Fourth
    (c) Fifth
    (d) Eighth
Page 70

40. The _____ Amendment states that powers not delegated to the national government or denied to the states are reserved for the states or the people.
    (a) Twelfth
    (b) Tenth
    (c) Seventh
    (d) Fourth
Page 70

BEFORE GOING ON

Check your answers against the answer key below. If you have missed some, go back and reread the relevant passages on the page of the book indicated below those questions.

Review Test Answers:

1: a	11: a	21: d	31: a
2: a	12: a	22: c	32: b
3: a	13: b	23: a	33: b
4: d	14: c	24: b	34: a
5: a	15: b	25: d	35: b
6: d	16: b	26: a	36: b
7: b	17: a	27: b	37: c
8: c	18: b	28: d	38: d
9: c	19: a	29: c	39: c
10: a	20: c	30: d	40: b

Again, no matter how well you've done on the test, be sure you have all the key terms listed on page 84 absolutely clear. This week I think dropping a few references to "natural rights" will do most to enhance your reputation as a theoretically well grounded intellectual.

CHAPTER 3

FEDERALISM

CHAPTER LEARNING OBJECTIVES

After reading Chapter 3, you should be able to:

1. Define and distinguish federalism from unitary and confederate forms of government.
2. Discuss why federalism is important to politics and policy.
3. Explain how the Constitution divides power between the national and the state governments.
4. Discuss the major court cases and resulting interpretations of Constitutional provisions that established national supremacy.
5. Identify the Constitutional obligations the states have to each other.
6. Distinguish the notions of dual federalism and cooperative federalism.
7. Define the concept of fiscal federalism.
8. Identify and define the forms of federal grants.
9. Discuss the advantages and disadvantages of federalism for democracy.
10. Explain the relationship between federalism and the growth of the national government.

PRETEST QUESTIONS

The pretest below will give you an idea of the state of your knowledge about federalism. The questions should also help you learn what to look for while studying the text. Take the whole pretest, then check your answers against the key that follows (don't peek!). As you read the chapter, watch for where these questions are addressed (indicated after each question) so that you may learn why the answer is what it is.

1. All of the following countries have federal systems of government EXCEPT:
   (a) the Soviet Union.
   (b) Australia.
   (c) Great Britain.
   (d) Mexico.

Page 87

2. The United States began as a confederation under:
    (a) the U.S. Constitution.
    (b) the Sixth Amendment.
    (c) the Virginia Plan.
    (d) the Articles of Confederation.
Page 87

3. According to _____, the supreme law of the land in any case is, first and foremost, the U.S. Constitution.
    (a) the supremacy clause
    (b) the Virginia Plan
    (c) the U.S. Constitution
    (d) the Articles of Confederation
Page 93

4. In 1941, the Supreme Court, in United States v. Darby, called the Tenth Amendment:
    (a) unconstitutional.
    (b) a constitutional truism.
    (c) proof that the states' powers are supreme to the national government.
    (d) null and void.
Page 94

5. In McCulloch v. Maryland, the Supreme Court held that: the national government's policies always take precedence
    (a) over state policies.
    (b) state policies always take precedence over national government policies.
    (c) state policies take precedence over national government policies if they are in accordance with the Constitution.
    (d) as long as the national government behaved in accordance with the Constitution, its policies took precedence over state policies.

Page 94

6. The lawyer who argued against the national bank and for the state of Maryland in McCulloch v. Maryland was:
    (a) Alexander Hamilton.
    (b) Daniel Webster.
    (c) Luther Martin.
    (d) James McCulloch.
Page 95

7. In McCulloch v. Maryland, the Supreme Court held that Congress had certain _____ powers, powers specifically listed in Article 1, Section 8 of the Constitution.
    (a) implied
    (b) enumerated
    (c) "false"
    (d) ceremonial
Page 95

8. What McCulloch v. Maryland pronounced constitutionally with regards to national government supremacy, _____ settled militarily.
   (a) the Civil War
   (b) the Mexican-American War
   (c) World War I
   (d) World War II
Page 96

9. The national government has exclusive control over:
   (a) road building.
   (b) law enforcement.
   (c) the postal system.
   (d) schools.
Page 100

10. _____ federalism describes a federal system with mingled responsibilities and blurred distinctions between the levels of government.
   (a) Dual
   (b) Singular
   (c) Cooperative
   (d) Fiscal
Page 100

11. Education was usually thought of as being a _____ responsibility.
   (a) local
   (b) state
   (c) local and state
   (d) national government
Page 100

12. In 1965, Congress passed the Elementary and Secondary Education Act, which:
   (a) provided money to build schools.
   (b) provided federal grants to college students.
   (c) provided federal aid to numerous schools.
   (d) provided federal loans to college students.
Page 101

13. _____ federalism involves shared costs, federal guidelines and shared administration.
   (a) Cooperative
   (b) Dual
   (c) Fiscal
   (d) Independent
Page 101-102

14. Ronald Reagan advocated a move toward a more _____ federalism.
    (a) cooperative
    (b) singular
    (c) fiscal
    (d) dual
Page 102

15. The pattern of spending, taxing and providing grants in the federal system is called:
    (a) dual federalism.
    (b) fiscal federalism.
    (c) wasteful in all cases.
    (d) cooperative federalism.
Page 103

16. Federal aid accounts for over _____ percent of all the funds spent by state and local governments.
    (a) 10
    (b) 18
    (c) 25
    (d) 49
Page 103

17. A _____ grant can vary from grant to grant and depends on a number of factors, including population, per capita income or some other criterion.
    (a) block
    (b) project
    (c) formula
    (d) policy
Page 105

18. A response to state and local unhappiness with categorical grants was revenue sharing, a favorite of the _____ administration.
    (a) Roosevelt
    (b) Eisenhower
    (c) Kennedy
    (d) Nixon
Page 105

19. The state of Illinois holds the current record for the largest number of individual governments -- _____ at the latest count.
    (a) 22
    (b) more than 1000
    (c) more than 6000
    (d) more than 10,000
Page 112

20. None of these countries have federal systems EXCEPT:
    (a) China

       (b)   Malaysia
       (c)   Portugal
       (d)   France
Page 87

Pretest Answers:

1: c	11: c
2: d	12: c
3: a	13: a
4: b	14: d
5: d	15: b
6: c	16: b
7: b	17: c
8: a	18: d
9: c	19: c
10: c	20: b

READING FOR CONTENT

Listed below are sets of questions associated with the content of
each major section of Chapter 3. Carefully review the questions
associated with each section of the text before reading the section.
Have the questions in mind as you read the section and, when you
reach the end of each section, stop and see if you can answer the
questions well. If not, reread the relevant paragraphs until you
are sure of your response to each of the questions.

I.   What Federalism is and Why It Is Important

      How can federalism be distinguished from unitary and
         confederate forms of government?
      Why is federalism so important for our politics and policies?

II.   The Constitutional Basis of Federalism

      What is the relationship of the supremacy clause to the Tenth
         Amendment?
      What is the significance of the McCulloch v. Maryland case?
      What is the difference between the Congress' enumerated and
         implied powers?
      What is the significance of the case of Gibbons v. Ogden?
      What are the constitutionally defined obligations of the
         states to one another?

III. Intergovernmental Relations Today

      What is the difference between the notions of dual federalism
         and cooperative federalism?
      What is meant by "fiscal federalism?"
      What is the difference between categorical and block grants?
      What is the difference between project and formula grants?

What are the advantages and disadvantages of fiscal federalism?

IV. Understanding Federalism

What are the advantages and disadvantages of federalism for democracy?
How is federalism associated with the growth of government?

CHAPTER OVERVIEW

I. Introduction (86-87)

This chapter explores the complex relationships between different levels of government in the United States. How the federal system has changed and why it remains at the center of important policy battles will be discussed.

II. What Federalism Is And Why It Is So Important (87-92)

A. What Federalism Is

FEDERALISM is a way of organizing a nation so that two or more levels of government have formal authority over the same area and people. This is not a very common form of governmental organization. Most governments are not federal but UNITARY GOVERNMENTS, in which all power resides in the central government. American states are unitary governments with respect to their local governments. Local governments get their authority from the state governments and can be altered or abolished by them. In the federal relationship between the national and state governments, neither can alter or abolish the other.

A third form of government organization is a confederation. In a confederation the national government is weak and most or all power resides in the hands of its components. The United States was a confederation under its first constitution, the Articles of Confederation. Today the form exists primarily in international organizations such as the United Nations.

B. Why Federalism Is So Important

The federal system decentralizes our politics. All elected officials in the national government, even the president, are nominated and elected in statewide elections or in districts within the states. The layers of government the system provides also provides more opportunities for political participation. The federal system also decentralizes our policies, creating a tension between the levels over who should control specific types of policy.

States are responsible for most public policies dealing with social, family, and menial issues. The national government cannot pass laws that directly regulate such matters. They can become national issues, however, when groups pressure the national government to attempt to influence state policy through its control of grants-in-aid monies.

The American states have always played an important role as policy innovators. Almost every policy the national government has adopted had its beginnings in the states.III. The Constitutional Bias Of Federalism (92-100)

Loyalty to state governments was too strong to allow a new Constitution to abolish the states in 1787. Thus, for practical and political reasons, the stronger national government the founders sought could not be unitary in form. In strengthening the national government while respecting the state, the founders found a middle ground between unitary and confederate forms.

A. The Division of Power

The Constitution ensures that the states would be vital cogs by giving them equal representation in the Senate, making them responsible for all elections, guaranteeing them protection against violence and invasion, and forbidding Congress from altering state boundaries without their permission.

The Constitution makes the national government supreme, however, in the SUPREMACY CLAUSE of Article VI which provides that the following are the supreme law of the land: 1) the Constitution; 2) Laws of the national government (when consistent with the Constitution); and 3) Treaties (made only by the national government).

The national government can only operate within its appropriate sphere, however. The boundaries of national power are suggested in part by the TENTH AMENDMENT, which states "powers not delegated to the United States by the Constitution, nor prohibited by it to the states, are reserved to the states respectively, or to the people." Though it seems to limit the national government to its enumerated powers, the courts have ruled that it does not give states powers supreme to the national government for activities not mentioned in the Constitution. Challenges to the authority of the national government occasionally arise, but there is little doubt about the supremacy of the national government.

B. Establishing National Supremacy

Three events have largely settled the issue of how national and state powers are related (in favor of the national level): the MCCULLOCK V. MARYLAND court case, the Civil War, and the civil rights movement.

1. McCulloch v. Maryland. State versus national power clashed in

this case when the state of Maryland passed a law placing a tax on a branch of the national bank, a national government agency. The State of Maryland argued that the Constitution does not list the power to create a national bank among Congress' powers. The national government argued that such a power was "implied" by the Constitution's "necessary and proper" clause. In deciding the case, John Marshall and the Federalist dominated court decided for the bank and in so doing set forth two great Constitutional principles. First, the supremacy of the national government and, second, that the national government did have certain implied powers that far beyond its ENUMERATED powers. Today the notion of IMPLIED powers has become like a rubber band - almost indefinitely stretchable. The "necessary and proper" clause is often called the ELASTIC clause, allowing extensive national government action, especially in the economic realm. Economic regulation rests on a broad interpretation of "commerce" established in the case of GIBBONS V. OGDEN. The interstate and international regulation of commerce is an enumerated power of the national legislature.

2. Federalism as the Battleground of the Struggle for Equality. The Civil War is often thought of as mainly a struggle over slavery, but it was also a struggle between states and the national government. The war asserted the national government's power over the southern states' claim of sovereignty.

A century later the issue of states' rights and national power again erupted over the issue of equality. The 1954 Supreme Court decision that school segregation was unconstitutional led to a long civil struggle, ultimately decided in favor of the national government's standards of racial equality.

C. States' Obligations to Each Other

The states must deal with each other as well as with the national government. The Constitution outlines certain obligations that each state has to every other state.

1. Full Faith and Credit. Article IV of the Constitution requires that states give FULL FAITH AND CREDIT to the public acts, records, and civil judicial proceedings of every other state. The society and economy could not function without this reciprocity.

2. Extradition. Almost all criminal law is state law. The Constitution says that states are required to return a person charged with a crime in another state to that state for trial or imprisonment. States cannot be forced to comply, but are usually happy to provide such EXTRADITION in expectation of similar consideration by other states.

3. Privileges and Immunities. The citizens of each state are entitled to all the PRIVILEGES AND IMMUNITIES of any other state in which they happen to be. Thus states cannot discriminate against citizens of other states. There are exceptions, however. Out of

state students may pay higher tuition, for instances, and states have residency requirements for voting privileges. The Supreme Court has never clarified just which privileges a state must guarantee.

IV. Intergovernmental Relations Today (100-108)

A. From Dual to Cooperative Federalism

One way to understand the changes in federalism in the nation's history is to contrast DUAL FEDERALISM with COOPERATIVE FEDERALISM. In dual federalism, the state and national level of government are distinctly separate and supreme within their own spheres. The states are responsible for some policies, the national government for others. This results in a relatively narrow interpretation of national government power.

Today the system is more likely to be described as cooperative federalism. Instead of the responsibilities distinctly separated, as in a layer cake, the system is thought of like a marble cake, with mingled responsibilities and blurred distinctions between the levels of government. The powers and policy assignments are shared between states and the national government. The national government may provide the money, for example, while the states provide the administration for a program.

Though dual federalism used to provide a more accurate description of American federalism than it does today, the system was never neatly separated into purely state and purely national responsibilities. Today, the federal government's presence is felt in most policy areas. For hundreds of programs, cooperative federalism involves: 1) Shared costs (where Washington foots part of the bill if the states and cities are willing to pay some of the costs); 2) Federal guidelines (or conditions that accompany grant money and allow the national government to influence state policy); and 3) Shared administration (in which states and localities retain administrative powers allowing latitude in spending national monies).

B. Fiscal Federalism

Fiscal federalism, the pattern of spending, taxing, and providing grants in the federal system, is the cornerstone of the national government's relations with the states. Money is the national government's principal source of influence over the states. State and local aid amounts to more that 120 billion dollars each year - about 18 percent of all the funds spent by state and local governments, and about 10 percent of the national budget.

1. The Federal Grant System: Distributing the Federal Pie. There are two major types of federal aid for states and localities. About 80 percent of aid comes in the form of CATEGORICAL GRANTS. They must be used for 1 of 422 specific purposes or "categories" of state and

local spending, and come with "strings" attached - rules and regulations about its use. A nondiscrimination provision to protect minorities is commonly attached, for example. Much federal regulation is accomplished through this indirect attachment of "strings" on grant monies.

There are two types of categorical grants. The most common type (288 of the 422) are PROJECT GRANTS. Project grants are awarded on the basis of competitive applications. This distinguishes them from the second type called FORMULA GRANTS, which are distributed according to a formula. These formulas vary from grant to grant and may be computed on the basis of population, per capita income, percentage of rural population, etc. There are 134 formula grant programs including Medicaid and Aid for Families with Dependent Children (AFDC).

Complaints about the cumbersome application process and strings associated with categorical grants led to the adoption of the second major type of grant - the BLOCK GRANT. Given more or less automatically to states and communities they are designed to support broad programs like community development and social services. The recipient government is allowed to decide the specific way the money will be spent in these broad areas.

A third form of grants, called "revenue sharing" returned national money to the states with no strings at all. Revenue sharing never amounted to a large part of state and local budgets, however, and was ended altogether by the Reagan Administration.

2. The Scramble for Federal Dollars. Hustling for federal dollars is an important task for states and communities. Full-time intergovernmental relations staffs in city halls and state capitols investigate grant programs and make applications. Most states and many cities have full-time staffs in Washington, D.C. They have even banded together in interest groups like the National League of Cities and Council of State Governments in order to better pursue their common interests.

Though some states and cities due better than others in capturing federal grant money, distribution follows the principle of universalism on the whole. There are not many things in America more equitably distributed than federal aid to states and cities.

3. The Mandate Blues. Though usually pleased to receive aid, it can sometimes become a burden to the states. Because they are required to "match" federal monies for many programs, when the national government decided to increase funding, so must the states if they wish to retain the program. States pay for 45 percent of Medicaid, for example, which the national government expanded by 146 percent during the 1980s placing a strain on many state government budgets.

V.   Understanding Federalism (108-116)

A. Federalism and Democracy

By decentralizing the system, federalism was designed to contribute to democracy - at least in the sense that it provided protection against possible tyranny by a powerful distant government.

1. Advantages for Democracy. The more levels of government the opportunity for participation in and access to government. This increases the likelihood that government will be responsive. Diversity of opinion in different regions of the country can be reflected in the public policy of the various states. Local problems can be handled locally in ways that reflect local values.

2. Disadvantages for Democracy. Diversity can also mean inequality, however. States differ in the resources they can devote to solving problems and providing services. A citizen's life chances and circumstances will depend on the chance of birthplace.

Local interests may be able to thwart national majority support of certain policies. Federalism greatly complicated and delayed efforts to end racial segregation and other forms of discrimination.

Finally, the sheer number of governments (83,237) can be a burden to democracy. In addition to the national and state governments are municipalities (or townships), counties, school districts and other special districts. Having so many governments makes it difficult to know which governments are doing what or extending democratic control over them.

B. Federalism and the Growth of the National Government

As the United States changed from an agricultural to an industrial nation, new problems arose and with them new demands for governmental action. The national government responded with a national banking system, subsidies, and a host of other policies that dramatically increased its role in the economy. The power of private corporations grew and many interests asked the national government to restrain monopolies and encourage open competition.

For many of the nation's problems only the authority and resources of the national government would be adequate. Thus turning to state governments was not a viable option. They could not address the needs for environmental protection or social security, for example. The national government has grown much more rapidly than the states in the past 60 years and now accounts for more public spending than all the states combined. Still, the states have not been supplanted by the national government. They carry out virtually all the functions they always have. National government growth has been in new responsibilities demanded by the people, and in aid to the states in carrying out their functions.

DOING RESEARCH ON FEDERALISM

Chapter 3

Federalism may not seem like a fascinating subject at first glance, but the nation/state relationship was the focal point of debate over the ratification of the Constitution, a contributing cause of civil war, and fertile source of controversy in American politics to this day. Thus, it is also a fertile source of research possibilities.

One such possibility is the fundamental question of whether state centered or nation centered federalism is best in the modern era. You could base a paper on the proposition that one or the other form is the more effective and appropriate and proceed to develop arguments to defend your position. The text provide a starting point in its discussions of the advantages and disadvantages of fiscal federalism and federalism's relationship to democracy and the size of government. Journal literature examining the efforts to return power and policy responsibility to the states during the Reagan era are many and provide more than enough material for your discussion.

Another alternative is to focus on a particular policy area and investigate how the state and national level governments "cooperate" in policy making and implementation. What is the national role in education, transportation, health, public safety, or economic development policies, to mention just a few possibilities?

The immense diversity of the fifty states also provides a rich source of interesting comparative studies. The impacts and consequences of different policy approaches to problems of education, corrections, abortion, business regulation, social welfare, or taxation could be explored. Select two to four states in different parts of the country or with sharply differing policy approaches to a similar problem, and compare their situations. Alternatively you may wish to examine the political and policy importance of the differing cultural, social, or economic characteristics of two or more states. Migration and rapid growth, ethnicity, population density, etc., may have important implications for a state's politics and policies. Comparative information about the states is available from a number of sources, but a good place to start is The World Almanac and Book of Facts under "states."

REVIEW TEST

Reread the chapter overview and quiz yourself with the "Reading for Content" questions. Review the learning objectives listed at the beginning of this chapter to be sure you have achieved them. When you feel like you are ready, take the Review Test below.

1.   _____ is a way of organizing a nation so that two or more levels of government have formal authority over the same area and people.
    (a)   Federalism
    (b)   Revenue sharing
    (c)   Dual federalism

(d)   Factionalism
Page 87

2.   Most governments in the world today are _____ governments, in
      which all power resides in the central government.
      (a)   federal
      (b)   feudal
      (c)   dualist
      (d)   unitary
Page 87

3.   States receive their authority directly from:
      (a)   the national government.
      (b)   the U.S. Constitution.
      (c)   state legislatures.
      (d)   the Articles of Confederation.
Page 87

4.   In a confederation, the national government is weak and most or
      all the power is in the hands of:
      (a)   the individual states.
      (b)   the president.
      (c)   Congress.
      (d)   the House of Representatives.
Page 87-88

5.   The electoral college system of voting for president makes it
      possible for a presidential candidate receiving the most
      popular votes to lose the election.   This has not happened
      since:
      (a)   1824.
      (b)   1876.
      (c)   1888.
      (d)   1960.
Page 89

6.   Candy Lightner, the woman who formed MADD (Mothers Against
      Drunk Drivers) realized that it was easier to raise the
      national drinking age by:
      (a)   getting key senators and legislators to sponsor her
             efforts on a national level.
      (b)   lobbying all fifty state legislatures separately.
      (c)   getting key senators and legislators to sponsor a
             constitutional amendment.
      (d)   lobbying all fifty state legislatures and coercing them
             to sponsor a constitutional amendment.
Page 90

7.   Almost every policy the national government has adopted had its

beginnings in:
(a)   Congress.
(b)   the states.
(c)   the White House.
(d)   the House of Representatives.
Page 90-91

8.   Judges in every state were told to obey the Constitution:
(a)   unless it conflicted with state constitutions.
(b)   unless it conflicted with state law.
(c)   even if it conflicted with state law or constitution.   (d)
only if it corresponded to state law.
Page 93

9.   The Tenth Amendment states that the "powers not delegated to
the United States by the Constitution:
(a)   are reserved to the states respectively."
(b)   are reserved to the people."
(c)   nor prohibited by it to the states, are reserved to the
states respectively, or to the people."
(d)   are left up to the courts' discretion."
Page d

10.   In 1941, the Supreme Court, in United States v. Darby,
called _____ a constitutional truism.
(a)   the Fifth Amendment
(b)   the Sixth Amendment
(c)   the Tenth Amendment
(d)   the Fourteenth Amendment
Page 91

11.   In 1985, the Supreme Court overturned National League of Cities
v. Usery in the case:
(a)   Griswald v. Connecticut.
(b)   Garcia v. San Antonio Metro.
(c)   Mapp v. Ohio.
(d)   Texas v. Johnson.
Page 94

12.   The chief justice of the Supreme Court, who wrote the majority
decision in McCulloch v. Maryland, was:
(a)   John Marshall.
(b)   John Jay.
(c)   Oliver Wendell Holmes.
(d)   William Howard Taft.
Page 94

13.   Other than arguing for the state of Maryland in McCulloch v.
Maryland, lawyer Luther Martin was famous for:
(a)   being a Revolutionary War hero.
(b)   firing the "shot heard around the world."
(c)   shooting Alexander Hamilton.

(d) signing the Declaration of Independence.
Page 95

14. In McCulloch v. Maryland, the Supreme Court ruled that the Constitution's "necessary and proper" clause gives Congress:
(a) unlimited powers.
(b) enumerated powers.
(c) implied powers.
(d) ceremonial powers.
Page 95

15. In McCulloch v. Maryland, the Supreme Court ruled that the Constitution's _____ clause gives Congress implied powers.
(a) "necessary and proper"
(b) war powers
(c) elastic
(d) both elastic and "necessary and proper" are correct
Page 95

16. Especially in the domain of _____ policy, hundreds of congressional policies involve powers not specifically mentioned in the Constitution.
(a) economic
(b) military
(c) foreign
(d) environmental
Page 96

17. In 1824, the Supreme Court defined commerce very broadly, encompassing virtually every form of commercial activity, in:
(a) McCulloch v. Maryland.
(b) Gibbons v. Ogden.
(c) Texas v. Johnson.
(d) Mapp v. Ohio.
Page 96

18. In 1954, the Supreme Court ruled that school segregation was:
(a) up to the states to decide.
(b) unconstitutional.
(c) constitutional.
(d) "morally improper but constitutionally sound."
Page 96

19. The national government, using federal marshals, made sure that black students were able to enroll at _____ in 1963.
(a) UCLA
(b) Tulane
(c) Duke
(d) the University of Alabama

Page 97

20. The conflict between states and the national government over equality issues:
    (a) was decided in favor of the national government.
    (b) is still being debated to this day.
    (c) was decided in favor of the states.
    (d) will never be resolved.
Page 97

21. _____ of the Constitution requires that states give full faith and credit to the public acts, records and civil judicial proceedings of every other state.
    (a) The elastic clause
    (b) The establishment clause
    (c) Article IV
    (d) Article II, Section 8
Page 98

22. The most complicated obligation among the states is the requirement that citizens of each state receive all the _____ of any other state in which they happen to be.
    (a) privileges
    (b) immunities
    (c) tax incentives
    (d) privileges and immunities
Page 99

23. States are exclusively responsible for:
    (a) law enforcement.
    (b) the postal system.
    (c) monetary policy.
    (d) military policy.
Page 100

24. In _____ federalism, powers and policy assignments are shared between the states and the national government.
    (a) dual
    (b) singular
    (c) fiscal
    (d) cooperative
Page 100

25. Dual federalism was a more appropriate description of the American federal system:
    (a) during the nineteenth century
    (b) during the revolutionary war
    (c) recently

(d)   during the colonial period
Page 100

26. Even though education was mainly a state responsibility, _____ set aside land to be used for schools in the Northwest Territory under the Articles of Confederation.
    (a)   Congress
    (b)   local authorities
    (c)   the Supreme Court
    (d)   the military
Page 101

27. In the 1950's and 1960's, the national government began supporting _____ education.
    (a)   public elementary
    (b)   public secondary
    (c)   college
    (d)   public elementary, secondary and even college
Page 101

28. Historically, _____ was/were responsible for building roads.
    (a)   cities
    (b)   Congress
    (c)   states
    (d)   cities and states
Page 101

29. Ronald Reagan argued that _____ had primary responsibility for governing in most policy areas and promised to "restore the balance between levels of government."
    (a)   the president
    (b)   the national government
    (c)   states
    (d)   Congress
Page 102

30. _____ is/are the main instrument(s) the national government uses for both aiding and influencing states and localities.
    (a)   Money
    (b)   Grants-in-aid
    (c)   Financial coercion
    (d)   all of these
Page 103

31. Federal aid to state and local governments accounts for about _____ percent of all federal government expenditures.
    (a)   three
    (b)   six
    (c)   ten

(d) eighteen

Page 103

32. _____ grants can be used for one of 422 specific purposes, or categories, of state and local spending.
(a) Categorical
(b) Revenue Sharing
(c) Block
(d) Special purpose

Page 104

33. Common _____ grants are those for Medicaid, Aid for Families with Dependent Children, and child nutrition programs.
(a) block
(b) policy
(c) project
(d) formula

Page 105

34. About _____ percent of all federal aid to state and local community governments is in the form of block grants.
(a) two
(b) eleven
(c) twenty-two
(d) thirty-five

Page 105

35. On the whole, federal grant distribution follows the principle of:
(a) universalism.
(b) categorization.
(c) formula grants.
(d) dual federalism.

Page 107-108

36. Medicaid receives wide support from both political parties and the national government picks up _____ of the bill. (a) 100 percent
(b) 75 percent
(c) 55 percent
(d) none

Page 108

37. The U.S. Bureau of the Census counts not only people but governments. Its latest count revealed _____ American governments.
(a) 51
(b) 102

         (c)   12,502
         (d)   83,237
Page 111

38.   State and localities spend _____ percent of the Gross National
      Product today in 1990.
      (a)   three
      (b)   six
      (c)   thirteen
      (d)   twenty
Page 115

39.   There are only _____ countries with federal systems.
      (a)   forty
      (b)   twenty-three
      (c)   nineteen
      (d)   thirteen
Page 87

40.   Of the following countries, only _____ has a unitary
      government instead of a federal system.
      (a)   Canada
      (b)   Switzerland
      (c)   China
      (d)   India
Page 87

BEFORE GOING ON

Check your answers against the answer key below. If you have missed
some, go back and reread the relevant passages on the page of the
book indicated immediately below those questions.

Review Test Answers:

1: a	11: b	21: c	31: c
2: d	12: a	22: d	32: a
3: b	13: d	23: a	33: d
4: a	14: c	24: d	34: b
5: c	15: d	25: a	35: a
6: a	16: a	26: a	36: c
7: a	17: b	27: d	37: d
8: c	18: b	28: d	38: c
9: c	19: d	29: c	39: d
10: c	20: a	30: d	40: c

Chapter 3

Knowing the Key Terms listed on page 117 remains an essential ingredient for success - wouldn't hurt to check them again. This week find a way to mention the important role of "intergovernmental relations" in today's political process. This will show that you are right up-to-date in your terminology, and leave the less well equipped wondering what you are talking about.

CHAPTER 4

CIVIL LIBERTIES AND PUBLIC POLICY

CHAPTER LEARNING OBJECTIVES

After reading Chapter 4, you should be able to:

1. Define civil liberties.
2. Identify the Bill of Rights
3. List the freedoms guaranteed in the First Amendment.
4. Discuss the process and implications of incorporation of the Bill of Rights.
5. Discuss the key issues and cases concerning freedom of religion.
6. Discuss the key issues and cases concerning freedom of expression.
7. Discuss the key issues and cases concerning rights of the accused.
8. Discuss the key issues and cases concerning the right of privacy and abortion.
9. Discuss the implications of civil liberties for democracy.
10. Discuss how civil liberties affect the size of government.

PRETEST QUESTIONS

The pretest below will give you an idea of the state of your knowledge about civil liberties. The questions should also help you learn what to look for while studying the text. Take the whole pretest, then check your answers against the key that follows (don't peek!). As you read the chapter, watch for where these questions are addressed (indicated after each question) so that you may learn why the answer is what it is.

1. In 1985, two men were convicted of murder and sentenced to life imprisonment. One man had hired the other to kill his wife. The killer responded to an ad in _____ magazine and this led the woman's family to sue the magazine (unsuccessfully) for letting the advertisement appear.
   (a) Soldier of Fortune
   (b) High Times
   (c) Newsweek
   (d) Cosmopolitan

Page 124

2.   In 1925, the Supreme Court overturned _____ with Gitlow v.
      New York and asserted that state government must respect First
      Amendment rights.
      (a)   Mapp v. Ohio
      (b)   Tinker v. Des Moines Independent
      (c)   Marbury v. Madison
      (d)   Barron v. Baltimore
Page 124-125

3.   "The provisions of the Bill of Rights have been held to apply
      to the states, not in their own right, but as implicit in the
      _____ Amendment," writes constitutional scholar Samuel
      Krislov.
      (a)   First
      (b)   Fifth
      (c)   Ninth
      (d)   Fourteenth
Page 125

4.   In _____, the Supreme Court declared that aid to church-
      related schools must have a secular purpose, not be used to
      advance or inhibit religion, and avoid excessive government
      "entanglement" with religion.
      (a)   Lemon v. Kurtzman
      (b)   Engle v. Vitale
      (c)   Mapp v. Ohio
      (d)   Schenck v. United States
Page 127

5.   In the 1970's, _____ formed an organization called the
      Moral Majority.
      (a)   Jimmy Swaggert
      (b)   Jim Bakker
      (c)   Jerry Falwell
      (d)   Larry Flynt
Page 129

6.   No fewer than three _____ laws sought to legalize school
      prayer by making it voluntary.
      (a)   Florida
      (b)   Alabama
      (c)   California
      (d)   Oregon
Page 129

7.   Supreme Court Justice _____ thought that American's freedom of
      expression, like their freedom of conscience, was absolute.
      (a)   William Howard Taft
      (b)   Anthony Kennedy
      (c)   Byron White
      (d)   Hugo Black
Page 130
8.   The Supreme Court was portrayed recently in the best- selling

book, _____, written by Bob Woodward and Scott Armstrong.
(a)   The Brethren
(b)   Veil
(c)   Wired
(d)   The Final Days
Page 132-133

9.   Supreme Court Justice _____ once remarked that he could not define obscenity but "he knew it when he saw it."
(a)   Byron White
(b)   Thurgood Marshall
(c)   Harry Blackmun
(d)   Potter Stewart
Page 133

10.   In 1973, the Court tried to clarify its doctrine concerning obscenity in:
(a)   Engel v. Vitale
(b)   Miller v. California.
(c)   Lynch v. Donnelly.
(d)   Falwell v. Flynt.
Page 133

11.   In 1988, all nine justices of the Supreme Court ruled against the Reverend Jerry Falwell when he tried to sue _____ magazine after they printed a humorous ad that depicted him in a manner he thought libelous.
(a)   Soldier of Fortune
(b)   Hustler
(c)   National Lampoon
(c)   Mad
Page 136

12.   _____ held that federal free speech guarantees did not apply when a person was on private property.
(a)   Hudgens v. National Labor Relations Board
(b)   Bakke v. the Board of Regents
(c)   Near v. Minnesota
(d)   Engel v. Vitale
Page 139

13.   The Supreme Court ruled that "the trial of a criminal case must be open to the public," in:
(a)   New York Times v. Sullivan.
(b)   Nixon v. United States.
(c)   Richmond Newspapers v. Virginia.
(d)   Schenck v. United States.
Page 141

14.   In one important case regarding the freedom of assembly,

_____ applied to march in the streets of Skokie, Illinois, where many survivors of Hitler's death camps lived.
    (a) the American Nazi Party
    (b) the Ku Klux Klan
    (c) the Palestine Liberation Front (PLO)
    (d) the Black Panthers
Page 143

15. To prevent abuse of police power, the Constitution requires that no court may issue a search warrant unless _____ exists to believe that a crime has occurred or is about to occur.
    (a) suspicion
    (b) certainty
    (c) proof
    (d) probable cause
Page 145

16. Although in federal courts, the _____ Amendment has always ensured the right to counsel, not until recently did people who were tried in state courts have this right.
    (a) Sixth
    (b) Fifth
    (c) Third
    (d) First
Page 148

17. The _____ Amendment ensures the right to a speedy trial by an impartial jury.
    (a) Fifth
    (b) Sixth
    (c) Eighth
    (d) Ninth
Page 149

18. Through the _____ Amendment, the provision of the Bill of Rights concerning cruel and unusual punishment applies to the states.
    (a) Fourteenth
    (b) Sixteenth
    (c) Nineteenth
    (d) Twenty-first
Page 150

19. The _____ Amendment states that the "right of the people to keep and bear arms shall not be infringed."
    (a) Second
    (b) Fourth
    (c) Sixth
    (d) Seventh
Page 123

20. Technical advancements, especially in the area of _____ are

presenting the court system with difficult new legal and
ethical issues.
(a)   space
(b)   social engineering
(c)   medicine
(d)   education
Page 152-156 (passim)

Pretest Answers:

1: a		11: b
2: d		12: a
3: d		13: c
4: a		14: a
5: c		15: d
6: b		16: a
7: d		17: b
8: a		18: a
9: d		19: a
10: b		20: c

READING FOR CONTENT

Listed below are sets of questions associated with the content of
each major section of Chapter 4. Carefully review the questions
associated with each section of the text before reading the section.
Have the questions in mind as you read the section and, when you
reach the end of each section, stop and see if you can answer the
questions well. If not, reread the relevant paragraphs until you
are sure of your response to each of the questions.

I.   The Bill of Rights - Then and Now

      What are "civil liberties."
      Which Constitutional amendments constitute the Bill of
        Rights?
      What are the First Amendment freedoms?
      How has the Bill of Rights been "incorporated" - extended to
        the states?

II.   Freedom of Religion

      What does the "establishment clause" prohibit?
      What does the "free exercise clause" protect?
      Who are the "fundamentalists" and what do they want?

III. Freedom of Expression

      What is the meaning and significance of the principle of no
        "prior restraint?"
      How has the Supreme Court defined obscenity?
      What are the key cases in which the Court dealt with
        obscenity?

What is libel and how is it defined for public figures?
What is symbolic speech and why is it important?
How are commercial speech and the public airwaves regulated?
How is free speech limited in the interests of public order?
How is free press limited in the interests of a fair trial?
What are shield laws and how are they related to free press?
What behavior does the freedom of assembly protect.
How is freedom of assembly limited in the interest of order?

IV. Defendant's Rights

What are the rights of the accused protected in the Bill of
   Rights?
What is the exclusionary rule and how has it been modified
   recently.
Which rights were protected by the decision in Miranda v.
   Arizona?
What right was protected by the decision in Gideon v
   Wainwright?
How has the Supreme Court dealt with the death penalty?
Which Supreme Court cases have dealt with the death penalty?

V. The Right To Privacy

How has the Supreme Court found a right to privacy in the
   Constitution?
How has the right to privacy shaped the Court's rulings on
   abortion?
What are the key Supreme Court cases dealing with abortion?

VI. Understanding Civil Liberties and the Constitution

How are civil liberties related to democracy?
How are civil liberties related to the size of government?

CHAPTER OVERVIEW

I. Introduction   (121-122)

CIVIL LIBERTIES are legal and constitutional protections against the
government. Americans' civil liberties are set down in the Bill of
Rights. These rights are applied and interpreted in specific cases
by the courts. The U.S. Supreme Court is the final interpreter of
the content and scope of our liberties.

II. The Bill Of Rights - Then And Now (122-125)

The first ten amendments to the Constitution comprise the BILL OF
RIGHTS. The Bill of Rights ensures Americans basic liberties:
freedom of speech and religion, protection against arbitrary
searches and rights when accused of a crime, etc. Americans have

always held the Bill of Rights in high esteem, viewing it as a central expression of the nation's creed. Political scientists have discovered, however, that people are more devoted to these rights in theory than in practice in specific cases. Americans believe generally in the freedom of speech, for example, but many citizens would not allow their public schools to teach about atheism or homosexuality.

A. Rights in Conflict: The Tough Cases

Cases involving civil liberties are often ambiguous and involve balancing conflicting rights.

B. The Bill of Rights and the States

The Bill of Rights was written to restrict the powers of the national government. What happens if a state government violates the national Bill of Rights? Originally the Supreme Court ruled, in BARRON V. BALTIMORE that the Bill of Rights restrained only the national government, not the states and cities. Almost a century later the Supreme Court began to extend the Bill of Rights to the states through the "due process" clause of the FOURTEENTH AMENDMENT. In GITLOW V. NEW YORK, the Court declared that freedoms of speech and press "were fundamental personal rights and liberties protected by the due process clause of the Fourteenth Amendment from impairment by the states." Since then most of the Bill of Rights has been extended to cover state governments by "incorporation" through the Fourteenth Amendment. Only the Second, Third, and Seventh have not been applied specifically to the states.

III. Freedom Of Religion (125-130)

The First Amendment makes two statements about religion and government. The "establishment clause" states that "Congress shall make no law respecting an establishment of religion." The "free exercise clause" protects the citizens' freedom to worship as they please. Controversy sometimes arises due to conflicts in these provisions.

A. The Establishment Clause

It is clear that the establishment clause prohibits Congress from creating an official national church, but it is less clear what else it prohibits. Does it mean only that the government cannot favor one religion over another, or does it create, as Thomas Jefferson believed, a "wall of separation" between church and state that forbids any support for religion at all? Debate in this area is especially intense over aid to church-related schools. In Lemon v. Kurtzman the Supreme Court approved such aid, but said it must not involve excessive government "entanglement" with religion.
No church-state issue is more controversial than school prayer. In ENGEL V. VITALE the Court ruled that such prayer violated the establishment clause when done as part of classroom exercises in

public schools. This ruling has generated much popular opposition and continues to be ignored in a considerable number of school districts.

B. The Free Exercise Clause

The guarantee of the free exercise of religion is not always simple. Religions can sometimes forbid action that society thinks necessary, or require actions that society finds disruptive or illegal. The Supreme Court has never permitted religious freedom to be an excuse for any and all behaviors. Instead the Court has taken the position that while people have an inviolable right to believe what they want, they do not necessarily have the right to practice a belief. The Court expects society to "reasonably accommodate" religious practices, but need not tolerate dangerous practices or those deeply offensive to social norms.

C. The Rise of the Fundamentalists

Religious issues and controversies have become much more salient in the nation's political debate in recent years. This is due, in part, to fundamentalist religious groups spurring their members to political action.   These religious groups have pressed a conservative view on several key issues including abortion, school prayer, and the teaching of "creation science" in conjunction with the theory of evolution. Though becoming weaker in recent years, these movements contributed to an atmosphere in which the Court has lowered, or poked some significant holes in, the "wall of separation" between church and state raised in the 1960s.

IV.   Freedom Of Expression (130-143)

A democracy depends on the free expression of ideas. In America the freedom of conscience is absolute - Americans can believe whatever they want to believe. Freedom of speech has normally been interpreted by the courts as subject to some limitation, however, especially when it conflicts with other rights or values such as public order. Obscenity and libel, for example, are not protected by the First Amendment.

The courts have also had to decide what constitutes speech (or press) within the meaning of the First Amendment. Certain forms of nonverbal speech, like picketing, are considered symbolic speech and receive First Amendment protection. Other forms of expression are considered "action," which is more easily limited under the Constitution.

A. Prior Restraint

One principle has been made clear by the Court in freedom of expression cases - there can be no PRIOR RESTRAINT on speech and the press.   Prior restraint refers to a government's actions that prevent material from being published at all. In other words, there can be no censorship. The one exception is in the area of national security.   The government has succeeded in censoring material thought damaging to the national security.   Even in this area, however, the courts are reluctant to issue injunctions that constitute prior restraint, and demand convincing argument that a significant threat to the national interest is involved.

B. Obscenity

In ROTH V. UNITED STATES the Supreme Court ruled that obscenity was not "within the area of constitutionally protected speech or press." Deciding just what is obscene, though, is not an easy matter. Public standards vary from time to time, place to place, and person to person.

The Court attempted to clarify the issue in 1973 in the MILLER V. CALIFORNIA case.   Materials were obscene if the work, taken as a whole, appealed to a prurient interest in sex; and if it showed "patently offensive sexual contact; and if it "lacked serious artistic, literary, political, or scientific merit." Decisions on obscenity, following these guidelines, should be made by local communities. The difficulty remains, however, in determining what is lewd or offensive. Rather than try to ban pornography, many communities merely try to regulate its availability to the young.

Recently some women's groups have argued that pornography discriminates against women, unfairly degrading and dehumanizing women by gender. Some cities have passed antipornography ordinances on this basis, but, so far, the courts have struck them down on First Amendment grounds.

C. Defamation: Libel and Slander

Libel, the publication of statements known to be false that are malicious and tend to damage a person's reputation, and slander (spoken defamation), are not protected by the First Amendment. Because of the need to encourage debate and criticism of government and politicians, statements about public figures are libelous only if made with malice and reckless disregard for the truth. Public figures must prove that those making an untrue statement knew it was untrue and intended harm. This is a difficult standard to attain.

Despite the leniency of American libel laws they probably do inhibit the press to some extent. Libel cases are expensive and there is evidence that publications sometimes limit themselves to stay on the safe side.

D. Symbolic Speech

Broadly interpreted, freedom of speech is a guarantee of freedom of expression. The Court has ruled that freedom of speech goes beyond the spoken word. Actions such as wearing a black arm band or burning the flag in protest of government actions are SYMBOLIC SPEECH, that express an opinion but do not consist of speaking or writing. Such acts are viewed as somewhere between pure speech and pure action. Precisely where the line is remains less than clear and continues to be defined by individual court decisions.

E. Commercial Speech

As COMMERCIAL SPEECH advertising is restricted far more extensively than expressions of opinion on religious, political or other matters. The Federal Trade Commission (FTC) regulates what kinds of goods can be advertised on broadcast media and the content of such advertising.

F. Regulation of the Public Airwaves

The Federal Communications Commission (FCC) regulates the content, nature, and existence of radio and television broadcasting. This sort of governmental interference would violate the First Amendment if applied to the print media. The regulation is justified on the basis that only a limited number of broadcast frequencies are available, and they are "owned" by the public.

G. Free Speech and Public Order

The Supreme Court has ruled that government can limit speech if it provokes a clear and present danger of substantive evils. What is a danger, when it is "clear and present" and if will cause "substantive" evil remain matters of interpretation. The courts have been generally quite supportive of the right to protest, pass out leaflets, or gather signatures on petitions - so long as the activity is confined to public places. Constitutional protections diminish dramatically on private property.

H. Free Press Versus Fair Trial

A trial may not be "fair" if press coverage inflames public opinion so much that an impartial jury cannot be found. Yet journalists wish to have their freedom to cover trials and the public its "right to know." The courts have sought to balance these conflicting rights.

Journalists also claim a right to keep their sources of information confidential. They argue that the free press would become merely a tool of the government or prosecutors if it had to reveal where it got information on illegal activities, for example. Moreover, its sources would be unwilling to come forward, damaging the people's right to know. Some states have passed SHIELD LAWS to protect reporters and their confidentiality. In most states, however, they have no right to withhold information when a case comes to trial. The Supreme Court has also ruled that the Constitution affords them no such right. Sometimes they have gone to jail for this principle of their profession.

I. Freedom of Assembly

The freedom to "peaceably assemble" is also granted by the First Amendment. It is the basis for the right to form interest groups and political parties as well as for picketing and protesting. There are two facets of the freedom of assembly.

1. Right to Assemble. This is the right to gather together in order to make a statement. Because this right poses a threat to order it is subject to the reasonable limits of time, place, and manner. Any group has a right to demonstrate, but not anytime, anyplace and any how it wishes. Usually a group must apply to the local city government for a permit and post a bond a few hundred dollars. The permit must be granted as long as the group pledges to hold its demonstration at a time and place that allows police to prevent major disruptions.

There are virtually no limitations on the content of the protest message. The balance between freedom and order is tested when the content of a protest verges on harassment, however. This problem has recently been raised when abortion protesters attempt to shame and intimidate clients outside abortion clinics.

2. Right to Associate. The second facet of the freedom of assembly is the right to associate with people who share a common interest, including an interest in political change.

V. Defendant's Rights (143-151)

Most of the rest of the Bill of Rights is concerned with the rights of people accused of crimes. Originally intended particularly for the protection of those accused in political arrests, today the protections in the Fourth, Fifth, Sixth, Seventh, and Eighth Amendments are mostly applied in criminal justice cases.

A. Interpreting Defendants's Rights

The Bill of Rights covers every stage of the criminal justice process. Any misstep may invalidate a conviction.

The language of the Bill of rights is often vague. The courts must continually rule on the constitutionality of actions by the police, prosecutors, judges and legislatures that may or may not violate these vaguely worded protections. One thing that is clear, however, is that these rights have been extended to the states and thus limit both national and state authorities.

B. Searches and Seizures

Police cannot arrest a citizen on a whim. Before making an arrest, police need what the courts call PROBABLE CAUSE for believing someone is guilty of a crime. To get a conviction they will need physical evidence to use in court. The Fourth Amendment is quite clear in forbidding UNREASONABLE SEARCHES AND SEIZURES. No court may issue a SEARCH WARRANT without probable cause to believe a crime has occurred or is about to occur. Warrants must specify the area to be searched and what is being searched for.

No search warrant is necessary for a "reasonable" search, however, and most searches take place without warrants. Warrantless searches are valid if probable cause exists, if the search is necessary to protect an officer's safety, or if the search is limited to material relevant to the suspected crime or within the suspect's immediate control.

Courts use an EXCLUSIONARY RULE to prevent illegally seized evidence from being introduced in the courtroom. No matter how incriminating a piece of evidence, it cannot be used if not constitutionally obtained. The reasoning for this is that police should only be rewarded with a conviction for competent and constitutional police work.

The Burger Court made some exceptions to the exclusionary rule. Police can use illegally evidence when this evidence led them to a discovery they would eventually have made without it. Also, evidence can be used if the police who seized it mistakenly thought (in "good faith") they were operating under a constitutionally valid warrant.

C. Self-incrimination

In the American system the burden of proof rests on the police and prosecutors. Suspects cannot be compelled to help with their own conviction. The FIFTH AMENDMENT specifically forbids forced SELF-INCRIMINATION. (If the government grants a suspect immunity from prosecution, however, they must testify regarding their own and others' crimes.)

Not only do citizens have a right against helping with their own conviction, they have the right to be made aware of this right at the time of arrest. In MIRANDA V. ARIZONA the Supreme Court set guidelines for police questioning of suspects: 1) suspects must be told that they have a constitutional right to remain silent and stop answering questions at any time; 2) they must be warned that what they say can be used against them in a court of law; and 3) they must be told that they have a right to have a lawyer present during questioning and that a public defender is available.

D. The Right to Counsel

The SIXTH AMENDMENT has always ensured the right to counsel in federal courts. But only relatively recently have people tried in state courts been afforded this right. Beginning with the GIDEON V. WAINWRIGHT case, Supreme Court decisions have universalized this right so every court is required to appoint a lawyer to represent anyone who does not have the money to hire one.

E. Trial by Jury

Though guaranteed a right to trial by jury, in America 90 percent of all cases begin and end with a guilty plea. Most cases are settled through a process called PLEA BARGAINING. A bargain is struck between a defendant's lawyer and a prosecutor to the effect that a defendant will plead guilty to a lesser crime in exchange for not being prosecuted for the more serious one. The process reduces punishments, but it saves time and money that would otherwise be spent on a trial.

About 300,000 cases per year do go to trial. These defendants have the Sixth Amendment right to a speedy trial by an impartial jury. The Constitution does not specify, however, how an impartial jury will be selected, the size of the jury, or the majority that will be required to convict. The 12 person jury and unanimous vote for criminal convictions is a tradition passed down from English practice.

F. Cruel and Unusual Punishment

The EIGHTH AMENDMENT forbids CRUEL AND UNUSUAL PUNISHMENT, but it does not define the phrase. This provision of the Bill of Rights has also been extended to the state through the Fourteenth Amendment.

Almost all the debate over cruel and unusual punishment has centered on the death penalty. In GREGG V. GEORGIA the Supreme Court ruled that the death penalty was not cruel and unusual punishment. Earlier decisions have limited its application, however, demanding that it not be applied in a discriminatory manner or arbitrarily and inconsistently. The Court also ruled that it could not simply be made mandatory for certain crimes.
Though an accepted part of the criminal justice system, the application of the death penalty remains a relative rarity.VI. The Right To Privacy (151-155)

Technology has expanded the power of government and private organizations to threaten citizens' privacy far beyond what the drafters of the Bill of Rights could have imagined. Today's hottest controversies concerning civil liberties involve privacy rights.

A. Is There a Right to Privacy?

The Bill of Rights does not explicitly state that Americans have a RIGHT TO PRIVACY. The concept of privacy clearly underlies many of the first ten amendments, however. Freedom of religion implies the right to private beliefs and protections against "unreasonable searches and seizures" ensures privacy in one's home, for example.

In Griswold v. Connecticut in 1965 the Court formally recognized that the Bill of Rights cast "penumbras" - unstated liberties on the fringes of the more explicitly stated rights - protecting a right to privacy. Supporters of the ruling argued that the protection of privacy must be the underlying purpose of the Fourth Amendment. Opponents saw the Supreme Court simply inventing protections not specified by the Constitution. This controversy was to be no mere academic exercise, for the right to privacy underlies the controversial ruling establishing abortion rights.

B. Firestorms over Abortion

In 1973 the Court ruled in ROE V. WADE that a state could not limit a woman' right to choose an abortion during the first trimester of her pregnancy. The decision argued that as the pregnancy progressed the state's "interest" increased so that it could regulate abortion during the second trimester, but only to ensure the health of the mother. Finally, during the third trimester the state could prohibit abortion, except when the mother's life was in danger.

The decision unleashed a storm of protest which has never subsided. Opponents of the decision have been successful in winning some legislative and judicial modifications on the right to abortion. In 1989 the Court upheld, in the WEBSTER V. REPRODUCTIVE HEALTH SERVICES case, state laws restricting the use of public funds for abortions. The Court has not yet "overturned" the Roe decision, however. If it should, the states would be able to recriminalize abortion in any way they see fit.

With the small victories for the anti-abortion forces, and with the Supreme Court becoming more conservative, the abortion rights forces are again becoming more active. Proponents of free choice on abortion believe that a woman's control of her own body is a fundamental right, necessary to be a fully autonomous human being. Opponents call themselves "pro-life" because they believe that the fetus is a fully autonomous human being, and that abortion therefore violates that person's right to life. It is an emotional and irreconcilable debate that promises to continue to challenge American politics and politicians for the foreseeable future.

C. A Time to Live and a Time to Die

Advances in medical technology allow the maintenance of vital life functions despite the absence of others. As a result states have been forced to address the problem of defining death. Procedures such as in-vitro fertilization, frozen embryos, and artificial insemination complicate efforts to define birth and parental rights and responsibilities. The Courts will bear the responsibility for sorting out these and many more legal quandaries in the future as medical science continues to advance.

VII. Understanding Civil Liberties And The Constitution (155-157)

America is democratic because it is governed by officials elected by the people. American government is constitutional because it has a fundamental law that limits the things government can do. Thus the Constitution limits what even the majority of the people can democratically empower the government to do. The democratic and constitutional components of government both conflict with and reinforce each other.

A. Civil Liberties and Democracy

Individual rights, such as those protected by the First Amendment, enhance democracy. If people are to govern themselves they need access to information and opinions to make informed decisions. But majority opinion can potentially conflict with individual rights. The majority may be willing to restrict or revoke the right of unpopular minorities to free expression, for example. Ultimately the courts decide what constitutional guarantees mean in practice. The courts enhance democracy by protecting liberty and equality from the excesses of majority rule.

B. Civil Liberties and the Size of Government

The size and efficiency made possible by modern information processing technologies make government a potentially greater threat to individual liberties than ever before. The strict limitations on governmental power provided by the Bill of Rights are increasingly essential to individual freedom.

DOING RESEARCH ON CIVIL LIBERTIES

Civil liberties raise an abundance of controversial issues, all of which have generated a wealth of opinion and scholarly literature. School prayer, free press versus fair trial, obscenity, symbolic speech (flag burning, for example), the exclusionary rule, plea bargaining, the death penalty, and abortion are all fertile ground for research papers. In addition, your text raises the emerging controversies surrounding the right-to-die and the new technology of birth (in-vitro fertilization, frozen embryos, etc.), which also could by explored in a research paper.

Alternatively, you may wish to exercise your rights in doing your research under the Freedom of Information Act (FOIA). The government collects information on an astounding array of subjects and, within certain limits, you have a right to access it. The FOIA applies to information held by administrative agencies, but not to records of Congress, the courts, or state governments. To use the act you need to know what information you want and which agency might have it. You need to provide a reasonable description of the information you are seeking. The better you can identify the material you want the quicker and more effectively the agency can respond. Thus, you may wish to look at <u>The United States Government Manual</u> to find the appropriate agency, and the <u>Federal Register</u> which lists the record systems the government keeps.

A couple of cautions. First, agencies are allowed to charge for providing information under the FOIA. There can be an hourly charge to pay for the costs of searching and a charge for copying the materials. Thus, the more specific your request the lower the cost - because it will include fewer materials and be easier to find. Agencies don't always charge, however. Also, some categories of information are "off limits" under the FOIA. Such things as agency personnel records, material on criminal investigations, and classified national security materials, for example.

REVIEW TEST

Reread the chapter overview and quiz yourself with the "Reading for Content" questions. Review the learning objectives listed at the beginning of this chapter to be sure you have achieved them. When you feel like you are ready, take the Review Test below.

1.   Supreme Court Justice _____ declared that government can limit speech if it provokes a clear and present danger of substantive evils.
     (a)   Oliver Wendell Holmes
     (b)   William Howard Taft
     (c)   Hugo T. Black
     (d)   William O. Douglas
Page 130

2.   When the national government was determined to jail the leaders of the Communist party, their vehicle was
     _____, which forbids the advocacy of violent overthrow of the American government.
     (a)   the Hatch Act
     (b)   the Smith Act
     (c)   the Sixth Amendment
     (d)   the First Amendment
Page 139

3.   _____ wrote that God gave the American people "the three precious gifts of freedom of speech, freedom of religion, and the prudence never to exercise either of them."
     (a)   James Madison
     (b)   John Quincy Adams
     (c)   H. L. Mencken
     (d)   Mark Twain
Page 122

4.   The Supreme Court case _____, in 1833, said that the Bill of Rights restrained only the national government, not states

and cities.
(a)   Mapp v. Ohio
(b)   Schenck v. United States
(c)   Barron v. Baltimore
(d)   Griswold v. Connecticut
Page 124-125

5.   The 1925 case Gitlow v. New York upheld First Amendment rights but based itself on:
(a)   the Fifth Amendment.
(b)   the Fourteenth Amendment.
(c)   the Sixteenth Amendment.
(d)   the Twenty-first Amendment.
Page 125

6.   It was the _____ Amendment, which was ratified in 1868, that contains the "due process" clause.
(a)   Fifth
(b)   Eleventh
(c)   Thirteenth
(d)   Fourteenth
Page 125

7.   As recently as 1985, then Attorney General _____ criticized Gitlow v. New York and called for "disincorporation" of the Bill of Rights.
(a)   John Mitchell
(b)   Edwin Meese
(c)   Richard Thornburg
(d)   Ramsey Clark
Page 125

8.   Gradually, especially during the 1960's when _____ was chief justice, the Supreme Court has applied most of the Bill of Rights to the states.
(a)   Oliver Wendell Holmes
(b)   Warren Burger
(c)   Earl Warren
(d)   William Rehnquist
Page 125

9.   All of the amendments to the Constitution have been applied specifically to the states EXCEPT:
(a)   the Second Amendment
(b)   the Third Amendment
(c)   the Seventh Amendment
(d)   all answers are correct
Page 125

10.   _____ argued that the First Amendment created a "wall of separation" between church and state.
(a)   Cotton Mather

    (b)   James Madison
    (c)   Thomas Jefferson
    (d)   Benjamin Franklin
Page 126

11. Twenty years after the 1962 and 1963 rulings, President _____
     pushed unsuccessfully for an amendment to permit prayer in
     schools.
     (a)   Nixon
     (b)   Johnson
     (c)   Carter
     (d)   Reagan
Page 127

12. _____ refused induction into the armed services during the
     Vietnam War because, he said, military service would violate
     his Muslim faith.
     (a)   Muhammed Ali
     (b)   Beach Boy Carl Wilson
     (c)   H. Rap Brown
     (d)   Stokely Charmichael
Page 128

13. In the 1970's, Jerry Falwell formed an organization called: (a)
     MADD (Mothers Against Drunk Driving).
     (b)   the American Nazi Party.
     (c)   the Ku Klux Klan
     (d)   the Moral Majority.
Page 129

14. No fewer than three Alabama laws sought to legalize school
     prayer by making it:
     (a)   mandatory.
     (b)   compulsory only once a week.
     (c)   voluntary.
     (d)   part of graduation requirements.
Page 129

15. Television evangelist _____ made a small but respectable
     showing in the Republican presidential primaries.
     (a)   Oral Roberts
     (b)   Pat Robertson
     (c)   Jim Bakker
     (d)   Jimmy Swaggert
Page 130

16. In 1919, Supreme Court Justice _____ said that "the most
     stringent protection of free speech would not protect a man
     from falsely shouting 'fire' in a theater and causing a panic."

(a) Oliver Wendell Holmes
(b) William O. Douglas
(c) Hugo Black
(d) William Howard Taft
Page 130

17. In 1988, the Supreme Court ruled, in Hazelwood School District v. Kuhlmeier, that a high school newspaper:
    (a) was NOT a public forum.
    (b) was subject to prior restraint by school officials.
    (c) could be regulated in any "reasonable manner" by school officials.
    (d) all answers are correct
Page 131-132

18. In Roth v. United States (1957), the Supreme Court ruled that _____ is not within the area of constitutionally protected speech or press.
    (a) a music recording
    (b) rock and roll music
    (c) obscenity
    (d) a racial slur
Page 133

19. The state of Georgia banned the acclaimed film _____, a ban the Supreme Court struck down in Jenkins v. Georgia.
    (a) Carnal Knowledge
    (b) Last Tango in Paris
    (c) Baby Doll
    (d) Behind the Green Door
Page 133

20. The Supreme Court has held, in cases such as _____, that statements about public figures are libelous only if made with malice and reckless disregard for the truth.
    (a) Marbury v. Madison
    (b) Texas v. Johnson
    (c) New York Times v. Sullivan
    (d) Miller v. California
Page 135

21. _____, once the commander of American troops in South Vietnam, sued CBS for libel.
    (a) William Westmoreland
    (b) Robert S. McNamara
    (c) Dean Rusk
    (d) McGeorge Bundy
Page 135-136

22. In the spring of 1986, the Los Angeles Times refused to publish several episodes of the syndicated cartoon strip, _____, on the grounds that they were "overblown and unfair" to members of the Reagan administration.

        (a)   Bloom County
        (b)   Shoe
        (c)   Doonesbury
        (d)   The Family Circus
Page 136-137

23.   The Supreme Court, in 1989, decided that Texas' law prohibiting
      flag desecration violated the First Amendment in:
      (a)   Roth v. United States.
      (b)   Johnson v. Johnson.
      (c)   Schenck v. United States.
      (d)   Texas v. Johnson.
Page 137

24.   In the 1960's, the source of the most bitter controversy in the
      nation was:
      (a)   the quest for civil rights.
      (b)   the ratification of the Equal Rights Amendment.
      (c)   the debate over prayer in schools.
      (d)   the Vietnam War.
Page 139

25.   Hudgens v. National Labor Relations Board (1976) held that
      federal free speech guarantees did not apply when a person: (a)
      was in another state.
      (b)   was on private property.
      (c)   was on public property.
      (d)   they had a criminal record.
Page 139

26.   The freedom of persons to peaceably assemble can conflict with
      other societal values when it disrupts:
      (a)   public order.
      (b)   traffic flow.
      (c)   peace and quiet.
      (d)   all answers are correct
Page 141

27.   The _____ Amendment is specific in forbidding unreasonable
      searches and seizures by the police upon any citizen.
      (a)   First
      (b)   Second
      (c)   Fourth
      (d)   Fifth
Page 145

28.   Constitutional protection against self-incrimination begins:
      (a)   at the arrest of a person.
      (b)   at the person's arraignment.
      (c)   at pre-trial hearings.

(d) at a person's trial.
Page 147

29. When a suspect is read their rights under law after arrest, this is due to the Supreme Court ruling:
   (a) Mapp v. Ohio.
   (b) Near v. Minnesota.
   (c) Miranda v. Arizona.
   (d) Texas v. Johnson.
Page 147

30. Today, _____ is required to appoint a lawyer to represent anyone who does not have the money to hire one.
   (a) national appellate courts
   (b) national trial courts
   (c) state appellate courts
   (d) every court
Page 148

31. In American courts, 90 percent of all cases begin and end with a _____ plea.
   (a) guilty
   (b) not guilty
   (c) nolo contendere (no contest)
   (d) dismissal
Page 149

32. The _____ Amendment forbids cruel and unusual punishment for convicted citizens.
   (a) Fourth
   (b) Sixth
   (c) Seventh
   (d) Eighth
Page 150

33. In _____, the Supreme Court first confronted the question of whether the death penalty is inherently cruel and unusual punishment (and sent a confusing message).
   (a) Furman v. Georgia
   (b) Powell v. Alabama
   (c) Schenck v. United States
   (d) Miller v. California
Page 150

34. The _____ Amendment protects a person against "double jeopardy" (being tried twice for the same crime).
   (a) First

(b) Fifth
(c) Sixth
(d) Seventh
Page 144

35. After a person has been arrested, the courts are forbidden from setting "excessive bail" by:
(a) Article I, Section 9
(b) Article III, Section 2
(c) the Fifth Amendment
(d) the Eighth Amendment
Page 144

36. The _____ Amendment reads that "this enumeration...of certain rights, shall not be construed to deny or disparage others retained by the people."
(a) Seventh
(b) Eighth
(c) Ninth
(d) Tenth
Page 123

37. The _____ Amendment reads that "no soldier shall, in time of peace be quartered in any house, without the consent of the owner, nor in time of war, but in a manner to be prescribed by law."
(a) First
(b) Second
(c) Third
(d) Fourth
Page 123

38. Like abortion, in-vitro fertilization involves the legal question of:
(a) when life begins.
(b) when live ends.
(c) the rights of the accused.
(d) freedom of religion.
Page 154

39. Ultimately the courts decide what constitutional guarantees mean in practice. The federal courts are also the branch least subject to:
(a) majority rule
(b) minority rights
(c) the Constitution
(d) the Tenth Amendment
Page 157

40. _____ guarantees that a "writ of habeas corpus" will not be suspended and forbids imprisonment without evidence.
(a) Article I, Section 9

(b)   The Eighth Amendment
(c)   Article III, Section 2
(d)   the Sixth Amendment
Page 144

BEFORE GOING ON

Check your answers against the answer key below. If you have missed
some, go back and reread the relevant passages on the page of the
book indicated immediately below those questions.

Review Test Answers:

1: a	11: d	21: a	31: a
2: b	12: a	22: c	32: d
3: d	13: d	23: d	33: a
4: c	14: c	24: d	34: b
5: b	15: b	25: b	35: d
6: d	16: a	26: d	36: c
7: b	17: d	27: c	37: c
8: c	18: c	28: a	38: a
9: d	19: a	29: c	39: a
10: d	20: c	30: d	40: a

By now most of the Key Terms listed on page 159 should be becoming
familiar to you.   Take a look at the list and see if you are
confident that you can define and discuss all of them. In addition,
it is important for this chapter to carefully review the list of Key
Cases also on page 159.   Court cases have played a central role in
defining civil liberties.   In some instances the name of the case
has become journalistic "short hand" for the rights it defines.
This is certainly true of "Miranda, "Schenck," "Roth," "Furman," and
"Roe v. Wade," for example. Knowledge of the McCleskey v. Kemp case
(and the ability to cite its name) will arm you well for your next
argument about the death penalty. A real load off your mind, right?

CHAPTER 5

CIVIL RIGHTS AND PUBLIC POLICY

CHAPTER LEARNING OBJECTIVES

After reading Chapter 5, you should be able to:

1. Define civil rights, distinguishing it from civil liberties.
2. Distinguish and discuss various definitions of equality.
3. Discuss the meaning and importance of the equal protection of the laws clause of the Fourteenth Amendment.
4. Identify the major historical milestones in the struggle for civil rights in America.
5. Identify the major milestones in the struggle for voting rights, and the devices historically used to deny such rights.
6. Identify and discuss the struggle for equal rights of groups other that African Americans.
7. Identify the major milestones in the battle for women's suffrage and equal rights in law and in the workplace.
8. Discuss the origins and fate of the Equal Rights Amendment.
9. Identify emerging groups demanding equal rights.
10. Define affirmative action.
11. Identify and discuss the major cases dealing with Affirmative Action.
12. Discuss the implications of civil rights for democracy and the size of government.

PRETEST QUESTIONS

The pretest below will give you an idea of the state of your knowledge about civil rights. The questions should also help you learn what to look for while studying the text. Take the whole pretest, then check your answers against the key that follows (don't peek!). As you read the chapter, watch for where these questions are addressed (indicated after each question) so that you may learn why the answer is what it is.

Chapter 5

1. In _____, the Supreme Court invalidated a law barring African
    Americans from jury service but refused to extend the amendment
    to more subtle kinds of discrimination.
    (a) Strauder v. West Virginia
    (b) Marbury v. Madison
    (c) Mapp v. Ohio
    (d) Roe v. Wade
Page 166

2. The Dred Scott decision invalidated the hard-won Missouri
    Compromise and was an important milestone on the road to:
    (a) civil rights for all men.
    (b) women's suffrage.
    (c) Civil War.
    (d) minority voting rights.
Page 167

3. The Supreme Court provided a constitutional justification for
    segregation in the 1896 case of:
    (a) Plessy v. Ferguson.
    (b) Bakke v. the Board of Regents.
    (c) Dred Scott v. Sandford.
    (d) Brown v. the Board of Education.
Page 169

4. _____ took many steps to forbid discrimination in the sale or
    rental of housing.
    (a) The Civil Rights Act of 1964
    (b) The Open Housing Act of 1968
    (c) The Voting Rights Act of 1965
    (d) The Smith Act
Page 173

5. In 1964 poll taxes were declared void by the _____ Amendment.
    (a) Sixteenth
    (b) Eighteenth
    (c) Twenty-first
    (d) Twenty-fourth
Page 175

6. The _____ resulted in hundreds of thousands of African-
    Americans being registered in southern states and counties.
    (a) Fifteenth Amendment
    (b) Twenty-fourth Amendment
    (c) Voting Rights Act of 1965
    (d) Civil Rights Act of 1964
Page 175

7. American Indians were not made citizens of the United States until:
    (a) 1872.
    (b) 1896.
    (c) 1907.
    (d) 1924.
Page 176

8. Asian Americans suffered during _____ when the U.S. Government, beset by fears of a Japanese invasion of the Pacific Coast, rounded up more than one hundred thousand Americans of Japanese descent and herded them into encampments.
    (a) the Sino-Soviet War
    (b) the Vietnam War
    (c) World War I
    (d) World War II
Page 176

9. The Seneca Falls Declaration set the groundwork for a movement that would culminate in the ratification of the Nineteenth Amendment, which:
    (a) led to the signing of the Emancipation Proclamation.
    (b) gave women the right to vote.
    (c) outlawed alcohol.
    (d) gave American Indians the right to vote.
Page 177

10. The Feminine Mystique, written by _____ and published in 1963, encouraged many women to question traditional assumptions and to assert their own rights.
    (a) Gloria Steinem
    (b) Erica Jong
    (c) Betty Friedan
    (d) Jacqueline Susanne
Page 178

11. Congress passed the Equal Rights Amendment in _____ although it has never been ratified.
    (a) 1968
    (b) 1972
    (c) 1982
    (d) 1987
Page 179

12. Women now comprise _____ percent of the armed forces and compete directly with men for promotion.
    (a) 2
    (b) 6
    (c) 11
    (d) 22
Page 182

13. Congress opened all armed service academies to women in:

    (a)   1975.
    (b)   1967.
    (c)   1963.
    (d)   1947.
Page 183

14. In 1915, _____ banned the grandfather clause that had been used to prevent blacks from voting.
    (a)   the Twenty-first Amendment
    (b)   Smith v. Allwright
    (c)   the Twenty-third Amendment
    (d)   Guinn v. United States.
Page 175

15. The _____ decision in 1950 held that the "separate but equal" formula was generally unacceptable in professional schools.
    (a)   Plessy v. Ferguson
    (b)   Guinn v. United States
    (c)   Smith v. Allwright
    (d)   Sweatt v. Painter
Page 169

16. The lawyer who argued Linda Brown's case before the Supreme Court in Brown v. the Board of Education (1954) was _____, who later became a Supreme Court justice.
    (a)   Thurgood Marshall
    (b)   Abe Fortas
    (c)   Harry Blackmun
    (d)   William Brennan
Page 170

17. Harper v. Virginia (1966) held that the _____ Amendment forbids making a tax a condition of voting in any election.
    (a)   Twenty-first
    (b)   Eighteenth
    (c)   Sixteenth
    (d)   Fourteenth
Page 174

18. Brown v. the Board of Education (1954) held that segregated schools are inherently unequal and that they violated:
    (a)   the Ninth Amendment.
    (b)   the Tenth Amendment.
    (c)   the Fourteenth Amendment.
    (d)   the Twenty-first Amendment.
Page 174

19. Of all eastern European countries, _____ has come the closest to full sexual equality.

(a)   East Germany
(b)   Poland
(c)   Czechoslovakia
(d)   Yugoslavia
Page 184

20. The 1857 _____ decision held that slaves could not gain
     freedom by escaping to a free state or territory. This upheld
     the constitutionality of the slave system.
     (a)   Plessy v. Ferguson
     (b)   Roth v. California
     (c)   Texas v. Johnson
     (d)   Dred Scott v. Sandford
Page 167

Pretest Answers:

1: a	11: b
2: c	12: c
3: a	13: a
4: b	14: d
5: d	15: d
6: c	16: a
7: d	17: d
8: d	18: c
9: b	19: a
10: c	20: d

READING FOR CONTENT

Listed below are sets of questions associated with the content of
each major section of Chapter 5. Carefully review the questions
associated with each section of the text before reading the section.
Have the questions in mind as you read the section and, when you
reach the end of each section, stop and see if you can answer the
questions well. If not, reread the relevant paragraphs until you
are sure of your response to each of the questions.

I.   Two Centuries of Struggle

      What is the meaning of equality of opportunity?
      What is the meaning of equality of result?
      How is the Fourteenth Amendment important for equality?
      What does the "equal protection of the laws" mean?
      What is meant by the term "suspect classification?"

II.   Race, The Constitution, and Public Policy

      What are the three eras of struggle for African American
         equality?
      Which amendment ended the era of slavery?
      What was the significance of the case of Plessy v. Ferguson?

What is the significance of the case of Brown v. Board of Education?

What is the significance of the case of Swann v. Charlotte-Mecklenberg County Schools?

How can de jure and de facto segregation be distinguished?

What was made illegal by the Civil Rights Act of 1964?

Which amendment guaranteed blacks the right to vote?

What devices were used to prevent blacks from effectively exercising the right to vote?

How did these devices function to limit or eliminate black voting rights?

What did the Voting Rights Act of 1965 accomplish?

What other minorities have suffered discrimination and benefit from civil rights legislation?

III. Women, The Constitution and Public Policy

How did women win the right to vote?

What is the Equal Rights Amendment (ERA)?

What happened to the ERA?

In what cases has the Court addressed sex discrimination?

In what ways have women been discriminated against?

What problem is the notion of "comparable worth" intended to address?

How are women treated differently in military service?

IV. New Groups Under the Civil Rights Umbrella

What new groups are arising to claim civil rights?

V. A New Equality Issue: Affirmative Action

What is the meaning of Affirmative Action?

In what cases has the court addressed Affirmative Action?

How did the Burger Court view Affirmative Action?

How did the Rehnquist Court view Affirmative Action?

How popular is Affirmative Action with the public?

VI. Understanding Civil Rights and the Constitution

What is the association between equality and democracy?

How can majority rule threaten civil rights?

What are the implications of civil rights policy for the size of government?

CHAPTER OVERVIEW

I. Introduction (162-163)

Americans have never fully come to terms with equality. Today, debates about equality center on these key types of inequality in America: 1) Racial discrimination, 2) Sexual discrimination, and 3)

Discrimination based on age, disability, and other factors. CIVIL RIGHTS are policies that extend basic rights to groups historically subject to discrimination.

II. Two Centuries Of Struggle (163-166)

The struggle for equality in America is older than the government itself and continues today. Philosophically, the struggle involves defining the term "equality." Constitutionally, it involves interpreting laws. Politically, it often involves power.

A. Conceptions of Equality

In America equality has never meant that there was or should be no differences among people. It has been linked to "natural" or "inalienable" rights to which all were equally entitled. This, in turn, is the foundation for a belief in "equality of opportunity" - an equal chance for all. What any person makes of that equal chance depends on his or her abilities and efforts. Thus, equal results or equal rewards have never been an emphasis in American society.

B. Early American Views of Equality

Equality was not a central issue of the American revolution nor of the Constitutional Convention. The delegates to the Convention did their best to avoid facing slavery, a central equality issue of the day, and women's rights got even less attention at the Convention.

C. The Constitution and Inequality

The word equality does not appear in the original Constitution. The delegates were intent on designing a plan for government, not guarantees of individual rights. Not even the Bill of Rights mentions equality. It does, however, have implications for equality, since it does not limit the scope of its guarantees to specified groups within society. As a result, the disadvantaged also share such political liberties as freedom of expression with which they can work effectively for greater equality. It was just this kind of political activism that led to the Fourteenth Amendment which enacts a guarantee of equality.

The first and only place in which the idea of equality appears in the Constitution is in the Fourteenth Amendment. The amendment forbids the states from denying to anyone EQUAL PROTECTION OF THE LAWS. As the courts began to apply a broader interpretation to the equal protection clause in the mid-twentieth century, this lone reference to equality proven sufficient to assure equal rights to all Americans.
The Court has ruled that most classifications that are "reasonable" - that bear a rational relationship to some legitimate governmental purpose - are constitutional. Thus, age is a reasonable classification for determining who may vote, for example.

95

Classifications that are arbitrary, however, are invalid. Normally, classifications are assumed to be reasonable. The burden of proving a classification arbitrary rests with the party that is challenging it.

The Court has ruled that racial and ethnic classifications are "inherently suspect." Such classifications are presumed to be invalid unless a compelling reason for them can be shown and there is no other way to accomplish the purpose of the law. Thus the burden of proof for such classifications is on the state. Classifications based on gender fall somewhere between the reasonable and inherently suspect presumptions. A law that discriminates on the basis of sex must bear a "substantial" relationship to an "important" legislative purpose.

The equal protection clause is interpreted expansively enough to forbid school segregation, prohibit job discrimination, reapportion state legislatures, and permit forced busing and affirmative action.

III. Race, The Constitution, And Public Policy (166-177)

African Americans have been the focus of the constitutional struggle for equal rights. The African American struggle for equality can be divided into three eras: 1) The era of slavery (colonization through 1865); 2) The era of reconstruction and resegregation (1865-1954); and 3) The era of civil rights (1954- present).

A. The Era of Slavery

For America's first 250 years of European settlement, African Americans were brought to America unwillingly as kidnap victims and lived in slavery. Perhaps the boldest official defense of slavery came in the Supreme Court's DRED SCOTT V. SANDFORD decision in 1857. Chief Justice Taney stated that a black man, whether slave or free, had no rights under a white man's government, and that Congress had no power to ban slavery in the western territories. This decision voided compromises that had helped to avoid civil war. The Union Civil War victory and the THIRTEENTH AMENDMENT ended slavery. This, with the Fourteenth and Fifteenth Amendments, together called the "Civil War amendments," seemed to promise full citizenship for African Americans.

B. The Era of Reconstruction and Resegregation

Immediately after the Civil War Congress imposed strict conditions on the former Confederate states and enforced them with military rule. The traditional white power holders were barred from office. After 1876, however, this period of "reconstruction" ended when, to ensure his election, Rutherford B. Hayes promised to withdraw federal troops and allow white Southerners to reclaim power. "Jim Crow laws" were passed which segregated and degraded blacks. These laws relegated African Americans to separate public facilities, school systems, restrooms, restaurants, and later, to "the back of the bus." Racial segregation came to affect every part of life during this period.

Legal justification for segregation came in the Supreme Court case PLESSY V. FERGUSON in 1896. The Court upheld a Louisiana law requiring segregation in railroad transportation, saying that segregation was not unconstitutional as long as the facilities were substantially equal. In subsequent practice the "separate" part of this principle was honored more than the "equal" part, however. For example, Southern states were allowed to maintain "whites only" high schools and professional schools despite providing none at all for blacks. Nevertheless, some progress on the long road to racial equality was made during the first half of the twentieth century (see Table 5.2).

C. The Era of Civil Rights

Legal segregation came to an end in 1954 when, in BROWN V. BOARD OF EDUCATION, the Supreme Court set aside its decision in Plessy v. Ferguson and held that segregation is "inherently" unequal and therefore unconstitutional under the Fourteenth Amendment.

The CIVIL RIGHTS MOVEMENT was the organized attempt by both blacks and whites to end the policies and practices of segregation. The catalyst for the movement came in 1955 when Rosa Parks, a black woman, refused to move to the back of a Montgomery, Alabama bus. She was ultimately forced off the bus creating an incident that led to a bus boycott led by Martin Luther King, Jr. This articulate and charismatic local minister soon became the best- known leader of the movement.

The civil rights movement used sit-ins, marches, and civil disobedience to bring attention to the problem of racial inequality and appeal to the national conscience. By the 1970s overwhelming majorities of Americans supported racial integration.

It was the courts, as much as the national conscience, that put civil rights on the national agenda. A string of Supreme Court decisions holding various forms of discrimination unconstitutional followed the Brown decision. Congress also passed a number of policies to foster racial equality. The CIVIL RIGHTS ACT OF 1964 made racial discrimination illegal in hotels, motels, restaurants, and other places of public accommodation as well as in all employment practices. The Voting Rights Act of 1965 cracked centuries old barriers to African-American voting in the South. The Open Housing Act of 1968 took steps to forbid discrimination in the sale or rental of housing.

One reason for all this activity was the fact that by the mid- 1960s federal laws effectively protected the right to vote. Thus members of minority groups had some power to hold their legislators accountable.

D. Getting and Using the Right to Vote

In the early Republic, SUFFRAGE, the legal right to vote, was mostly limited to property-holding white males. While property qualifications disappeared in the first-half of the nineteenth century, the vote was extended to others only slowly and painfully after the Civil War.

The FIFTEENTH AMENDMENT, adopted in 1870, guaranteed blacks the right to vote in principle. States invented many ingenious methods of circumventing the Amendment, however, and its principle was not fully realized for a full century.

Southern states used a "grandfather clause," which exempted whites but not blacks, from literacy tests as a qualification to vote. The literacy tests could then be very rigorous to effectively exclude blacks. POLL TAXES were used to discourage blacks from registering to vote. The WHITE PRIMARY, which allowed political parties to exclude blacks from primary elections, barred blacks from participating in the most important election in the heavily one-party Democratic South.

The grandfather clause was declared unconstitutional in Guinn v. Oklahoma in 1913. The white primary was declared unconstitutional in 1941. Poll taxes were made unconstitutional by the TWENTY-FOURTH AMENDMENT to the Constitution in 1964. The federal government took action to reverse the enduring effects of these practices with the VOTING RIGHTS ACT OF 1965. This Act sent federal election registrars to states and counties that had histories of discrimination. The number of African American office holders from the South has increased from 70 to more than 2500 as a result.

E. Other Minority Groups

American Indians are the oldest and, perhaps, the historically the most mistreated minority group. Though benefitting from the gains won by the African Americans, many remained huddled in relative poverty on reservations. Asian Americans were singled out for special mistreatment during World War II when they were herded into internment camps. Hispanic Americans have also had need of the nondiscrimination policies won during the civil rights movement. Hispanics will soon be the largest minority group in an America in which minorities constitute a majority of the population. With each of these minorities organized to participate, they will play an increasingly important role in shaping American political outcomes.

IV. Women, The Constitution, And Public Policy (177-183)

In the nineteenth century women faced a world in which they were not only denied the vote, but also subjected to patriarchal family law and the denial of educational and career opportunities. Two early women's rights activists, Lucretia Mott and Elizabeth Cady Stanton, organized a meeting in Seneca, New York, that would prove to be the genesis of the movement for women's rights. The meeting produced the Seneca Falls Declaration of Sentiments and Resolutions. It would be 72 years before women would receive the right to vote with the NINETEENTH AMENDMENT in 1920.

A. The Battle for the Vote

The battle for women's suffrage was fought mostly in the late nineteenth and early twentieth centuries. Leaders like Stanton and Susan B. Anthony led the movement which also addressed women's other grievances. The feminists lobbied, marched, protested and used civil disobedience in the effort to win the right to vote.

B. The "Doldrums": 1920-1960

While there was broad consensus within the feminist movement on the demand for the vote, there was considerable division with regard to other issues. As a result, once the vote was won the movement lost momentum. Public policy toward women continued to be dominated by the principle of protectionism rather than equality. "Protected" women were less attractive in the employment market than men. Family law reflected the value of preserving traditional motherhood, including providing custody of children to women in case of divorce, combined with child support.

Only a minority of feminists challenged these assumptions. Alice Paul, the author of the EQUAL RIGHTS AMENDMENT (ERA), claimed that the real result of protectionist law was to perpetuate sexual inequality.

C. The Second Feminist Wave

Betty Friedan's book "The Feminine Mystique," published in 1963, led many women to question traditional assumptions. Groups like the National Organization for Women (NOW) and the National Women's Political Caucus were organized. The Civil Rights Act of 1964 banned sex discrimination. The Pregnancy Discrimination Act of 1978 made it illegal for employers to exclude pregnancy and childbirth from their sick-leave programs. Title IX of the Education Act of 1972 forbade sex discrimination in federally subsidized programs. The ERA was revived and, though passed by Congress, it fell three states short of ratification.In REED V. REED in 1971 the Court ruled that any "arbitrary" sex- based classification violated the equal protection clause of the Fourteenth Amendment. In 1976 in CRAIG V. BOREN it established a "medium scrutiny" standard: sex discrimination would be presumed to be neither valid nor invalid. This invalidated exclusive male legal control of property, and laws allowing alimony payments only to women among other matters. (See Table 5.5)

D. Wage Discrimination and Comparable Worth

Despite the vast growth in women's share of the work force, protectionism is not dead. Demands for equality, however, keep nudging protectionism into the background.

Traditional women's jobs often pay much less than men's jobs demanding comparable skill. The issue of COMPARABLE WORTH was raised to the forefront in 1983 when the Washington state Supreme Court ruled that its state government had discriminated against women by denying them equal pay for jobs of comparable worth. The Supreme Court has yet to address this controversial concept.

E. Women in the Military

Women have served in every branch of the military since World War II. Recently they have become a part of the regular service and begun to comprise a significant part of the armed forces (11 percent). The service academies were opened to women in 1975.

Two important differences between men and women persist in military service. Only men must register for the draft at age eighteen, and women are prohibited by statute and regulations from serving in combat. (Some women did take part in combat in the Panama invasion in 1989, however.)

V. New Groups Under The Civil Rights Umbrella (183-187)

Racial minorities and women are not the only Americans who can claim civil rights. Policies enacted to protect one group can be applied to others. New groups have emerged with claims to rights.

A. Civil Rights and the Graying of America

America's population is aging rapidly. Aging Americans have claimed space under the civil rights umbrella. Since 1967 Congress has passed a variety of laws limiting discrimination on the basis of age. No one over the age of 40 may be denied employment because of their age, and compulsory retirement is being phased out altogether.

B. Are the Young a Disadvantaged Group Too?

The young have also suffered from inferior treatment under the law. There are obvious difficulties in organizing an autonomous children's rights movement, but young people are not silent in asserting their rights.

C. Civil Rights and the Disabled

Disabled Americans, who comprise about 17 percent of the population, have suffered from both direct and indirect discrimination. They have been denied services, education and jobs. But they have also been kept poor and isolated without overt discrimination because public and private facilities have been hostile to their needs.

An inaccessible environment was defined as discrimination in the Rehabilitation Act of 1973. With the Americans with Disabilities Act of 1989 protections have been strengthened, requiring employers and public facilities to make "reasonable accommodations" for the handicapped.

D. Gay Rights

Homosexual activity is illegal in some states and homosexuals often face prejudice in hiring, education, access to public accommodations, and housing. Both gay men and women began organizing seriously in the 1970s and 1980s and, while not always successful, have won important victories.

Homosexual activists may face the toughest battle for equality. The reluctance to appear hostile to the aged or the disabled, which bridles the tongue of many potential opponents, has no apparent equivalent with respect to gay America. Homosexuals are safe targets and are likely to remain so for years to come.

VI. A New Equality Issue: Affirmative Action (187-190)

Affirmative Action extends the protections for women and minorities in an attempt to counteract the effects of past discrimination. Some state and federal laws thus provide for discrimination in favor of previously discriminated against groups. Such laws are taking "affirmative action" to correct for unequal conditions created by past discrimination that might otherwise continue indefinitely. Efforts to increase minority enrollment, job holding, or promotion are common examples.

These programs have brought charges of "reverse discrimination." The Court's position on these programs, while never perfectly clear, was more sympathetic in the past. The Rehnquist Court has emerged as a clear opponent of affirmative action. As a result, civil rights activists are turning increasingly to Congress in the hope of furthering the cause of equality.

VII. Understanding Civil Rights And The Constitution (190-191)

The only mention of equality in the Constitution is the "equal protection of the laws" clause of the Fourteenth Amendment. It has been the basis for civil rights statutes and judicial rulings protecting the rights of minorities and women. These laws and decisions have empowered groups to seek and gain more victories.

A. Civil Rights and Democracy

Equality is a basic principle of democracy. Every citizen is given one vote on the presumption that the needs and preferences of each

are of equal importance. Individual liberty is an equally important principle, however, that often conflicts with equality.
Equality tends to favor majority rule. Majorities can threaten minority rights, however. The principle of equality thus invites the denial of minority rights, while the principle of liberty condemns such a denial. The democratic process, when such rights as the First Amendment freedoms are guaranteed, facilitates the fight by minorities for equality.

B. Civil Rights and the Size of Government

Civil Rights laws increase the size and power of government. These laws tell individuals and institutions that there are things they must do and cannot do. Libertarians and conservatives object to the expansion in government inherent in these laws.

The founders might well also be perturbed. These policies do not appear to conform to the eighteenth century idea of limited government. Like civil liberties, however, civil rights have contributed to greater checks on the government by those who benefit from such protections.

DOING RESEARCH ON CIVIL RIGHTS

The struggle for civil rights has been, perhaps, the single most important story of the second half of the twentieth century in America. As a result, there is probably no subject that has received more attention or provides more opportunities for research. The effort to achieve a more equal society has generated many controversies that you could explore. Busing, reverse discrimination, the ERA, comparable worth, the role of women in the military, and even the impact of the use of "run-off" election systems would provide good subjects for inquiry.

Looking more carefully at the struggles of some "other" minorities, or some of the "new" claimants for civil rights might also be interesting. Hispanics, Asians, or Native Americans may be the more significant minority in your area. What have been the major milestones in their struggle for equal rights? What have been their tactics? What are their present circumstances and goals? How do they compare with the experiences of African Americans? Similar questions could underlie research on the elderly, the young, disabled or homosexuals.

Having been born after the institution of most of the landmark legislation against formal segregation and discrimination, many students today have little sense for the way the world was before. Research might profitably focus on "the way it was" culturally, socially and legally in the nation or your particular region or state - say sixty years ago. While there is plenty to read, both about that time and that was written in that time - don't overlook older folks that grew up in the '30s, '40s and '50s as a resource.

Interviewing relatives, neighbors, or elders of the church or community can provide unique and invaluable insights into the way things were, what has changed, and how much things have - and have not - changed.

REVIEW TEST

Reread the chapter overview and quiz yourself with the "Reading for Content" questions. Review the learning objectives listed at the beginning of this chapter to be sure you have achieved them. When you feel like you are ready, take the Review Test below.

1. The first and only place in which the idea of equality appears in the Constitution is in:
    (a) the Bill of Rights
    (b) the First Amendment
    (c) the Fourteenth Amendment
    (d) the Twenty-first Amendment
Page 165

2. The _____ Amendment extends the right to vote to black males over twenty one.
    (a) Fifteenth
    (b) Thirteenth
    (c) Ninth
    (d) Sixth
Page 175

3. Over the last one hundred years, _____ has become the vehicle for more expansive constitutional interpretations, especially those regarding discrimination.
    (a) the due process clause
    (b) the establishment clause
    (c) the clear and present danger test
    (d) the equal protection clause
Page 166

4. The Supreme Court has ruled that racial and ethnic classifications are:
    (a) invalid at all times
    (b) always upheld
    (c) inherently suspect
    (d) valid at all times
Page 166

5. During the slavery era, any public policy of the slave states or the federal government had to accommodate _____ of slave owners.
    (a) purely financial interests
    (b) civil rights

      (c)   civil liberties
      (d)   property interests
Page 167

6.   The boldest Supreme Court decision in defense of slavery was:
      (a)   Dred Scott v. Sandford
      (b)   Brown v. the Board of Education
      (c)   Miranda v. Arizona
      (d)   Bakke v. the Board of Regents
Page 167

7.   In the Dred Scott decision, Chief Justice _____ bluntly announced that a black man, slave or free, had no rights under a white man's government.
      (a)   John C. Marshall
      (b)   Hugo L. Black
      (c)   Earl Warren
      (d)   Roger Taney
Page 167

8.   To ensure his election in 1876, _____ promised to pull the troops out of the South and let the old slave states resume business as usual.
      (a)   Ulysses S. Grant
      (b)   Samuel J. Tilden
      (c)   Rutherford B. Hayes
      (d)   James A. Garfield
Page 168

9.   The Supreme Court's decision to outlaw legal segregation in Brown v. the Board of Education in 1954 set aside its earlier precedent in:
      (a)   Marbury v. Madison.
      (b)   Plessy v. Ferguson.
      (c)   Mapp v. Ohio.
      (d)   the Slaughterhouse Cases.
Page 169

10.   The practice of busing students to achieve racially balanced schools was upheld by the Supreme Court in:
      (a)   Swann v. Charlotte-Mecklenberg County Schools.
      (b)   Texas v. Johnson.
      (c)   Johnson v. Johnson.
      (d)   Schenck v. the United States.
Page 171

11.   _____, meaning "in reality," segregation results, for example, when children are assigned to schools near their homes and the homes are in racially segregated neighborhoods.
      (a)   De jure
      (b)   De facto

(c) Fiduciary
(d) Certiorari
Page 171

12. Adopted in 1870, the _____ Amendment guaranteed blacks the right to vote -- at least in principle.
    (a) Tenth
    (b) Thirteenth
    (c) Fourteenth
    (d) Fifteenth
Page 175

13. All of the following were used by southern states to exclude blacks from voting EXCEPT:
    (a) poll taxes
    (b) literacy tests
    (c) white primaries
    (d) health examinations
Page 175

14. _____ were declared void in the Twenty-fourth Amendment passed in 1964.
    (a) Poll taxes
    (b) Literacy tests
    (c) White primaries
    (d) Grandfather clauses
Page 175

15. _____ are the fastest growing minority group; their representation rising from .5 percent to 3 percent in the last three decades.
    (a) Asian Americans
    (b) African Americans
    (c) Hispanic Americans
    (d) Indian Americans
Page 176

16. Not until _____ did Congress establish the Indian Claims Act to settle financial disputes arising from lands taken from the Indians.
    (a) 1907
    (b) 1924
    (c) 1946
    (d) 1964
Page 176

17. The one hundred men and women who signed the Seneca Falls Declaration began a movement that would culminate in the ratification of the:
    (a) Fifteenth Amendment.

   (b)   Equal Rights Amendment.
   (c)   Nineteenth Amendment.
   (d)   Smith Act.
Page 177

18.   Alice Paul, the author of _____, was one activist who claimed
      that the real result of protectionist law was to perpetuate
      sexual inequality.
      (a)   the Equal Rights Amendment
      (b)   the Feminine Mystique
      (c)   Silent Spring
      (d)   Bury My Heart at Wounded Knee
Page 178

19.   The Pregnancy Discrimination Act of 1978 made it illegal for
      employers to:
      (a)   fire women because they were pregnant.
      (b)   hire women because they were pregnant.
      (c)   exclude pregnancy and childbirth from sick-leave plans.
      (d)   assign stressful and arduous duties to pregnant women.
Page 179

20.   In Reed v. Reed (1971) the Court ruled that any
      "arbitrary" sex-based classification violated:
      (a)   the equal protection clause.
      (b)   the establishment clause.
      (c)   the Twenty-first Amendment.
      (c)   the Twenty-fourth Amendment.
Page 179

21.   In 1988, the female civilian labor force amounted to :
      (a)   3 million.
      (b)   10 million.
      (c)   25 million
      (d)   54 million.
Page 181

22.   In 1987, the median annual earnings for full-time women workers
      was _____, compared to $26,722 for men.
      (a) $12,834
      (b) $14,872
      (c) $17,504
      (d) $23,935
Page 182

23.   The United States has had a volunteer armed force since: (a)
      1982.
      (b)   1973.
      (c)   1962.
      (d)   1946.

Page 183

24. Statutes and regulations prohibit women from serving in combat but several women did participate in combat during the American invasion of:
    (a) Vietnam.
    (b) Grenada.
    (c) Beirut.
    (d) Panama.

Page 183

25. Disabled Americans comprise about _____ percent of the population and have been known to suffer from both direct and indirect discrimination.
    (a) 17
    (b) 12
    (c) 8
    (d) 3

Page 185

26. Many Americans still believe that they do not know any gay people, yet the best estimate is that about ____ percent of the American population is homosexual.
    (a) 5
    (b) 10
    (c) 15
    (d) 20

Page 187

27. Guinn v. United States (1915) banned the _____ that had been used to prevent blacks from voting.
    (a) grandfather clause
    (b) poll tax
    (c) literacy test
    (d) establishment clause

28. The 1944 _____ decision banned all-white primaries in elections.
    (a) Plessy v. Ferguson
    (b) Guinn v. United States
    (c) Smith v. Allwright
    (d) Sweatt v. Painter

Page 169

29. The 1950 Sweatt v. Painter decision, declaring that the "separate but equal" formula was generally unacceptable, did much to repudiate the earlier case _____ that provided the constitutional basis for segregation.
    (a) Guinn v. United States

(b)   Near v. Minnesota
(c)   Smith v. Allwright
(d)   Plessy v. Ferguson
Page 169

30.   The year 1877 marked the end of _____.   After this,
      African-Americans made gains in the South that were reversed
      after Confederates returned to power.
      (a)   the Civil War
      (b)   Reconstruction
      (c)   segregation
      (d)   slavery
Page 169

31.   The Supreme Court case that ended segregation once and for all
      (and also struck down Plessy v. Ferguson) was:
      (a)   Near v. Minnesota.
      (b)   Roe v. Wade.
      (c)   Brown v. the Board of Education.
      (d)   Bakke v. the Board of Regents.
Page 170

32.   The chief justice of the Supreme Court at the time of the Brown
      v. the Board of Education decision in 1954 was:
      (a)   Warren Burger.
      (b)   William Howard Taft
      (c)   Earl Warren
      (d)   Abe Fortas
Page 170

33.   The _____ Amendment ended the poll tax in federal elections.
      (a)   Fifteenth
      (b)   Nineteenth
      (c)   Twenty-second
      (d)   Twenty-fourth
Page 175

34.   Cleveland, Ohio, became the first city to elect a black mayor,
      _____, in 1967.
      (a)   L. Douglas Wilder
      (b)   Carl Stokes
      (c)   Harold Washington
      (d)   Adam Clayton Powell, Jr.
Page 174

35.   The Swann v. Mecklenberg County Schools decision approves
      _____ as a means of combating state-enforced segregation. (a)
      busing
      (b)   taxing of the states
      (c)   taxing of the cities
      (d)   taxing of the states and the cities

Page 174

36. In 1984, _____ was nominated as the first woman vice-presidential candidate of a major party.
    (a) Gloria Steinem
    (b) Elizabeth Dole
    (c) Shirley Chisholm
    (d) Geraldine Ferraro

Page 180

37. The only system of government that assures, or has assured, that there will be no sexual inequality is:
    (a) capitalism.
    (b) none.
    (c) socialism.
    (d) communism.

Page 184

38. In Bakke v. the UC Board of Regents (1978) there were _____ different opinions written by the Court.
    (a) three
    (b) five
    (c) six
    (d) eight

Page 189

39. The 1971 _____ decision approved of busing as a means of combating state-enforced segregation.
    (a) Swann v. Charlotte-Mecklenberg County Schools
    (b) Bakke v. UC Board of Regents
    (c) Harper v. Virginia
    (d) Grove City College v. Bell

Page 174

40. After Reconstruction ended in 1877, white southerners lost little time reclaiming power and imposing a code of _____ laws, or segregational laws, upon blacks.
    (a) Dred Scott
    (b) Nat Turner
    (c) Jim Crow
    (d) Marcus Garvey

Page 168

BEFORE GOING ON

Check your answers against the answer key below. If you have missed some, go back and reread the relevant passages on the page of the book indicated immediately below those questions.

Review Test Answers:

1: c	11: b	21: d	31: c
2: a	12: d	22: c	32: c
3: d	13: d	23: b	33: d
4: c	14: a	24: d	34: b
5: d	15: a	25: a	35: a
6: a	16: c	26: b	36: d
7: d	17: c	27: a	37: b
8: c	18: a	28: c	38: c
9: b	19: c	29: d	39: a
10: a	20 a	30: b	40: c

Before declaring yourself an expert on civil rights, take another look at the Key Terms listed on page 192. Can you define and discuss all of them? Next time you are sitting around reviewing the dastardly deeds of government, impress your friends by knowing that it was in Korematsu v. United States that the Supreme Court ruled constitutional the "internment" of Japanese (certainly one of the darkest chapters in U.S. history) during World War II.

CHAPTER 6

PUBLIC OPINION AND POLITICAL ACTION

CHAPTER LEARNING OBJECTIVES

After reading Chapter 6, you should be able to:

1. Describe generally the demographic make-up of the U.S.
2. Describe generally the historical patterns of immigration.
3. Describe generally the pattern of internal migration.
4. Identify and discuss the major agents of political socialization.
5. Describe the basic techniques of public opinion polling.
6. Assess the role of public opinion polls in American politics.
7. Assess the distribution and importance of ideology in structuring the political behavior of Americans.
8. Assess the implications of the level of political information held by Americans.
9. Describe the types and extent of participation in politics.
10. Assess the role of popular participation in democratic politics.

PRETEST QUESTIONS

The pretest below will give you an idea of the state of your knowledge about public opinion and political action. The questions should also help you learn what to look for while studying the text. Take the whole pretest, then check your answers against the key that follows (don't peek!). As you read the chapter, watch for where these questions are addressed (indicated after each question) so that you may learn why the answer is what it is.

1. The most valuable tool for understanding demographic changes in America is the:
    (a) demograph.
    (b) statistician.
    (c) census.
    (d) gerrymander.
    Page 203

2. Before the Civil War, all of the following were in the first

wave of immigration to the United States EXCEPT:
(a)   Mexicans
(b)   Germans
(c)   Irish
(d)   Scandinavians
Page 204

3.   Strongly anticommunist _____ in Miami are the near-majority of the city's population.
(a)   Cubans
(b)   Vietnamese
(c)   Mexicans
(d)   Jews
Page 204-205

4.   The largest component of the minority majority currently is the African-American population -- one in _____ Americans.   (a) five
(b)   eight
(c)   twelve
(d)   twenty
Page 206

5.   Nearly 33 percent of blacks currently live under the poverty line compared to about _____ percent of whites.
(a)   10
(b)   18
(c)   23
(d)   44
Page 206

6.   The number of black elected officials has increased from 1,479 in 1970 to _____ in 1987.
(a)   2,346
(b)   3,589
(c)   4,001
(d)   6,384
Page 206

7.   War and disease reduced the number of American Indians to _____ by 1910.
(a)   210,000
(b)   520,000
(c)   1.5 million
(d)   3 million
Page 208

8.   The process of reapportionment, which causes states to gain or

lose congressional representation based on population changes, occurs after every:
- (a) six years.
- (b) census is taken.
- (c) presidential election.
- (d) two years.

Page 209

9. After reapportionment in 1990, these three states will have one-fourth of the seats in the House of Representatives:
- (a) California, Texas and Florida
- (b) Massachusetts, New Jersey and Pennsylvania
- (c) Texas, New York and Florida
- (d) Florida, Georgia and Alabama

Page 209

10. By the year 2020, there will be just _____ working Americans for every person over the age of sixty five.
- (a) two
- (b) three
- (c) four
- (d) five

Page 210

11. _____ are the "new parents" according to many observers. (a) Schools
- (b) Churches
- (c) Social groups
- (d) The Mass Media

Page 213

12. A typical poll of about fifteen hundred to two thousand respondents has a sampling error of + or - _____ percent. (a) 10
- (b) 6
- (c) 5
- (d) 3

Page 215

13. The well-established magazine _____ became a laughingstock and was soon out of business when it predicted a victory for Alf Landon over Franklin Roosevelt in 1936.
- (a) Literary Digest.
- (b) Harper's Weekly.
- (c) Vanity Fair.
- (d) Ramparts.

Page 216

14. Probably the most criticized type of poll is the:

(a)   random sample poll.
(b)   random digit dialing poll.
(c)   door to door poll.
(d)   election day exit poll.
Page 218

15.   Thomas Jefferson trusted people's good sense and believed that
      _____ would enable them to take the tasks of citizenship ever
      more seriously.
      (a)   education
      (b)   political participation
      (c)   voting
      (d)   mandatory conscription
Page 220

16.   According to a recent 1988 opinion poll, only 14% of the people
      knew that _____ was then Speaker of the House (before his
      resignation).
      (a)   Thomas P. "Tip" O'Neil
      (b)   Thomas Foley
      (c)   Jim Wright
      (d)   Carl Albert
Page 220

17.   On an average, according to recent polls, only _____ percent
      of the public can name both of their U.S. senators, much less
      say how these senators generally vote.
      (a)   30
      (b)   45
      (c)   50
      (d)   72
Page 220

18.   The authors of the classic study The American Voter classified
      people who could connect their opinions and beliefs with broad
      policy positions taken by parties or candidates as:
      (a)   ideologues
      (b)   nature of the times voters.
      (c)   groups benefit voters.
      (d)   a "no issue content" group
Page 223

19.   Ronald Reagan made his first mark in politics by giving a
      televised speech on behalf of presidential candidate:
      (a)   Dwight D. Eisenhower.
      (b)   Barry Goldwater.
      (c)   Richard M. Nixon.
      (d)   Gerald R. Ford.
Page 225

20.   The reason that the Reagan years were popular and that George
      Bush was elected is that many swing voters are classified,

according to the book The American Voter, as: (a) nature of
the times voters.
(b) ideologues.
(c) group benefits voters.
(d) a "no issue content" voter.
Page 228-229

Pretest Answers:

1: c	11: d
2: a	12: d
3: a	13: a
4: b	14: d
5: a	15: a
6: d	16: c
7: a	17: a
8: b	18: a
9: a	19: b
10: a	20: a

READING FOR CONTENT

Listed below are sets of questions associated with the content of
each major section of Chapter 6. Carefully review the questions
associated with each section of the text before reading the section.
Have the questions in mind as you read the section and, when you
reach the end of each section, stop and see if you can answer the
questions well. If not, reread the relevant paragraphs until you
are sure of your response to each of the questions.

I.   The American People

      What were the three waves of immigration and when did they
        occur?
      What is the general demographic make-up of the U.S.?
      How is the demographic make-up of the U.S. changing?
      What does the Simpson-Mazzoli Act provide for?
      How is the population of the U.S. shifting regionally?
      What is reapportionment and why is it important?
      What are the implications of the aging of America?

II.   What Americans Learn About Politics: Political Socialization

      What is political socialization?
      How does political learning take place?
      What are the major agents of socialization?

III. What Americans Believe: Public Opinion and Policy

How is public opinion measured?
How do public opinion polls affect elections and the behavior
   of political elites?
How well informed is the American public according to polls?
What is the role of ideology in guiding political behavior?
What have been the trends of public opinion about the size of
   government and other issues during the Reagan years?

IV.   How Americans Participate in Politics

How much do Americans participate in politics?
In what ways do Americans participate in politics?
What is civil disobedience and how is it different from other
   forms of protest?

V.   Democracy, Public Opinion, and Political Action

What is the role of public opinion in democracy?
What is the role of political participation in democracy?

CHAPTER OVERVIEW

I.   Introduction   (202-203)

America is a diverse society of about 250 million people. Such
diversity makes the study of American public opinion especially
complex.   For the American government to work efficiently and
effectively, the diversity of the American public and its opinions
must be faithfully channeled through the political process.

II. The American People (203-210)

The most valuable tool for understanding demographic changes in
America is the CENSUS. The U.S. Constitution requires this actual
enumeration of the population every ten years. This count is very
important, for it determines the apportionment of Congressional
seats and the dispersal of money in many federal aid programs.

A. The Immigrant Society

The United States has always been a nation of immigrants. Today
630,000 new immigrants can be legally admitted each year.   There
have been three great waves of immigration to the United States: 1)
Before the Civil War came northwestern Europeans; 2) After the Civil
War came southern and eastern Europeans; and 3) After World War II
came Hispanics and Asians.

Immigrants bring with them aspirations and their own political
beliefs.   Some, like Cubans and Vietnamese are fleeing communist
regimes and are strongly anti-communist. Others, like Mexicans, are
fleeing poverty and seek equality. Mexican-American leaders have

pushed for bilingual education as part of the fight for equality. Thus, immigration can affect the policy agenda.

B. The American Mosaic

America has been called a "melting pot" in reference to its mixture of cultures, ideas, and peoples. Today, America is developing a "minority majority" - meaning America will soon cease to have a white, generally Anglo-Saxon majority. If current trends continue, nonwhites will be in the majority by the middle of the twenty-first century.

The largest minority group is currently the African American population. Descendants of slaves, the legacy of racism and discrimination has left them economically and politically disadvantaged as a group. They have recently been exercising a good deal of political power, however.

By the year 2000, the Hispanic population should outnumber the black population. Like African Americans they tend to be concentrated in cities. They are also exercising increasing political clout, especially in the Southwest.

An issue involving the Hispanic community is illegal immigration. The Simpson-Mazzoli Act was designed to combat such immigration by requiring employers to document the citizenship of their employees. The law causes concern among leaders of immigrant groups, who fear that employers might simply decline to hire members of such groups rather than take chances that they are in the country illegally.

By far the worst off among American ethnic minorities are native Americans. Today there are about 1,000,000 descendants of the original Americans. As a group, they are the least healthy, poorest, and least-educated in the American "melting-pot."

Despite its diversity Americans retain general agreement on what it means to be American. Minorities continue to assimilate most basic American values.

C. The Regional Shift

Between the 1970 and 1990 censuses, growth in the Sunbelt surged while growth in the Frostbelt sagged. The Census Bureau estimates that 87 percent of all the nation's population growth from 1980 to 1988 took place in the South and West.

Because states gain or lose congressional representation as their population changes, power shifts with population. This process is called reapportionment and occurs after each census. California, Texas and Florida will be the big gainers after the 1990 census, and among them will have one-fourth of the seats in the House of Representatives.

D. The Graying of America

Nationwide, the fastest growing age group in America is composed of citizens over sixty-five. This is a result of both medical advances and the fact that the birth rate has dropped substantially. This trend is likely to intensify as we approach the year 2020, when the post-World War II baby boom generation reaches their "golden years." This new political interest is already being mobilized politically, and by 2020 "gray power" will be substantial indeed. With the pressure an older population will bring to Social Security and medical and other elderly care programs, the political agenda will certainly be greatly affected.

III. What Americans Learn About Politics:
     Political Socialization (210-215)

Political socialization is "the process through which an individual acquires his [or her] particular political orientations -- his [or her] knowledge, feelings, and evaluations regarding his [or her] political world." Authoritarian regimes use formal and overt means to indoctrinate their citizens at an early age. In contrast, socialization is a much more subtle process in the United States.

A. How Americans Learn: The Process of Political Socialization

Informal learning is really much more important than formal, classroom learning about politics. Most informal socialization is unintentional or accidental. Words like "pick up, absorb, and acquire" best describe the informal side of socialization. Among the most important agents of socialization are the family, the media, and the schools.

1. The Family. The family's role is central because of its monopoly on time and emotional commitment in the early years. The powerful influence of the family is not easily broken. Most children adopt and retain the political values and leanings of their parents. These are modified somewhat in later life by other socialization agents, but rarely changed fundamentally.

2. The Mass Media. To some extent the mass media are "the new parents" - able to enter the home and speak directly to children from an early age. Contrary to popular impression, heavy television watching increases, rather than decreases, knowledge about politics and government. As children get older, television displaces parents as the chief agent of socialization.

3. School. Political socialization is important to the stability and legitimacy of governments. This is one reason governments (including America's) often use the schools to promote loyalty to the country and support for its basic values.

Education exerts a profound influence on a variety of political attitudes and behavior. The better educated are more likely to support the system by voting, being informed about politics, and more tolerant of diverse opinions. School thus pays off for the system not only economically, but also in citizens who more closely approximate the democratic model.

B. Political Learning Over a Lifetime

Politics is a lifelong activity. Increasing age does not mean increasing levels of knowledge about politics. It does, however, increase one's political participation and strength of partisan attachment.

IV. What Americans Believe: Public Opinion and Policy (215-223)

For our purposes PUBLIC OPINION concerns the distribution of the population's beliefs about politics and policy issues. Understanding the content of public opinion on controversial issues is especially important for politicians in elections.

A. Measuring Public Opinion

Sophisticated technology is now available for measuring public opinion. Polls rely on a SAMPLE of the population - a relatively small proportion of people who are chosen as representative of the whole. In public opinion polling a sample of about fifteen hundred to two thousand people can faithfully represent the "universe" of potential voters. The key to the accuracy of opinion polls is the technique of RANDOM SAMPLING, which operates on the principle that everyone should have an equal probability of being selected. If the sample is randomly drawn its make-up should match the population as a whole.

No sample will perfectly reflect the whole, however. The level of confidence we have in the sample is known as the SAMPLING ERROR, which depends on the size of the sample. The larger the sample the smaller will be the sampling error, i.e., the more confident we are that it is like the whole. A sample of fifteen hundred has a sampling error of plus or minus 3 percent. This means that 95 percent of the time the poll results will be within 3 percent of what the population's opinion actually is.

The newest computer and telephone technology has made surveying less expensive and more commonplace. Now most polling is done on the telephone with samples selected through RANDOM DIGIT DIALING. Calls are placed to phone numbers within randomly chosen exchanges around the country. It has some disadvantages, but is much cheaper than person-to-person interviewing. Public-opinion polling has become affordable to even minor candidates, and thus has become a big business.

B. The Role of Polls in American Democracy

Polls help political candidates distinguish which way people are leaning. Supporters of polling argue that this helps politicians keep in touch with constituents and is therefore a tool for democracy. Critics think that the information polling provides makes politicians more concerned with following than leading. Polling may help discourage bold leadership.

Some argue that polls actually weaken democracy. The public views registered in polls are passive and often ill-informed opinions. Expressions of opinion in voting, letter-writing and other political behavior takes some effort and is likely to be of higher quality. Polls can also weaken democracy by distorting the election process. They can create both "bandwagon" and "underdog" effects. They lend to the media's tendency to focus on who's hot and who's not rather than issues and positions.

Probably the most criticized type of poll is the election-day EXIT POLL that randomly samples people leaving the polling place. These polls allow networks to project all but very close races very early on election night - sometimes before the polls have even closed. Critics worry that this discourages voting and may alter results, though there is little empirical evidence that voters are influenced by exit poll results.

The most common criticism of polling is that by altering the wording of a questions pollsters can get pretty much the results they want. Being an informed consumer of poll results requires thought about whether the questions are fair and unbiased before accepting the results.

C. What Polls Tell Americans About Political Information

Public opinion analysts agree that the level of public knowledge about politics is dismally low. Only 30 percent can name both their senators, much less say how these senators generally vote.
Some argue that Americans are ill-informed despite living in an information rich society because of a misguided educational policy. They blame the schools for failing to teach "cultural literacy." Lacking basic contextual knowledge about history and geography, for example, people can't understand and use the information they receive from the news media.

Part of the reason mass politics works as well as it does, despite the lack of public knowledge about politics, is that people do know generally what basic values they want upheld.

V.   What Americans Value: Political Ideologies (223-229)

A coherent set of values and beliefs about public policy is a POLITICAL IDEOLOGY. Political ideology results in a set of coherent and consistent policy preferences.

A. Do People Think in Ideological Terms

In the 1950s a study found that only 12 percent of the people showed evidence of thinking in ideological terms. These "ideologues" could connect their opinions with broad policy positions of parties or candidates. More Americans were "group benefits voters" who thought of politics mainly by the groups they liked or disliked. Partisan choice was a matter of that party's support of a group with which these voters identified. About 24 percent of the population were "nature of the times" voters. Their voting behavior hinged on whether the times seemed good or bad. Finally, 22 percent were devoid of any ideological or issue content in their political evaluations. These were called the "no issue content" group. They voted solely out of loyalty to party or judged candidates wholly by their personalities.

Studies done in the 1970s suggest that the public has become only a little more sophisticated. While there seem to be somewhat more ideologues, the general picture remains pretty much the same. Relatively few people have ideologies which organize their political beliefs. (See Table 6.3) Thus, election results do not really indicate a conservative or liberal shift, because most voters do not think in such terms, and those that do are the least likely to shift from election to election.

B. Public Attitudes on the Size of Government

Does Ronald Reagan's electoral success indicate a shift of public opinion to the right - a greater hostility toward big government? For much of the population the size of government elicits no opinion at all. In 1988, 47 percent of those interviewed said they had not thought about the question.

Nor do public opinions on different aspects of this issue hold together well. While more people today think the government is too big than too small, a plurality has consistently called for more spending on programs like health care, education, aid to cities, environmental protection, and fighting crime. Thus, people seem to oppose the idea of big government in principle but favor it in practice. Political scientists say that "Americans are ideological conservatives but operational liberals."

C. People Liked Reagan but Not His Policies

Ronald Reagan was able to appeal to the ideological conservatism of Americans in his rhetoric. He followed up with a thoroughly conservative policy agenda, however, that was far less popular with America's operational liberalism. With the exception of a rise in support for military spending during the 1980 campaign, public opinion specialists have been unable to document any shift toward conservative attitudes during the 1980s.

Instead of an ideological shift, Reagan's (and Bush's) success reflects the fact that swing voters, "nature of the times voters," care more about results than ideology. In this analysis, the 1980 election was about voting Carter out rather than Reagan's ideology in. With relative peace and prosperity during the 1980s, Republicans could preserve and maintain the votes of this group.

VI. How Americans Participate in Politics (229-233)

POLITICAL PARTICIPATION encompasses the many activities used by citizens to influence the selection of political leaders or the policies they pursue. Political participation can be violent or peaceful, organized or individual, casual or consuming. Despite rather low levels of voting turnout, especially in state and local elections, the United States can be said to have a generally participatory political culture.

A. Conventional Participation

Political scientists distinguish between two broad types of participation: conventional and unconventional. Conventional participation includes many widely accepted modes of influencing government: voting, writing members of Congress, ringing doorbells, running for office, and so on. Unconventional participation includes such more dramatic action as protesting, civil disobedience, and even violence.

The number of Americans for whom political activity is an important part of their everyday life is very small. They are the political elites, the activists, the party leaders, the interest- group leaders, the judges, and the members of Congress, etc.

One study of American political participation found that of twelve common political activities the majority of Americans participated in only one - voting in presidential elections. Less than one-fifth had ever contacted a public official, given money to a candidate or party, or helped form a political group.

B. Protest as Participation

PROTEST is a form of political participation designed to achieve policy change through dramatic and unconventional tactics. From the Boston Tea Party to burning draft cards, Americans have engaged in countless political protests. Today, the goal of protest is often to attract media attention that will make a broader range of people aware of the protesters' grievances.

CIVIL DISOBEDIENCE is the intentional breaking of a law thought to be unjust in order to protest it. A nonviolent tactic, its users accept arrest and punishment for their action. The Reverend Martin Luther King, Jr. advocated the use of civil disobedience against segregationist law in the 1950s and 1960s. His efforts earned him the Nobel Peace Prize.

Sometimes political participation can be violent. Protests sometimes become violent when they lead to confrontation with other groups or the police. Although supported by few people throughout American history, violence has not been an uncommon means of pressuring the government to change its policies.

C. Class, Inequality, and Participation

Participation is very unequal in American political life. Citizens of higher social economic status participate more in politics. Because minority groups generally have lower education and economic status, they generally have lower political participation rates. They are not as much lower than average as might be expected, however, because minorities feel a group consciousness that provides an extra incentive to vote. In fact, when blacks, Hispanics, and whites of equal incomes and educations are compared, the participation rates of the minorities are actually higher than those of comparable whites.

VII. Democracy, Public Opinion, And Political Action (233-234)

American democracy is representative rather than direct. The public decides "not what government shall do but rather who shall decide what government shall do." If people know little about where the candidates stand on the issues, how can they make rational choices about who is to lead? In the case of a president, citizens typically go on a general sense of what life has been like during the incumbent's administration. They do not need to know the precise economic or foreign policies of the incumbent in order to see or feel the results. Even if people are only voting on the basis of the nature of the times, their voices are heard - holding presidents accountable for the consequences of their actions.

DOING RESEARCH ON PUBLIC OPINION AND POLITICAL ACTION

Students often find exploring public opinion a most enjoyable way to meet a class research requirement. There is a lot of data available and the possibilities for investigation in the patterns of opinion holding almost endless. You could compare opinions held on different issues or trace the changes in opinion on an issue over time. In the latter case, the impact of significant events on public opinion holding might be assessed.
Sources for national data on public opinion include polls done by ABC/New York Times, CBS/Washington Post, the Harris and Roper organizations, and the famous Gallop Poll. Check with your library about the availability of these data sources. The Gallop Poll publishes a monthly report of the results of its surveys and these, if nothing else, should be in the reference section of your library.

Of course, with a bit more initiative you could conduct your own survey. If you are interested in the opinions of your fellow students on an issue (or two) of national importance, concern to the campus community, or even if you are just curious about the level of political knowledge of your classmates, a survey may be of interest to you. Develop your own schedule of questions and draw your own sample! Before you begin, however, talk to your professor about what you wish to ask and how you wish to conduct your survey to be sure it is OK. Your prof can also help you with phrasing valid questions and drawing an accurate sample. No sense in doing all that work if it is flawed for the lack of a few pointers! When you compile your data you may just be surprised by what you find.

REVIEW TEST

Reread the chapter overview and quiz yourself with the "Reading for Content" questions. Review the learning objectives listed at the beginning of this chapter to be sure you have achieved them. When you feel like you are ready, take the Review Test below.

1. There are about _____ Americans, forming a mosaic of racial, ethnic and cultural groups.
    (a)   250 million
    (b)   2 billion
    (c)   6 billion
    (d)   150 billion
Page 202

2. The U.S. Constitution requires that the government conduct an "actual enumeration," of the population every _____ years.
    (a)   two
    (b)   four
    (c)   five
    (d)   ten
Page 203

3. The first required census of the United States took place in:
    (a)   1790.
    (b)   1800.
    (c)   1824.
    (d)   1900.
Page 203

4. _____ said that America is "not merely a nation, but a nation of nations."
    (a)   John F. Kennedy
    (b)   Lyndon B. Johnson
    (c)   Martin Luther King, Jr.,
    (d)   Ronald Reagan
Page 204

5. Today, federal law allows up to _____ new immigrants to be

legally admitted every year.
(a) 150,000
(b) 220,000
(c) 630,000
(d) 980,000
Page 204

6. There have been _____ great waves of immigration to the United States.
(a) two
(b) three
(c) five
(d) six
Page 204

7. After World War II, all of the following made up the third wave of immigrants to the United States EXCEPT:
(a) Hispanics
(b) Jews
(c) Asians
(d) Central Americans
Page 204

8. The _____ saw the largest number of immigrants in any decade in American history.
(a) 1850's
(b) 1920's
(c) 1940's
(d) 1980's
Page 204

9. As the third wave of immigration continues, policy-makers have come to speak of a new _____, a clever phrase meaning that America will soon cease to have a white, generally Anglo-Saxon majority.
(a) counter culture
(b) "shining hope"
(c) subculture
(d) minority majority
Page 206

10. The largest component of the minority majority currently is the _____ population -- one in eight Americans.
(a) African-American
(b) Italian-American
(c) Hispanic American
(d) Asian-American
Page 206

11. Nearly 33 percent of _____ currently live under the poverty

line compared to about 10 percent of whites.
(a)   Hispanics
(b)   Asian-Americans
(c)   Italian-Americans
(d)   African-Americans
Page 206

12.   In 1989, _____ became the nation's first elected African-American governor.
(a)   David Dinkens
(b)   Harold Washington
(c)   L. Douglas Wilder
(d)   Carl Stokes
Page 206

13.   By the year 2000, the _____ population should outnumber the black population.
(a)   Hispanic
(b)   Asian
(c)   Irish
(d)   Italian
Page 206-207

14.   A new immigration law, called the _____ Act, required that employers document the citizenship of their employees.
(a)   Smith
(b)   Pendleton
(c)   Rico
(d)   Simpson-Mazzoli
Page 207

15.   Before Europeans arrived in America, _____ American Indians lived here.
(a)   500,000-750,000
(b)   1 to 3 million
(c)   5 to 7 million
(d)   12 to 15 million
Page 208

16.   Today, about _____ descendants of the original Americans, the Indians, are left.
(a)   500,000
(b)   1 million
(c)   3 million
(d)   4 million
Page 208

17.   All of the following states have shown an increase in

population according to census figures EXCEPT:
(a)   New York.
(b)   California.
(c)   Texas.
(d)   Florida.
Page 209

18.   After reapportionment, California, Texas and Florida will have
_____ of the seats in the House of Representatives.   (a)   10%
(b)   14%
(c)   25%
(d)   32%
Page 209

19.   The Social Security system is exceeded only by _____ as
America's most costly public policy.
(a)   interest on the national debt
(b)   Medicare
(c)   national defense
(d)   foreign aid
Page 210

20.   The current group of older Americans and can lay claim to
nearly _____ dollars guaranteed by Social Security.
(a)   5 billion
(b)   50 billion
(c)   500 billion
(d)   5 trillion
Page 210

21.   When it comes to guessing how young people will vote, the most
important indicator comes from examining:
(a)   the voting patterns of their home state.
(b)   their socio-economic background.
(c)   the political leanings of their parents.
(d)   their education.
Page 212

22.   Heavy TV watching by children _____ knowledge about
politics and government.
(a)   decreases
(b)   drastically decreases
(c)   increases
(d)   has no effect on
Page 213

23.   Political socialization is so important to governments that
they often use _____ to promote loyalty to the country and

support for its basic values.
(a) schools
(b) television
(c) movies
(d) religion
Page 213

24. Today, American educational policy consumes more than _____ dollars annually.
(a) 10 billion
(b) 70 billion
(c) 170 billion
(d) 700 billion
Page 214

25. In public opinion polling, a sample of about _____ people can faithfully represent the "universe" of potential voters.
(a) 200 to 500
(b) 600 to 1,000
(c) 1,500 to 2,000
(d) 5,000 to 7,500
Page 215

26. _____ is the most important aspect of an opinion survey.
(a) A large response
(b) A small response
(c) Accurate representation
(d) Selective representation
Page 216

27. In recent years, the public's confidence in public opinion polling has:
(a) dropped slightly.
(b) risen substantially.
(c) dropped drastically.
(d) risen slightly.
Page 217

28. Now, most polling is done on the telephone with samples selected though:
(a) the phone book.
(b) random digit dialing.
(c) motor-vehicle records.
(d) voter registration records.
Page 217

29. In a(n) _____ poll, workers are sent out to voting places and told to ask every tenth person how they voted.

(a) random digit dialing
(b) exit
(c) selective
(d) summary
Page 218

30. A great criticism of polling is that pollsters can get the
     results they want easily by:
     (a) calling all their friends.
     (b) polling only those registered by the party affiliation
          they want polled.
     (c) altering the wording of a question.
     (d) lying about the results.
Page 219

31. _____ said that "it is true that you may fool all of the
     people some of the time, and some of the people all of the
     time, but you can't fool all of the people all of the
     time."
     (a) Alexander Hamilton
     (b) H. L. Mencken
     (c) Abraham Lincoln
     (d) Mark Twain
Page 219-220

32. Thomas Jefferson trusted the people's good sense and believed
     that education would enable them to take the tasks of
     citizenship even more seriously. Toward that end, he founded:
     (a) Harvard University.
     (b) the University of Virginia.
     (c) Yale University.
     (d) the Annapolis Naval Academy.
Page 220

33. _____ held a contrasting view to that of Thomas Jefferson's
     regarding the common people of America. He told Jefferson that
     "your people, sir, are a great beast."
     (a) George Washington
     (b) James Madison
     (c) Alexander Hamilton
     (d) Aaron Burr
Page 220

34. In a recent 1988 public opinion poll, only 39% knew that _____
     was then Reagan's secretary of state.
     (a) George Shultz
     (b) Caspar Weinberger
     (c) Alexander Haig
     (d) Henry Kissinger
Page 220

35. In a 1988 public opinion poll, only 4% of the people could
     properly identify _____ as the chief justice of the Supreme
     Court.

      (a)   Byron White
      (b)   William Brennan
      (c)   Antonin Scalia
      (d)   William Rehnquist
Page 220

36. E.D. Hirsch, Jr., criticizes the schools for a failure to teach:
      (a)   political identification.
      (b)   "basic moral values."
      (c)   "cultural literacy."
      (d)   more courses on the mass media.
Page 220-222

37. The authors of The American Voter classified people who voted for people simply based on their personalities and generally not regarding ideology or issues are:
      (a)   ideologues.
      (b)   group benefits voters.
      (c)   nature of the times voters.
      (d)   the "no issue content" group.
Page 223

38. _____, although formerly an FDR liberal in the 30's and 40's, led a conservative revolution in the 1980's against big government.
      (a)   Ronald Reagan
      (b)   William F. Buckley, Jr.,
      (c)   Jerry Falwell
      (d)   R. Emmett Tyrell
Page 225

39. Many political scientists have concluded that a vast majority of Americans are:
      (a)   ideological and operational conservatives.
      (b)   in favor of big government but disdain it in practice.
      (c)   in opposition to big government in principle and in practice.
      (d)   ideological conservatives but operational liberals.
Page 226

40. _____ won a Nobel Peace Prize for his civil disobedience against segregationist law in the 1950's and 1960's and wrote a classic defense of civil disobedience.
      (a)   Malcolm X
      (b)   Martin Luther King, Jr.,
      (c)   James Baldwin
      (d)   Stanley Crouch
Page 232

BEFORE GOING ON

Check your answers against the answer key below. If you have missed some, go back and reread the relevant passages on the page of the book indicated immediately below those questions.

Review Test Answers:

1: a	11: d	21: c	31: c
2: d	12: c	22: c	32: b
3: a	13: a	23: a	33: c
4: b	14: d	24: c	34: a
5: c	15: d	25: c	35: d
6: b	16: b	26: c	36: c
7: b	17: a	27: b	37: d
8: d	18: c	28: b	38: a
9: d	19: c	29: b	39: d
10: a	20: d	30: c	40: b

No matter how well you did on the Review Test, it would be sheer folly not to go back and go through those Key Terms (page 235) just one more time. The good news is there aren't that many of them for Chapter 6, so it won't take a practiced scholar like yourself very long at all. May I recommend "minority majority" for the "college word" to find a way to mention this week. Your authors call it a "clever phrase" so, who knows, maybe some of the cleverness will rub off on its user. In any case, if used casually in a complex sentence, it is sure to set the listeners mind to spinning - sorting out just what it means. Besides, if all else fails, one can have hours of fun just trying to say it ten times fast.

CHAPTER 7

POLITICAL PARTIES

CHAPTER LEARNING OBJECTIVES

After reading Chapter 7, you should be able to:

1. Identify and discuss the three components of parties.
2. Identify and discuss the tasks of political parties.
3. Discuss the implications of rational choice theory for the behavior of political parties.
4. Identify major milestones in the history of the American party system.
5. Discuss the three major changes in the party system since the New Deal that shape the character of parties today.
6. Discuss the key characteristics that distinguish the Democratic and Republican parties today.
7. Discuss the types of third parties and their impact on electoral and political outcomes.
8. Discuss the impacts of the two-party system on the processes of politics.
9. Describe the state of party identification among the electorate.
10. Describe the organizational structure of American parties.
11. Discuss the importance of parties for democratic government.
12. Discuss the relationship between strong parties and the size of government.

PRETEST QUESTIONS

The pretest below will give you an idea of the state of your knowledge about political parties. The questions should also help you learn what to look for while studying the text. Take the whole pretest, then check your answers against the key that follows (don't peek!). As you read the chapter, watch for where these questions are addressed (indicated after each question) so that you may learn why the answer is what it is.

1. A widely adopted way of thinking about political parties in political science is as "three headed political giants." The three heads include all of the following EXCEPT:
    (a) the party in the electorate.
    (b) the party and the individual.
    (c) the party as an organization.
    (d) the party in government.
Page 239

2. What punctuates party eras is a _____ that shakes the foundation and divides the majority party.
    (a) critical election
    (b) gerrymander
    (c) electoral upheaval
    (d) coalition fracture
Page 244

3. In the _____, James Madison warned strongly against the dangers of "factions," or parties.
    (a) Declaration of Independence
    (b) Constitution
    (c) Federalist Papers
    (d) Bill of Rights
Page 245

4. The Federalist party failed to be a major force in American politics after their candidate _____ failed in his reelection bid for president in 1800.
    (a) John Adams
    (b) Thomas Jefferson
    (c) James Madison
    (d) James Monroe
Page 245

5. More than anyone else, it was _____ who founded the modern American political party.
    (a) George Washington
    (b) Thomas Jefferson
    (c) Andrew Jackson
    (d) James Madison
Page 246

6. While Andrew Jackson was the charismatic leader, the Democrats' behind-the-scenes architect was:
    (a) Henry Clay.
    (b) John Quincy Adams.
    (c) Martin Van Buren.
    (d) John C. Calhoun.
Page 246

7. The _____ party contained notables such as Henry Clay and Daniel Webster but was only able to win the presidency when they ran war heroes William H. Harrison in 1840 and Zachary Taylor in 1848.
    (a) Democratic
    (b) Republican
    (c) Federalist
    (d) Whig
Page 246

8. After _____, the Republican party was in ascendancy for more than sixty years.
    (a) the Mexican-American War
    (b) the Civil War
    (c) Reconstruction
    (d) the Spanish-American War
Page 247

9. In the election of 1896, the Democrats nominated _____, populist proponent of "free silver."
    (a) Grover Cleveland
    (b) Woodrow Wilson
    (c) Samuel J. Tilden
    (d) William Jennings Bryan
Page 247

10. President _____'s handling of the Great Depression turned out to be disastrous for the Republicans.
    (a) Warren G. Harding
    (b) Calvin Coolidge
    (c) Herbert Hoover
    (d) Dwight D. Eisenhower
Page 247

11. _____, who succeeded Roosevelt in 1945, promised a Fair Deal.
    (a) Harry S. Truman
    (b) Adlai Stevenson
    (c) John F. Kennedy
    (d) Lyndon B. Johnson
Page 248

12. _____ was picked as Kennedy's vice-president to help win southern votes and became president upon Kennedy's death in 1963. He was overwhelmingly elected in 1964.
    (a) Hubert Humphrey
    (b) Lyndon B. Johnson
    (c) Stuart Symington
    (d) George C. Wallace
Page 249

13. Since 1968, the Republicans have won _____ out of six

presidential elections.
   (a)   two
   (b)   three
   (c)   five
   (d)   six
Page 249

14.   Political scientists agree that all of the following are major changes that have occurred to the party system since Roosevelt's New Deal EXCEPT:
   (a)   party loyalty has declined.
   (b)   those who do belong to a party are more likely to belong to the party that matches their ideology.
   (c)   party loyalty has increased.
   (d)   party organizations have become more energetic and effective.
Page 251

15.   The most recent restructuring of the Democratic party began in _____, the year of the rowdiest national convention ever.
   (a)   1960
   (b)   1968
   (c)   1972
   (d)   1976
Page 253

16.   Demonstrators at the Democratic National Convention in the city of _____ battled the police sent by Mayor Richard Daley.
   (a)   Miami
   (b)   New York City
   (c)   Chicago
   (d)   Los Angeles
Page 253

17.   In both 1984 and 1988, about 15 percent of the Democratic delegates were so-called:
   (a)   pseudo-delegates.
   (b)   "shadow" delegates.
   (c)   superdelegates.
   (d)   subdelegates.
Page 254

18.   In 1968, the American Independent party became an important third party. This was the party of segregationist:
   (a)   J. Strom Thurmond.
   (b)   Jesse Helms.
   (c)   Fielding Wright.
   (d)   George Wallace.
Page 257

19.   The Bull Moose Progressives of 1912 were formed by _____ in his efforts to win the presidency from Republican

136

William Howard Taft.
(a) Woodrow Wilson
(b) Warren G. Harding
(c) Theodore Roosevelt
(d) Robert La Follette
Page 256

20. The _____ Party of the 1850's were the first true antislavery party.
(a) Free Soil
(b) Whig
(c) Democratic
(d) "Know-Nothing"
Page 256

Pretest Answers:

1: a	11: a
2: a	12: b
3: c	13: c
4: a	14: c
5: c	15: b
6: c	16: c
7: d	17: c
8: b	18: d
9: d	19: c
10: c	20: a

READING FOR CONTENT

Listed below are sets of questions associated with the content of each major section of Chapter 7. Carefully review the questions associated with each section of the text before reading the section. Have the questions in mind as you read the section and, when you reach the end of each section, stop and see if you can answer the questions well. If not, reread the relevant paragraphs until you are sure of your response to each of the questions.

I. The Meaning of Party

How is political party defined?
What are the three components of an American party?
What are the basic tasks of political parties?
What are the implications of the rational-choice theory for party behavior?

II. Party Eras in American History

What are party eras and how many have there been?
What is a critical election?
What is a coalition?
What is a party realignment?

Chapter 7

How many party systems have there been and when did they
   begin?
What groups made up the New Deal coalition?

III. The Parties Today: Dealignment and Renewal

How have things changed since the New Deal that affect the
   nature of parties and the party system today?
How are the Republican and Democratic parties distinct?
What types of third parties emerge in American politics?
How have third parties been important to politics and
   elections?
What are the political effects of the two party system?

IV. The Party in the Electorate

What is party identification?
What has been the recent trends in party identification?
What has been the result of the trends in party
   identification?

V.   The Party Organizations: From the Grass Roots to Washington

What are the key characteristics of American party
   organizations?
What were party machines and on what were they built?
What are the roles of the state party organizations?
What are the key elements of the national party organization?

VI. The Party in Government: Promises and Policy

To what extent do party leaders keep their promises when in
   government?

VII. Understanding Political Parties

What are the elements of the responsible party model?
Why are responsible parties important for democratic
   governance?
How well do American parties measure up to the responsible
   party model?
How do weak parties contribute to big government?
How has high-tech campaigning contributed to weakening
   American political parties.

CHAPTER OVERVIEW

I. Introduction   (238-239)

Political scientists and politicians alike believe that a strong
party system is desirable and bemoan the weakening of the parties in
recent decades.   PARTY COMPETITION is the battle between Democrats

and Republicans for the control of public offices. Americans have had a choice between two major parties ever since the early 1800s.

II. The Meaning of Party (239-243)

Almost all definitions of political parties have one thing in common: Parties try to win elections. This is their core function and the key to their definition, distinguishing them from other political organizations such as interest groups. Anthony Downs defined a POLITICAL PARTY as a "team of men [and women] seeking to control the governing apparatus by gaining office in a duly constituted election."

Parties are not as unified in America as the term "team" may imply, however, and might be better thought of as "three-headed political giants." The three heads are: 1) the party-in-the- electorate, 2) the party as an organization, and 3) the party-in- government. The "party-in-the-electorate" is by far the largest component. American parties do not require dues or membership cards to distinguish members. To be a member of a party all you need to do is claim to be a member. If you say you are a Democrat or a Republican, you are. The "party as an organization" includes the national, state and local party offices and staff. These are the people who keep the party running between elections and make its rules. The "party-in-government" consists of elected officials who label themselves as members of the party. Despite sharing a single party label officeholders of the same party do not always agree on policy.

A. Tasks of the Parties

In a large democracy, LINKAGE INSTITUTIONS translate inputs from the public into outputs from the policy-makers. In the United States there are four main linkage institutions: parties, elections, interest groups, and the media. Among the tasks parties perform, or should perform, if they are to serve as effective linkage institutions are: 1) Picking policy-makers; 2) Running campaigns; 3) Giving cues to voters (through a PARTY IMAGE that suggests to voters what each party stands for; 4) Articulating policies; and 5) Coordinating policy-making.

B. Parties, Voters, and Policy: The Downs Model

Anthony Downs has provided a working model of the relationship among citizens, parties, and policy employing a rational-choice perspective. "Rational-choice theory" assumes political actors have goals and pursue those goals sensibly and efficiently. Voters want to maximize the chance that policies they favor will be adopted. Parties want to win office. Thus, in order to win office, the wise party selects policies that are widely supported. Since the majority of the American electorate is neither extremely liberal nor conservative, Downs' model suggests that centrist parties will tend to win. The long history of American party competition has shown that successful parties rarely stray far from the midpoint of public opinion. Thus, the difference between the Republican and Democratic party is not great because, as rational political actors, they have little choice but to remain close to the middle. They try to distinguish themselves only enough to forge separate identities to build voter loyalty around.

III. Party Eras In American History (243-250)

America is a two-party system and always has been. There have always been minor parties, but they have rarely had a chance to win major office. Though a two-party system, American history has witnessed long periods during which one party has been the dominant majority. Political scientist call these PARTY ERAS.

What marks the beginning and end of party eras is a CRITICAL ELECTION. A critical election reveals new issues that create fissures in each party's coalition and lead to the formation of new coalitions for each party. This process is called PARTY REALIGNMENT, a rare event in American political life. Realignments are normally associated with a major crisis or trauma in the nation's history.

A. 1796-1824: The First Party System

Alexander Hamilton, co-author of the Federalist Papers and the nation's first secretary of the treasury, founded the Federalist party as part of his effort to organize support for his policies. The nation's first political party, the Federalists were opposed, and eventually crushed, by the Democratic-Republicans (also known as Jeffersonians) led by Virginians Jefferson, Madison and Monroe. Every political party depends upon a COALITION, a set of individuals and groups supporting it. The Democratic-Republican party derived its coalition from agrarian interests rather than the growing number of capitalists, who supported the Federalists.

B. 1828-1860: Jackson and the Democrats versus the Whigs

General Andrew Jackson, more than anyone else, founded the modern American political party. In 1828 he forged a new coalition that included westerners, southerners, new immigrants as well as settled Americans. A Democratic-Republican, after his ascension to the presidency his party became known as simply the Democratic party. This is the same Democratic party we have today. It was opposed by the Whig party which included such leaders as Henry Clay and Daniel Webster. The Whigs had two distinct wings - northern industrialists and southern planters - who were united more by opposition to Democratic policies than by agreement with each other.

C. 1860-1932: The Republican Era

In the 1850s the issue of slavery split both the Democrats and the

Whigs. The Republicans rose in the late 1850s as "the" antislavery party. Folding in abolitionist elements of several minor parties, the Republicans by 1860 were strong enough to elect Abraham Lincoln president in a four candidate race. In the aftermath of the civil war that followed, the Republican party was in ascendancy for more than sixty years.

Despite Republican dominance, the Democrats remained competitive until 1896. Political scientists call the 1896 election a realigning one, because it shifted the party coalitions and entrenched the Republicans more firmly as the majority party. The election, a bitter class based battle, brought the new working classes and moneyed interests into the Republican fold. The Republican dominance lasted until the Great Depression brought about another fissure in the crust of the American party system.

D. 1932-1968: The New Deal Coalition

President Hoover's inaction in the face of the depression was a disaster for the Republicans. New York Governor Franklin D. Roosevelt handily defeated him in 1932 promising a "New Deal." The popularity of Roosevelt and his New Deal programs brought new voters into the electorate, and new blood to Democratic ranks. The resulting NEW DEAL COALITION was basically made up of urban dwellers, labor unions, Catholics and Jews, the poor, Southerners, African Americans, and intellectuals. Aspects of this coalition continue to shape the party coalitions today (see Figure 7.3).
The New Deal coalition made the Democratic Party the clear majority party until President Johnson's Vietnam War policies tore the party apart in 1968.

E. 1968-Present: The Era of Divided Government

Since 1968 the Republicans have won five out of six presidential elections. At the same time, they have consistently been the minority party in the House of Representatives, and have had the majority in the Senate only six years - from 1981-1986. This extended period of divided government is unprecedented in American history. Divided government is common at the state level as well, with only eighteen states having unified control of governorship and state legislature in 1989. Once an oddity, divided government is now a commonplace.

IV.   The Parties Today: Dealignment and Renewal (250-258)

The recent pattern of divided government has led many political scientists to believe that the party system has dealigned. Whereas realignment involves people changing from one party to another, PARTY DEALIGNMENT means that people are gradually moving away from both.

There are signs of both party decay and revitalization, however, so there is no simple answer about the future of the party system. Political scientists generally agree that three major changes have occurred to the party system since Roosevelt's New Deal. First, party loyalty has declined. Party loyalty has been replaced not with negative attitudes, but with neutrality. Second, those who do identify with a party are more likely to belong to the party that matches their ideology. Once both liberals and conservatives in the south allied with the Democrats and the Republicans had strong liberal wing centered in the Northeast. Today, however, the Republican party is more consistently conservative, and liberals are concentrated in the Democratic party. Third, even while party loyalty has lagged, party organizations have become more energetic and effective. First the Republicans and then the Democrats have learned the secrets of high-tech fund-raising. As a result, the parties' national, congressional, and senatorial campaign committees are now wealthier and better organized than ever before.

Thus, the past few years has witnessed the emergence of what has been called the SPLIT-LEVEL PARTY - a party with a strong, vigorous organization but a weak following on the mass level.

A. The Democrats: Party of Representation

In the aftermath of their riotous 1968 Convention, the Democrats responded to demands for greater representation for minorities and women in their leadership. The McGovern-Fraser Commission adopted guidelines to assure more equal representation for minorities and women, but disfranchised some of the party's traditional leaders in the process. In 1982, the Hunt Commission set aside about 15 percent of delegate slots as so-called SUPERDELEGATES for party leaders and elected officials.

In the 1990s the Democrats must face the question of how to translate their broad representation into presidential election victories. Having won only one (by a narrow margin) of five elections since the McGovern-Frasier reforms, many feel that divisiveness of the Democrat's open procedures has hurt their ability to unite for the fall campaign against the Republicans.

B. The Republicans: Party of Efficiency

Though racked by the Watergate scandal and resignation of President Nixon in 1974, the Republicans were not distracted by questions of fairness of representation within their ranks. Thus, they could focus on winning elections rather than being balanced by race, sex, age, and ethnicity. As party Chairman Bill Brock made the Republican organization more effective and efficient. The advantage they built in computerized high-tech fund raising in the late seventies, though growing smaller, is still visible today.

C. Third Parties: Their Impact on American Politics

THIRD PARTIES pop up every year and occasionally attract the public's attention. Third parties come in two basic varieties - those that promote certain causes (a controversial single issue or an extreme ideology) and "splinter" parties, which are offshoots of a major party.

Though they rarely win offices, scholars believe third parties are often important. They have drawn enough votes in one-third of the last thirty-six presidential elections to have decisively tipped the electoral college vote. They have brought new groups into the electorate and new issues to the political agenda. If the issues prove popular enough, they are often adopted and their supporters absorbed by one of the major parties.

D. Two Parties: So What?

What difference would it make if America had a multi-party system as many European countries have? The most obvious consequence of two-party governance is the moderation of political conflict. With just two, both must attempt to cling to a centrist position in order to succeed.

Unfortunately this also means that parties often cling to political ambiguity. Taking a clear and strong stand on controversial issues is dangerous and even politically foolhardy.

Given the social diversity of America, we would surely have many parties if we had a multi-party system. America could have religious parties, union-based parties, farmer's parties, ethnic and racial based parties, environmentalist parties, and so on.

V. The Party In The Electorate (258-261)

Because we have no formal party membership in America, the party-in-the-electorate consists largely of symbolic images and ideas. For most citizens party is a psychological label consisting of images which provide a picture of where a party stands on issues and whose interests it represents. These party images shape people's PARTY IDENTIFICATION, their self proclaimed preference for one or the other party.

The clearest trend in party identification over the past three decades has been the decline of both parties and resultant upsurge of independence (mostly at the expense of the Democrats). In 1988, for the first time, independents outnumbered both Democrats and Republicans. Virtually every major social group has moved toward a position of increased independence, with the exception of African Americans, who have become even more Democratic.

In addition, those who still identify with a party are no longer as loyal in the voting booth as used to be the case. One result of this is a greater tendency toward TICKET-SPLITTING - voting with one party for one office and another for other offices.

Chapter 7

VI. The Party Organizations:
From The Grass Roots To Washington (261-268)

As organizations, American political parties are decentralized and
fragmented.   They lack the top-down authority, control and
efficiency usually associated with large organizations. Top leaders
have little power to reward or punish those at lower levels in the
structure. Candidates in the United States can get elected on their
own. They do not need the help of the party most of the time, and
hence the party organization is relegated to a limited role.

A. Local Parties: The Dying Urban Machines

County and city organizations may be the grass roots of the party
but, except in a few places, grass roots party volunteers are hard
to find. This is particularly true for the minority party where one
party is consistently dominant. Some areas have both parties with
well oiled precinct, city, and county organizations, but local
politics is no longer a hot bed of party organization.

From the late nineteenth century through the New Deal of the 1930s,
the situation was very different, however. Scores of cities were
dominated by PARTY MACHINES - a "party organization that depends
crucially on inducements that are both specific and material."
"Specific" in that it can be given to one person and withheld from
another, and "material" in that it involved, directly or indirectly,
money.   PATRONAGE was one of the key inducements offered by
machines. A patronage job is one that is given for political
reasons rather than for merit or competence. Patronage can also take
the form of lucrative government contracts let for political
reasons.

B. The Fifty State Party Systems

American national parties are a loose aggregation of state parties,
which are themselves a fluid association of individuals, groups, and
local organizations.   There are fifty state party systems,
characterized by great variation in level of organization, and no
two exactly alike. Most are becoming better organized, however,
establishing permanent physical headquarters and substantially
increasing their budgets. They remain small compared to nationally
organized interest groups based in Washington, however.C. State
Parties as Legal Organizations

State, not federal, statutes define a party and specify how it is to
be organized. Parties are more closely regulated in America than in
other western democracies. Recently the federal courts have upheld
the power of national parties when national party policy has
conflicted with state law, however.

D. The National Party Organizations

144

The supreme power within each of the parties is its NATIONAL CONVENTION. Meeting every four years, its main task is to write the party's platform and then nominate its candidates for president and vice-president. Keeping the party operating between conventions is the NATIONAL COMMITTEE, composed of representatives from the states and territories. Day-to-day activities of the national party are the responsibility of the NATIONAL CHAIRPERSON of the party. The national chairperson is elected by the national committee, but in the case of the party holding the presidency the person chosen will be the personal choice of the president.

VII.   The Party In Government: Promises And Policy (268-270)

The party that wins control of government, and the elected officials that represent it, generally try to turn campaign promises into action. Sometimes voters suspect that political promises are made to be broken, and there are notable instances of politicians turning from their policy promises. It is all too easy to forget how often parties and presidents do exactly what they say they will do. The impression that politicians and parties never produce policy out of promises is largely erroneous.
Gerald Pomper has shown that party platforms are excellent predictors of a party's actual policy performance in office. Only 10 percent of a party's platform promises were ignored altogether. The party platforms adopted at the national conventions represent blueprints for action, and reflect the differences between the two major parties. (See Figure 7.3)

VIII.   Understanding Political Parties (270-272)

Today, political parties are considered essential elements of democratic government. The founders were wary of parties, however and designed a system which has greatly restrained their political role in America to this day. Whether American parties should continue to be so loosely organized is at the heart of today's debate concerning their role in American democracy.

A. Democracy and Responsible Party Government

Ideally, in a democracy candidates should say what they mean to do if elected and be able to do what they promised once they are elected. Because this is all too often not the case in the American party system critics have called for a "more responsible two-party system." The RESPONSIBLE PARTY MODEL would meet the following conditions: 1) parties must present distinct, comprehensive programs for governing the nation; 2) each party's candidates must be committed to its program; 3) the majority party must implement its programs and the minority party must state what it would do if it were in power; and 4) the majority party must accept responsibility for the performance of the government.

A two-party system operating under these conditions would make it easier for party promises to be turned into governmental policy. A party's officeholders would have control of the government and they would be collectively (rather than individually) responsible for their actions. Voters would know whom to blame for what the government does and does not accomplish.

American parties fall far short of these conditions. They are too decentralized to take a single national position and enforce it. Not everyone thinks America's decentralized parties are a problem, however. They argue that the complexity and diversity of American society is too great to be captured by a simple black and white model of party politics. In this view, America's decentralized parties are appropriate for the type of limited government the founders sought to create.

B. Big Government and Weak Parties

It can be argued that weak parties have not limited government but fostered big government. Because no single party can ever be said to have firm control over the government, the hard choices necessary to limit the growth of government are rarely addressed. A disciplined and cohesive governing party would have the power to say no to various demands on government. The lack of a strong party structure makes it easier for politicians to pass the buck than bite the bullet.

C. Is the Party Over?

The key problem of the parties today is this: the parties are low-tech institutions in a high-tech political era. The technology for campaigning - television, polls, computers, political consultants, media specialists, and the like - is available for hire to candidates. They need not rely on parties.

The media also frees the party-in-the-electorate from parties. With the advent of television, voters no longer need the party to find out what the candidates are like and what they stand for. The parties have had a rough time of late, but there are indications that they are beginning to adapt to the high-tech age. Parties are likely to continue to play an important - but significantly reduced - role in American politics.

DOING RESEARCH ON POLITICAL PARTIES

Many college students, perhaps you among them, fail to see why there is such a fuss over the decline of political parties as guides to the electorate in voting. They see party based voting as rather mindless and even demeaning - unsuitable all-in-all for an educated voter. Instead, they tend to see "voting for the person" as a good thing. If you share this view, investigating the role of parties and the costs and dangers of a highly disaggregated election process might be a worthwhile research focus. Researching the question might not change your opinion, but it would give you a much greater appreciation for the complexities of the matter.

You may wish to investigate party coalitional behavior and realignments of the past. It is a fascinating process and one that is the subject of considerable speculation at the present point in party history. An in depth look at a realignment might provide you with insights valuable for understanding what is - and is not - going on now. James L. Sundquist's <u>Dynamics of the Party System</u> is an excellent place to begin.

A useful study can focus on party platforms. Though often dismissed as vague collections of "campaign promises," they are fairly accurate indications of the party's positions on important policy questions. The major parties' platforms are printed in the <u>New York Times</u> shortly after each party's national convention. By tracing the changes in a single party over-time, or carefully comparing the similarities and difference between the parties, you can learn a lot about the philosophical and ideological make up of each party, and the power of various groups within each party.

REVIEW TEST

Reread the chapter overview and quiz yourself with the "Reading for Content" questions. Review the learning objectives listed at the beginning of this chapter and take on the Review Test below.

1.　By far the largest component of an American party is the:
    (a)　party and the individual.
    (b)　party as an organization.
    (c)　the party in government.
    (d)　party in the electorate.
Page 240

2.　The _____ has a national office, a full-time staff, rules and bylaws and budgets. It also has state and local offices. (a) party in the electorate
    (b)　party and the individual
    (c)　party in government
    (d)　party as an organization
Page 239

3.　All of the following are linkage institutions EXCEPT:
    (a)　parties.
    (b)　the bureaucracy.
    (c)　interest groups.
    (d)　the media.
Page 241

4.　Political parties perform all of the activities EXCEPT:
    (a)　running campaigns.
    (b)　giving cues to voters.

(c) articulating policies.
(d) running elections.
Page 241

5. In the American electorate, the majority of voters are:
    (a) in the middle of the road.
    (b) extremely liberal.
    (c) extremely conservative.
    (d) slightly libertarian.
Page 242

6. While studying American political parties, it is wise to remember that:
    (a) America is a one-party system with two branches.
    (b) America is a multi-partied system.
    (c) America is a two party system and always has been.
    (d) America has always had a three party system with the third party always being weak.
Page 243

7. All of the following events, or traumas, have split political parties and caused party realignment EXCEPT:
    (a) the Civil War.
    (b) the Spanish-American War.
    (c) the Great Depression.
    (d) Watergate.
Page 244

8. In the Federalist Papers, _____ warned strongly against the dangers of "factions," or parties.
    (a) Alexander Hamilton
    (b) Thomas Jefferson
    (c) John Jay
    (d) James Madison
Page 245

9. _____ was the nation's first secretary of the treasury.
    (a) Aaron Burr
    (b) Alexander Hamilton
    (c) John C. Marshall
    (d) Thomas Jefferson

10. Every political party depends on a _____, or a set of individuals or groups supporting it.
    (a) referendum
    (b) consortium
    (c) bureaucracy
    (d) coalition
Page 246

11. All of the following men became two-term presidents as Democratic-Republicans EXCEPT:

    (a)   Thomas Jefferson
    (b)   James Madison
    (c)   James Monroe
    (d)   John Quincy Adams
Page 245

12.   _____ left his mark by stating that Democrats must "see that their only hope for maintaining the purity of their own principles was to admit the existence of an opposing party."
    (a)   Daniel Webster
    (b)   Andrew Jackson
    (c)   James Knox Polk
    (d)   Martin Van Buren
Page 246

13.   The Whig party contained many notables but was not able to win the presidency until they nominated _____ in 1840.
    (a)   Henry Clay
    (b)   William Henry Harrison
    (c)   John Tyler
    (d)   Millard Fillmore
Page 246

14.   The last Whig elected president was _____ in 1848.
    (a)   William Henry Harrison
    (b)   John Tyler
    (c)   Zachary Taylor
    (d)   Daniel Webster
Page 246

15.   Combining several minor parties, in 1860 the Republicans forged a coalition strong enough to elect _____.
    (a)   James Buchanan
    (b)   Stephen Douglas
    (c)   Everett Edwards
    (d)   Abraham Lincoln
Page 247

16.   After the Civil War, the _____ party controlled the South.
    (a)   Republican
    (b)   Whig
    (c)   Democratic
    (d)   American Independent
Page 247

17.   The Republican party, in 1896, made clear its positions in favor of the gold standard and put _____ in the White House.
    (a)   Theodore Roosevelt

(b) William McKinley
(c) Benjamin Harrison
(d) William Howard Taft
Page 247

18. Political scientists call the 1896 election a realigning one, because it shifted the party coalitions and entrenched the _____ party for another generation.
    (a) Democratic
    (b) Whig
    (c) Populist
    (d) Republican
Page 247

19. _____ handily defeated President Hoover in 1932 and promised a New Deal.
    (a) Al Smith
    (b) Harry S. Truman
    (c) Woodrow Wilson
    (d) Franklin D. Roosevelt
Page 247

20. Immigrant groups in Boston and other cities had been initially attracted to the Democratic presidential candidacy of New York Governor _____, a Catholic, in 1928.
    (a) Fiorello H. LaGuardia
    (b) Al Smith
    (c) Robert H. Moses
    (d) James M. Cox
Page 247

21. All of the following were basic elements of the New Deal coalition EXCEPT:
    (a) urban dwellers in big cities like Chicago and Philadelphia.
    (b) labor unions.
    (c) aristocratic northern industrialists.
    (d) Catholics and Jews.
Page 248

22. World War II hero and Republican _____ broke the Democrats' grip on power by being elected president twice during the 1950's.
    (a) Thomas E. Dewey
    (b) Richard M. Nixon
    (c) Dwight D. Eisenhower
    (d) Barry M. Goldwater
Page 248

23. President Lyndon Johnson's _____ programs included a major

expansion of government programs to help the poor, the dispossessed and the minorities.
(a) New Federalism
(b) New Frontier
(c) Fair Deal
(d) Great Society
Page 249

24. Johnson's Vietnam War policies split the Democratic party in 1968 and left the door to the presidency open for Republican candidate:
(a) Barry Goldwater.
(b) Richard Nixon.
(c) Gerald Ford.
(d) Ronald Reagan.
Page 249

25. From 1968 to 1990, the Republicans have won most of the presidential elections but have consistently been the minority party in:
(a) the House of Representatives.
(b) the U.S. Senate.
(c) both the House and the Senate.
(d) none of the answers are true.
Page 249

26. By 1989, a twentieth-century low of only _____ states had unified control of their governorship and legislature?
(a) forty-two
(b) thirty-three
(c) twenty-four
(d) eighteen
Page 250

27. Today, it is true that:
(a) southern liberals and conservatives alike still vote with the Democratic party.
(b) there is a strong liberal wing of the Republican party centered in the Northeast.
(c) conservative southerners no longer shy away from the Republican label.
(d) the Democrats' "Solid South" is as solid as ever.
Page 251

28. Both Reagan in 1984 and Bush in 1988 did about 5 percent better in the _____ than in the rest of the country.
(a) Northeast
(b) Midwest
(c) West Coast
(d) South
Page 251

29. Demonstrators at the Democratic National Convention in Chicago fought the police sent by Mayor:

(a) Abe Beam.
(b) Ed Koch.
(c) John V. Lindsey.
(d) Richard Daley.
Page 253

30. After the 1968 convention, the _____ Commission brought great changes to the Democratic party and tried to make future conventions more representative.
    (a) McGovern-Fraser
    (b) Humphrey-Muskie
    (c) Jackson-Udall
    (d) Shriver-Eagelton
Page 254

31. Democratic party superdelegates provided a key source of support for presidential candidate:
    (a) Walter F. Mondale.
    (b) Jesse Jackson.
    (c) Michael Dukakis.
    (d) Both Mondale and Dukakis.
Page 254

32. In the five elections since the McGovern-Fraser reforms, the Democratic party has won _____ of them.
    (a) one
    (b) two
    (c) three
    (d) four
Page 254

33. In 1968, Governor George Wallace of Alabama formed the _____ party and ran as their presidential candidate.
    (a) American Independent
    (b) States' Rights
    (c) Progressive
    (d) Bull Moose
Page 257

34. A walkout by southerners at the Democratic convention of 1948 led to the formation of the States' Rights, or Dixiecrat, Party whose presidential candidate was:
    (a) Fielding Wright.
    (b) J. Strom Thurmond.
    (c) Curtis LeMay.
    (d) Glenn Taylor.
Page 256

35. The variously named Independent Party in 1980 represented

Republican _____'s efforts to win the presidency.
(a) Howard H. Baker, Jr.,
(b) Philip Crane
(c) Robert Dole
(d) John Anderson
Page 256

36. Teddy Roosevelt's Bull Moose Progressive Party was a splinter from the _____ party.
(a) Republican
(b) Democratic
(c) Federalist
(d) Libertarian
Page 256

37. All of the following were active political parties who offered candidates for president in 1860 EXCEPT:
(a) the Republican party.
(b) the Democratic party.
(c) the Confederate party.
(d) the Constitutional Union party.
Page 256

38. This third party was formed in 1831 and based its platform on its opposition to the Masons.
(a) The Republican Party
(b) the Whigs
(c) the "Know-Nothings"
(d) the Anti-Masonic Party
Page 256

39. As of 1988, only _____ percent of blacks identified themselves as Republicans.
(a) two
(b) seven
(c) eighteen
(d) twenty-three
Page 260

40. The supreme power within each of the parties is its:
(a) national convention.
(b) presidential candidate.
(c) national chairman.
(d) national signing committee.
Page 267

BEFORE GOING ON

Chapter 7

Hopefully, the routine of studying the book and using the Study Guide are, by now, beginning to make it easier to be well prepared for the Review Test. The style of the authors of both the text and the questions should be becoming familiar, and the process of preparation more efficient and effective. As always, you can check your answers against the answer key below. Go back and reread the relevant passages on the indicated page for any you have missed.

Review Test Answers:

1: d	11: d	21: c	31: d
2: d	12: d	22: c	32: a
3: b	13: b	23: d	33: a
4: d	14: c	24: b	34: b
5: a	15: d	25: a	35: d
6: c	16: c	26: d	36: a
7: b	17: b	27: c	37: c
8: d	18: d	28: d	38: d
9: b	19: d	29: d	39: b
10: d	20: b	30: a	40: a

It should by now also be second nature to go back and review those Key Terms (page 273) just one more time. The best test is to use them as well as to formally define them. Again, the importance of knowing the vocabulary can't be overstated in a basic introductory survey course like this one. (Besides, it will keep me from feeling responsible for your grade if I have missed one in the Overview and sample questions.) If you feel comfortable with the terms, it is time to select that special one that will most graphically demonstrate your burgeoning knowledge. This chapter has a lot of impressive sounding key terms but, for practical reasons I suggest "rational-choice theory." Not only is it a theory, which always sounds impressive, but the basic notion is generalizable to all sorts of life circumstances. You can, for example, complement someone by saying their behavior conforms to rational-choice theory - or, of course, suggest that someone's behavior is less than that which would fulfill the tenets of rational-choice theory. If that really makes them angry, you can always retreat by saying that it is just something thought up by a bunch of social scientists.

CHAPTER 8

NOMINATIONS AND CAMPAIGNS

CHAPTER LEARNING OBJECTIVES

After reading Chapter 8, you should be able to:

1. Describe the steps in the nomination process and the strategies associated with each step.
2. Distinguish the caucus and primary delegate selection processes.
3. Discuss the principle criticisms of the nomination process.
4. Describe the modern purposes and processes of the national convention.
5. Identify the basic elements of campaign organization.
6. Describe campaign finance regulations.
7. Assess the role of money in campaigns.
8. Describe the role of the media in the modern campaign.
9. Identify the basic effects of campaigns, and assess the importance of each.
10. Assess the effect of the nomination and campaign processes on democracy and the size of modern government.

PRETEST QUESTIONS

The pretest below will give you an idea of the state of your knowledge about nominations and campaigns. The questions should also help you learn what to look for while studying the text. Take the whole pretest, then check your answers against the key that follows (don't peek!). As you read the chapter, watch for where these questions are addressed (indicated after each question) so that you may learn why the answer is what it is.

1. After Ronald Reagan's 1984 campaign, Jeff Carter said that, "_____ are the biggest thing to hit politics since television."
   (a) TelePrompTers
   (b) opinion polls
   (c) mass mailings
   (d) computers
Page 278

2.   In 1968, _____ caused his bid to be the Republican presidential nominee to self-destruct after he stated that he had been "brainwashed" about the Vietnam War.
     (a)   Barry Goldwater
     (b)   Nelson Rockefeller
     (c)   George Romney
     (d)   Henry Cabot Lodge
Page 278

3.   The goal of the nominating game is to win the majority of delegates' support at the:
     (a)   grassroots level.
     (b)   primary election level.
     (c)   superdelegate level.
     (d)   national party convention.
Page 281

4.   Today, most of the delegates to the Democratic and Republican conventions are selected in _____ primaries.
     (a)   presidential
     (b)   closed
     (c)   open
     (d)   precinct-level
Page 282

5.   The presidential primary season begins during the winter in:
     (a)   New Hampshire.
     (b)   Virginia.
     (c)   Idaho.
     (d)   Minnesota.
Page 283

6.   In the 1980 delegate chase, one memorable term was coined by George Bush. After he scored a victory over Ronald Reagan in the Iowa caucus, he claimed to possess:
     (a)   "the big mo"
     (b)   "firepower"
     (c)   "the little mo"
     (d)   "the mo better blues"
Page 283

7.   _____, in his 1987 autobiography, Looking Forward, defended the current system of picking presidential candidates.
     (a)   George Bush
     (b)   George McGovern
     (c)   Mario Cuomo
     (d)   Edward M. Kennedy
Page 287

8.   _____, the 1988 presidential candidate who barely lost in Iowa and carried only his native Illinois, argues that the best place to start the presidential race is in small states where "candidates of limited means have a chance."
      (a)   Paul Simon
      (b)   Jesse Jackson
      (c)   Richard Gephardt
      (d)   Joseph Biden
Page 287

9.   The third day of today's national conventions is devoted to:
      (a)   drafting the party platform.
      (b)   hearing opposition speeches regarding the party platform.
      (c)   the keynote speech.
      (d)   choosing the presidential candidate through delegate voting.
Page 290

10.   In order to effectively organize their campaigns, candidates must do all of the following EXCEPT:
      (a)   line up a campaign manager.
      (b)   get a fund raiser.
      (c)   make sure all important delegates support you in advance.
      (d)   hire a pollster.
Page 291

11.   As California Treasurer Jesse Unruh used to say, "_____ is the mother's milk of politics."
      (a)   money
      (b)   honesty
      (c)   integrity
      (d)   constituent service
Page 293

12.   According to the Federal Election Commission, presidential candidates who raise five thousand dollars on their own in at least _____ states can get individual contributions of up to two hundred fifty dollars matched by the federal treasury.
      (a)   ten
      (b)   fifteen
      (c)   twenty
      (d)   twenty five
Page 294

13.   The FEC counted _____ PACs in 1988.
      (a)   253
      (b)   572
      (c)   897
      (d)   9,100
Page 295

14. A _____ is formed when a business association or some other interest group decides to contribute to candidates they believe will be favorable toward their goals.
    (a) country club
    (b) caucus
    (c) PAC
    (d) fund club
Page 295

15. _____ is absolutely crucial to electoral victory.
    (a) Polling
    (b) Money
    (c) A computer
    (d) Integrity
Page 298

16. Television advertising accounts for about _____ of the total budget for a presidential or senatorial campaign.
    (a) 25%
    (b) 50%
    (c) 75%
    (d) 90%
Page 299

17. News coverage is disproportionately devoted to all of the following during a campaign EXCEPT:
    (a) poll results.
    (b) campaign strategies.
    (c) position stands.
    (d) "what will happen next."
Page 299

18. The idea of holding a national primary to select party nominees was first proposed to Congress in 1913 by:
    (a) President Woodrow Wilson.
    (b) President Theodore Roosevelt.
    (c) President William Howard Taft.
    (d) Supreme Court Justice Oliver Wendell Holmes.
Page 288

19. According to legend, Congressman _____ lost a Florida Senate race in 1950 after his opponent made a series of vague charges about his character.
    (a) George Smathers
    (b) Claude Pepper
    (c) Strom Thurmond
    (d) Lester Maddox
Page 292

20. In 1984, _____ percent of all TV news stories about the nomination campaigns were about Iowa and New Hampshire.
     (a) 2
     (b) 12
     (c) 18
     (c) 34
Page 286

Pretest Answers:

1: d	11: a
2: c	12: c
3: d	13: d
4: a	14: c
5: a	15: b
6: a	16: b
7: a	17: c
8: a	18: a
9: d	19: b
10: c	20: d

READING FOR CONTENT

Listed below are sets of questions associated with the content of each major section of Chapter 8. Carefully review the questions associated with each section of the text before reading the section. Have the questions in mind as you read the section and, when you reach the end of each section, stop and see if you can answer the questions well. If not, reread the relevant paragraphs until you are sure of your response to each of the questions.

I.   The High-Tech Campaign

     Which of high-tech have had the greatest impact on campaigns?

II. The Nomination Game

     What is a nomination?
     How do you define "campaign strategy?"
     What factors discourage most politicians from seeking the
        presidency?
     What is the difference between a caucus and a primary?
     What criticisms are directed at the present delegate
        selection process?
     What are the functions of the National Convention?
     How have the functions of the National Convention changed in
        recent years?

III. The Campaign Game

     What are the basic elements of a campaign organization?
     What are the provisions of the Federal Election Campaign Act?

What do Political Action Committees do?
Why are Political Action Committees important?
What criticisms are directed at Political Action Committees?
What is the impact of money on elections?
What is the impact of the media in campaigns?
What effects do campaigns have, and which are most important?
Why are campaigns not more effective than they are?

IV.   Understanding Nominations and Campaigns

Why can it be argued that campaigns are too democratic?
Why does the campaign process help to foster big government?

CHAPTER OVERVIEW

I.   Introduction   (276-276)

There are two types of campaigns in American politics: campaigns for
party nominations (nomination campaigns) and campaigns between
nominees for public office (election campaigns). Campaigning today
is an art and a science, heavily dependent on technology.

II. The High-Tech Campaign (276-278)

Today, television, rather than travel, is the most prevalent means
used by candidates to reach voters. For a majority of voters,
today's presidential campaign has little reality apart from its
media version. The computer revolution has also reached the
political campaign. Between 15 and 25 percent of presidential
campaign expenses now goes to computer services and their related
tool, direct mail. The high-tech campaign for the presidential
nomination is no longer a luxury. Use of the media and computer
technology is a must to be competitive.

III. The Nomination Game (278-291)

A NOMINATION is a party's official endorsement of a candidacy for
office. Success in the nomination game requires money, media
attention, and momentum. CAMPAIGN STRATEGY is the way in which
candidates attempt to manipulate each of these elements to achieve
the nomination. A campaign, whether for a nomination or the
election, is often unpredictable. Both conscious choices and slips
of the tongue help determine outcomes.

A. Deciding to Run

Not every politician wants to run for president. One reason is that
campaigns have become more taxing than ever. The prospective
candidate faces a four year full time task. A presidential
candidacy needs to be either officially announced or an "open

35. Which of the following factors does NOT tend to weaken campaigns' impact on voters.
    (a) incumbents, even with established track records and name recognition, have no real substantial advantage.
    (b) most people pay relatively little attention to campaigns.
    (c) people have a remarkable capacity for selective perception -- paying most attention to things they already agree with.
    (d) factors such as party identification still influence voting behavior.
Page 301

36. In an apology to the state he governed in January, 1990, Governor _____ apologized for running for office and managing the state simultaneously.
    (a) Reuben Askew
    (b) Bob Kerrey
    (c) Charles S. Robb
    (d) Michael Dukakis
Page 276

37. In 1984, _____ complained that his wife got to campaign in California while he was stuck in New Jersey. He won in California but got trounced in New Jersey for this remark.
    (a) Gary Hart
    (b) Walter Mondale
    (c) George Bush
    (d) Ronald Reagan
Page 288

38. To personalize the argument against prison furloughs in the 1988 campaign, the Bush campaign used the case of _____ --a murderer who raped a Maryland woman one weekend while on a prison furlough.
    (a) Willie Horton
    (b) Richard Speck
    (c) Ted Bundy
    (d) Roger Dale Stafford
Page 292

39. In 1984, 34 percent of all TV news stories about the nomination campaigns were about:
    (a) Iowa.
    (b) New Hampshire.
    (c) Iowa and New Hampshire.
    (d) California.
Page 286

40. By appealing directly to the people, a candidate can emerge

from nowhere to win the White House as did _____ in 1976.
(a)   Jimmy Carter
(b)   Ronald Reagan
(c)   Gerald Ford
(d)   John F. Kennedy
Page 301

BEFORE GOING ON

By now these review tests must be a snap! Just to be on the safe
side check your answers against the answer key below anyway. If,
somehow, you got fooled - go back and reread the relevant passages
on the indicated page - to get schooled.

Review Test Answers:

1: b	11: c	21: a	31: d
2: a	12: b	22: d	32: d
3: d	13: d	23: d	33: b
4: a	14: c	24: c	34: d
5: b	15: c	25: a	35: a
6: d	16: d	26: d	36: d
7: a	17: c	27: b	37: a
8: c	18: b	28: a	38: a
9: b	19: c	29: b	39: c
10: d	20: c	30: c	40: a

As you review the Key Terms on page 303 (just one more time for
luck), you will notice that this time there are relatively few.
Thus your task will be quickly accomplished and you can soon lay
down your weary head and dream of the FEC chasing PACs through the
national party convention on Super Tuesday. Seriously, the term to
take with you on the streets is "selective perception." Practiced
by practically everyone, it can be applied to practically all of
those who hold viewpoints radically different from your own. You
can suggest that selective perception of the evidence has led them
to their erroneous view. Of course, it is important that you've
examined all the evidence, even that which is inconvenient, lest
selective perception leads you into a trap of your own design.

CHAPTER 9

ELECTIONS AND VOTING BEHAVIOR

CHAPTER LEARNING OBJECTIVES

After reading Chapter 9, you should be able to:

1. Discuss the functions of elections.
2. Identify unique features of elections in America.
3. Identify the factors associated with voting and nonvoting.
4. Describe the rational choice (Downs) explanation of voting.
5. Discuss how the rational choice can explain the inequalities in voting.
6. Identify the three major elements determining how voters vote.
7. Identify the conditions that must be met for policy voting to occur.
8. Describe the way the electoral college system works today.
9. Discuss the impact of the electoral college on the presidential election.
10. Discuss the impact of elections on public policy.
11. Discuss the impact of public policy on elections.
12. Discuss the implications of elections for the growth of government.

PRETEST QUESTIONS

The pretest below will give you an idea of the state of your knowledge about elections and voting behavior. The questions should also help you learn what to look for while studying the text. Take the whole pretest, then check your answers against the key that follows (don't peek!). As you read the chapter, watch for where these questions are addressed (indicated after each question) so that you may learn why the answer is what it is.

1. Unlike most other democracies, the United States has three kinds of elections, including all of the following EXCEPT: (a) those which select party nominees.
    (b) those which elect federal judges.
    (c) those which select officeholders among the nominees.
    (d) those in which voters engage in making or ratifying legislation.
Page 308

2. Presidential primaries are _____ primaries because they choose only delegates to go to a national convention.
    (a) indirect
    (b) secondary
    (c) runoff
    (d) direct
    Page 308

3. The most famous example of an initiative petition is California's _____, which in 1978 put a limit on the rise in property taxes in California.
    (a) Proposition 13
    (b) House Bill 1017
    (c) Miller/Roth Act
    (d) Smith Act
    Page 309

4. In the election of 1800, both incumbent president John Adams and challenger Thomas Jefferson were nominated by:
    (a) their parties' elected representatives in Congress.
    (b) direct primaries.
    (c) a national convention.
    (d) local primaries.
    Page 310

5. Not wanting John Adams to be his vice-president, Thomas Jefferson made sure that all his electors also voted for his vice-presidential choice:
    (a) Alexander Hamilton.
    (b) John Jay.
    (c) Aaron Burr.
    (d) James Madison.
    Page 311

6. In 1896, the Democrats' blamed their incumbent President _____ for the 1893 Depression.
    (a) Samuel J. Tilden
    (b) Chester A. Arthur
    (c) Grover Cleveland
    (d) Woodrow Wilson
    Page 312

7. The winner of the 1896 presidential election was:
    (a) William Jennings Bryan.
    (b) Theodore Roosevelt.
    (c) William McKinley.
    (d) Woodrow Wilson.
    Page 312

8. In 1988, presidential candidate _____ dropped out of the race after allegations of being unfaithful to his wife.
    (a) Pat Robertson
    (b) Gary Hart
    (c) Joseph Biden
    (d) Jesse Jackson
Page 313

9. The presidential campaign of _____ hit a snag in 1988 after he came in third to Robert Dole and Pat Robertson in the Iowa caucus.
    (a) Jack Kemp
    (b) Alexander Haig
    (c) George Bush
    (d) Pierre S. "Pete" DuPont IV
Page 313

10. George Bush hammered away at Michael Dukakis on issues such as Dukakis' veto of a bill requiring teachers to lead students in the Pledge of Allegiance and the furlough of murderer:
    (a) Richard Speck.
    (b) Huey Newton.
    (c) Charles Manson.
    (d) Willie Horton.
Page 314

11. In the 1988 election, the "solid south" went for:
    (a) Bush and Dukakis equally.
    (b) Dukakis overwhelmingly.
    (c) Bush overwhelmingly.
    (d) Dukakis, with Bush picking up several states.
Page 315

12. The nearly two centuries of American electoral history have witnessed expanded:
    (a) suffrage, the right to vote.
    (b) segregation.
    (c) abuses of power.
    (d) colonialism.
Page 316

13. Largely to prevent corruption associated with stuffing ballot boxes, states adopted _____ around the turn of the century.
    (a) primary elections
    (b) voter registration
    (c) runoff elections
    (d) the Federal Election Campaign Act
Page 319

14. In 1948, _____ won a race for the U.S. Senate by a total of
    87 - very suspicious - votes.
    (a) Robert S. Kerr
    (b) Hubert Humphrey
    (c) Lyndon Johnson
    (d) Richard Nixon
Page 321

15. The following groups support the Democratic party EXCEPT:
    (a) Mexican Americans.
    (b) Jews.
    (c) intellectuals.
    (d) upper-income voters.
Page 323

16. In 1976, _____ told Americans, "I'll never lie to you."
    (a) Richard Nixon.
    (b) Edward M. Kennedy
    (c) Jimmy Carter
    (d) Ronald Reagan
Page 325

17. In support of the new voter registration House bill passed in
    1990, Democratic Majority Whip _____, said that "each
    generation has widened the circle of participation."
    (a) Tony Coelho
    (b) George Mitchell
    (c) William Gray
    (d) Richard Gephardt
Page 327

18. The uniquely American electoral college is created by:
    (a) President Jefferson.
    (b) the Constitution.
    (c) the Bill of Rights.
    (d) Alexander Hamilton.
Page 327

19. The highest voter turnout for industrial nations in recent
    times has been in _____ with a turnout of 93% in 1990.
    (a) East Germany
    (b) Great Britain
    (c) Japan
    (d) the United States
Page 318

20. The state with the highest voter turnout in the elections of
    1988 was _____ with 66.3 percent of the electorate voting.
    (a) Alaska
    (b) Oklahoma
    (c) Minnesota
    (d) Georgia
Page 320

Pretest Answers:

1:	b	11:	c
2:	a	12:	a
3:	a	13:	b
4:	a	14:	c
5:	c	15:	d
6:	c	16:	c
7:	c	17:	c
8:	b	18:	b
9:	c	19:	a
10:	d	20:	c

READING FOR CONTENT

Listed below are sets of questions associated with the content of each major section of Chapter 9. Carefully review the questions associated with each section of the text before reading the section. Have the questions in mind as you read the section and, when you reach the end of each section, stop and see if you can answer the questions well. If not, reread the relevant paragraphs until you are sure of your response to each of the questions.

I.   How American Elections Work

     What important functions do elections serve?
     Why is electoral legitimacy so important?
     How do American elections perform some unique functions?

II.   A Tale of Three Elections

     Why was the election of 1800 important?
     Why was the election of 1896 important?
     How does the election of 1988 illustrate the characteristics
        of the modern electoral process?

III. Whether To Vote: A Citizen's First Choice

     What has happened to the voting rate as suffrage expanded?
     What factors are related to the decision on whether to vote?
     What is the purpose of voter registration systems?
     What is the effect of voter registration systems on voter
        turnout?
     Under what conditions can voting be a rational behavior?
     How can viewing voting as a rational behavior help explain
        the inequalities in voting?

IV. How Americans Vote: Explaining Citizen's Decisions

     What is the mandate theory of elections?
     What are the three major elements of voter's decisions on how

to vote?

What is the relative importance of each of the three
   elements?

What conditions must be met for policy voting to take place?

V.   The Last Battle: The Electoral College

Why did the founders create the electoral college system for
   the election of the president?

How does the electoral college system work today?

What bias does the electoral college system introduce into
   the campaign and electoral process?

How can the electoral college system produce a result that
   does not reflect the popular vote?

VI.   Democracy and Elections

What tasks do elections accomplish according to democratic
   theory?

Under what circumstances do elections affect public policy?

How do politicians seek to avoid conditions that would allow
   elections to affect public policy?

How does public policy affect election outcomes?

How are elections related to the size of government?

CHAPTER OVERVIEW

I.   Introduction   (306-307)

This chapter focuses on how elections function in the American
system and how voters generally behave. Though we search for
meaning in elections, they may not be quite the expression of
popular will we assume they are.

II. How American Elections Work (307-309)

Elections serve many important functions in American society. They
socialize and institutionalize political activity, providing a
peaceful channel for participation in place of spontaneous
demonstrations, riots or revolutions. Because elections provide
regular access to political power, leaders can be replaced without
being overthrown. The peaceful transfer of power is possible when
elections have LEGITIMACY in the eyes of the people - that is, it is
almost universally accepted as a fair and free method of selecting
political leaders.

A. The Importance of Electoral Legitimacy

The importance of electoral legitimacy is illustrated by the
difference between the Mexican and U.S. elections of 1988. The
Mexican election results, which were delayed for days, were widely

viewed as tainted by fraud. When the government finally announced that its candidate had won a narrow victory, the result was a massive protest march in the nation's capital. Doubts about the legitimacy of the victory of Carlos Salinas de Cortari have clearly hampered the effectiveness of his administration.

In contrast, the results of the U.S. election were reported the evening of the vote, Michael Dukakis conceded the election publicly shortly after all the polls had closed and, though disappointed, his supporters went about their daily business the next day with never a thought about protest or disruption. Such is the importance of electoral legitimacy.

B.   Some Unique American Electoral Features

There are a number of features of the American electoral system that are unique. The United States has three kinds of elections: those that select party nominees, those which select officeholders from among the nominees, and those in which voters engage in making or ratifying legislation.

Elections held for the purpose of picking party nominees are called PRIMARIES. Primaries are used to select the nominees in states for Congressional elections as well as state and local offices. These are DIRECT PRIMARIES because party nominees are chosen directly by the people, while presidential primaries are indirect because they choose delegates to go to a national convention.

Also virtually unique to the United States are state-level elections that permit voters to enact legislation. The INITIATIVE PETITION enables voters in twenty-three states to put proposed legislation on the ballot. In this way citizens can force a decision on an issue upon which the state legislature has failed to act. Another example of direct legislation is the REFERENDUM, whereby voters are given the chance to approve or disapprove some legislative act or constitutional amendment.

Primaries, initiative petitions, and referendums have all been reforms of the election system. Modern electronic technology could allow even broader and deeper direct participation if fully utilized. The history of American elections has been a history of increasing technological sophistication and increasing democracy.

III.   A Tale Of Three Elections (309-316)

Times change, and so do elections. Modern campaigns are slick, high-tech affairs. A glance at three American elections gives a good idea of how they have changed over the past two centuries.

A. 1800: The First Electoral Transition of Power

By modern standards the election of 1800 was not much of an election at all: no primaries, no nominating conventions, no candidate speeches, and no entourage of reporters. President John Adams and challenger Thomas Jefferson were both nominated by their parties' elected representatives in Congress, and state and local organizations promoted their cause. The focus of the campaign was not on voters, but on the state legislatures which had the responsibility for choosing members of the electoral college. Personal campaigning by the candidates was considered below the dignity of the presidential office.

B.   1896: A Bitter Fight over Economic Interests

By 1896 nominating conventions had become well established, and each party coalesced around a clear, and distinct, economic agenda. The Republicans favored the gold standard and high tariffs. The gold standard linked money to gold, which was scarce; thus debtors never got a break the devaluation of the currency associated with inflation. Tariffs protected capitalists and their workers from foreign competition. The Democrats favored unlimited coinage of silver. Unlike the Republicans, who had a frontrunner in William McKinley, they had no consensus candidate.

The Democrats finally nominated William Jennings Bryan, who had galvanized the convention with his "Cross of Gold" speech. Bryan broke with tradition and took to the stump in person, giving six hundred speeches in twenty-six states. McKinley remained at home in Ohio. Bryan's campaign was a harbinger of things to come, but McKinley won the election and cemented an electoral majority for the Republicans that lasted until 1932.

C. 1988: Bush Wins One for the Gipper

By 1988 the convention procedure had become only a formality to ratify the decisions of presidential primaries. Despite a field of several candidates in both parties, the 1988 conventions ultimately proved no exception to this rule. The campaign was less bitter than those of 1800 or 1896, but commentators and voters complained that it was far too negative. Unlike the nineteenth century contests, it was the candidates themselves that were hurling the charges back and forth. The Bush campaign was especially successful in using a few "hot button" issues to paint a negative picture of the opposing candidate. However, political scientists concluded that Bush's victory owed more to the positive performance of the economy than the negative tone of his campaign.
The voters continued to demonstrate a penchant for "split-ticket" voting that was absent in earlier elections. The result was continuing dominance of the House and Senate by the Democrats, who actually picked up a few seats in each house despite the Republican presidential victory. Voters also demonstrated their indifference to voting. About 50 percent of the eligible voters turned out in 1988 as opposed to nearly 80 percent in 1896.

IV. Whether To Vote: A Citizen's First Choice (316-323

The two centuries of American electoral history have witnessed dramatic expansion in SUFFRAGE, the right to vote. Once limited to property owning white males of more than twenty-one years of age, today all over the age of eighteen are guaranteed the right to vote. As the right to vote has been extended, however, proportionally fewer of those eligible have chosen to exercise that right.

A. Who Votes and Who Stays Home?

Several conclusions are apparent from the research on nonvoting. Among these are: 1) voting is a class-biased activity (higher educational and income people are more likely to vote); 2) young people have the lowest turnout rate; 3) whites vote with greater frequency than members of minority groups (largely due to differences in income and education levels); 4) Southerners do less voting than Northerners; 5) government employees are heavy participators in the electoral process; and 6) voting is not strongly related to gender.

The best predictor of whether a person will vote is whether that person is registered. America's unique registration system is partly to blame for lower turnout than seen in other democracies.
B. The Registration System

VOTER REGISTRATION was adopted around the turn of the century to prevent corruption associated with the widespread practice of stuffing ballot boxes. Requiring early registration made elections more ethical and more legitimate.

Registration procedures differ greatly from state to state. Presently registration is easiest and least restrictive in the upper Great Plains states and Northwest. Not coincidentally turnout tends to be higher in these states as well. Some political scientists feel that less restrictive registration nationwide could increase turnout by as much as 9 percent. It is not the whole solution, however, for even in those states with liberalized election laws, turnout has declined since the reforms were instituted. The will to vote seems lower than it once was.

C. A Policy Approach to Deciding Whether to Vote

Realistically, when ninety million people vote in a presidential election, the chance of one vote affecting the outcome is very, very small. Not only does your vote not make much difference to the outcome, but voting is somewhat costly. You have to spend time and energy getting informed and getting to the polls. Indeed, all other things being equal, it can be argued that a rational person would not vote. Anthony Downs argues that rational people vote if they believe that the policies of one party will bring more benefits than the policies of the other. Thus, people who see POLICY DIFFERENCES between the parties will vote. Even if one sees no differences or

is indifferent to them, one might also vote because of a sense of
CIVIC DUTY.

Why the difference in voting between the higher and lower socio-
economic status people? First, higher status people are more
likely, on nearly every issue, to recognize and understand policy
differences and their consequences. Second, higher status people
also score higher on POLITICAL EFFICACY, the belief that ordinary
people can influence the government. Third, lower status people
find the bureaucratic hurdles of the registration process especially
difficult.

V. How Americans Vote: Explaining Citizen's Decisions

Election outcomes are often explained as reflecting voter's
agreement with the policy views of one candidate more than the
other. The winner thus has a "mandate" to carry out promised
policies. This MANDATE THEORY OF ELECTIONS is favored by
journalists and politicians.

Political scientists are very skeptical of the mandate theory of
elections. They know that different people rarely vote the same way
for the same reasons. They focus on three major elements of voter's
decisions: 1) voters party identification; 2) voters evaluation of
the candidates; and 3) the match between voter's policy positions
and those of the candidates and parties.

A. Party Identification

Party identifications are crucial for many voters in that they
provide a regular perspective through which they can view the
political world. They can rely on their party identification to
guide them without concerning themselves with every issue. With the
emergence of television and candidate-centered politics, however,
the hold of the party on the voter has eroded greatly. Voting along
strict party lines is no longer common, and voters feel they no
longer need parties to guide their choices.

B. Candidate Evaluations: How Americans See the Candidates

All candidates try to present a favorable personal image. Research
has shown that the three most important dimensions of candidate
image are integrity (honest), reliability (dependable, strong and
decisive), and competence (ability and experience). Such evaluations
of candidate personality are sometimes seen as superficial and
irrational. Others argue that such judgments actually concentrate
on the manner in which a candidate would conduct governmental
affairs. Indeed, college educated voters are most likely to see the
candidates in terms of personal attributes.

C. Policy Voting

POLICY VOTING can only take place when several difficult conditions are met. First, voters must possess their own policy positions. Second, voters must know where the candidates stand on policy issues. Third, voters must actually cast a vote for the candidate whose policy positions coincide with their own.

Two "real world" factors make these conditions even more difficult to meet. First, candidates often decide that the best way to handle an issue is to cloud their positions so as to avoid alienating anyone. Second, media typically focuses more on the "horse-race" aspects of a campaign than on policy issues.

Early voter studies showed voters rarely voted on policies. Policy voting has become easier than in the past, however, with the disappearance of party bosses and the rise of issue-oriented activists in primaries influencing the choice of party nominees. Thus issues are more important, and policy voting more possible.

VI.   The Last Battle: The Electoral College

It is the ELECTORAL COLLEGE, not the popular vote, which actually determines the president of the United States. The continued use of this complex system is opposed by the American Bar Association and many political scientists. The electoral college reflects the fact that the founders wanted the president to be selected by the nation's elite rather than directly by the people. Fortunately, political practice has made the vote of the electoral college more responsive to popular majorities than was originally intended.

The following summarizes the way in which the electoral college system works today:
- Each state has as many electoral votes as it has U.S. senators and representatives. State parties select slates of electors, appointment a being for faithful service.
- Aside from Maine, each state has a winner-take-all system. The winning party's slate votes as a bloc for the winner.
- Electors cast their ballots in their states in December, then the votes are sent to the vice-president (who is also the president of the Senate), who reports the count at the opening of the new session. -If no candidate receives a majority of the electoral vote, the election is thrown into the House of Representatives, which must choose (each state delegation having one vote) from among the top three candidates.

The electoral college is important to the presidential election for two reasons. First, it introduces a bias into the campaign and electoral process in favor of the bigger states and their urban centers. Second, it has the capability of producing a winner who has received fewer popular votes. Both these problems are associated with the winner-take-all voting system. As a result of this practice, winning big states, even by a few votes, is far more important to the candidate than piling up big leads in small states. It also means that a candidate can lose the popular vote yet still win in the electoral college by winning the large states by small margins while losing the small states by large margins.

Until a popular vote winner loses in the electoral college, which hasn't happened since 1888, or the election is thrown into the house of representatives, which hasn't happened since 1824, reform of the Electoral College seems unlikely.

VII. Democracy and Elections (328-332)

Elections accomplish two tasks according to democratic theory. First, they select the policy-makers. Second, elections are supposed to help shape public policy. It is more accurate to describe the connection between elections and public policy as a two-way street: elections - to some degree - affect public policy, and public-policy decisions partly affect electoral outcomes.

A. Elections Affect Public Policy

While there may never be a definitive answer to the question of how much elections affect public policy, the broad contours of an answer are clear: The greater the policy differences between the candidates, the more likely voters will be able to steer government policies by their choices. Of course candidates, for their own purposes, often practice the "art of ambiguity" making policy differences less rather than more clear.

B. Public Policy Affects Election Outcomes

If elections affect policies, then policies can also affect elections. Most policies have consequences, and those who feel better off as a result of a policy tend to support candidates who pledge to continue that policy. This is known as RETROSPECTIVE VOTING, in which voters are asking the candidates "What have you done for me lately?"

The state of the economy is an important part of the answer to that question for many voters. When the economy takes a downturn, the call to punish the people and party in power often sweeps the nation. Herbert Hoover and more recently Jimmy Carter are prominent examples of presidents that were victims of poor economic management. Certainly the perception of economic policy impacts can affect elections.

C. Elections and the Size of Government

While elections provide the threat of electoral punishment which serves to constrain policy-makers, they also help to increase general support for government and its powers. Because voters know that the government can be replaced at the next election, they are much more likely to feel that it will be responsive to their needs. Therefore, rather than wishing to be protected from the state, citizens in a democracy often seek to benefit from it. They are comfortable granting government more power and demanding more services from it. As a result government tends to grow.

DOING RESEARCH ON ELECTIONS AND VOTING BEHAVIOR

This chapter presents two particularly interesting avenues for inquiry. One is the phenomenon of nonvoting and the other is the electoral college system. (Indeed, one might want to look into the possibility that the latter has something to do with the former in presidential elections.) Nonvoting offers a number of possible foci for research, an interesting one you may wish to explore is whether nonvoting makes any real difference in the outcomes of elections. Would higher voting rates elect different candidates or produce different directions for government? What sort of evidence is there that a systematic bias exists in the patterns of nonvoting that is policy or candidate related? If you find such evidence, what does it suggest about the strategies of differing candidates in parties in "getting out the vote?"

Another interesting question is why the young are among the least likely to vote. You may wish to explore this question on campus by finding and surveying nonvoters (statistics suggest there should be a lot of them) about why they have chosen not to vote. You will need to carefully plan your survey in advance, so that you can ask relevant questions. If you can find some common threads in the reasons students have for not voting, you may have the beginnings of an explanation. Based on this information, you may wish to speculate on some reforms that might tend to stimulate more participation among the young.

The electoral college is an often-debated and much maligned feature of the Constitution. It has had a decisive, and controversial, impact on several presidential elections. The electoral college offers several avenues for research. Most basically, the system's features could be fully described and its advantages and disadvantages fully explored. Some of these may surprise you, and make you somewhat more sympathetic to the institution.

If you are sure you want to get rid of it, however, a paper could explore the possible alternatives, explain the virtues and vices of each, who is likely to gain and lose with each, and present an argument for the adoption of one or the other.
Alternatively, you could take a look at the electoral college from the vantage point of one planning a presidential campaign. Such a paper could analyze the features of the electoral college in terms of their impact on campaign strategy. You may wish to assess whether the electoral college makes running for president simpler or more complicated than would be the case with direct election.

Chapter 9

REVIEW TEST

Time for the "test." If you have done the "Reading for Content" questions and feel like you have achieved the learning objectives listed at the beginning of the chapter, you should be ready. If you have not been using the test as a practice exam (you know, looking ahead at the answers as you go) stop it! Try hard to think through items you aren't sure of rather than going to the answer list quickly. It you can't get to feeling sure of it, take your best guess - just like in the real exam. This will be much better practice for the real thing. Ok, have at it.

1.   _____ socialize and institutionalize political activity by making it possible for most political participation to be channeled through the electoral process.
   (a)   Elections
   (b)   Senators
   (c)   Congressmen
   (d)   Parties
Page 307

2.   The 1988 elections in Mexico were controversial because Mexico's foreign debt had topped:
   (a) $10 million
   (b) $100 million
   (c) $1 billion
   (d) $100 billion
Page 307-308

3.   In the American election of 1988, George Bush defeated Massachusetts Governor:
   (a)   Lloyd Bentsen
   (b)   Jesse Jackson
   (c)   Michael Dukakis
   (d)   Walter Mondale
Page 308

4.   State primaries to choose congressional and state offices are called _____ primaries because party nominees are chosen directly by the people.
   (a)   people
   (b)   local
   (c)   runoff
   (d)   direct
Page 308

5.   All that is required for an initiative petition is for signatures to be gathered in numbers equaling _____ percent of the voters in the previous election.
   (a)   50
   (b)   40
   (c)   35
   (d)   10
Page 309

6. An example of a provision for direct legislation is the _____, whereby voters are given the chance to approve or disapprove some legislative act or constitutional amendment.
    (a) recall petition
    (b) secondary primary
    (c) referendum
    (d) runoff primary
Page 309

7. In the election of 1800, incumbent President _____ was challenged by then Vice-President Thomas Jefferson.
    (a) George Washington
    (b) James Madison
    (c) James Monroe
    (d) John Adams
Page 310

8. The focus of the 1800 campaign was not on voters, but rather on _____, on which the responsibility of choosing members of the electoral college rested.
    (a) state legislatures
    (b) the U.S. House of Representatives
    (c) the U.S. Senate
    (d) the House and the Senate
Page 311

9. In 1796, _____ had become John Adams' vice-president by virtue of finishing second.
    (a) Thomas Jefferson
    (b) Aaron Burr
    (c) James Madison
    (d) Alexander Hamilton
Page 311

10. On March 4, 1801, the transition from Adams to Jefferson marked the first peaceful transfer of power between parties via the electoral process since:
    (a) Napoleon Bonaparte was elected Emperor of France.
    (b) Robert Walpole was elected Britain's first Prime Minister.
    (c) George Washington was elected the United States' first president.
    (d) ever -- this is the first time in history.
Page 311

11. The Republicans, in 1896, had a clear frontrunner in former Congressman _____, who supported the gold standard and high tariffs.
    (a) Benjamin Harrison
    (b) William McKinley
    (c) Rutherford B. Hayes
    (d) Theodore Roosevelt
Page 311

12. The main issue that the Democratic party came up with in the 1896 election was:
    (a) American imperialism.
    (b) farm subsidies.
    (c) high tariffs and the gold standard.
    (d) unlimited coinage of silver.
Page 312

13. The winner of the 1896 Democratic presidential nomination was:
    (a) Adlai Stevenson.
    (b) William Jennings Bryan.
    (c) Samuel J. Tilden.
    (d) Woodrow Wilson.
Page 312

14. The 1988 election was similar to the election of _____ in that the Republicans nominated their incumbent vice- president and the Democrats nominated a relatively unknown candidate from Massachusetts.
    (a) 1800
    (b) 1896
    (c) 1912
    (d) 1960
Page 312

15. In 1988, George Bush won the presidency. He became the first sitting vice-president to win a presidential election since:
    (a) Martin Van Buren in 1836.
    (b) Millard Fillmore in 1850.
    (c) William Howard Taft in 1908.
    (d) Richard Nixon in 1960.
Page 312

16. In the 1988 presidential race, Democratic candidate _____ dropped out after being accused of plagiarizing a speech.
    (a) Richard Gephardt
    (b) Albert Gore, Jr.,
    (c) Gary Hart
    (d) Joseph Biden
Page 313

17. In 1988, only the Democrats managed to keep much of a race going until their convention. _____ continued to challenge Michael Dukakis even though he trailed by a large margin.
    (a) Jesse Jackson
    (b) Albert Gore, Jr.,
    (c) Paul Simon
    (d) Bruce Babbitt
Page 313

18. Republican vice-presidential candidate Dan Quayle was severely

admonished during a debate with Democratic vice-presidential candidate Lloyd Bentsen when Quayle compared his experience in office to that of:
(a) John F. Kennedy.
(b) Ronald Reagan.
(c) Richard Nixon.
(d) Michael Dukakis.
Page 314

19. George Bush clenched the Republican nomination for president after:
(a) the national convention in New Orleans.
(b) Super Tuesday.
(d) the Iowa caucus.
(c) the New Hampshire primary.
Page 313

20. _____ states were carried by the Bush/Quayle ticket in 1988, thus giving them a wide margin in the electoral college.
(a) Forty
(b) Forty five
(c) Forty seven
(c) Forty nine
Page 315

21. In 1988, only 50 percent of the adult population voted for president -- the lowest figure since:
(a) 1896.
(b) 1908.
(c) 1924.
(d) 1944.
Page 316

22. In the study of voting behavior, all of the following have been found to be true EXCEPT:
(a) government employees are heavy participators in the electoral process.
(b) young people have the lowest turnout rate.
(c) voting is very strongly related to gender.
(d) voting is a class-biased activity -- those with higher educational and income levels vote more than those who have lower educational and income levels.
Page 316-317

23. Since 1960, it is true that:
(a) voter turnout has increased.
(b) voter registration has been made much easier.
(c) states that have liberalized election laws now have much higher turnouts than before the reforms came.
(d) America's voter turnout rate is higher than every Western European country.
Page 321

24. _____ class people score higher on political efficacy, the

belief that ordinary people can influence the government.
    (a) Upper
    (b) Middle
    (c) Lower
    (d) Upper-middle
Page 322

25. Until some factors which inhibit voting change dramatically, it
     is likely that American elections will be decided by about
     _____ of the eligible voters.
    (a) 75%
    (b) 50%
    (c) 25%
    (d) 10%
Page 322

26. The idea that an election winner has a mandate from the people
     to carry out his promised policies is called the _____ theory
     of politics.
    (a) mandate
    (b) referendum
    (c) basic
    (d) classical
Page 323

27. Today, the most important factor in elections for the House of
     Representatives is:
    (a) constituent service.
    (b) incumbency.
    (c) money.
    (d) character or charisma.
Page 324

28. With the emergence of television and candidate centered
     politics, the hold of the party on the voter _____ during
     the 1960's and 1970's.
    (a) increased substantially
    (b) increased slightly
    (c) decreased substantially
    (d) decreased slightly
Page 323

29. On the political dimension of "reliability," Ronald Reagan had
     a clear edge over Carter in 1980 and _____ in 1984.
    (a) Michael Dukakis
    (b) Gerald Ford
    (c) John Glenn
    (d) Walter Mondale
Page 325

30. In 1988, Michael Dukakis proudly proclaimed that the major
     election issue was not ideology but:

(a)   reliability.
(b)   competence.
(c)   integrity.
(d)   fiscal flexibility.
Page 325

31.   In 1988, _____ made it clear where he stood on the tax issue
      with his famous line, "Read my lips.   No new taxes!"   (a)
      Ronald Reagan
      (b)   George Bush
      (c)   Robert Dole
      (d)   Pat Robertson
Page 325

32.   In the 1968 campaign, both candidates -- _____ --were
      deliberately ambiguous about what they would do to end the
      Vietnam War.
      (a)   Kennedy and Nixon
      (b)   Johnson and Goldwater
      (c)   Humphrey and Nixon
      (d)   McGovern and Nixon
Page 325

33.   In opposition to the 1990 House bill that would make voter
      registration easier, House Minority Leader _____ maintained
      that the new process would virtually invite those who wanted to
      vote under several names to do so.
      (a)   Robert Dole
      (b)   Newt Gingrich
      (c)   Alan Simpson
      (d)   Robert Michel
Page 306

34.   A new bill passed by the House of Representatives in 1990 would
      establish national standards for voter registration for the
      first time and authorize _____ dollars to help states cover
      the cost of new procedures.
      (a)   1 million
      (b)   50 million
      (c)   1 billion
      (d)   50 billion
Page 306

35.   Electors meet in their states in December, following the
      November election, and then mail their votes to:
      (a)   the Speaker of the House.
      (b)   the Senate president pro tempore.
      (c)   the President.
      (d)   the Vice-President.
Page 328

36.   The last time the House of Representatives decided the winner
      of a presidential election was in:

(a)   1800.
(b)   1824.
(c)   1876.
(d)   1960.
Page 328

37.   It is true that the members of the electoral college:
      (a)   are bound to vote for the state's popular vote winner
      (b)   can vote for whomever they choose if the state's popular
            vote winner did not exceed a fifty percent win.
      (c)   can vote for anyone they want to.
      (d)   are bound to vote only for the presidential nominee, if he
            won   the   state's   popular   vote,   but   not   the
            vice-presidential nominee.
Page 328-331 (passim)

38.   _____ was in office when the stock market crash of 1929
      sparked the Great Depression, resulting in defeat in 1932.
      (a)   Calvin Coolidge
      (b)   Warren G. Harding
      (c)   Herbert Hoover
      (d)   William Howard Taft
Page 331

39.   In the 1988 elections, voter turnout in the United States
      averaged about _____ percent.
      (a)   35
      (b)   50
      (c)   67
      (d)   74
Page 318

40.   The state with the lowest voter turnout in the election of 1988
      was _____ with 38.8 percent of the electorate voting.   (a)
      Montana
      (b)   Colorado
      (c)   Kentucky
      (d)   Georgia
Page 320

BEFORE GOING ON

Feel pretty good about the "exam?"   Now is the time to use the
answer key below to "grade" your exam and see how you did.   As
always, go back and reread the relevant passages on the indicated
page for any you have missed.

Review Test Answers:

1: a	11: b	21: c	31: b
2: d	12: d	22: c	32: c
3: c	13: b	23: b	33: d
4: d	14: d	24: a	34: b
5: d	15: a	25: b	35: d
6: c	16: d	26: a	36: b
7: d	17: a	27: b	37: c
8: a	18: a	28: c	38: c
9: a	19: b	29: d	39: b
10: d	20: a	30: b	40: d

Take another look at the short list of Key Terms on page 333. Be especially sure that you understand the significance of each in the context of the chapter. This is particularly true for the meaning of "legitimacy" and "political efficacy" for the process of elections and the explanation of voting behavior. To help with that let me recommend "political efficacy" and its more generic root "efficacy" as your "college word" of the week. In addition to sounding sophisticated, it is an extremely handy little word. To get a better sense of all its possibilities look it up in your dictionary. You may find that you feel more efficacious just having this little wonder in your verbal arsenal.

CHAPTER 10

INTEREST GROUPS

CHAPTER LEARNING OBJECTIVES

After reading Chapter 10, you should be able to:

1. Define interest group and distinguish it from political party.
2. Distinguish the key elements of the three theories of interest group politics.
3. Discuss the extent, nature, and reasons for increase in interest groups.
4. Discuss the most common lobbying activities of groups.
5. Identify the functions interest groups perform for members of Congress.
6. Discuss the effectiveness of lobbying.
7. Discuss the role of PACs in electioneering.
8. Discuss the importance of litigation and going public as techniques.
9. Identify the types of interest groups and their concerns.
10. Discuss the factors that help to make a group successful.
11. Discuss the role of interest groups in democracy.
12. Discuss how interest groups contribute to government growth.

PRETEST QUESTIONS

The pretest below will give you an idea of the state of your knowledge about interest groups. The questions should also help you learn what to look for while studying the text. Take the whole pretest, then check your answers against the key that follows (don't peek!). As you read the chapter, watch for where these questions are addressed (indicated after each question) so that you may learn why the answer is what it is.

1. A(n) _____ is an organization of people with similar policy goals entering the political process to try to achieve those goals.
    (a) caucus
    (b) referendum
    (c) interest group
    (d) faction
Page 337

197

2.   It is true today that many political scientists believe that:
     (a)   dishonest lobbying far outpaces honest lobbying.
     (b)   there are no longer any honest transactions in lobbying.
     (c)   honest lobbying poses greater problems for democracy than dishonest lobbying.
     (d)   interest groups are looked upon far more favorably today than at any time in American history.
Page 338-339

3.   Pluralists argue that lobbying is not a problem because:
     (a)   one or two groups generally dominate anyway.
     (b)   lobbying is open to all.
     (c)   so few people engage in it, or are able to.
     (d)   it is heavily regulated.
Page 341

4.   Real power, _____ say, is held by relatively few people, key groups, and institutions.
     (a)   populists
     (b)   liberals
     (c)   elitists
     (d)   hyperpluralists
Page 341

5.   The majority of interest groups have their headquarters in:
     (a)   Washington, D.C.
     (b)   New York City.
     (c)   San Francisco.
     (d)   Boston, MA.
Page 345

6.   In 1960, about _____ percent of the interest groups in the Walker study were headquartered in Washington, D.C.
     (a)   52
     (b)   66
     (c)   72
     (d)   89
Page 346

7.   Most lobbyists are extremely well educated and those of a major group paid well in excess of _____ dollars a year.
     (a)   1,000,000
     (b)   150,000
     (c)   90,000
     (d)   50,000
Page 348

8.   In 1974, there were only _____ PACs in the United States.
     (a)   608
     (b)   432
     (c)   209
     (d)   157
Page 350

9. During the 1987-88 election cycle, PACs gave _____ dollars to House incumbents compared with nine million dollars to the challengers.
    (a) 15 million
    (b) 32 million
    (c) 56 million
    (d) 82 million
Page 351

10. If a lobbyist fails in Congress or gets only a vague piece of legislation, the next step is to:
    (a) go to court.
    (b) start lobbying new legislators.
    (c) renew lobbying efforts on legislators who had not voted on the matter.
    (d) disband the PAC.
Page 352

11. One tactic that lawyers employ to make the views of interest groups heard by the judiciary is the filing of _____ briefs.
    (a) writ of certiorari
    (b) writ of habeas corpus
    (c) amicus curiae
    (d) curiae certiorari
Page 352

12. One lawyer of note stated that _____ lawsuits were the "greatest, most effective legal engine to remedy mass wrongs."
    (a) multiple deposition
    (b) class action
    (c) amicus
    (d) certiorari
Page 353

13. Only on rare occasions has the government imposed wage and price controls. The _____ administration recently, but briefly, used wage and price controls to combat inflation. (a) Reagan
    (b) Carter
    (c) Ford
    (d) Nixon
Page 354

14. Nearly _____ workers are members of unions belonging to the AFL/CIO, itself a union of unions.
    (a) 13 million
    (b) 5 million
    (c) 900,000
    (d) 500,000
Page 355

15. The American labor movement reached its peak in 1970, when _____ percent of the work force belonged to a union.

199

(a)   7
(b)   12
(c)   25
(d)   50
Page 355

16. Since its peak membership in 1970 when 25 percent of the work force belonged to a union, membership in American unions has declined to about _____ percent of the labor force.
(a)   23
(b)   19
(c)   16
(d)   9
Page 355

17. All of the following are examples of major business interest groups EXCEPT:
(a)   the National Organization of Manufacturers
(b)   the Chamber of Commerce
(c)   AT&T
(d)   Common Cause
Page 356

18. Consumer groups include good-government groups such as _____ that push for openness and fairness in government.   (a)   the Sierra Club
(b)   the National Urban League
(c)   the NAACP
(d)   Common Cause
Page 358

19. The _____ Amendment guaranteed women the right to vote.
(a)   Fifteenth
(b)   Seventeenth
(c)   Eighteenth
(d)   Nineteenth
Page 360

20. A _____ group can be defined as having a narrow interest, dislikes compromise, and single- mindedly pursues its goal.
(a)   single-issue
(b)   multiple-issue
(c)   free-rider
(d)   compromise
Page 363

Pretest Answers:

1: c	11: c
2: c	12: d
3: b	13: b
4: c	14: a
5: a	15: c
6: b	16: c
7: c	17: d
8: a	18: d
9: d	19: d
10: a	20: a

READING FOR CONTENT

Listed below are sets of questions associated with the content of each major section of Chapter 10. Carefully review the questions associated with each section of the text before reading the section. Have the questions in mind as you read the section and, when you reach the end of each section, stop and see if you can answer the questions well. If not, reread the relevant paragraphs until you are sure of your response to each of the questions.

I.   The Role and Reputation of Interest Groups

     How are interest groups defined?
     How are interest groups different from political parties?
     Why are interest groups generally unpopular?

II.   Theories Of Interest Group Politics

     What are the essential arguments of pluralist theory?
     What are the essential arguments of elite theory?
     What are the essential arguments of hyperpluralist theory?

III.   The Interest Group Explosion

     What are the major characteristics of modern interest groups?
     Why have the number of interest groups expanded rapidly?

IV.   How Groups Try To Shape Policy

     What are the principal general strategies of interest groups?
     What are the most commonly used lobbying techniques?
     How are lobbyists useful to members of Congress?
     How effective is lobbying?
     What is the role of Political Action Committees (PACs) in
       electioneering?
     How are interest groups involved in litigation?
     What do interest groups do when they "go public?"

V.   Types Of Interest Groups

What are the major types of interest groups?
What are the principal strengths and problems of each type of
  economic interest?
How are energy and environmental interests in conflict?
What are the principal concerns of the equality interests?

VI. What Makes an Interest Group Successful?

What are the principal characteristics that contribute to the
  strength and success of interest groups?
What is Olsen's law of large groups?
Why is intensity important to the success of groups?
How does money contribute to the success of groups?

VII. Understanding Interest Groups

How do interest groups contribute to democratic government?
How do interest groups distort the democratic process?
How do interest groups contribute to government growth?

CHAPTER OVERVIEW

I.   Introduction (336-337)

Our nation's capital has become a hub of interest group activity.
While participation in elections has declined, participation in
interest groups has mushroomed. This chapter will explore the
factors behind the interest group explosion, how these groups enter
the policy-making process, and what they get out of it.

II. The Role and Reputation of Interest Groups (337-339)

Organizing to promote interests is an essential part of democracy.
The right to organize groups is protected by the Constitution,
which guarantees the right "peaceably to assemble, and to petition
the Government for a redress of grievances."

A. Defining Interest Groups

An INTEREST GROUP is an organization of people with similar policy
goals entering the political process to try to achieve those aims.
The state and local levels of government as well as the national
congress, bureaucracy, and courts are all potential policy arena
targets. This multiplicity of policy arenas helps distinguish
interest groups from political parties. Parties fight their battles
through the electoral process, while American interest groups may
support candidates for office but will not run their own slate of
candidates. Another key difference between parties and interest
groups is that interest groups are often policy specialists, whereas
parties are policy generalists. Most groups have a handful of key
policies to push and have no need to be concerned with broad popular

appeal.

B. Why Interest Groups Get Bad Press

Interest groups traditionally have received bad press in America because their activities are commonly linked with the influence of money and the presence of corruption in the policy process. There is little doubt, however, that honest lobbying outpaces dishonest lobbying by a wide margin. Many political scientists now believe, however, that honest lobbying poses greater problems for democracy than dishonest lobbying.

III. Theories of Interest Group Politics (339-344)

Understanding the debate over the implications of interest groups for American government requires an examination of PLURALIST THEORY, ELITE THEORY and HYPERPLURALIST THEORY.

A. Pluralism and Group Theory

Pluralist Theory argues that interest group activity brings representation to all. It rests its case on the many centers of power in the American political system. Pluralist theorists offer a "group theory of politics" which contains several essential arguments including: 1) Groups provide a key linkage between people and government (all legitimate interests can get a hearing from government once organized); 2) Groups compete with one another constantly; 3) No one group is likely to become too dominant; 4) Groups usually play by the "rules of the game;" and 5) Groups weak in one resource can use another (all groups are able to affect policy by one means or another). Pluralists do not deny that some groups are stronger than others, but argue that lobbying is open to all and is therefore not a problem.

B. Elites and the Denial of Pluralism

Whereas pluralist are impressed by the vast number of organized interests, elitists are impressed by how insignificant most of them are. They argue that real power is held by very few people, key groups, and institutions. In sum, the elitist view of the interest group system makes the following points: 1) The fact that there are numerous groups proves nothing, because groups are extremely unequal in power; 2) Awesome power is controlled by the largest corporations; 3) The power of a few is fortified by an extensive system of interlocking directorates; (Elitists point out that about one-third of top institutional positions are held by people with more than one such position); 4) Other groups may win many minor policy battles, but the corporate elites prevail when it comes to the big decisions. Thus, even honest lobbying is a problem because it benefits the few at the expense of the many.
C. Hyperpluralism and Interest Group Liberalism

Hyperpluralist theory asserts that too many groups are getting too much of what they want, resulting in government policy that is often contradictory and lacking in direction. This excessive deference of government toward groups has also been termed "interest group liberalism" by Theodore Lowi. Lowi argues that now virtually all pressure group demands are legitimate and that the job of the government has become to advance them all.

Interest group liberalism is promoted by the network of "subgovernments" in the political system, that link interest groups, subcommittees of Congress, and agencies of the bureaucracy concerned with a particular policy. All elements composing subgovernments have a similar goal: protecting their self- interest. Relationships between groups and the government become too cozy, and hard choices about national policy rarely get made. In short, the hyperpluralist position on group politics is that: 1) Groups have become too powerful in the political process with government trying to please all interests; 2) Interest group liberalism is aggravated by numerous subgovernments; 3) Trying to please every group results in contradictory and confusing policy.

IV. The Interest Group Explosion (344-346)

A number of points can be made about the rapidly expanding number of interest groups in America: 1) The majority of groups now have their headquarters in Washington D.C.; 2) There are an enormous number of highly specialized and seemingly trivial groups; and 3) Almost every group - large or small - has a staff and publications. About 80 percent of the groups listed in the Washington Information Directory originated from occupational, industrial, or professional memberships. Half of these groups have been established since World War II. One of the major reasons for the expansion of interest groups is that technology has made it easier to organized them for political influence.

V. How Groups Try to Shape Policy (346-354)

The three traditional strategies are lobbying, electioneering, and litigation. In addition, groups have recently developed a variety of techniques to appeal to the public for widespread support.

A. Lobbying

The term LOBBYING comes from the place where petitioners used to collar legislators. Today, lobbying refers to a "communication, by someone other than a citizen acting on his [or her] own behalf, directed to a governmental decision-maker with the hope of influencing his [or her] decision." Lobbyists are political persuaders who represent organized groups, normally work in Washington, and handle groups' legislative business.
Ornstein and Elder list five ways lobbyists can help a member of Congress: 1) They are an important source of information; 2) They

can help a member with political strategy; 3) They can help formulate campaign strategy and get the group's members behind a politician's reelection campaign; 4) They are a source of ideas and innovations; 5) They provide friendship.

Political scientists are not in agreement about the effectiveness of lobbying. Much evidence suggests that lobbyists' power over policy is greatly exaggerated. Sometimes lobbying can persuade legislators to support a certain policy, however. It is clear that lobbying works best on those already committed to the policy position, however. Thus most lobbying, like most campaigning, is directed toward activating and reinforcing supporters.

B. Electioneering

Because lobbying works best on those already on the same side, getting the right people into office is also a key strategy of interest groups. Many groups therefore get involved in ELECTIONEERING, aiding candidates financially and getting their members out to support them.

Recently, POLITICAL ACTION COMMITTEES (PACs) have provided a means for groups to participate in electioneering more than ever before. The number of PACs have mushroomed from 608 in 1974 to 4,268 in 1988. As campaign costs have risen in recent years, PACs have come along to help pay the bill. Most of their money goes to incumbents. In 1987-88 they gave incumbents nine times ($82 million) as much as they did challengers ($9 million) in races for the House of Representatives. PAC contributions are investments for the future, and incumbents are the most likely to be able to return the investment.

C. Litigation

If a group fails in Congress or gets only a vague piece of legislation, the next step is to go to court in the hope of getting specific rulings. The successes of environmental groups and civil rights groups have come largely in the courts.

A tactic that lawyers employ to make the views of interest groups heard by the judiciary is the filing of AMICUS CURIAE ("friend of the court") briefs. Amicus briefs consist of written arguments submitted to the courts in support of one side of a case.

A more direct judicial strategy employed by interest groups is the filing of CLASS ACTION LAWSUITS, enabling groups of similarly situated plaintiffs to combine like grievances into a single suit.

D. Going Public

Public opinion ultimately makes its way to policy-makers, and so interest groups carefully cultivate their public image. They market not only their stand on issues but their reputations as well. In this way, increasing numbers of groups are trying to create a reservoir of goodwill with the public at large.

VI. Types of Interest Groups (354-361)

Interest groups can be clustered by the type of issues they focus on. Some groups deal mainly with economic issues, others with issues of energy and the environment, and still others with equality issues. Though all groups do not fit neatly within these categories, most do concern themselves with a limited range of issues.

A. Economic Issues

Public policy in America has economic effects through regulations, tax advantages, subsidies and contracts, and international trade policy. Business, labor, and farmers all fret over the impact of such governmental policies on their economic interests.

1. Labor. Numerically, labor has more affiliated members than any other interest group. These organizations press for policies to ensure better working conditions and higher wages. Unions have fought hard for the UNION SHOP, which requires new employees to join the union representing them. Business groups have supported RIGHT-TO-WORK LAWS, which outlaw union membership as a condition of employment. The union shop helps unions combat the "free- rider" problem that undermines their effectiveness. Business claims that such a practice denies basic freedoms.

The American labor movement reached its peak in 1970, when 25 percent of the work force belonged to a union; since then the percentage has declined to about 16 percent.

2. Agriculture. Only 3 percent of Americans now make their living as farmers. The family farm has given way to giant agribusinesses, often heavily involved with exports. There are several broad-based agricultural groups (the American Farm Bureau Federation, the National Farmers' Organization), but equally important are the commodity associations formed of peanut farmers, potato growers, dairy farmers, and other producers.

3. Business. If elite theorists are correct about the existence of a power elite, it would be made up of business groups. Elitists' views may or may not be exaggerated, but business is certainly well organized for political action. Business PACs have increased more than any other category of PACs. Business' interests are overseen by two large umbrella groups - the National Association of Manufacturers (NAM) and the Chamber of Commerce.

Different business interests compete on specific issues, however. The hundreds of trade and product associations are far less visible than the NAM and the Chamber of Commerce, but they are at least as important to their members in pursuing policy goals.

4. Consumers and Public Interest Lobbies. Today over two thousand organized groups are championing various causes or ideas "in the public interest." These PUBLIC INTEREST LOBBIES can be defined as organizations that seek "a collective good, the achievement of which will not selectively and materially benefit the membership or activists of the organization." Consumer groups have won many legislative victories in recent years. Among the most important was the creation of the Consumer Product Safety Commission in 1973. Other groups speak for those who cannot speak for themselves such as children, animals, and the mentally ill.

B. Energy and Environmental Interests

Some environmental groups have been around since the nineteenth century, but most have been formed in the last twenty years. They have promoted pollution-control policies, wilderness protection, and population control and opposed strip-mining, supersonic aircraft, offshore oil drilling and nuclear power plants.

The concerns of the environmentalists often come into direct conflict with energy goals. Their efforts have had a profound impact on public policy in the area of nuclear power. No new plants have been built since 1977. Given no sign of a drop in the demand for energy, producers argue that some risks must be taken with oil exploration and nuclear power. Group politics intensifies when two public interests clash, such as environmental protection and an assured supply of energy.

C. Equality Interests

The Fourteenth Amendment guarantees equal protection under the law. American history, though, shows that this is easier said than done. Two sets of interest groups, representing women and minorities, have made equal rights their main policy goal.

Equality at the polls, in housing, on the job, in education, and in all other facets of life has long been the dominant goal of African-American groups. The oldest and largest of these groups is the National Association for the Advancement of Colored People (NAACP). This organization argued and won the landmark Brown v. Board of Education case in 1954 that declared segregation unconstitutional. The NAACP and other civil rights groups have won many victories in principle, but must continue to press to realize equality in practice. Today, they push for more effective affirmative action programs to ensure educational and employment opportunities for minorities.

The Nineteenth Amendment guaranteed women the vote, but other guarantees of equal protection for women remained absent from the Constitution. The National Organization for Women (NOW) has been central in the struggle against sexual discrimination in recent years. Their primary goal has been the passage of the Equal Rights Amendment (ERA), which states that "equality of rights under the law shall not be abridged on account of sex." The ERA seems dead for the moment, and NOW is attempting to enact the protections it would constitutionally guarantee through a variety of individual statutes. This is just one example of the truth that in American interest group politics issues are rarely settled once and for all, rather they shift to different policy arenas.

VII. What Makes an Interest Group Successful? (361-365)

There are many factors that affect how successful an interest group is. Among them are the size of the group (the smaller the better), its intensity, and its financial resources.

A. The Surprising Ineffectiveness of Large Groups

There are good reasons why consumer groups, for example, are less effective than producer groups - small groups have organizational advantages over large groups.

To shed light on this point it is important to distinguish between a potential and an actual group. A POTENTIAL GROUP is composed of all people who might be group members because they share some common interest. In contrast the ACTUAL GROUP is composed of whatever portion of the potential group chooses to join. Consumer groups are minuscule when compared with the total number of consumers, while many business organizations organize virtually all of their potential members.

This is important because all groups are in the business of providing collective goods. A COLLECTIVE GOOD is something of value that cannot be withheld from a potential group member. In other words, members of the potential group share in the benefits of the collective good that members of the actual group work to secure. Under these circumstances why should potential members work for something if they are just as likely to get it for free? This is commonly known as the FREE-RIDER PROBLEM. The bigger the potential group, the more serious the free-rider problem. That is the gist of OLSON'S LAW OF LARGE GROUPS: "The larger the group, the further it will fall short of providing an optimal amount of a collective good." Small groups thus have an organizational advantage. In a small group a given member's share of the collective good may be great enough that he or she will try to secure it. The old saying that "everyone can make a difference" is much more credible in the case of small groups.

This distinct advantage of small groups helps explain why public interest groups have a tougher time than business groups. They seek "public interest" goals, the gains of which are spread thinly over millions of people. In contrast, the lobbying costs and benefits for business are concentrated. The power of business is thus due to more than just money, large corporations also enjoy an inherent size advantage.

B. Intensity

One way a large potential group may be mobilized is through an issue that people feel intensely about, such as abortion. Intensity is a psychological advantage that can be enjoyed by small and large groups alike. Single-issue groups focus intensely on an issue members care intensely about.

A SINGLE ISSUE GROUP can be defined as a group that has a narrow interest, dislikes compromise, and single-mindedly pursues its goal. Anti-Vietnam War activists may have formed the first modern single-issue groups. The most emotional contemporary issue is that of abortion. Groups opposed to abortion rights organized in response to the Roe v. Wade decision in 1973 that made abortion a right during the first trimester of pregnancy. For years intensity was on the side of these "pro-life" groups. With the 1989 Webster v. Reproductive Services decision that gave states greater freedom to restrict abortion, the "pro-choice" side has become better mobilized than ever before.

C. Financial Resources

A major indictment of the American interest group system is that it is biased toward the wealthy. Those who have money certainly get heard in and enjoy greater access to the policy process.

It is important to emphasize, however, that even on some of the most important issues the big interests do not always win. An example was the Tax Reform Act of 1986.

VIII. Understanding Interest Groups (365-367)

A free society must allow for the representation of all groups that seek to influence political decision making; yet, because groups are usually more concerned with their own self-interest rather than with the needs of society as a whole, for democracy to work well it is important that they not be allowed to assume a dominant position.

A. Interest Groups and Democracy

James Madison's solution to this problem was to create a wide-open system in which many groups with opposing interests would counterbalance one another. Pluralist theorists believe that a rough approximation of the public interest emerges from this competition, and that with the growth of interest representation in recent years we have more fully than ever achieved this goal.

Elite theorists disagree pointing to the proliferation of business PACs as evidence that the interest group system both corrupts and biases our policy process.

B.   Interest Groups and the Size of Government

America's two most recent past presidents both remarked at the end of their time in office that their attempts to cut waste in federal spending had been frustrated by interest groups. This is because, above all else, most special interest groups strive to maintain established programs which benefit them - and thus help promote and maintain larger government.

One can also make the argument that the growth in the size of government in recent years helps to account for the proliferation of interest groups. The more areas government becomes involved in, the more need interests have in organizing to influence public policy. For example, once the government got seriously into the business of protecting the environment, many groups sprang up to lobby for strong standards and enforcement. In response, many others representing industry and business emerged to defend their markets and profits.

DOING RESEARCH ON INTEREST GROUPS

A lot can be learned about the role of interest groups in the American policy process by conducting an in depth study of one group. You might choose a group that promotes an interest you share or one that you are particularly interested in. Such a case study could explore the goals, tactics, resources, problems, successes and failures of the group. For many groups there will be background material available in your library. For other, your best source will be the group itself. You may need to contact members of a local organization or the local chapter of a national organization. Groups are often more than happy to provide information to those interested, but it will be part of their "going public" and be designed to promote their interest - so beware. Because of this, if the group is opposed by a organized counter-interest, this group's views of your group's goals, tactics, and so on might also be useful in providing some balance.

The most controversial entrants in the interest group struggle in recent years have been "single-issue" groups. A paper focusing on the kinds of single-issue groups, their tactics, and their special impact on the policy process would be something that would deepen your understanding of the role of interest groups in democracy. You might also wish to explore the types of reforms that might help solve the problems that single-issue groups present to the policy process.   Tackling a question like this well will impress any professor!   Your "For Further Reading" list is, again, a good starting point.   The books by Jeffrey Berry, Allan Cigler and Burdett Loomis, Kenneth Godwin, and Kay Schlozman and John Tierney are particularly relevant.

Political Action Committees (PACs) have also been a focus of rising concern. A paper that addresses how PACs are formed and how they work would be refreshing. A good basic reference source for such a paper is <u>PAC Handbook</u> by Edith Fraser. A more common approach to PACs is to examine their scope and impact. A great deal has been written in the popular press and academic literature on the impact of PACs.

REVIEW TEST

Time for the "test." Treat the test below as a real "trial run" and try hard to figure out the ones that you aren't sure of without looking at the answers. Hopefully, if you have done the thinking and studying necessary to respond to the "Reading for Content" questions you'll be ready. Ok, have at it.

1. Since 1960, it is true that:
    (a) voter turnout and participation in interest groups has declined.
    (b) voter turnout has declined while participation in interest groups has risen drastically.
    (c) voter turnout has increased while participation in interest groups has fallen off drastically.
    (d) voter turnout and participation in interest groups have mushroomed.
Page 337

2. The authors of _____ thought that interest groups were no better than political parties, which they also disliked.
    (a) The Federalist Papers
    (b) the Declaration of Independence
    (c) the U.S. Constitution
    (d) Common Sense
Page 338

3. _____, used the derogatory term 'faction' to describe his dislike for both interest groups and political parties.
    (a) Thomas Jefferson
    (b) James Madison
    (c) Benjamin Franklin
    (d) John Adams
Page 338

4. All of the following are key arguments to the group theory of politics EXCEPT:
    (a) groups compete.
    (b) groups usually play by the "rules of the game."

211

    (c)   groups weak in one resource can use another.
    (d)   it is likely that one or two groups can dominate the rest.
Page 340

5.   Whereas pluralists are impressed by the vast number of organized interests, _____ are impressed by how insignificant most of them are.
    (a)   hyperpluralists
    (b)   populists
    (c)   conservatives
    (d)   elitists
Page 341

6.   According to the _____ theory, honest lobbying is a problem because it benefits the few at the expense of the many.
    (a)   hyperpluralist
    (b)   elite
    (c)   pluralist
    (d)   populist
Page 342

7.   Theodore Lowi coined the phrase interest group _____, to refer to the government's excessive deference to groups.
    (a)   populism
    (b)   conservatism
    (c)   liberalism
    (d)   libertarianism
Page 342

8.   Interest group liberalism is promoted by the network of _____ in the American political system.
    (a)   marketing agents
    (b)   communication specialists
    (c)   subsidizers
    (d)   subgovernments
Page 342

9.   The _____ theory position on group politics is that relations between interest groups and government has become too cozy.
    (a)   pluralist
    (b)   populist
    (c)   hyperpluralist
    (d)   elite

10. The trade, commercial and business section of the Encyclopedia of Associations lists _____ interest groups. (a)   342
    (b)   578
    (c)   973
    (d)   3,806
Page 345

11. A study of interest groups found that _____ percent of the groups originated from occupational, industrial or professional memberships.
    (a) 80
    (b) 75
    (c) 60
    (d) 45
Page 345-346

12. In 1960, about _____ percent of the interest groups in the Walker study were headquartered in Washington, D.C.
    (a) 52
    (b) 66
    (c) 72
    (d) 89
Page 346

13. One of the major factors for the explosion of interest groups has been:
    (a) new issues.
    (b) the growth of government bureaucracy.
    (c) the development of sophisticated technology.
    (d) the Vietnam War and Watergate.
Page 346

14. Although women are increasingly seen in the public interest lobbying role, _____ percent of the representatives of business and professional associations are men.
    (a) 94
    (b) 79
    (c) 66
    (d) 52
Page 348

15. Lobbying is a high pressure job. The average Washington lobbyist lasts less than _____ year(s).
    (a) ten
    (b) five
    (c) two
    (d) one
Page 348

16. In the election of 1896, silver-mining interests poured millions of dollars into the presidential campaign of _____ who advocated unlimited coinage of silver.
    (a) William Jennings Bryan
    (b) William McKinley
    (c) Garrett A. Hobart
    (d) Grover Cleveland
Page 350

213

17.   Lobbying works best with:
      (a)   people who are easily converted to join their side
            because of their own uneasy stance.
      (b)   those already on the same side.
      (c)   those who adamantly oppose one's side.
      (d)   people who are neutral to a cause.
Page 350

18.   The number of PACs has mushroomed from 608 in 1974 to _____ in
      1988.
      (a)   722
      (b)   1,089
      (c)   3,456
      (d)   4,268
Page 350

19.   According to a Common Cause study, _____ out of 435 members of
      the House of Representatives elected in 1988 received the
      majority of their campaign funds from PACs.
      (a)   150
      (b)   210
      (c)   378
      (d)   430
Page 351

20.   During the 1987-88 election cycle, PACs gave 82 million dollars
      to House incumbents compared to _____ dollars to the
      challengers.
      (a)   52 million
      (b)   36 million
      (c)   15 million
      (d)   9 million
Page 351

21.   After his defeat for a House seat, Steve Sovern formed
      _____, which urged candidates to shun PAC campaign
      contributions.
      (a)   Common Cause
      (b)   the National Consumers League
      (c)   LASTPAC
      (d)   the National Urban League
Page 352

22.   Traditionally, PAC money has gone to _____ because they are
      sound investments for the future.
      (a)   people challenging Republican seats
      (b)   people challenging Democratic seats
      (c)   new candidates
      (d)   incumbents
Page 351

23.   _____ legislation typically includes a written provision

allowing ordinary citizens to sue for enforcement.
(a)   Environmental
(b)   Civil Rights
(c)   Law enforcement
(d)   Property
Page 352

24. _____ briefs consist of written arguments submitted to the courts in support of one side of a case.
(a)   Deposition
(b)   Habeas corpus
(c)   Certiorari
(d)   Amicus curiae
Page 352

25. In the emotionally charged case of Regents of the University of California v. Bakke, which challenged affirmative action programs as reverse discrimination, over a hundred different groups filed _____ briefs.
(a)   certiorari
(b)   habeas corpus
(c)   fiduciary
(d)   amicus curiae
Page 353

26. All _____ interest groups are ultimately concerned with wages, prices and controls.
(a)   economic
(b)   consumer
(c)   energy
(d)   equality
Page 353

27. Numerically, _____ has more affiliated members than any other interest group.
(a)   agriculture
(b)   energy
(c)   labor
(d)   environment
Page 353

28. Unions have fought hard for _____, which requires new employees to join the union representing them.
(a)   affirmative action
(b)   right to work laws
(c)   union shop
(d)   union labels
Page 355

29. In 1947, Congress passed the Taft-Hartley Act, which permitted

states to adopt _____ laws.
(a) affirmative action
(b) right to work
(c) union shop
(d) civil union
Page 355

30. Once the occupation of the majority of Americans, only _____ percent now make their living as farmers.
(a) 3
(b) 12
(c) 15
(d) 24
Page 355

31. _____ theory holds that for virtually every interest in society there is an organized group.
(a) Pluralist
(b) Elite
(c) Hyperpluralist
(d) all answers are correct
Page 356

32. There are over _____ groups organized that champion various causes for the "public interest."
(a) 500
(b) 2,000
(c) 12,000
(d) one million
Page 356

33. _____ was propelled to prominence by a book, Unsafe at Any Speed, which attacked General Motors' Corvair as a mechanically deficient and dangerous automobile.
(a) Lee Iacocca
(b) Ralph Nader
(c) Ron Nessen
(d) Donald Trump
Page 357

34. Among the newest interest groups are the _____, although a few have been around since the nineteenth century.
(a) energy lobbies
(b) environmentalists
(c) equal rights lobbies
(d) consumer lobbies
Page 358

35. Equality interest groups base their power on the _____

Amendment which guarantees equal protection under the law. (a)
First
(b)   Fifth
(c)   Eleventh
(d)   Fourteenth
Page 359

36.   In 1954, the _____ argued and won the landmark Brown v.
the Board of Education case, which made segregated schools
illegal.
(a)   the ACLU
(b)   the National Urban League
(c)   the NAACP
(d)   Common Cause
Page 359

37.   The relatively quiet, consensual politics of the ERA movement
was disrupted when _____, a conservative activist from
Alton, Illinois, started up a highly visible STOP ERA movement.
(a)   Sarah Weddington
(b)   Norma McCorvey
(c)   Tammy Faye Baker
(d)   Phyllis Schlafly
Page 360

38.   A _____ is something of value, such as clean air, that cannot
be withheld from a potential member of a interest group.
(a)   collective good
(b)   free-rider
(c)   promised good
(d)   proven good
Page 361

39.   Olson's law of large groups holds that:
(a)   the larger the potential group, the greater the
participation.
(b)   small groups will always have 100% participation.
(c)   the larger the potential group, the less likely potential
members are to contribute.
(d)   the free-rider problem always happens in small, elite
groups.
Page 363

40.   After the collapse of many Savings and Loans in the late 1980's,
the Lincoln Savings and Loan chairman _____ was charged
with fraud and accused of giving 1.3 million dollars to five
U.S. Senators to help his situation.
(a)   T. Boone Pickens
(b)   Armand Hammer
(c)   Charles Keating
(d)   Neil Bush
Page 365

Chapter 10

BEFORE GOING ON

Feel pretty good about the "exam?" Now is the time to use the
answer key below to "grade" your exam and see how you did. As
always, go back and reread the relevant passages on the indicated
page for any you have missed.

Review Test Answers:

1:	b	11:	a	21:	c	31:	a
2:	a	12:	c	22:	d	32:	b
3:	b	13:	c	23:	a	33:	b
4:	d	14:	a	24:	d	34:	b
5:	d	15:	b	25:	d	35:	d
6:	b	16:	a	26:	a	36:	c
7:	c	17:	b	27:	c	37:	d
8:	d	18:	d	28:	c	38:	a
9:	c	19:	b	29:	b	39:	c
10:	d	20:	d	30:	a	40:	c

After you have reviewed and made certain of those Key Terms on page
368, you may wish to take a look at a really entertaining book on
politics (really!). Jeffrey Birnbaum and Alan Murray's Showdown at
Gucci Gulch: Lawmakers, Lobbyists, and the Unlikely Triumph of Tax
Reform comes with my highest recommendation (and I wouldn't steer
you wrong). This is a sugarcoated way to learn a lot about
"realpolitik." My recommendation for the term of the week is
"amicus curiae" briefs. Not only is this one of the more esoteric
(a good term itself) interest group activities, it is always good to
drop a little Latin here and there.

CHAPTER 11

THE MASS MEDIA AND THE POLITICAL AGENDA

CHAPTER LEARNING OBJECTIVES

After reading Chapter 11, you should be able to:

1. Discuss the purpose and importance of media events.
2. Summarize the development of the mass media.
3. Describe the nature of the print media business.
4. Describe the nature of the broadcast media business.
5. Describe the processes of reporting the news.
6. Discuss the existence and nature of news biases.
7. Discuss the impact of the media on public opinion.
8. Describe the role of the media in setting the policy agenda.
9. Discuss the role of the media in democratic governance.
10. Describe the impact of media on the size of government.

PRETEST QUESTIONS

The pretest below will give you an idea of the state of your knowledge about the mass media and politics. The questions should also help you learn what to look for while studying the text. Take the whole pretest, then check your answers against the key that follows (don't peek!). As you read the chapter, watch for where these questions are addressed (indicated after each question) so that you may learn why the answer is what it is.

1. Few media encounters made as much news as the profile, by CBS anchor Dan Rather, of _____. The January, 1988, interview became heated as Rather tried to question his alleged involvement in the Iran-Contra affair.
    (a) George Bush
    (b) Ronald Reagan
    (c) Gary Hart
    (d) Oliver North
    Page 373

219

2. All of the following were principles of managing news coverage of President Reagan EXCEPT:
    (a) limit reporter's access to the president.
    (b) control the flow of information.
    (c) stay on the offensive.
    (d) talk about the issues the reporters want to talk about.
Page 375-376

3. In 1987, reporters literally stalked _____ after stories emerged concerning his alleged womanizing.
    (a) Jesse Jackson
    (b) George Bush
    (c) Gary Hart
    (d) Edward Kennedy
Page 376-377

4. Lyndon Johnson was one of the two recent presidents (the other was Richard Nixon) to feel that he was hounded out of office by:
    (a) the Vietnam War.
    (b) Democrats.
    (c) Republicans.
    (d) the press.
Page 378

5. President _____ stated that "the President of the United States will not stand and be questioned like a chicken thief by men whose names he does not even know."
    (a) Ronald Reagan
    (b) Richard Nixon
    (c) F.D. Roosevelt
    (d) Herbert Hoover
Page 378

6. President _____ held 337 press conferences in his first term and 374 in his second.
    (a) Ronald Reagan
    (b) Richard Nixon
    (c) Dwight Eisenhower
    (d) F.D. Roosevelt
Page 378

7. In 1944, President Roosevelt played a trick on his Republican opponent, _____, and left one minute of radio air time dead after his address. Many listeners changed the dial before the opponent's own address came on.
    (a) Herbert Hoover
    (b) Alf Landon
    (c) Wendell Wilkie
    (d) Thomas Dewey
Page 378-379

8. In 1851, the _____, one of the nation's most influential

newspapers (even today) was founded.
   (a)   New York Times
   (b)   Boston Globe
   (c)   Washington Post
   (d)   Wall Street Journal
Page 381

9. Today's massive media conglomerates control newspapers with
    _____ percent of the nation's daily circulation.
   (a)   24
   (b)   56
   (c)   68
   (d)   78
Page 381

10. The best selling magazine in the United States is:
   (a)   TV Guide.
   (b)   Time.
   (c)   Playboy.
   (d)   Newsweek.
Page 383

11. During World War II, _____ took an early lead in broadcasting
    news on the radio.
   (a)   CBS
   (b)   NBC
   (c)   ABC
   (d)   BBS
Page 384

12. By 1949, there were _____ television sets in American homes.
   (a)   50,000
   (b)   100,000
   (c)   500,000
   (d)   1 million
Page 384

13. In 1960, Richard Nixon made a poor showing due to appearance
    live broadcast presidential debates with:
   (a)   Adlai Stevenson.
   (b)   Nelson Rockefeller.
   (c)   John F. Kennedy.
   (d)   Lyndon Johnson.
Page 384

14. Polls taken after the 1960 presidential debates showed that
    people who watched the debates on television thought that: (a)
    Kennedy won.
   (b)   nobody did particularly well.
   (c)   both candidates did very well.
   (d)   Nixon won.
Page 384
5. After a CBS news special, President Johnson sadly

remarked that if he had lost the support of _____ then he had lost the support of the American people.
(a) Charles deGaulle
(b) Walter Cronkite
(c) Everett Dirksen
(d) Robert Kennedy
Page 385

16. In his book, News from Nowhere, Edward J. Epstein tracked down the sources of 440 major stories. He found that news correspondents accounted for exactly _____ percent of news stories.
(a) 50
(b) 25
(c) 10
(d) 1
Page 387

17. For in-depth analysis of the news, there is very little of substance on television. All of the following provide a careful examination of important public policies, EXCEPT:
(a) the MacNeil-Lehrer Newshour.
(b) Nightline.
(c) A Current Affair.
(d) This Week with David Brinkley.
Page 388

18. Surveys show that people are most fascinated by stories with all of the following EXCEPT:
(a) violence.
(b) political content.
(c) disaster.
(d) scandal.
Page 390

19. People in power can use a _____, or a carefully placed bit of inside information given to a friendly reporter.
(a) sound bite
(b) "chip"
(c) leak
(d) marker
Page 393

20. When _____, Nixon's top foreign policy advisor, arranged Nixon's famous trip to China, he was reminded that domestic appearances were as important as foreign policy gains.
(a) Henry Kissinger
(b) William Rogers
(c) Cyrus Vance
(d) Caspar Weinberger
Page 393

Pretest Answers:

1: a	11: a
2: d	12: d
3: c	13: c
4: d	14: a
5: d	15: b
6: d	16: d
7: d	17: c
8: a	18: b
9: d	19: c
10: a	20: a

READING FOR CONTENT

Listed below are sets of questions associated with the content of each major section of Chapter 11. Carefully review the questions associated with each section of the text before reading the section. Have the questions in mind as you read the section and, when you reach the end of each section, stop and see if you can answer the questions well. If not, reread the relevant paragraphs until you are sure of your response to each of the questions.

I. The Mass Media Today

How does the media make news as well as report it?
How has the media affected the behavior of political elites?

II. The Development of the Mass Media

When did media politics first become important?
How has the relationship between the media and politicians changed over the years?
How has the structure of the print media changed over the years?
What are the most important print media outlets in America?
How has the structure of the broadcast media changed over the years?
When did the broadcast media rise to central importance in American politics?

III. Reporting The News

Why does the fact that reporting the news is a business shape how journalists define, get and present the news?
How are ratings related to what is defined as "news."
How are costs related to finding the news?
Why do business considerations result in news being superficial?
What are the biases of the news?
How are the biases of the news related to business demands?

IV. The News and Public Opinion

What is the impact of the media's news reporting on public opinion?

V.   The Policy Agenda and the Special Role of the Media

What is the special role of the media in setting the agenda of government?
How do political activists and politicians use the media to affect the political agenda?

VI.   Understanding the Mass Media

Why is the media important to democracy?
How does the media help keep government small?
How does the media help to expand the size of government?

CHAPTER OVERVIEW

I.   Introduction (372-372)

The American political system has entered a new period of HIGH- TECH POLITICS, a politics in which the behavior of citizens and policy-makers, as well as the POLITICAL AGENDA itself, is increasingly shaped by technology. The MASS MEDIA is a key part of that technology. Television, radio, newspapers, magazines, and other means of popular communication are called "mass media" because they reach and profoundly influence not only the elites but the masses.

II.   The Mass Media Today (372-378)

These days media often makes news as well as reports it. Mass media are today such powerful political players that politicians plot careful media strategies to control how their message and image are conveyed. Candidates have learned that the secret to controlling the media's focus is limiting what they can report on to carefully scripted events. These are known as MEDIA EVENTS. A media event is staged primarily for the purpose of being covered. If the media were not there, the event would probably not happen.

Nor does image making stop with the campaign - it is also a critical element in day-to-day governing. Politicians' images in the press are often seen as good indicators of their clout.   This is especially true of presidents, who have devoted great attention to maintaining a good public image in recent years. The Reagan White House managed media relations on the following seven principles: 1) plan ahead; 2) stay on the offensive; 3) control the flow of information; 4) limit reporters' access to the president; 5) talk about the issues you want to talk about; 6) speak in one voice; and 7) repeat the same message many times.

More and more of American government and politics hinge upon the media. Some critics of the media fear that it can determine the American political agenda and aid some political issues and candidacies while ignoring or ruining others. Others worry that it tends to reduce all of politics to theater, both complicating the process of understanding politics, and trivializing it at the same time.

III. The Development of the Mass Media (378-386)

While we live in a mass media age, it has not always been so. There was virtually no daily press during Washington's presidency. Daily newspapers emerged late in the nineteenth century, radio and television only in the first half of the twentieth century. Franklin D. Roosevelt practically invented media politics during his terms as president (1933-1945). He viewed the media as a potential ally and carefully cultivated the press. He promised reporters two PRESS CONFERENCES - presidential meetings with reporters - a week, and delivered them. He thus made certain that he became "the" newsmaker. He knew how to feed the right story to the right reporter to get the stories he wanted reported and in the way he wanted them reported.

This relatively cozy relationship between politicians and the press lasted until the early 1960s. The press saw themselves as an extension of the government and were accepting of what officials told them. The Vietnam War and the Watergate scandal soured the press on government, however. Today's newspeople work in an environment of cynicism. They see politicians as seldom telling the whole story, and their own job as ferreting out the truth. This INVESTIGATIVE JOURNALISM - the use of detective-like reporting methods to unearth scandals and malfeasance - pits reporters against political leaders. The media has a unique ability to expose government's dirty linen, and there is evidence that TV's fondness for investigative journalism has contributed to greater public cynicism and negativism about politics and government.

A. The Print Media

The PRINT MEDIA includes newspapers and magazines and has been around in some form for a very long time. The first newspaper appeared in ancient Rome some fifteen hundred years ago. The first American daily newspaper appeared in Philadelphia in 1783, but dailies remained rare until technological advances and cheap paper made possible the "penny press" in the mid nineteenth century. By the 1840s the development of the telegraph made possible a primitive "wire service" capable of rapidly relaying news stories from city to city.

Newspapers consolidated in CHAINS during the early part of the twentieth century. Today's massive media conglomerates control newspapers with 78 percent of the nation's daily circulation. These chains control many radio and television stations as well.

Among the press there is a pecking order. From the beginning the New York Times has been considered a cut above the rest, America's "newspaper of record." Its clearest rival today is the Washington Post, offering perhaps the best coverage of Washington politics. Most smaller papers depend on the Associated Press as a source of news. Eighty percent of the non-communist world's news comes from just four sources, the Associated Press, the United Press International, the New York Times news service, and the Los Angeles Times/Washington Post news service.

Magazines - the other component of the print media - are popular, but not so much as a source of political information. The newsweeklies - mainly Time, Newsweek, and U.S. News and World Report - rank well behind the popular general interest magazines in circulation. Serious magazines of political news and opinion - such as the New Republic, the National Review, and Commentary - reach basically only the educated elite.

B. The Broadcast Media

The BROADCAST MEDIA, consisting of television and radio, has gradually displaced the print media as Americans' principal source of news and information. Invented in 1903, radio achieved its first commercial broadcast in 1920 when the first radio station, KDKA in Pittsburgh reported the Harding-Cox election returns. During World War II, led by CBS, radio went into the news business in earnest.

Whereas CBS pioneered radio news, NBC pioneered television news. The 1950s and 1960s were the adolescent years of American television. The political career of Richard Nixon was made and unmade on television during those years. Nixon used television to make his career in his famous "checkers speech" saving his place on the Republican ticket as Eisenhower's vice-presidential running-mate. In 1960 Nixon's career was damaged by his haggard appearance in the first PRESIDENTIAL DEBATE against Senator John F. Kennedy. Looking awful compared to the crisp, clean, attractive Kennedy, Nixon's poll ratings declined sharply. This debate illustrates the visual power of television, for whereas people listening on radio gave the edge in the debate to Nixon, those who saw it thought Kennedy had won.

Television had a dramatic impact on the conduct of the Vietnam War. It not only exposed governmental incompetence and deception about the progress of the war, but it brought the horrors of war into American homes every night in living color. With the growth of cable TV, particularly the Cable News Network (CNN), television has recently entered a new era of bringing the news to people - and political leaders - as it happens. Leaders increasingly rely on television news as their most immediate source of information and communication.

Since 1963, surveys have consistently shown that more people rely on TV for news than any other medium. People also think, by two to one margins, that television reports are more believable than newspaper stories.

IV. Reporting the News (386-391)

Regardless of the medium, it cannot be overemphasized that news reporting is a business in America. The drive for profit shapes how journalists define the news, where they get the news, and how they present it. Because some news stories attract more viewers and readers, and thus more revenues, there are inherent biases in what the public sees and reads about.

A. Defining News

News is what is timely and different. The odd episode is more newsworthy than the commonplace or mundane. This focus can lead to a peculiar view of events and policy-makers. TV news also caters to its audience to maintain high ratings. As a result, news shows are tailored to a fairly low level of audience sophistication. The TV networks largely define news as what is entertaining.

B. Finding the News

Edward J. Epstein studied NBC's news department and called the resulting book "News From Nowhere" to make the point that the organizational processes shape the news. The popular image of correspondents ferreting out the news is not entirely inaccurate, but a surprising amount of news comes from well-established sources. Much comes tailor-made in press releases or in TRIAL BALLOONS - information leaked to the media to see what the political reaction will be. Most TV news stories originate from other news media. Correspondents accounted for only 1% in Epstein's study, while the AP and UPI wire services accounted for 70 percent. Print reporters also rely heavily on established sources. So rare is the major story resulting from original investigative research and reporting that they are the basis of major journalistic awards.

C. Presenting the News

Once the news has been "found" it must be compressed into a short broadcast news segment or fit in among the newspaper advertisements. Most news coverage is superficial as a result. TV analysis of news events rarely lasts more than a minute. Complex issues are given little coverage partly because they don't fit into the time framework of the evening news.

Oddly, as technology has enabled the media to pass along information with greater speed, coverage has become less complete. For example, newspapers once routinely reprinted the entire text of speeches, while Americans now hear SOUND BITES of fifteen seconds or less of TV. Politicians have learned that it is unnecessary to build a carefully crafted case for his or her point of view when a catchy line will serve as well or better.

Chapter 11

D. Bias in the News

The vast majority of social science studies have found that the media is not systematically biased toward a particular ideology or party. This reflects several factors: 1) reporters' belief in journalistic objectivity; 2) rotation of reporter assignments and awards for objectivity; 3) media's stake in attracting viewers and readers making them careful not to lose their audience by appearing biased.

This is not to say, however, that news coverage does not distort reality, however. Journalists must select which stories to cover and to what degree. Because news is a business, the overriding bias is toward stories that will draw the largest audience. These tend to be stories focusing on conflict, violence, disaster, or scandal. Television is biased toward stories that generate good pictures as well. Seeing a TALKING HEAD is boring compared to something that involves action and color.

V. The News and Public Opinion (391-392)

Determining the effects of the news media on people's opinions and behaviors is a difficult task, in part because it is hard to separate the media from other influences. For many years experts doubted that the media had much effect on public opinion. They were looking for "direct impacts" - for example, whether or not the media affected how people voted. When the focus turned to how the media affects "what Americans think about", more positive results were uncovered. This effect is of no small consequence. By increasing public attention to specific problems, television news can influence the criteria by which the public evaluates political leaders. Indeed, research indicates that the impact of news commentators on opinion change is quite high - higher than that of presidents. If so, the news media is a very potent factor in opinion change in America.

VI. The Policy Agenda and the Special Role of the Media (392-393)

A POLICY AGENDA is "the list of subjects or problems to which government officials, and people outside of government closely associated with those officials, are paying some serious attention at any given time." Political activists depend heavily upon the media to get their ideas place high on the governmental agenda. Political activists are often called POLICY ENTREPRENEURS - people who invest their political "capital" in an issue. Policy entrepreneurs' weapons include press releases, press conferences, and letter writing; buttonholing reporters and columnists; trading on personal contacts; and even doing something dramatic. In addition, people in power can use a LEAK - a carefully placed bit of inside information given to a friendly reporter.

Because so much of politics is theater, the staging of political events to attract media attention is a political art form. Dictators, revolutionaries, prime ministers, and presidents alike all play to the cameras. The media is not monopolized by political elites, however. The poor and otherwise powerless can use it too. Civil rights groups in the 1960s relied heavily on the media to tell their stories of unjust treatment. Protest groups of all types have come to appreciate the importance of an interesting media event in publicizing their causes.

More important than a few dramatic events is conveying a long term, positive image via the media. Policy entrepreneurs depend on good will and good images, and they often turn to public relations firms to improve their image and convey their message.

VII. Understanding The Mass Media (393-396)

Often referred to as the "fourth branch of government" because of its importance, the media acts as a key linkage institution between the people and the policy-makers. As such it profoundly affects the policy agenda.

A. The Media and the Size of Government

The watchdog function of the media can be argued to help keep government small. With journalists distrustful of politicians and their policy proposals, every new proposal is met with skepticism. Such skepticism acts as a constraint on the growth of government.

The watchdog orientation of the press is often reformist, however. Reporters see their job as crusading against foul play and unfairness in government and society. When they focus on injustice in society they inevitably encourage the growth of government. Once the media identifies a problem in society, it usually begins to ask what the government is doing about it. The media thus portrays the government as responsible for the problem and encourages it to take on more and more tasks in response.

B. Democracy and the Mass Media

The widespread access to information possible through the mass media could be a great boon to democracy. Most observers think that the media has fallen far short of realizing this potential, however. The rise of the "information society" has not brought about the "informed society." Difficult issues, like the economy, nuclear power, and biotechnology are not well covered in the media.

Whenever it is criticized for being superficial, the media's defense is to say that this is what people want. If the American people want (and will actually watch and read) serious coverage of the issues, the media will be happy to give it to them. Blame the profit oriented nature of the business, or blame the people - most of whom like news to be more entertaining than informative. In this sense one can say that the people really do rule through the media.

DOING RESEARCH ON THE MASS MEDIA AND POLITICS

Your text points out that there is no consistent liberal or conservative or partisan bias in the news. This may not be true of your local news outlets, however. You may wish to systematically study the content of your local media to see if you can detect any consistent liberal or conservative ideological patterns. In doing so, it is important that you first carefully define "conservative" and "liberal" and what sorts of things would indicate evidence of bias, however. Otherwise, your subjective judgment of various articles or broadcast reports may say more about your own ideological biases than that of the media.

You may wish to investigate how the media has covered major events or specific media events, and evaluate its tone and the extent of its attention. Major media events like presidential debates might be one focus for such a project. Looking through back issues of newsmagazines and newspapers following the Kennedy-Nixon, Carter-Ford, Carter-Reagan, Reagan-Mondale, and/or Bush Dukakis debates can reveal how well each side did controlling the "spin" of the press story.

Or you might wish to look at a major news event to see how it was covered or how coverage changed over time. One interesting project might be to compare the press coverage in tone and content on the Vietnam War at different times. Compare stories on the conflict in the early 1960s with those shortly before and after the commitment of combat troops in 1965. Finally, compare these periods with news reports late in the experience, say 1970 or 1971. Alternatively, reports on some period in Vietnam could be compared with reports on World War II, the Korean War, or even the recent crisis in the Persian Gulf.

Regardless of the research you do, you should be aware that not all media is unbiased, or even pretends to be unbiased. Some outlets, particularly opinion magazines, are intended to be proponents of a particular point of view. These can be very valuable sources of ideas and arguments, but their biases should be recognized by those that are using them. Opinion journals like The National Review, The Public Interest, and Commentary represent various aspects of the conservative side of the spectrum, for example. The New Republic, The American Prospect, and The Progressive represent various shades of liberal opinion. In using such sources, you should always seek to look at both sides and provide some balance in your discussions of the issues.

REVIEW TEST

Go back and review the "Reading for Content" questions if you haven't already done so.   If you feel like you have achieved the learning objectives listed at the beginning of the chapter, you should be ready for the Review Test.   Try hard to think through items you aren't sure of rather than going to the answer list quickly.   Taking the Review Test seriously will help you prepare.

1.   At the 1988 summit, _____ got to visit with Mikhail Gorbechev before Ronald Reagan did.
     (a)   Dan Rather
     (b)   Tom Brokaw
     (c)   Diane Sawyer
     (d)   Sam Donaldson
Page 373

2.   Few media encounters made as much news as the profile of then-Vice-President George Bush by CBS anchor _____ in January of 1988.   Questions about Bush's alleged role in the Iran-Contra affair led to a heated exchange.
     (a)   Peter Jennings
     (b)   Bernard Shaw
     (c)   Tom Brokaw
     (d)   Dan Rather
Page 373

3.   The most effective method of putting across a candidate's platform and/or image in today's presidential campaign is:
     (a)   radio spots.
     (b)   favorable news coverage.
     (c)   thirty-second TV commercials.
     (d)   personal appearances and fund-raisers.
Page 374

4.   In the 1988 presidential elections, the _____ campaign was far more skillful than others in influencing what issues were discussed by the media and what was reported about their candidate.
     (a)   Bush
     (b)   Dukakis
     (c)   Jackson
     (d)   Dole
Page 374

5.   Few, if any, administrations devoted so much concern and energy to the president's media appearances than did the administration of:
     (a)   John F. Kennedy.
     (b)   Lyndon Johnson
     (c)   Ronald Reagan.
     (d)   Jimmy Carter.
Page 375

6.   The task of applying the seven principles of news management

231

for President Reagan was:
(a)   Ed Meese.
(b)   Michael Deaver.
(c)   Donald Regan.
(d)   James Baker.
Page 372

7.   In 1989, when _____ was nominated for secretary of defense, the media extensively investigated allegations of a drinking problem.
(a)   Richard Cheney
(b)   James Baker III
(c)   Caspar Weinberger
(d)   John Tower
Page 377

8.   Some see politics as national theater. _____ outscored the soap operas in his televised Iran- Contra testimony.
(a)   John Poindexter
(b)   Oliver North
(c)   Richard McFarland
(d)   Eugene Hasenfus
Page 378

9.   _____, stated that the biggest change in politics in his long career was "all you guys in the media."
(a)   Lyndon Johnson
(b)   Hubert Humphrey
(c)   Robert Kennedy
(d)   George McGovern
Page 378

10.   As recently as the presidency of _____, reporters submitted their questions to the president in writing, and he responded in writing -- if at all.
(a)   Woodrow Wilson
(b)   Herbert Hoover
(c)   Harry S. Truman
(d)   John F. Kennedy
Page 378

11.   The daily newspaper is largely a product of:
(a)   the late eighteenth century.
(b)   the early nineteenth century.
(c)   the late nineteenth century.
(d)   the early twentieth century.
Page 378

12.   Franklin Roosevelt promised reporters two _____ a week.
(a)   radio addresses
(b)   speeches

    (c)   press conferences
    (d)   major stories
Page 378

13.   The United Press news syndicate carried _____ times as much
       Washington news under FDR as it had under Hoover.
       (a)   six
       (b)   four
       (c)   three
       (d)   two
Page 378

14.   _____ was the first president to use radio, broadcasting a
       series of "fireside chats."
       (a)   F.D. Roosevelt
       (b)   Herbert Hoover
       (c)   Calvin Coolidge
       (d)   Woodrow Wilson
Page 378

15.   To reporters, politicians rarely tell the whole story and the
       press sees ferreting out the truth as their job. No one
       epitomized this attitude in the 1980's better than:
       (a)   Sam Donaldson.
       (b)   Diane Sawyer.
       (c)   Bryant Gumbel.
       (d)   Peter Jennings.
Page 329

16.   Guaranteed freedom of speech by the _____ Amendment, the
       American media has a unique ability to hang the government's
       dirty linen.
       (a)   First
       (b)   Third
       (c)   Fifth
       (d)   Ninth
Page 380

17.   The first newspaper was the Roman gazette Acta Diurna, a kind
       of house organ for the regime of _____ in 59 b.c.
       (a)   Romulas
       (b)   Caligula
       (c)   Constantine
       (d)   Julius Caesar
Page 381

18.   In 1841, the New York Tribune, published by _____,
       started up.

    (a) William Randolph Hearst
    (b) William Franklin
    (c) Joseph Pulitzer
    (d) Horace Greeley
Page 381

19. By the 1840's, the _____ permitted a primitive "wire service," which relayed news stories from city to city faster than ever before.
     (a) telegraph
     (b) pony express
     (c) telephone
     (d) radio
Page 381

20. The newspaper editor _____ sent an artist to cover the Spanish-American conflict in Cuba, telling him,"you furnish the pictures and I'll furnish the war."
     (a) Joseph Pulitzer
     (b) Katherine Graham
     (c) Charles Foster Kane
     (d) William Randolph Hearst
Page 381

21. Newspapers consolidated into chains during:
     (a) the mid-nineteenth century.
     (b) the late nineteenth century.
     (c) the early twentieth century.
     (d) the late twentieth century.
Page 381

22. The _____ is known as the "nation's newspaper of record" and stands a cut above most newspapers in its influence.
     (a) Washington Post
     (b) New York Times
     (c) Los Angeles Times
     (d) Wall Street Journal
Page 381

23. Serious magazines of political news and opinion are basically reserved for the educated elite in America. All of the following magazines, EXCEPT ONE, fit this description.
     (a) The New Republic
     (b) Reader's Digest
     (c) Commentary
     (d) National Review
Page 384-385

24. The _____ was invented in 1903, the same year as the Wright

brothers' famous flight.
(a) telegraph
(b) television
(c) radio
(d) film projector
Page 384

25. The first television station actually appeared in:
(a) 1913.
(b) 1922.
(c) 1931.
(d) 1945.
Page 384

26. By 1949, there were a million TV sets in American homes. Just two years later, there were:
(a) 2 million
(b) 3 million
(c) 5 million
(d) 10 million
Page 384

27. In 1952, while running as Dwight Eisenhower's vice-presidential candidate, _____ made a famous speech denying that he took under-the-table gifts and payments.
(a) Estes Kefauver
(b) Richard Nixon
(c) Robert A. Taft
(d) Nelson Rockefeller
Page 384

28. Polls taken after the 1960 presidential debates showed that people who listened to the debates on radio thought that:
(a) Kennedy had won.
(b) nobody had done very well.
(c) both candidates did equally well.
(d) Nixon had won.
Page 384

29. In 1968, CBS anchorman _____ after a tour of Vietnam reported that he thought the war was unlikely to be won.
(a) Walter Cronkite
(b) Mike Wallace
(c) David Brinkley
(d) Chet Huntley
Page 385

30. According to a book by Edward J. Epstein, TV networks (to a large extent) define news as:

(a) something new and different.
(b) what is relevant and important.
(c) what effects the average viewer.
(d) what is entertaining to the average viewer.
Page 387

31. In their pursuit of high ratings, news shows are tailored to:
    (a) a fairly low level of audience sophistication.
    (b) an average intelligence level of audiences.
    (c) a high level of audience sophistication.
    (d) an understandable but complex approach to viewers.
Page 387

32. Edward J. Epstein's study of news sources found that the wire services accounted for _____ percent of TV news stories.
    (a) 15
    (b) 50
    (c) 70
    (d) 95
Page 387

33. Columnists like _____ regularly expose the uglier side of government corruption and inefficiency.
    (a) Jack Anderson
    (b) Maury Povich
    (c) Diane Sawyer
    (d) Connie Chung
Page 387

34. In place of political speeches, Americans now hear _____ of fifteen seconds or less on TV.
    (a) clips
    (b) chips
    (c) snapshots
    (d) sound bites
Page 389

35. Seeing a shot of a person's face talking directly to the camera, or a _____, is boring to the average viewer and the viewer will normally switch channels rather than watch it.
    (a) talking head
    (b) head room
    (c) head shot
    (d) dim bulb
Page 390-391

36. In studies, researchers found that the impact of news

commentators such as John Chancellor and David Brinkley seemed _____ in affecting opinion change.
   (a)   insignificant
   (b)   slightly significant
   (c)   particularly significant
   (d)   to encourage negative backlash
Page 392

37.   Political activists are often called _____, or people who invest their political "capital" in an issue.
   (a)   political capitalists
   (b)   policy entrepreneurs
   (c)   policy sharks
   (d)   troubleshooters
Page 392

38.   Though skeptical of what politicians say and do, _____ looks at America's social problems in a manner that encourages government to take on more and more tasks.
   (a)   the media
   (b)   the people
   (c)   an interest group
   (d)   a PAC
Page 395

39.   Just before he announced his candidacy in 1944, _____ was examined by a doctor who said that the prognosis for his living for four years was very bleak.   The report was suppressed and the candidate won the election -- dying four months into his term.
   (a)   Robert A. Taft
   (b)   John F. Kennedy
   (c)   Franklin D. Roosevelt
   (d)   Warren G. Harding
Page 377

40.   In the 1980's, Prime Minister Margaret Thatcher, of Great Britain, banned the book _____ by Peter Wright because it claimed a past high government official been a double agent.
   (a)   Spycatcher
   (b)   Master Spy
   (c)   Veil
   (d)   From Russia With Love
Page 380
BEFORE GOING ON

Use the answer key below to "grade" your exam and see how you did. As always, go back and reread the relevant passages on the indicated page for any you have missed. Why just be good when with a little effort you can be perfect?

Review Test Answers:

1: b	11: c	21: c	31: a
2: d	12: c	22: b	32: c
3: c	13: c	23: b	33: a
4: a	14: a	24: c	34: d
5: c	15: a	25: c	35: a
6: b	16: a	26: d	36: c
7: d	17: d	27: b	37: b
8: b	18: d	28: d	38: a
9: a	19: a	29: a	39: c
10: b	20: d	30: d	40: a

Take another look at the short list of Key Terms on page 397. Notice how many of these terms have to do with the process of the politicians using the media for their purposes. Media events, press conferences, trial balloons, policy entrepreneurs, and leak all involve the contrivances of politicians to use the media. Another, which is not stressed by your text, is "spin control," which refers to the efforts of campaign officials to color the media's interpretation of a media event. Knowing that these interpretations will determine how the event is see and evaluated by the public, the politicians work very hard to make that interpretation what they wish it to be. Major presidential campaigns have "spin doctors" who handle this vital job of handling the press and coloring its views. They are nowhere more in evidence than just after a presidential debate. After all, who won the debate will be, to a large degree, who the media says won the debate.

To emphasize the importance of the media as a political tool of political activists and elites, let me offer the press "leak" as this week's term to take to the streets. Reference to "leaks" shows that you are hip to the process. Besides, the term "leak" conjures up such appropriate graphic imagery that it is just too compelling a choice to pass up.

CHAPTER 12

CONGRESS

CHAPTER LEARNING OBJECTIVES

After reading Chapter 12, you should be able to:

1. Describe the basic characteristics of the member's job.
2. Describe the personal characteristics of members of Congress.
3. Describe the importance of incumbency for reelection.
4. Discuss why incumbency is so great an advantage for reelection.
5. Discuss the sources and importance of money in congressional elections.
6. Describe the organizational structure of Congress.
7. Identify the major institutional and party leadership positions in Congress.
8. Identify the four general types of committees.
9. Discuss the role of committees in the policy process.
10. Define and discuss the role of informal organizations (caucuses).
11. Describe the steps in the process of a bill becoming a law.
12. Discuss the factors that influence Congressional decisions.
13. Discuss the dilemma of representation and effectiveness as it relates to Congress's role in democracy.
14. Explain why the nature of Congress contributes to the growth of government.

PRETEST QUESTIONS

The pretest below will give you an idea of the state of your knowledge about Congress. Take the whole pretest, then check your answers against the key that follows (don't peek!). As you read the chapter, watch for where these questions are addressed so that you may learn why the answer is what it is.

1. In 1989, House Majority Whip _____ resigned after charges of financial improprieties.
   (a) Richard Gephardt
   (b) Tom Foley
   (c) Jim Wright
   (d) Tony Coelho

Page 410

2. The salary for a seat in the U.S. Senate is:
   (a) 14,400 a year.
   (b) 19,400 a year.
   (c) $51,400 a year.
   (d) $101,400 a year.

3. The dominant occupation of most members of Congress is:
   (a) law.
   (b) academia.
   (c) business.
   (d) political in nature.
Page 413

4. It is better stated that Congress engages in _____ representation, or representing the interests of groups.
   (a) reflective
   (b) deceptive
   (c) descriptive
   (d) substantive
Page 414

5. A(n) _____ is a person who is already holding an office in Congress.
   (a) gerrymander
   (b) "dictator"
   (c) planter
   (d) incumbent
Page 414

6. In Gary Jacobsen's study of congressional elections, he found that fewer than _____ percent of the House members seeking reelection lose the general elections.
   (a) 2
   (b) 7
   (c) 12
   (d) 20
Page 415

7. The average member of Congress will make about _____ trips back to their home district every year to increase visibility.
   (a) 5
   (b) 15
   (c) 25
   (d) 35
Page 417

8. The total cost for 1988 U.S. Senate races was $_____ million.
   (a) 5
   (b) 55
   (c) 100
   (d) 190
Page 422

9. About _____ percent of the funds raised by candidates for

Congress in 1988 came from the more than four thousand PACs.
(a) 10
(b) 25
(c) 33
(d) 50
Page 422

10. The U.S. Congress and every American state legislature except _____ are bicameral legislatures.
(a) Oklahoma's
(b) Hawaii's
(c) Nebraska's
(d) Maine's
Page 426

11. Party loyalty to leadership and party-line voting are more common in the:
(a) Senate.
(b) House.
(c) conference committee.
(d) ad hoc committee.
Page 427

12. The _____ now directly appoints the members of the Rules Committee.
(a) Speaker of the House
(b) House Majority leader
(c) president
(d) House Majority Whip
Page 427

13. Today, a filibuster can be halted if _____ members of the Senate vote to cut off debate.
(a) sixty
(b) seventy five
(c) eighty three
(d) ninety
Page 428

14. The Speaker's principal partisan ally is the _____, a job that has been the main stepping stone to the Speaker's seat.
(a) President pro tempore
(b) house majority leader
(c) majority whip
(d) minority leader
Page 429

15. In 1989, controversial Republican congressman _____was

elected House Republican whip.
(a) Robert Walker
(b) Newt Gingrich
(c) Jim Inhofe
(d) Ike Skelton
Page 429

16. In 1989, the Democrats selected the current Senate majority leader, _____, who uses his polished speaking style on behalf of his party in public and on television.
(a) Robert Byrd
(b) George Mitchell
(c) Edward Kennedy
(d) Daniel P. Moynihan
Page 430

17. Committees and subcommittees stay busy in legislative _____, the process of monitoring the bureaucracy and its administration of policy.
(a) hindsight
(b) watchdogging
(c) oversight
(d) "hide and seek"
Page 432

18. Members of congress seek committees that will help them reach three goals, which include all of the following EXCEPT:
(a) important contacts with PACs (to finance the next election).
(b) reelection in general.
(c) influence in Congress.
(d) the opportunity to make policy in important areas.
Page 433

19. The person most referred to as the chief legislator in congress is the:
(a) Speaker of the House.
(b) Senate majority leader.
(c) president.
(d) House majority leader.
Page 440

20. _____ had started the ball rolling with regards to reform in Congress while he was majority leader from 1955-1961. He originated the rule that gave each senator a seat on at least one key committee.
(a) Everett M. Dirksen
(b) Lyndon B. Johnson
(c) Robert S. Kerr
(d) John F. Kennedy
Page 447

Pretest Answers:

1: d	11: b
2: d	12: a
3: a	13: a
4: d	14: b
5: d	15: b
6: b	16: b
7: d	17: c
8: d	18: a
9: c	19: c
10: c	20: b

READING FOR CONTENT

Listed below are sets of questions associated with the content of each major section of Chapter 12. Carefully review the questions associated with each section of the text before reading the section. Have the questions in mind as you read the section and, when you reach the end of each section, stop and see if you can answer the questions well. If not, reread the relevant paragraphs until you are sure of your response to each of the questions.

I.   The Representatives and Senators

What are the burdens and perquisites of the job?
What are the dominant personal characteristics of members?
Why do incumbents win most congressional elections?
What is the role of party identification in congressional
     elections?
Under what circumstances can incumbents be defeated?
What are the sources and importance of money in congressional
     elections?

II. How Congress is Organized To Make Policy

What is the nature of American bicameralism?
How are the roles of the House and Senate distinct?
How is the Speaker of the House selected?
What are the powers of the Speaker of the House?
What is the role of the party leadership positions in each
     house?
What is the role of the party whips in each house?
What types of committees does Congress have?
What is the purpose and number of standing committees?
What is the purpose of conference committees?
What are the basic functions of standing committees?
How do members of Congress get on committees?
How are committee chairs selected?
What are the informal organizations called caucuses?
Why are caucuses important?

III. The Congressional Process

What are the steps involved in a bill becoming a law?
How does the president influence congressional decisions?
When does party influence congressional decisions?
How much does constituency influence the behavior of members?
When do members follow their own ideology and beliefs?
How do lobbyists and interest groups influence legislators?
How are lobbyists regulated?

IV.   Understanding Congress

What is the dilemma of representation versus effectiveness?
How is the dilemma of representation versus effectiveness
   related to the role of Congress in a democracy?
How does the responsiveness of Congress contribute to the
   growth in government?

CHAPTER OVERVIEW

I.   Introduction (408-410)

The framers of the Constitution conceived of Congress as the center
of policy-making in America. Congress's prominence has ebbed and
flowed over the course of American history, and has been on the
increase in recent years. Congress faces a rush of increasingly
complex legislation each year. To deal with its business Congress
has decentralized most important activities, but the policy process
remains frustratingly slow and inefficient. Members are accosted by
lobbyists, frustrated by the fragmentation of power, and tainted by
ethical problems. Nonetheless, there is no shortage of men and
women running for congressional office.

II.   The Representatives and Senators (410-414)

A. The Job

Perhaps the most prominent characteristic of a member of Congress's
job is hard work. The typical representative is a member of about
six committees and subcommittees; a senator is a member of about
ten. The foremost attraction of the job is power. Members of
Congress make key decisions about important matters of public
policy. The salary and perquisites are also attractive.

B. The People

There are 535 members of Congress - 100 Senators and 435
Representatives. The Constitution specifies only that members of
the House must be a least twenty-five years old and have been
American citizens for seven years, that senators must be at least
thirty and have been American citizens for nine years, and that all
must be residents of the states from which they are elected.
The members of Congress cannot be called typical or average

Americans. They come mostly from occupations with high status and usually have substantial incomes. Only a handful are members of minority groups (24 African-Americans, 12 Hispanics). Women are the most under-represented group, having only twenty-five in the House and two in the Senate.

Obviously, members of Congress cannot claim "descriptive" representation, that is, representing constituents through mirroring their personal, politically relevant characteristics. They can engage in "substantive" representation, however, representing the interests of groups. Most members have lived among their constituents for many years and share their general beliefs and attitudes.

III. Congressional Elections (414-425)

A. Who Wins?

Like all politicians, members of Congress have their eyes on the next election. INCUMBENTS are those already holding office. The most important fact about congressional elections is that, when they choose to run for reelection, incumbents usually win. Not only do more than 90 percent of the incumbents seeking reelection win (99 percent won in 1988), but they tend to win with big margins. In 1988 more than 87 percent of the House incumbents won more than 60 percent of the vote. Incumbent Senators are also advantaged but not so much as House members. Senator's are less advantaged because they represent larger more heterogeneous constituencies, have less personal contact with their constituents, receive more media attention on controversial and divisive issues, and tend to draw more visible challengers.

Despite their success at reelection, incumbents have a strong feeling of vulnerability. Thus they have been raising and spending more campaign funds, traveling home more, and staffing more local offices than ever before.

B. The Advantages of Incumbents

Voters do not send incumbents back because they agree with their votes on important policy matters. Evidence suggests they are unaware of how they vote. Nor do voter assessments of presidential performance or the ups and downs of the economy have much impact. Members of Congress engage in three primary activities that increase the probability of their reelection: advertising, credit claiming, and position taking.

1. Advertising. Advertising is more than placing ads in newspapers and TV. Most congressional advertising takes place between elections and takes the form of contact with constituents. The goal is visibility. They use the mails and frequent trips home to maintain visibility.

2. Credit Claiming. Congresspersons also engage in credit claiming, which involves personal and district service. Not how members vote but how many folks know them and how these people size up their service to them are what count for reelection. Policy stands and voting records make enemies as well as friends, service and visibility produce only support.

As a result of the advantages of incumbency in advertising and credit claiming, incumbents, especially in the House, are usually better known and have a more favorable image than their opponents.

3. Position Taking. Members must also engage in position taking - taking policy stands when they vote and responding to constituents' questions about issues. The positions they take may make a difference in the outcome of an election, especially if the issues are salient to voters and their positions are inconsistent with the views of their constituents. This is especially true for the Senate, in which issues are likely to play a greater role.

4. Weak Opponents. Another advantage for incumbents is that they are likely to face weak opponents. The advantages of incumbency discourage potentially effective opponents from challenging members of the House.

C. The Role of Party Identification

Although party loyalty at the voting booth is not as strong as it was a generation ago, it is still a good predictor of voting behavior. About three-fourths of voters who identified with a party in 1988 voted for Senate and House members of their party.

D. Defeating Incumbents

Given the advantages of incumbency, incumbents almost have to beat themselves, and some do. An incumbent tarnished by scandal is vulnerable. Incumbents may also be redistricted out of their familiar turfs. Congress reapportions its membership after every federal census. States that have gained population gain seats; states that have lost population lose states. In both cases redistricting may move one incumbent into another's district, pitting them against one another. In such circumstances an incumbent must lose. However, most of the turnover in the membership of Congress is the result of vacated seats.

E. Money in Congressional Elections

The cost of the congressional elections in the 1987- 88 election cycle was $410 million. Given the amounts involved, it is important to ask where this money comes from and what it buys. Most of the money comes from individuals, but about 33 percent came from the more than four thousand Political Action Committees (PACs). Incumbents receive the vast bulk of the money ($118 million to $14 million for incumbents in 1988).

Clearly, PACs are seeking access to policy-makers. Thus they give most of their money to incumbents who are likely to win anyway. PACs want to keep the lines of communication open. Since each PAC is limited to contributions of five thousand dollars per candidate, a single PAC can at most account for only a small percentage of a winner's total spending.

What does money buy the candidates who spend it? Spending a lot of money in a campaign is no guarantee of success. Money is important, however, for challengers. The more they spend the more votes they receive. It buys name recognition and a chance to be heard. Incumbents already possess these advantages and benefit less from spending. Nonetheless, incumbents normally out spend challengers by a wide margin. In open seats, the candidate who spends the most usually wins.

F. Stability and Change

The success of incumbents in reelection results in stability in the membership of Congress. Incumbent security and stability provide experience and expertise to address the complex problems of public policy. They also insulate Congress from the winds of change, however.

IV. How Congress Is Organized To Make Policy (425-437)

For Congress making policy means considering bills, voting intelligently for policy in the national interest, and doing one's legislative homework. Policy-making is the toughest role for members of Congress because of the volume and complexity of legislative work. Overwhelmed and often uncertain of their position on specific and complex legislation, members seek out for advice one or two other members serving on the committee reporting a bill whose judgment they trust. Congressional policy-making is so varied and confusing that members frequently resort to these "cue givers" who can help them make up their minds.

Congress is a collection of generalists trying to make policy on specialized topics. Members are short of time and expertise. Congress tries to cope with the demands of their work load and its complexity through its elaborate committee system.

A. American Bicameralism

A BICAMERAL LEGISLATURE is one divided into two houses. The bicameral Congress creates another check and balance - for no bill can be passed unless both House and Senate agree on it.

1. The House. More than four times larger than the Senate the House is also more institutionalized, that is, more centralized, more hierarchical, and less anarchic. Loyalty to party leadership and party-line voting are more common than in the Senate. Both the

House and Senate set their own agendas, but the House has a unique institution that plays a key role in the process, the HOUSE RULES COMMITTEE. This committee reviews most bills coming from House committees before they go to the full House. It gives each bill a "rule," which schedules the bill on the calendar, allots time for debate, and sometimes even specifies what kind of amendments may be offered.

2. The Senate. The Founders thought the Senate would protect elite interests against the popular tendencies of the House. Thus to the House they gave the power of initiating all revenue bills and of impeaching officials; to the Senate they gave the power of ratifying all treaties, of confirming important presidential nominations, and of trying impeached officials.

The Senate is less disciplined and less centralized than the House. Today's senators are also more equal in power than representatives are. Committees and the party leadership are important in determining the Senate's legislative agenda, just as they are in the House. Party leaders do for the Senate what the Rules Committee does for the House. Priding itself on freedom of discussion, the Senate permitted unlimited debate on a bill. Opponents of bills sometimes used this custom to try to "talk a bill to death" or FILIBUSTER, a practice unique to the Senate. Today, sixty members present and voting can halt a filibuster.

B. Congressional Leadership

Much of the leadership in Congress is party leadership. Those who have real power in the congressional hierarchy are those whose party put them there. Chief among these in the House of Representatives is the SPEAKER OF THE HOUSE. This office is mandated by the Constitution. In practice the majority party does the choosing, because that party's candidate will receive the unanimous support of the party - by definition enough to elect. The Speaker's powers have waxed and waned over the nation's history. Today the Speaker: 1) presides over the House when in session; 2) plays a major role in making committee assignments; 3) appoints or plays a key role in appointing the party's legislative leaders and leadership staff; 4) exercises substantial control over assigning bills to committees. In addition, the Speaker has a great informal clout inside and outside Congress.

The principal ally of the Speaker in the House party leadership structure is the MAJORITY LEADER. The majority leader is responsible for scheduling bills in the House and rounding up votes in support of the party's position on legislation. The party's WHIPS help the leader in this latter task. The minority party has similar roles for its MINORITY LEADER and whips.
1. The Senate. The vice-president of the United States is the president of the Senate. In practice, vice-presidents usually ignore their senatorial chores, leaving power in the Senate up to party leaders. Thus, the Senate majority leader, aided by party

whips, is the most important leadership position in the Senate. The leader corrals votes, schedules floor action, influences committee assignments, and is (along with the Speaker of the House) a major national spokesperson for the party.

2. Congressional Leadership in Perspective. Despite their positions, congressional leaders easily influence members. Both houses of Congress are highly decentralized and leaders are elected by members and must remain responsive to them. Leaders have little power to punish those who fail to support the party.

C. The Committees and Subcommittees

Most of the real work of Congress goes on in committees. Committees control the congressional agenda and guide legislation through the legislative process. Committees can be grouped into four types, the first of which is by far the most important. STANDING COMMITTEES are formed to handle bills in different policy areas. The Senate has 16 standing committees with 85 subcommittees, the House 22 standing committees with 140 subcommittees. JOINT COMMITTEES exist in a few policy areas; their membership is drawn from both the Senate and the House. CONFERENCE COMMITTEES are formed when the Senate and the House pass a particular bill in different forms. A conference committee consists of members of each house chosen by party leadership to iron out differences in the bill and report back a compromise bill. SELECT COMMITTEES are appointed for a specific purpose.

1. The Committees at Work: Legislation and Oversight. Every bill goes to a committee, which then has life and death power over it. Most of the more than 11,000 bills submitted by members every two years die in committee. The number is reduced to a relative few that are favorably reported for action by the whole House or Senate. Bills sent to committee go directly to a subcommittee that may have hearings on a bill and can rewrite or kill a bill.

The committees and subcommittees do not leave the scene even after legislation is passed. They engage in legislative OVERSIGHT, the process of monitoring the bureaucracy and its administration of policy. Oversight is handled mainly through hearings. Congress keeps tabs on more routine activities of the executive branch through its committee staff members. These staffers will have expertise in the specialized fields of the agencies that their committees oversee, and will maintain an extensive network of formal and informal contacts with the bureaucracy. Congress has increased its oversight activities in recent years. The larger size and complexity of the national bureaucracy and tighter budgets have provided incentive for more interest in oversight.

2. Getting on a Committee. Members seek committees that will help them achieve three goals: reelection, influence in Congress, and the opportunity to make policy in areas they think are important. Shortly after their election, new members write to their party's

congressional leadership, indicating their committee preferences. They will want something relevant to their home state or district to help with their effectiveness and reelection. The parties try to grant these requests as far as possible.

3. Getting Ahead on the Committee: Chairs and the Seniority System. COMMITTEE CHAIRS are the most important influences on the committee agenda - scheduling hearings, hiring staff, appointing subcommittees, and managing committee bills before the whole house. Until the 1970s the simple rule for picking committee chairs was the SENIORITY SYSTEM. The committee chair was that member of the majority party who had served on the committee the longest - regardless of their competence. This system decisively favored members from "safe" districts. Reforms in the 1970s modified the seniority system and took some of the powers of the committee chairs away.

D. The Mushrooming Caucuses: The Informal Organization of Congress

The informal organization of Congress - the informal networks of trust and mutual interest - can be as important as the formal structures to legislative outcomes. Lately these informal groupings have been dominated by a growing number of caucuses. A CAUCUS is a grouping of members of Congress sharing some interest or characteristic. There were more than seventy of these in the last Congress. Their goal is to shape the agenda of Congress by elevating their particular issues or interests to a prominent place. They are like interest groups made up of members of Congress. Examples include caucuses based on personal characteristics like the Black Caucus; on region like the Sunbelt Caucus; on ideology like the Moderate/Conservative Democrats; or on economic interest such as the Steel Caucus. The activities of these caucuses are directed toward their fellow members of Congress and toward administrative agencies. They press for committees to hold hearings, they push particular legislation, and they pull together votes on bills they favor.

V. The Congressional Process (437-446)

A BILL is a proposed law, drafted in precise, legal language. While only members of the House or Senate can formally submit a bill, the White House and interest groups are common sources of bills. What happens to a bill as it works its way through the legislative process is depicted in Figure 12.2 in your text. Most bills are killed off early in the process. Many are not even expected to be passed, their introduction having been a symbolic favor to a group or a constituent.

Also complicating the progress of legislation is the "rider," an amendment, typically unrelated to the bill itself, intended to be carried along on the back of another bill. This is used to attach a measure that could not pass on its own to a bill likely to pass.

Basically, Congress is a reactive and cumbersome decision-making body, whose many rules and procedures leave it open to countless external influences.

A.   Presidents and Congress: Partners and Protagonists

Presidents have their own legislative agenda. Their task is to persuade Congress that their agenda should also be Congress's. In their role as "chief legislator" presidents have many resources to influence Congress. They can try to influence members directly, by phoning wavering members, lobbying through their congressional liaison office, or by meeting with the party's congressional leadership.

Presidential leadership of Congress is normally "at the margins" in the sense that it involves being a "facilitator" of coalitions and an exploiter of opportunities, rather than a creator of entirely new political landscapes. Popular presidents or those with a large majority of their party in each house have a good chance of getting their way. Presidents are an important influence on Congress, especially on foreign policy matters, but they rarely dominate and they often lose on individual issues.

B.   Party, Constituency, and Ideology

Because parties remain while presidents come and go and constituents are more responsible for a congressperson's electoral fortunes than presidents, party and constituency are often more important influences on Congress than is the President.

1. Party Influence. On some issues, like electing congressional leadership positions, party members stick together in straight party-line votes. Differences between the parties are sharpest on questions of social welfare and economic policy. Traditionally Democrats tend to vote on the side of unions on labor issues, while Republicans favor business. On social welfare issues - poverty, unemployment aid, help for the cities - Democrats tend to be more generous with national money than Republicans.

Party leaders try to "whip" their members into line on these and other issues, but their power to do so is limited. The leadership's influence lies in its control of committee assignments, power to help with members' pet projects, and the control of some important legislative information. Recently, the parties (especially the Republicans) have become a more important source of money for congressional campaigns, as well. The rising importance of the Democratic and Republican congressional campaign committees allow party leadership to have an impact on the kinds of people who sit in Congress, and creates IOUs among those who benefit from their aid.

2. Constituency versus Ideology. Members of Congress are expected by their constituents to represent their interests in Washington. What does "representation" mean? Does it mean acting as a

"trustee," using their best judgment to make policy in the interest of the people? Or does it mean acting only as an "instructed delegate," mirroring the preferences of their constituents? Most members of Congress are "politicos," playing both roles at different times and with different issues.

The best way constituents can influence congressional voting is to elect a representative or senator who agrees with their views. Congressional candidates do take differing positions on important issues, and the winners do vote as they say they will, so voters can influence congressional policy.

If voters elect someone out of step with their thinking it may be difficult to influence their votes. It is hard for even well intentioned legislators to know what people want. Once elected, those who wish to vote in a manner out of step with the views of their constituents are still hard to defeat. Most voters do not know their representative's policy votes and even those that do know tend not to evaluate representatives on a policy basis.

On some controversial issues, however, legislators ignore constituent opinion at great peril. Legislators often will vote as "delegates" on such issues. But most issues are obscure, and on such issues legislators can safely ignore constituency opinion. On a typical issue the prime determinant of congressional member's vote is personal ideology.

C. Lobbyists and Interest Groups

Lobbyists have a dismal image, but they have a job to do - to represent the interests of their organization. In addition to being a source of campaign funds, however, they also perform the positive function of providing legislators with vital information.

Washington lobbyists can be a formidable force, but they do not hold all the high cards in their dealings with Congress. Congressmen can simply ignore them. Lobbyists are ineffective with those that oppose them, and concentrate on supporting and activating those that already are sympathetic with their interests. Members of Congress can also embarrass lobbyists by exposing heavy-handed tactics or informing an organization's members that they are being poorly represented in Washington.

Congress can also regulate lobbyists, although it has never done so very strictly. Lobbyists are regulated mainly by the 1946 Federal Regulation of Lobbying Act. Under the act paid lobbyists must register and file reports with the secretary of the Senate and the clerk of the House. These reports indicate who they are, who finances them, and what bills they are trying to pass or defeat. The theory is that making such information public will prevent shady deals and curb the influence of lobbyists. In fact, however, the law has been largely unenforceable and has limited scope because it applies only to direct contacts with Congress by those organizations whose principal activity is lobbying. These limits miss many organizations and much of the activity designed to influence legislation in Washington.

VI. Understanding Congress (446-447)

A. Congress and Democracy

In a large nation, the success of democratic government depends on the quality of representation. Some aspects of Congress make it very unrepresentative. For example, its members are an American elite and its leadership is chosen by those members not the people. Nevertheless, the evidence in this chapter demonstrates that Congress does try to listen to the American people. Members are responsive if the people make it clear what they want.

B. Reforming Congress

Reformers have tried to promote a more open, democratic Congress, and to a large degree they have succeeded.

1. Democratization. The reform movement of the 1970s tried to create more democracy by spreading power around. They got rid of the automatic and autocratic dominance of the most senior members as committee chairs. They made committee chairs elected by caucus of the majority party and weakened the power of the position of chair. As a result, subcommittees became the new centers of power in Congress.

These reforms and the proliferation of informal caucuses have greatly decentralized and fragmented power in Congress. This has opened Congress to greater interest group influence. Interest groups attach themselves to committees important to them, developing intimacy and influence with "their" committee. The committee system links policy making to the multiplicity of interests, rather than to a majority's preferences.

2. Representativeness versus Effectiveness. Supporters see Congress as a representative forum in which many interests compete for policy influence. Critics wonder if Congress is so responsive to so many interests that policy is as uncoordinated, fragmented, and decentralized as Congress itself. Agricultural committees, for example, busily tend to the interests of tobacco farmers while committees on health and welfare spend millions for lung cancer research.

In addition, some observers feel Congress is too representative - so much so that it is incapable of taking decisive action to deal with difficult problems. One reason Congress cannot balance the budget, they say, is that Congress is protecting the interests of too many people. With each interest trying to preserve the status quo, bold reforms cannot be enacted.

C. Congress and the Size of Government

If Congress is responsive to a multitude of interests and those interests desire government policies to aid them in some way, does the nature of Congress predispose it to increase the size of the public sector? Further, do the benefits of servicing constituents provide an incentive for members of Congress to tolerate, even to expand, an already big government? The more policies the more ways to help constituents. The more bureaucracies the more red tape to cut. Big government helps members of congress do the things that help them get reelected.

Government has also grown because of the responsiveness of Congress. Americans may want to balance the budget and pay low taxes, but they also support most government programs. Congress does not impose programs upon a reluctant public; instead, it responds to demands for them.

DOING RESEARCH ON CONGRESS

Congress presents a wealth of possible topics and a wealth of sources as well. One of the most obvious topics involves reforming Congress. You can look at some of the reforms of the past, or at the proposed reforms of the present. The important reforms of 1974 which brought the "subcommittee bill of rights" might be one focus. An investigation of the causes and consequences of these reforms will greatly deepen your understanding of the legislative process.

Reforms presently being proposed include most prominently suggestions to tinker with the terms of the members. One suggestion involves lengthening the terms of members of the House of Representatives from two to four years. Investigation of the sources of these suggestions and the likely consequences could make a good argumentative paper. Another good argumentative paper can be built around a reform being suggested lately that is a lot less popular with members of Congress - term limitation. Should members of Congress enjoy unlimited eligibility for reelection? What would be the effect of ten or twelve year limits on tenure? Is this a good solution to the problem of the incumbency effect, or is the cure worse than the disease? It is a hot issue right now, so most of the information you will find in recent periodicals.

Nearly all reforms are aimed at either improving the representativeness or the lawmaking effectiveness of Congress. As your text points out, however, improving one often damages the other. Complaints about the inefficiency of Congress are often related to the highly decentralized character of the legislative process. The decentralization is a reflection of Congress' effort to represent a highly diversified nation with many interests and concerns. Can congressional effectiveness and efficiency be improved without sacrificing representativeness? An interesting, text related, and challenging research question for the ambitious student of Congress.

Another area of reform involves the general question of ethics. This is also presently a hot issue in the wake of the ethics cases involving Speaker Jim Wright, Congressman Barney Frank, and the Keating Five. You might want to base a research paper on the nature of the Congress's procedures for policing ethics and the problems they pose. Alternatively you might look into one or more of these recent ethics cases, all of which deal with the difficult questions of gray areas in the law, and the fine line between ethical and unethical behavior. When a member's behavior crosses the line between representation of a constituents interests and influence peddling is a fascinating one, that some members have obviously misjudged.

Many other ideas for research on Congress can be found in the many reference sources on the institution. A useful starting point is Congressional Quarterly's Guide to Congress. It has information on the structure, origins and development, procedures, and members of Congress. Congressional Quarterly Weekly Reports is a good current guide to what is going on in Congress and the current issues and controversies. Once you have selected a topic, don't overlook your own congressional representative as a possible source. A letter to the member's local or Washington office detailing questions you wish answered or information you wish delivered will normally receive a timely response from the staff.

REVIEW TEST

Read through the Chapter Overview and review the "Reading for Content" questions if you haven't already done so. If you feel like you have achieved the learning objectives listed at the beginning of the chapter, you should be ready for the Review Test. Again, take the test as if you were taking it in class. Take your time and think carefully about your responses. Sounds stupid, but practice makes perfect.

1. The power to declare war lies with:
    (a) the Joint Chiefs of Staff
    (b) Congress
    (c) the president
    (d) the president's cabinet
Page 408
2. In 1989, _____ resigned from his post as Speaker of the House after questions of ethics tainted his office.
    (a) Tip O'Neil
    (b) Carl Albert
    (c) Jim Wright
    (d) Tom Foley
Page 410

3. Nineteenth century humorist _____ said that "it's easy to see why a man goes to the poorhouse or the penitentiary. ..he can't help it. But why he should voluntarily go live in Washington is beyond my comprehension."
   (a) Artemus Ward
   (b) H.L. Mencken
   (c) Mark Twain
   (d) Horace Greely
   Page 410

4. Perhaps the most prominent characteristic of a member of Congress' job is:
   (a) franking privileges.
   (b) travel allowances
   (c) hard work.
   (d) a lot of leisure time.
   Page 410

5. The salary for a seat in the House of Representatives is:
   (a) $24,400 a year.
   (b) $624,400 a year.
   (c) $124,400 a year.
   (d) $924,400 a year.
   Page 411

6. There are currently _____ members of the U.S. House.
   (a) 50
   (b) 100
   (c) 435
   (d) 535
   Page 412

7. The Constitution specifies that members of the House must be all of the following EXCEPT:
   (a) married.
   (b) twenty five years old.
   (c) American citizens for seven years.
   (d) residents of the states from which they are elected.
   Page 412-413

8. It is difficult for Congress to claim _____ representation, or representing constituents through mirroring their personal, politically relevant characteristics.
   (a) substantive
   (b) deceptive
   (c) descriptive
   (d) actual
   Page 414

9. As an example of substantive representation, members of Congress with a background of wealth can be champions of poor people's interests, such as:
   (a) Newt Gingrich.
   (b) Edward Kennedy.
   (c) Pat Robertson.
   (d) John Silber.
Page 414

10. The most important resource a candidate for Congress has is:
    (a) having more money than the opponent.
    (b) being photogenic.
    (c) being the incumbent.
    (d) being charismatic with audiences.
Page 414-415

11. In Gary Jacobsen's study of Congress, he found that, on the average, fewer than _____ percent of House members running for reelection are defeated in primary elections.
    (a) 2
    (b) 7
    (c) 12
    (d) 20
Page 415

12. Generally, more than _____ percent of House incumbents win.
    (a) 50
    (b) 75
    (c) 90
    (d) 98
Page 415

13. It is far easier for members of the _____ to win reelection as incumbents than it is for members of the _____.
    (a) House, Judiciary
    (b) House, Senate
    (c) Senate, House
    (d) Senate, Presidency
Page 416

14. In 1988 congressional elections, about _____ of the voters who identified with a party voted for Senate or House candidates of their own party.
    (a) 25%
    (b) 50%
    (c) 75%
    (d) 100%

15. An incumbent tarnished by scandal or corruption becomes

instantly vulnerable. Representative _____ of Georgia faced election while under indictment for involvement in a money laundering scheme.
  (a) Pat Swindall
  (b) Ben Jones
  (c) Tony Coelho
  (d) Jim Inhofe
Page 422

16. Each of the two presidential candidates in 1988 received about _____ dollars from the federal treasury.
  (a) 2 million
  (b) 17 million
  (c) 22 million
  (d) 46 million
Page 422

17. The total cost for U.S. House races in 1988 was $_____ (a) 222 million
  (b) 444 million
  (c) 567 million
  (d) 900 million
Page 422

18. The total cost for congressional elections in the 1987- 88 election cycle was $_____.
  (a) 220 million
  (b) 410 million
  (c) 5 billion
  (d) 17 billion
Page 422

19. In the late 1980's _____ contributed $1.3 million to the campaigns of five senators who, he hoped, would help avoid investigation of his failing savings and loan.
  (a) Charles Keating
  (b) Donald Trump
  (c) Neil Bush
  (d) T. Boone Pickens
Page 424

20. _____ at the Constitutional Convention created a bicameral Congress.
  (a) The First Amendment
  (b) Article II, Section 8
  (c) The Virginia Plan
  (d) The Connecticut Compromise
Page 426

21. According to the Constitution, the number of U.S. senators for

each state is determined by:
(a) two per state.
(b) one per state.
(c) population percentage.
(d) three per state.
Page 426

22. Bills are passed when:
(a) the president okays it, despite what Congress says.
(b) the Senate okays it.
(c) the House okays it.
(d) the House and Senate agree and send it to the president to be signed.
Page 426

23. A unique House committee central to agenda setting is:
(a) the Appropriations Committee.
(b) the Ways and Means Committee.
(c) the House Rules Committee.
(d) the Armed Services Committee.
Page 427

24. The Constitution's framers thought the _____ would protect elite interests against the tendency of other branches to protect the masses.
(a) House
(b) Senate
(c) Supreme Court
(d) president
Page 427

25. The _____ is the less disciplined and less centralized house.
(a) House
(b) Senate
(c) conference
(d) caucus
Page 427

26. Senator _____ once filibustered a full twenty four hours.
(a) Lyndon Johnson
(b) Robert S. Kerr
(c) Everett Dirksen
(d) J. Strom Thurmond
Page 428

27. _____, of Washington state, was elected Speaker of the House in 1989 and had been in Congress since 1964.
(a) Thomas Foley
(b) Thomas P. "Tip" O'Neil
(c) Jim Wright
(d) Carl Albert
Page 428

28. The _____, in practice, puts forth the candidate for

Speaker, which generally turns out to be a shoo-in.
(a) president
(b) full House
(c) outgoing Speaker
(d) majority party
Page 428

29. A great revolt in 1910, during the speakership of _____, whittled away many of the Speaker's powers and gave much power to committees.
(a) "Uncle" Joe Cannon
(b) "Alfalfa Bill" Murray
(c) Sam Rayburn
(d) Joe Martin
Page 429

30. The Republicans have been in the minority in the House since:
(a) 1910.
(b) 1933.
(c) 1955.
(d) 1973.
Page 429

31. A group of younger, more conservative Republicans banded together in the 1980's to make life difficult for Democrats and the House minority leader:
(a) Robert Michel.
(b) Alfonse D'Amato.
(c) Robert Dole.
(d) Alan Simpson.
Page 429

32. No Senate majority leader quite left the imprint that _____ did when he was leader from 1955 to 1961. He used his legendary "treatment" to keep his party in line and enacted many reforms in the Senate.
(a) Lyndon B. Johnson
(b) Everett M. Dirksen
(c) Mike Mansfield
(d) Barry Goldwater
Page 430

33. New bills sent to a committee typically go to:
(a) the majority whip.
(b) a joint committee.
(c) a conference committee.
(d) a subcommittee.
Page 432

34. An example of a congressional oversight would be:
(a) the Select Committee on Campaign Activities to

investigate 1972 campaign abuses.
  (b) the House Judiciary Committee's hearings on the impeachment of President Nixon.
  (c) the special joint committee investigating the 1987 Iran/Contra affair.
  (d) all answers are correct

Page 433

35. The most important influence on a committee agenda is:
  (a) the president.
  (b) the committee chair.
  (c) the Speaker of the House.
  (d) the majority leader.

Page 435

36. In the 101st Congress, there were more than _____ caucuses representing specific interests, many of them containing members from both parties and both houses of congress.
  (a) 25
  (b) 40
  (c) 70
  (d) 120

Page 437

37. Most members of Congress are thought to be _____, striving to be both representatives of the people and independent policy makers.
  (a) delegates
  (b) politicos
  (c) trustees
  (d) instructed delegates

Page 444

38. After the 1970's the new centers of power in Congress became the:
  (a) subcommittees.
  (b) select committees.
  (c) standing committees.
  (d) joint committees.

Page 448

39. The term of office for members of the U.S. House of Representatives is _____ years.
  (a) two
  (b) four
  (c) six
  (d) eight

Page 426

40. The Senate minority leader in the 101st Congress is Republican:

    (a)   Robert Dole.
    (b)   Alan Simpson.
    (c)   Robert Michel.
    (d)   Newt Gingrich.

Page 428

BEFORE GOING ON

Use the answer key below to "grade" your exam and see how you did. As always, go back and reread the relevant passages on the indicated page for any you have missed. Knowing why you missed what you missed will help you to remember the correct information.

Review Test Answers:

1: b	11: a	21: a	31: a
2: c	12: c	22: d	32: a
3: a	13: b	23: c	33: d
4: c	14: c	24: b	34: d
5: c	15: a	25: b	35: b
6: c	16: d	26: d	36: c
7: a	17: d	27: a	37: b
8: c	18: b	28: d	38: a
9: b	19: a	29: a	39: a
10: c	20: d	30: c	40: a

Take another look at the list of Key Terms on page 397. Be sure none of these terms are still a mystery to you. None of these terms are going to make you sound like a genius, but probably the most promising choice for this week is "pork barrel." This one is familiar to almost everyone but, again, it is such a deliciously graphic description of the representative function in America that it cannot be overlooked. Maybe you can ask your Senator or Representative what pork they have brought home to the barrel lately?

CHAPTER 13

THE PRESIDENCY

CHAPTER LEARNING OBJECTIVES

After reading Chapter 13, you should be able to:

1. Describe the ways an individual can become president.
2. Describe the means and justification for impeachment.
3. Describe the provisions of the 25th Amendment for succession.
4. Discuss the limits of formal constitutional powers and the informal expansion of powers by presidents over the years.
5. Describe the powers of the president as chief executive.
6. Describe the structure of the executive.
7. Discuss the president's role as chief legislator.
8. Identify the factors that contribute to presidential success in the role of chief legislator.
9. Discuss the presidents powers in national security policy.
10. Discuss the conflict between the president and Congress over the war powers.
11. Discuss the importance of public support for presidential power.
12. Describe the president's advantages in shaping public opinion.
13. Discuss the relationship of the president with the press.
14. Discuss the threat posed by executive power to democracy.
15. Discuss the impact presidents can have on the growth of government.

PRETEST QUESTIONS

The pretest below will give you an idea of the state of your knowledge about the Presidency. The questions should also help you learn what to look for while studying the text. Take the whole pretest, then check your answers against the key that follows (don't peek!). As you read the chapter, watch for where these questions are addressed (indicated after each question) so that you may learn why the answer is what it is.

1. _____ became president because Republican leaders thought he looked like one. After he died in office, he was almost everyone's choice for worst president.
   (a) Ulysses S. Grant
   (b) Warren G. Harding
   (c) Herbert Hoover
   (d) Benjamin Harrison
   Page 457

2. James David Barber has suggested that one examines presidents by looking at their:
   (a) past voting records.
   (b) early family life.
   (c) medical records and past illnesses.
   (d) presidential "character."
   Page 458

3. An example of an active-negative president, according to James David Barber, is:
   (a) Calvin Coolidge.
   (b) Franklin D. Roosevelt.
   (c) Lyndon B. Johnson.
   (d) Dwight D. Eisenhower.
   Page 459

4. The _____ Amendment, passed in 1951, limits a president to two terms in office.
   (a) Nineteenth
   (b) Twenty-first
   (c) Twenty-second
   (d) Twenty-fifth
   Page 460

5. All of the following presidents completed two full terms of office EXCEPT:
   (a) John Quincy Adams.
   (b) James Monroe.
   (c) Ronald Reagan.
   (d) Grover Cleveland.
   Page 460

6. After President _____'s debilitating stroke, almost everyone agreed that Vice-President Thomas Marshall would be a disaster as acting president so he did not assume the role.
   (a) Dwight Eisenhower
   (b) F.D. Roosevelt
   (c) William G. Harding
   (d) Woodrow Wilson
   Page 461

7. Because he was a Washington outsider, Ronald Reagan chose a Washington insider, _____, as his vice-president.
   (a) Nelson Rockefeller
   (b) Howard Baker
   (c) George Bush
   (d) Don Regan
Page 461

8. Only one president has been impeached: _____.
   (a) Andrew Johnson
   (b) Warren G. Harding
   (c) Herbert Hoover
   (d) Richard Nixon
Page 462

9. The _____ Amendment provides that if the vice-presidency becomes vacant a replacement is nominated by the president and must be approve by both houses of Congress.
   (a) Sixteenth
   (b) Nineteenth
   (c) Twenty-first
   (d) Twenty-fifth
Page 463

10. One of George Bush's former political rivals, _____, became his Secretary of Housing and Urban Development (HUD).
    (a) Robert Dole
    (b) Pierre S. "Pete" DuPont
    (c) Paul Laxalt
    (d) Jack Kemp
Page 468

11. The formal membership of the National Security Council includes all of the following position-holders EXCEPT:
    (a) the president.
    (b) the chairman of the joint chiefs of staff.
    (c) the secretary of defense.
    (d) the vice-president.
Page 469

12. President Franklin Roosevelt's aide _____ became very well known because of his importance to the president.
    (a) Colonel Edward M. House.
    (b) Sherman Adams.
    (c) Harry Hopkins.
    (d) Theodore Sorensen.
Page 472

13.   Congress can pass a vetoed law if two-thirds of _____ vote
       to override the president.
       (a)   the Senate
       (b)   the House of Representatives
       (c)   each house
       (d)   the house of Congress that sent the bill originally
Page 474

14.   Between 1953 and 1988, there were _____ years in which
       Republican presidents faced a Democratic House of
       Representatives.
       (a)   twenty-two
       (b)   sixteen
       (c)   twelve
       (d)   nine
Page 478

15.   President _____ was one of the most skilled politicians
       ever to walk the Capitol corridors. As president, he conducted
       the War on Poverty and escalated the Vietnam War (which
       eventually caused him to announce his decision not to run for
       re-election).
       (a)   Dwight D. Eisenhower
       (b)   John F. Kennedy
       (c)   Lyndon B. Johnson
       (d)   Richard M. Nixon
Page 458

16.   All of the following men were involved in the Watergate scandal
       EXCEPT:
       (a)   Spiro T. Agnew.
       (b)   H.R. "Bob" Haldemann.
       (c)   John Ehrlichman.
       (d)   G. Gordon Liddy.
Page 464

17.   The most popular president in the past twenty years, in terms
       of highest public approval rating and personal popularity: (a)
       George Bush.
       (b)   Lyndon Johnson.
       (c)   Ronald Reagan.
       (d)   Richard Nixon.
Page 490

18.   Out of concern for what was said about him in the media,
       President _____ installed a special television in the oval
       office so he could see what all three networks were saying
       about him at once.
       (a)   Lyndon Johnson
       (b)   Richard Nixon
       (c)   Jimmy Carter
       (d)   Ronald Reagan
Page 494-495

19. Andrew Johnson became president in 1865 after the assassination of President:
    (a) Zachary Taylor.
    (b) Abraham Lincoln.
    (c) William McKinley.
    (d) John F. Kennedy.
Page 461

20. _____ became president after the unexpected death of President Zachary Taylor in 1850.
    (a) James Knox Polk
    (b) John Tyler
    (c) Millard Fillmore
    (d) Andrew Johnson
Page 461

Pretest Answers:

1: b		11: b	
2: d		12: c	
3: c		13: c	
4: c		14: a	
5: a		15: c	
6: d		16: a	
7: c		17: a	
8: a		18: a	
9: d		19: b	
10: d		20: c	

READING FOR CONTENT

Listed below are sets of questions associated with the content of each major section of Chapter 13. Carefully review the questions associated with each section of the text before reading the section. Have the questions in mind as you read the section and, when you reach the end of each section, stop and see if you can answer the questions well. If not, reread the relevant paragraphs until you are sure of your response to each of the questions.

I.   The Presidents

     How much do we expect of presidents given their powers?
     How varied have been the occupants of the White House?
     In what ways do individuals come to be president?
     What roles does the vice-president play?
     What are the procedures and justifications for impeachment?
     How does the 25th Amendment provide for presidential
        succession?

II. Presidential Powers

     What are the president's Constitutional powers?

267

Chapter 13

How have individual presidents expanded these powers?

III. Running the Government: The Chief Executive

What are the president's powers and responsibilities as chief
 executive?
What is the cabinet and what does it do?
What important policy-making bodies are in the Executive
 Office of the President?
Why is the Office of Management and Budget so important?
Who makes up the White House staff?

III. Presidential Leadership of Congress: The Politics
 of Shared Powers.

What legislative powers are given to the President by the
 Constitution?
What role does party leadership play in presidential
 influence with Congress?
Why is public support such an important resource for
 presidential leadership of Congress?
What are legislative skills presidents need to lead Congress?

IV. The President and National Security Policy

What Constitutional powers make the president chief diplomat?
What prerogatives do presidents have as commander in chief of
 the armed forces?
What restrictions on the president are made by the War Powers
 Resolution?
What are the problems with the War Powers Resolution?

V. Power from the People: The Public Presidency

Why is public opinion so important for presidential power?
How do presidents go about maintaining high public approval?
What causes swings in presidential approval?
Why have presidential efforts to directly lead public opinion
 on policy matters been relatively unsuccessful?
Why is it so difficult to mobilize the public?

VI. The President and the Press

What is the usual relationship between the president and the
 press?
Who is the person who deals directly with the press for the
 president?
What is the character of most news coverage of the
 presidency?
How can it be argued that the press is biased against the
 presidency?
How can it be argued that the press is biased toward the
 presidency?

VII. Understanding the American Presidency

How can it be argued that the presidency is a threat to
    democracy?
How does the presidency affect the size of government?

CHAPTER OVERVIEW

I. Introduction (455-455)

Although presidents have vast powers, they are not as powerful as
they seem because other policy-makers have their own sources of
power. The Congress, cabinet members, private interest groups and
others have the power to resist the president's agenda and pursue
their own. Presidents operate in an environment filled with checks
and competing centers of power. Presidential power is the power to
persuade, not to command. Thus, to be effective, the president must
have highly developed political skills to mobilize influence, manage
conflict, negotiate, and fashion compromises.

II. The Presidents (455-463)

The presidency is an institution composed of the roles presidents
must play, the powers at their disposal, and the large bureaucracy
at their command. It is also a highly personal office in which the
personality of the individual occupying it makes a difference.

A. Great Expectations

Americans expect a lot of their presidents. They expect successful
policies from the Administration. The president personally should
be an extraordinary individual with an exemplary public and private
life.

Americans are of two minds about the presidency. On the one hand,
they want to believe in a powerful president, who can do good for
the country.   On the other hand, Americans do not like
concentrations of power. Perhaps as a result, though there has been
a substantial enlargement of presidential responsibilities in recent
decades, there has been no corresponding increase in presidential
power. It is in this environment of contradictory views and limited
power that the president must attempt to lead.

B. Who They Are

The Constitution requires only that the president must be a
natural-born citizen at least thirty-five years old and have resided
in the United States for at least fourteen years. In fact, all have
also been white, male, and except for John Kennedy, Protestant. In
other ways, especially in terms of social origins occupational
background, and personality, presidents have varied considerably,

however.

Political scientist James David Barber suggests that we examine presidents by looking at their "presidential character." Presidents, he claims, vary in their activity or passivity toward the job. Some working furiously (Lyndon Johnson), others taking it very easy (Calvin Coolidge). Presidents also vary in their positive or negative response to politics. Some love politics and enjoy the job (Franklin Roosevelt), others are driven only by a sense of duty and do the job relatively joylessly (Richard Nixon). Barber argues that those presidents who are both active and negative, like Lyndon Johnson and Richard Nixon, are prone to tragedy. Their psychological needs will cause them to persist in failed policies. Barber's typology is controversial, however, and there is no single answer to what makes a successful president.

C. How They Got There

1. Elections: The Normal Road to the White House. Most presidents travel to the presidency by the familiar path of running for election. They are guaranteed a four year term, and limited (by the TWENTY-SECOND AMENDMENT) to two such terms. Only nine presidents have actually served two or more successive terms in the White House.

2. The Vice-Presidency: Another Road to the White House. For more than ten percent of American history, the presidency has actually been occupied by an individual not elected to the office. One in five presidents got the job through the vice-presidency (almost one in three during the 20th century). Despite its importance, the choice of vice-presidents is usually an effort to placate some important symbolic constituency.

The occupants have rarely enjoyed the job, which consists mainly of waiting. The Constitution assigns the office the minor task of presiding over the Senate and voting in case of a tie. Recent presidents have made a greater effort to involve their vice-presidents in policy discussions and important diplomacy.

3. Impeachment and Succession. Getting rid of a discredited president before the end of a term is difficult. The Constitution provides a way to do it through IMPEACHMENT, which is roughly the equivalent of an indictment in criminal law. The House may, by majority vote, impeach the president for "Treason, Bribery, or other high Crimes and Misdemeanors." Once the House votes for impeachment, the case goes to the Senate, which tries the accused president, with the chief justice presiding. A two-thirds vote of the Senate is required for conviction and removal of the president. Only once has a president been impeached: Andrew Johnson in 1868. He escaped conviction by a single vote in the Senate. Richard Nixon escaped a certain vote of impeachment as a result of the WATERGATE scandal by resigning in 1974.

Several times a president has lain disabled, incapable of doing the job for weeks or months at a time. The TWENTY-FIFTH AMENDMENT (1967) clarified some of the Constitution's vagueness about disability. It permits the vice-president to become acting president if the vice-president and the president's cabinet determine that the president is disabled, and it outlines how a recuperated president can reclaim his powers. It also creates a means for selecting a new vice-president when the office becomes vacant. The president nominates a new vice-president, who assumes the office when both houses of Congress approve the nomination.

III. Presidential Powers (463-466)

The executive office conceived by the founders had more limited authority, fewer responsibilities, and much less organizational structure than the presidency of today.

A. Constitutional Powers

The Constitution says remarkably little about presidential power. The office is granted the "executive power" and lists just a few specific powers. There is little presidents can do on their own - they share executive, legislative, and judicial power with the other branches of government.

B. The expansion of Power

The role of the president has changed as America increased in prominence on the world stage and technology has also reshaped the presidency. Presidents themselves have taken the initiative in developing new roles for the office. Strong and activist presidents, like Thomas Jefferson, Andrew Jackson, Abraham Lincoln, Theodore Roosevelt, Woodrow Wilson, and Franklin Roosevelt enlarged the power of the presidency by expanding the president's responsibilities and political resources.

IV. Running The Government: The Chief Executive (466-473)

The Constitution charges the president to "take care that the laws be faithfully executed." Today this involves overseeing a sprawling bureaucracy that spends more than one trillion dollars a year. One resource the president has for controlling this bureaucracy is the power to appoint top-level administrators. Presidents also have the power to recommend agency budgets to Congress.

A. The Cabinet

Although the group of presidential advisors known as the CABINET is not mentioned in the Constitution, every president has had one. It is not a collective board of directors - decisions remain in the president's hands alone. The cabinet has changed in size and composition over the years, and presidents compose and use the

cabinet in different ways. Though subject to Senate approval,
presidents are usually granted considerable latitude in appointing
their trusted close political associates to these positions.

B. The Executive Office

The Executive Office of the President is a loose collection of
offices and organizations designed to serve the president. Three
major policy-making bodies are in the Executive Office. The
NATIONAL SECURITY COUNCIL (NSC) is the committee that links the
president's key foreign and military policy advisors. The COUNCIL
OF ECONOMIC ADVISORS (CEA) has three members appointed by the
president. They help the president make policy on economic matters.
The OFFICE OF MANAGEMENT AND BUDGET (OMB) is responsible for
preparing the president's budget. The OMB reviews and assesses all
the budgetary requests coming from the executive agencies, and
advises the president on their consistency with the president's
overall program.

C. The White House Staff

The White House staff consists of the key aides the president sees
daily - the chief of staff, congressional liaison people, press
secretary, national security advisor, and a few other administrative
and political assistants. Top aides in the White House hierarchy
are completely loyal to the president, and presidents rely heavily
on them for information, policy options, and analysis. This does
not absolve the president from responsibility, however. The
president sets the tone for the White House staff, and must demand
quality staff work to avoid policy mistakes and embarrassments.

V.   Presidential Leadership Of Congress:
The Politics Of Shared Powers (473-483)

Since the American system of separation of powers is actually one of
shared powers, if presidents are to succeed they must try to lead
the legislature to support their initiatives.

A. Chief Legislator

The president is required to give a State of the Union Address to
Congress and has the power to VETO congressional legislation. Once
Congress passes a bill the president may 1) sign it, making it law;
2) veto it, sending it back to Congress with the reasons for its
rejection; or 3) let it become law in 10 working days without a
signature. If Congress adjourns within ten days after submitting a
bill, the president can let it die by neither signing nor vetoing
it. This is called a POCKET VETO.

Congress can pass a vetoed law if two-thirds of each house vote to
override the president's veto. Only about 4 percent of all vetoed
bills have been overridden by Congress, however. Thus, even the

threat of a veto is an effective tool for persuading congress to respect a president's views. The veto is a blunt instrument, however. A president must sign or veto a bill in its entirety; they cannot select out objectionable parts for veto. Thus objectionable provisions must often be accepted to get those that are desired. Nor can this negative power resource accomplish the Administration's positive legislative goals.

B. Party Leadership

Presidents are highly dependent upon their party to move their legislative programs.

1. The Bonds of Party. For most senators and representatives, being in the same political party as the president creates a psychological bond to the president. They also desire to see the president's administration succeed because its failure might damage their chances for reelection.

2. Slippage in Party Support. Despite the pull of party ties, all presidents experience substantial slippage in the support of their party in Congress. Presidents usually can count on their own party member's support no more than two-thirds of the time. Presidents are forced to be active in party leadership and devote effort to converting even fellow partisans on policy matters. The diversity of policy positions often reflect the diversity of constituencies the party members represent. If the president is not popular in their constituencies, congressional party members may avoid identifying too closely with the White House.

3. Leading the Party. The president has some assets as party leader, including congressional party leaders, services and amenities for party members, and campaign aid. Each is of limited utility, however. Party leaders are predisposed to support the president, but are relatively weak in influencing members themselves. The president also controls many amenities and services, ranging from photos with the president to rides on Air Force One. The impact such favors have on congressional position holding is very questionable, however. Finally, there are the PRESIDENTIAL COATTAILS, a term that refers to voters casting their ballots for congressional candidates of the president's party because they support the president. Most recent studies show a diminishing connection between presidential and congressional voting, however, and few congressional races are determined by coattails. To add to these burdens the president's party has often lacked majorities in one or both houses of Congress in recent years. The president then must seek support from the opposition party to marshall the required majorities.

C. Public Support

One of the president's most important resources for leading Congress is public support.

1. Public Approval. Public approval makes the president's leadership resources more efficacious. If the president is high in the public's esteem, the president's party is more likely to be responsive (because supporting the president may help with reelection), the public is more easily moved, and legislative skills become more effective. Thus members of Congress will watch the president's standing in the polls as an indicator of the ability of the president to mobilize public opinion against presidential opponents. Public approval gives the president leverage, but not control.

2. Mandates. An electoral mandate accords added legitimacy and credibility to the newly elected president's proposals. Merely winning an election does not provide a mandate, however. Even winning by a large margin is no guarantee that Congress will interpret the results as a mandate to support the president's programs. The programs may not have been an issue in the campaign, or the people may also have elected majorities of the other party to the House and Senate, for example.

D.   Legislative Skills

Presidential legislative skills include bargaining, making personal appeals, consulting with Congress, setting priorities, exploiting "honeymoon" periods, and structuring congressional votes. Bargaining may take the form of trading support on policies, but it will be focused on a few key members of Congress whose support will have the greatest impact. A president is also wise to send legislation to the Hill early in the first year in office, to take strategic advantage of the goodwill that typically characterizes this "honeymoon" period. Presidents must also carefully establish priorities among their legislative proposals. They will have political resources to be fully effective on only a few bills at a time, thus it is sensible to focus on a limited number of really important issues.

VI. The President And National Security Policy (483-488)

Constitutionally, the president has the leading role in American defense and foreign policy.

A. Chief Diplomat

The president alone extends and terminates diplomatic recognition with foreign governments. The president also has the sole power to negotiate treaties with other nations (though ratification requires a two-thirds vote of the Senate). As the leader of the Western world, the president must try to lead America's allies on matters of both economics and defense. Presidents also help settle disputes among other nations in their diplomatic role.

B. Commander in Chief

The Constitution provides for civilian control of the military by making the president the commander in chief of the armed forces. When the Constitution was written, the United States did not have, nor expected to have, a large standing or permanent army. Today the president is commander in chief of two million uniformed men and women. His ability to "command" them can raise controversy in regard to the Congress's power to declare war.

C. War Powers

Though charged by the Constitution with declaring war and voting on the military budget, Congress long ago became accustomed to presidents making short-term military commitments of troops or navel vessels. Since World War II, however, Presidents have made long-term commitments of large forces in Korea and Vietnam with little attention to constitutional niceties.

In response, Congress passed the WAR POWERS RESOLUTION (1973) intended to give Congress a greater voice in the introduction of American troops into hostilities. It required presidents to consult with Congress, whenever possible, prior to using military force, and it mandated the withdrawal of forces after sixty days unless Congress declared war or granted an extension. Congress could at any time pass a concurrent resolution (which could not be vetoed) ending American participation in hostilities.

The War Powers Resolution cannot be deemed a success, however. There is reason to believe the Supreme Court would consider the law's use of the LEGISLATIVE VETO to end American involvement in fighting a violation of the separation of powers. Presidents have felt it to be an unconstitutional infringement on their powers, and have ignored its provisions in many instances.

The relevance of our two-hundred year old constitutional mechanisms for engaging in war are at issue. Modern technology allows the president to engage in hostilities so quickly that opposing points of view do not receive proper consideration, undermining the separation of powers. On the other hand, it is vital for the commander in chief to have the flexibility to meet America's global responsibilities and combat international terrorism without unnecessary hindrances and checks.

D. Crisis Manager

A CRISIS is a sudden, unpredictable, and potentially dangerous event. Most occur in the realm of foreign policy. Crises put a premium on rapid action, secrecy, constant management, consistent judgment, and expert advice. As a result, the president, who can come to quick and consistent decisions, confine information to a small group, carefully oversee developments, and call upon experts in the executive branch, has become more prominent than Congress in handling crises.

E. Working with Congress

In recent years Congress has challenged presidents on many national security issues. Congress has a central constitutional role in making national security policy, although this role is often misunderstood. The allocation of responsibilities for such matters is intended to prevent the concentration and subsequent potential for abuse of power. Congress's role has typically been oversight of the executive rather than initiation of policy. Presidents are not accorded automatic support on national security policy, but they usually end up obtaining much, often most, of what they request from Congress in this issue area.

VII.   Power From The People: The Public Presidency (488-494)

Because presidents are rarely in a position to command others to comply with their wishes, they must rely on persuasion. Public support is perhaps the greatest source of influence a president has, for it is difficult for other power holders to deny the legitimate demands of a president who has popular backing.

A. Going Public

Presidents are not passive followers of public opinion. The White House is a virtual whirlwind of public relations activity - educating, persuading and mobilizing public opinion. Often the president's appearances are staged purely to obtain the public's attention. The president's ceremonial role as "head of state" - including such activities as tossing out the season's first baseball or lighting the national Christmas tree - provide opportunities for building public support. Ceremonial activities give them an important symbolic aura and a great deal of favorable press coverage, contributing to their public support.

B. Presidential Approval

Much of the energy the White House devotes to public relations is aimed at increasing the president's public approval. Because of the connection between public support and presidential influence, the president's standing in the polls is monitored closely by the press, members of Congress, and others in Washington.

Presidential approval is the product of many factors. At the base is the predisposition of many people (especially the president's partisan identifiers) to support the president. Changes in approval levels appear to be due primarily to the public's evaluation of how the president is handling policy areas such as the economy, war, energy, and foreign affairs. Job-related personal characteristics, such as integrity and leadership skills, also play an important role in influencing presidential approval.

Sometimes the presidential approval rate takes a sudden jump. One explanation is "rally events" that relate to international relations, directly involve the United States and the president, and are specific, dramatic, and sharply focused. Such occurrences are rare and isolated, and they have little enduring impact on a president's public approval.

C. Policy Support

Commentators on the presidency often refer to it as a "bully pulpit," implying that presidents can persuade and mobilize the public to support their policies if they are skilled communicators. Despite their efforts and that of their staff aids, however, presidential speeches aimed at directly leading public opinion have typically been rather unimpressive. Only Franklin Roosevelt, John Kennedy, and Ronald Reagan have been effective speakers in the modern era.

Moreover, the public is not always receptive to the president's message. Absent a crisis, which is (fortunately) most of the time, people are not terribly interested or attentive to policy matters. Even Ronald Reagan, an effective communicator who tried to influence opinion on behalf of such policies as deregulation, decreased domestic spending and increased military spending, had little impact. Support for such regulatory programs as health care, education, and environmental protection actually increased.

D. Mobilizing the Public

Sometimes the president wants not only to change public opinion, but to mobilize the public to communicate its views directly to Congress. It is a potent potential weapon for the president, for when the people speak directly to Congress it listens attentively. It is difficult, however, for it involves the double burden of obtaining both opinion support and political action from a generally inattentive and apathetic public. It is risky as well, because if the attempt fails, the lack of response will send a clear message to Congress. Because of these difficulties and risks it has rarely been successfully used.

VIII. The President And The Press (494-497)

It is the media that provides people with most of what they know about chief executives and their policies. The media also interprets and analyses presidential activities. As the principal intermediary between the president and the public, relations with the press are an important aspect of the president's efforts to lead public opinion.

No matter who is in the White House or who reports on presidential activities, presidents and the press tend to be in conflict. Presidents want to control the amount and timing of information about their administration, whereas the press want all the information that exists immediately.

The White House monitors the press closely. About one-third of the high-level White House staff members are directly involved in media relations of one type or another. The person who most often deals directly with the press in the president's PRESS SECRETARY, who serves as a daily and routine conduit of information from the White House to the press. The most dramatic direct interaction between the president and the press is the presidential press conference. Despite their visibility, press conferences are not very useful means of eliciting information because presidents tend to anticipate questions and prepare carefully limited answers.
Most of the news coverage of the White House comes under the heading of "body watch" - that is, reporters focus on the most visible layer of presidents' personal and official activities and provide step-by-step accounts. Many feel that there is bias in media coverage, but studies show no systematic bias toward a particular person, party, or ideology. Some feel news coverage of the presidency often tends to emphasize the negative. Others argue that the press is inherently biased in favor of the White House because the president is typically portrayed with an aura of dignity and treated with deference.

IX. Understanding The American Presidency (497-499)

A. The Presidency and Democracy

From the time the Constitution was written there was a fear that the presidency would become too powerful. Still, we look for and favor presidents who are strong leaders. Concern about whether the presidency is too strong has waxed and waned throughout history. Such concerns are generally closely related to policy views. Those who oppose the president's policies are the most likely to be concerned about too much presidential power. Other than acting outside the law and the Constitution, there is little prospect of the presidency becoming a threat to democracy.

B. The Presidency and the Size of Government

Some of the most noteworthy presidents in the twentieth century (including Theodore Roosevelt, Woodrow Wilson, and Franklin Roosevelt) have successfully advocated substantial increases in the role of the national government. Supporting an increased role for government is not inherent in the presidency, however. All five of the presidents since Lyndon Johnson have championed constraints on government and limits on spending.
DOING RESEARCH ON THE PRESIDENCY

The president and presidency is always a favorite topic for research papers. The focal point of American politics, a great deal has been written about the presidency and presidential power. You may wish to select a particular president and investigate various aspects of his administration. A president's decision making style can be explored, for example, or compared with that of another. President Kennedy's handling of the Cuban Missile Crisis illustrates his approach to making decisions, and has been the focus of a great deal of literature. A great deal has also been written about the "hands-on" decision making style of Jimmy Carter as opposed to the remote "chairman-of-the-board" style of Ronald Reagan. A paper could examine the two and discuss the advantages and disadvantages of each.

As pointed out in the text, the powers of the president have grown beyond what was indicated in the Constitution. A paper could, after identifying the limited powers granted by the Constitution, trace the process of growth in power. Which presidents expanded these powers, how was it done and for what reasons? In light of your findings, you may wish to conclude with an argument that the powers of the presidency are, or are not, appropriate for the modern American governmental system.

Another interesting research project would be to compare the issue positions of a president as candidate with their activities as president. Look at the party platforms and election issues of a recent president, and compare these the policy efforts made by the president in office. The former can be found by carefully looking at the journalistic accounts of the campaign and in the platform reprinted in the <u>New York Times</u> shortly after the convention. The president's effort can be assessed in the same sources, of course, but can be supplemented as well by looking in the <u>Weekly Compilation of Presidential Documents</u> published by the <u>Federal Register</u>. You may wish to limit your inquiry to just one or two major issues. Your findings may surprise you about the nature of campaign promises.

REVIEW TEST

Read through the Chapter Overview and review the "Reading for Content" questions if you haven't already done so. If you feel like you have achieved the learning objectives listed at the beginning of the chapter, you should be ready for the Review Test. Again, take the test as if you were taking it in class. Keep going over the Review Tests until you know them all - and know why the answers are correct. They are good preparation for exams.

1. As Richard Neustadt has argued, the main source of a president's power is in his:

     (a)   power to persuade.
     (b)   constitutional powers.
     (c)   charisma.
     (d)   electoral mandate.
Page 455

2. When President Bush, or any president in the past, took the oath of office, the most daunting task before him was:
     (a)   the economy.
     (b)   living up to the expectations of the American people.
     (c)   a "do-nothing" Congress.
     (d)   the military complex.
Page 456

3. A famous presidential motto was captured in the sign that President _____ had on his desk: "The buck stops here."
     (a)   Franklin D. Roosevelt
     (b)   Dwight D. Eisenhower
     (c)   Harry S Truman
     (d)   Lyndon B. Johnson
Page 457

4. _____ was the only political scientist to become president and combined a Presbyterian moral fervor with a professor's intimidating style of leadership and speech making.
     (a)   Theodore Roosevelt
     (b)   Grover Cleveland
     (c)   Woodrow Wilson
     (d)   Jimmy Carter
Page 457

5. An example of an active-positive president, according to James David Barber is:
     (a)   Calvin Coolidge.
     (b)   Franklin D. Roosevelt.
     (c)   Lyndon B. Johnson.
     (d)   Richard Nixon.
Page 458-459

6. Once in office, presidents are guaranteed a _____ year term.
     (a)   two
     (b)   four
     (c)   six
     (d)   eight
Page 460

7. Only _____ of the thirty four presidents before George Bush have actually served two or more full terms in the White House.

(a) five
(b) nine
(c) seventeen
(d) twenty
Page 460

8. All of the following presidents served two or more full terms
    EXCEPT:
    (a) Franklin D. Roosevelt.
    (b) Ulysses S. Grant.
    (c) Thomas Jefferson.
    (d) Theodore Roosevelt.
Page 460

9. All of the following presidents attempted reelection but were
    defeated at the polls and served only one term EXCEPT:
    (a) Jimmy Carter.
    (b) Herbert Hoover.
    (c) Calvin Coolidge.
    (d) Martin Van Buren.
Page 460

10. Gerald Ford was nominated vice-president by President
    Nixon when Vice-President _____ resigned.
    (a) John C. Calhoun
    (b) Spiro T. Agnew
    (c) Nelson A. Rockefeller
    (d) Robert Dole
Page 461

11. _____, one of Franklin Roosevelt's vice-presidents, said
    the vice-presidency was "not worth a warm bucket of spit."
    (a) Harry S Truman
    (b) Henry A. Wallace
    (c) John Nance Garner
    (d) Alben W. Barkley
Page 461

12. Jimmy Carter was an outsider to Washington so he chose a
    vice-president, _____, with substantial Washington
    experience.
    (a) Geraldine Ferraro
    (b) Walter Mondale
    (c) Hubert Humphrey
    (d) George McGovern
Page 461

13. When his turn came to choose a vice-president, George Bush
    chose _____, who maintained a low profile while performing
    his duties after the 1988 election.

(a)   Pete Dominici
(b)   Robert Dole
(c)   Jack Kemp
(d)   Dan Quayle
Page 462

14.   If a president is impeached, the case goes to the _____, which tries the accused president with the chief justice presiding.
(a)   Supreme Court
(b)   combined Congress
(c)   Senate
(d)   House of Representatives
Page 462

15.   After President _____ suffered a stroke, his wife became virtual acting president.
(a)   John Adams
(b)   William Henry Harrison
(c)   James A. Garfield
(d)   Woodrow Wilson
Page 463

16.   The person in line after the president, in the event of death or disability, is the:
(a)   Speaker of the House.
(b)   vice-president.
(c)   Senate president pro tempore.
(d)   Secretary of State.
Page 463

17.   Of the Constitutional framers, _____ of Pennsylvania argued that only a single individual could combine the necessary characteristics of "energy, dispatch and responsibility." His argument led to a one-person presidency.
(a)   Alexander Hamilton
(b)   James Wilson
(c)   Eldridge Gerry
(d)   Thomas Jefferson
Page 463

18.   President Nixon was almost impeached and had to resign because of his involvement in:
(a)   the Vietnam War.
(b)   the Watergate scandal.
(c)   the invasion of Cambodia.
(d)   the "Christmas" bombing of Hanoi.
Page 464

19.   The federal bureaucracy spends more than $_____ a year.
(a)   one trillion
(b)   500 billion
(c)   50 billion

(d)   1 billion
Page 467

20. In George Washington's day, the cabinet consisted of three secretaries and the attorney general. Today, the cabinet consists of _____ secretaries and the attorney general.
(a)   25
(b)   13
(c)   10
(d)   7
Page 468

21. George Bush appointed _____ to be his secretary of state.
(a)   Richard Cheney
(b)   Caspar Weinberger
(c)   James A. Baker III
(d)   Brent Scowcroft
Page 468

22. President Bush met resistance when he nominated _____, to be Secretary of Defense. He was rejected by the Senate.
(a)   John Tower
(b)   Richard Cheney
(c)   Robert Bork
(d)   James Baker III
Page 468

23. The Executive Office of the President was established by:
(a)   Theodore Roosevelt.
(b)   Woodrow Wilson.
(c)   Franklin Roosevelt.
(d)   Dwight Eisenhower.
Page 469

24. The Office of Management and Budget grew out of the Bureau of the Budget (created in _____).
(a)   1921
(b)   1877
(c)   1825
(d)   1801
Page 470

25. President _____ changed the Bureau of the Budget to the Office of Management and Budget, giving it management duties. (a) Woodrow Wilson
(b)   F.D. Roosevelt
(c)   John F. Kennedy
(d)   Richard Nixon
Page 470

26. The White House staff include all of the following EXCEPT:
(a)   the chief of staff.
(b)   the national security advisor.
(c)   the press secretary.

(d)   the vice-president.
Page 471

27.   President Woodrow Wilson's well known chief advisor was:
      (a)   Colonel Edward M. House.
      (b)   Harry Hopkins.
      (c)   Hamilton Jordan.
      (d)   Sherman Adams.
Page 472

28.   All of the following men were important influences on President
      Reagan's presidency EXCEPT:
      (a)   James Baker III.
      (b)   Edwin Meese.
      (c)   Michael Deaver.
      (d)   Jody Powell.
Page 472

29.   About _____ percent of all vetoed bills since the nation's
      founding have been overridden by Congress.
      (a)   four
      (b)   fifteen
      (c)   twenty-two
      (d)   thirty
Page 475

30.   According to the text a president's three most useful resources
      include all of the following EXCEPT:
      (a)   their party leadership.
      (b)   their electoral mandate.
      (c)   public support.
      (d)   their own legislative skills.
Page 475

31.   Presidents can count on their own party members for support
      about _____ of the time.
      (a)   90%
      (b)   three-fourths
      (c)   one-third
      (d)   two-thirds
Page 476

32.   The frequent defection by _____ from support for presidents of
      their party is a prominent feature of American politics.
      (a)   Southern Democrats
      (b)   Liberal Republicans
      (c)   Northern Democrats
      (d)   West Coast moderate Democrats
Page 477

33.   Between 1953 and 1988, there were _____ years in which a
      Republican president faced a Democratic Senate.
      (a)   twenty-two
      (b)   sixteen

(c) twelve
(d) nine
Page 478

34. _____ operates mostly in the background and sets the limits of what Congress will and won't do for the president.
    (a) The Bureaucracy
    (b) The White House staff
    (c) The Cabinet
    (d) Public approval
Page 480

35. President _____ reestablished American links with China.
    (a) Dwight D. Eisenhower
    (b) John F. Kennedy
    (c) Lyndon B. Johnson
    (d) Richard Nixon
Page 459

36. From 1953 to 1990, President _____ held the record of the most vetoes -- 73, with only 2 being overridden.
    (a) Eisenhower
    (b) Johnson
    (c) Ford
    (d) Reagan
Page 475

37. Treaties are approved when:
    (a) the president signs them.
    (b) the House approves them with a two-thirds vote.
    (c) the Senate approves them with a two-thirds vote.
    (d) the whole Congress approves them with a two thirds vote.
Page 483

38. The Constitution states that only _____ can declare war.
    (a) the president
    (b) the Senate
    (c) Congress
    (d) the House of Representatives
Page 485

39. President _____ was responsible for ordering the invasion of Grenada, the settlement of troops in Beirut and the bombing of Libya during his presidency.
    (a) Gerald Ford
    (b) Richard Nixon
    (c) Jimmy Carter
    (d) Ronald Reagan
Page 485

40. Chester Alan Arthur became president after the assassination of President:
    (a) Abraham Lincoln.
    (b) William McKinley.

    (c)   James A. Garfield.
    (d)   Warren G. Harding.
Page 461

BEFORE GOING ON

Use the answer key below to "grade" your exam and see how you did. Be sure to, go back and reread the relevant passages on the indicated page for any you have missed. If you were sort of "asleep" when you read that passage, there may be something else you missed there as well.

Review Test Answers:

1: a	11: c	21: c	31: d
2: b	12: b	22: a	32: a
3: c	13: d	23: c	33: b
4: c	14: c	24: a	34: d
5: b	15: d	25: d	35: d
6: b	16: b	26: d	36: a
7: b	17: b	27: a	37: c
8: d	18: b	28: d	38: c
9: c	19: a	29: a	39: d
10: b	20: b	30: b	40: c

The Key Terms (that I know you are reviewing) on page 500 don't include James David Barber's presidential character types, mentioned briefly on page 458. Barber's book, listed in the For Further Reading section, is an entertaining, though methodologically controversial, look at past presidents. It comes with my recommendation if you are interested. The dimensions and categories of his typology of character can be applied to your attitude and approach to your work as well as that of the presidents to theirs. Are you an active-positive student? I think most of us aren't, unfortunately. You may wish to keep these categories in mind when selecting a career - try to pick something in which you can be an active-positive. Not only will you likely be more successful, but you'll certainly be happier. Though important to know, I don't think any of these terms have any street value, so I'm skipping the term of the week this week.

CHAPTER 14

CONGRESS, THE PRESIDENT, AND THE BUDGET: THE POLITICS OF TAXING AND SPENDING

CHAPTER LEARNING OBJECTIVES

After reading Chapter 14, you should be able to:

1. Compare the size of government in America to that in other nations.
2. Describe the rise of the social welfare state.
3. Describe the rise of the national security state.
4. Identify the players and strategies of budgetary politics.
5. Discuss the role of the president and the Congress in the budgetary process.
6. Identify the sources of government revenues.
7. Identify the general sites of government spending.
8. Describe the spending and appropriations processes.
9. Explain why much of the governments expenditures are considered "uncontrollable."
10. Explain the possible link between democratic politics and budgetary politics.

PRETEST QUESTIONS

The pretest below will give you an idea of the state of your knowledge about the politics of taxing and spending. The questions should also help you learn what to look for while studying the text. Take the whole pretest, then check your answers against the key that follows (don't peek!). As you read the chapter, watch for where these questions are addressed (indicated after each question) so that you may learn why the answer is what it is.

1. About _____ percent of all budget expenditures go to paying just the interest on the national debt.
   (a) four
   (b) eight
   (c) fourteen
   (d) twenty-two
Page 505

2. The national government alone spends about _____ percent of

the Gross National Product (GNP).
(a) 15
(b) 23
(c) 52
(d) 76
Page 507

3. In 1940, the Social Security system was financed with a _____ percent tax on payrolls.
(a) 3
(b) 5
(c) 7
(d) 12
Page 508

4. The final decisions on what to propose to Congress lie with:
(a) the Office of Management and Budget.
(b) the Senate Appropriations Committee.
(c) the president.
(d) the House Budget Committee.
Page 515

5. The _____ sets the parameters of the congressional budget process - examining overall revenues and expenditures and proposing resolutions binding Congress to certain limits.
(a) Congressional Budget Office
(b) Senate Budget Committee
(c) House Budget Committee
(d) all answers are correct
Page 515

6. All these have major roles in the budgetary process EXCEPT:
(a) the Senate Budget Committee.
(b) the House Ways and Means Committee.
(c) the Senate Finance Committee.
(d) the Treasury Department.
Page 515

7. Until _____, the various agencies of the executive branch sent their budget requests to the secretary of the treasury, who in turn forwarded them to the Congress.
(a) 1865
(b) 1897
(c) 1921
(d) 1945
Page 516

8. The president must submit a budget on the fifteenth day of the

new congressional session. Preparation of the presidential budget is begun by the OMB:
(a) almost a month before.
(b) about six months before.
(c) almost a year before.
(d) more than two years before.
Page 516

9. For years, Congress budgeted in a piecemeal fashion. Each agency request was handled by:
(a) the Secretary of the Treasury.
(b) the House Appropriations Committee.
(c) a subcommittee of the House and Senate Appropriations Committees.
(d) the Senate Appropriations Committee.
Page 518

10. By _____, Congress is to agree on the total size of the budget, which guides the Appropriations Committees in juggling figures for the individual agencies.
(a) April 15
(b) June 15
(c) August 15
(d) October 15
Page 518

11. The _____ advises Congress on the likely consequences of its budget decisions, forecasts revenues, and is a counterweight to the president's OMB.
(a) Congressional Budget Office
(b) General Accounting Office
(c) Treasury Department
(d) Senate Finance Committee
Page 518

12. Appropriations bills usually cover _____ and cannot exceed the money authorized for a program.
(a) five years
(b) three years
(c) eighteen months
(d) one year
Page 520

13. In _____, appropriations bills were lumped together in one enormous and complex bill rather than the thirteen separate appropriations bills that are supposed to pass.
(a) 1974
(b) 1981
(c) 1984
(d) 1987
Page 520

14. In 1989, automatic cuts went into effect for several weeks at

the end of the year until Congress and the president could agree on a budget. This was because of the cuts mandated by the _____ Act of 1985.
(a)   Congressional Budget and Impoundment
(b)   Congressional Election Reform
(c)   Gramm-Rudman-Hollings
(d)   Pendleton
Page 520

15.   Every American taxpayer must mail their income tax forms to the government by midnight every:
(a)   January 1.
(b)   April 15.
(c)   September 15.
(d)   October 1.
Page 523

16.   In _____, the Sixteenth Amendment was added, explicitly permitting Congress to levy an income tax.
(a)   1865
(b)   1894
(c)   1915
(d)   1934
Page 523

17.   In 1990, the government in Washington estimated that it would collect $_____ in Social Security taxes out of nearly $1.1 trillion collected in taxes altogether.
(a)   900 billion
(b)   565 billion
(c)   385 billion
(d)   105 billion
Page 523-524

18.   When President Reagan took office in 1981, the federal debt was about _____ percent of the GNP.
(a)   12
(b)   34
(c)   52
(d)   75
Page 525

19.   President _____ was elected on a platform that endorsed the Kemp-Roth bill, which favored cutting federal income taxes, and proceeded to incorporate elements of the bill into his administration's actions.
(a)   Gerald Ford
(b)   Jimmy Carter
(c)   Ronald Reagan
(d)   Richard Nixon
Page 528

20.   The federal budget document estimates that fully _____ of the

federal budget is uncontrollable.
- (a)   one-third
- (b)   one-fourth
- (c)   one half
- (d)   three-fourths

Page 536

Pretest Answers:

1: c	11: a
2: b	12: d
3: a	13: d
4: c	14: c
5: d	15: b
6: d	16: c
7: c	17: c
8: c	18: b
9: c	19: c
10: a	20: d

READING FOR CONTENT

Listed below are sets of questions associated with the content of each major section of Chapter 14. Carefully review the questions associated with each section of the text before reading the section. Have the questions in mind as you read the section and, when you reach the end of each section, stop and see if you can answer the questions well. If not, reread the relevant paragraphs until you are sure of your response to each of the questions.

I.   Big Governments, Big Budgets

What is the size of the American public sector compared to that of other nations?
What are the major milestones in the rise of the social welfare state?
What are the major milestones in the rise of the national security state?

II. The Budgetary Process

What are the states and strategies of budgetary politics?
Who are the major players in budgetary politics?
How does the budget process in the executive work?
What have been the major reforms of the congressional budget process?
What are the major steps in the present congressional budget process?

III. The Budget: Where it Comes From and Where it Goes

291

What are the principal sources of government revenues?
What are the problems involved with each of the sources of
government revenues?
What are tax expenditures and who do they generally benefit?
What are the trends in government spending?
What is incrementalism and its implications for the budget
process?
What are uncontrollable expenditures and entitlements?

IV. Understanding Budgeting

What is the relationship between democracy and the process of
budget-making?
How can budget realities limit the size of government?

CHAPTER OVERVIEW

I. Introduction   (504-505)

Every year the Congress and the president must produce a budget. The
budget outlines what government will spend money for and how much.
The central political issue in recent years has been how to pay for
what the government does.   The president and Congress have been
caught in a budgetary squeeze.   A budget DEFICIT occurs when
EXPENDITURES exceed REVENUES. The total of the yearly deficits, the
national debt, rose sharply during the 1980s, from less than one
trillion dollars to over three trillion dollars by 1990. Americans
want to balance the budget, maintain or increase government spending
on most policies and keep taxes low.   The president and Congress are
preoccupied trying to cope with these contradictory budgetary
demands.

II. Big Governments, Big Budgets (505-512)

Among Western nations, America has one of the smallest public
sectors relative to the size of the GNP.   Nevertheless, with a
budget of $1.2 trillion per year, it is difficult to characterize
the national government as anything by large.   The growth of
government in the United States, as elsewhere, has been dramatic.

A principal reason that government grows is in response to changes
in the public's preferences as well as changes in economic and
social conditions that affect the public's level of demand for
governmental activity.   This is why the rise of big government has
been so resistant to reversal: citizens like government services.

A. The Rise of the Social Service State

The rise of the social service state in the United States dates from
the passage of the SOCIAL SECURITY ACT in 1935.   The act was
intended to provide a minimal level of sustenance to older Americans

and thus to save them from poverty. In the 1950s disability insurance was included in the Social Security program, allowing workers who had not retired but who were disabled to collect benefits. In 1965, MEDICARE was added to the system, which provides both hospital and physician coverage to retirees and to some poor persons. Social security has slowly become the most expensive public policy in the world.

Social security is not, of course, the only social policy of the federal government that costs money. In health, education, job training, and many other areas, the rise of the social service state has contributed to America's growing budget. Liberals often favor such programs to assist individuals and groups in society; conservatives see them as a drain on the federal treasury.

B. The Rise of the National Security State

Before World War II, the United States largely disbanded its military forces at the end of wars. Since World War II, however, the "cold war" with the Soviet Union has resulted in a permanent military establishment and expensive military technology. Fueling the military machine has greatly increased the cost of government. Payrolls and pensions constitute a large component of the defense budget. The greatest expenditure of defense funds, however, is for research, development, and procurement of military hardware. The costs of military procurement in this age of high tech are great, even though total military expenditures have declined as a percentage of American GNP since the end of World War II. While American social services have expanded less than such services in Western European nations, American military expenditures have expanded more rapidly than in these nations.

III. The Budgetary Process (512-522)

There is more to public budgets than bookkeeping because such a BUDGET is a policy document allocating burdens (taxes) and benefits (expenditures). Thus budgeting is concerned with translating financial resources into human purposes - a series of goals with price tags attached.

A. Budgetary Politics

Public budgets are the supreme example of Harold Lasswell's definition of politics as "who gets what, when, and how."

1. Stakes and Strategies. Every political actor has a stake in the budget. Mayors want federal grants-in-aid; defense contractors want big defense budgets; agencies within the government also work to protect their interests, etc. You can think of budgetary politics as resembling a game in which players choose among strategies. Agencies pad their budget requests and interest groups try to link their demands to the national interest, for example. All the

players have their own strategies in the game of budgetary politics, and in the pluralistic politics of budget making, there are plenty of players.

2. The Players. The main actors in the budgetary process include: 1) The interest groups - lobbyists focus on agencies, congressional committees and even presidents; 2) The agencies - convinced of the importance of their mission they push for higher allocations; 3) The Office of Management and Budget (OMB) - influence on agency distributions make them major actors in the process; 4) The president - makes final decisions on what to propose to Congress and thus sets the agenda for discussion; 5) The tax committees in Congress - the HOUSE WAYS AND MEANS COMMITTEE and the SENATE FINANCE COMMITTEE write the tax codes that distribute the burdens of cost; 6) The Budget Committees and the Congressional Budget Office (CBO) - the CBO, the congressional equivalent of the OMB, and the Senate and House Budget Committees set the parameters of the congressional budget process, binding Congress to certain limits; 7) The subject-matter committees - write new laws which require new expenditures; 8) The Appropriations Committees and their subcommittees - decide who gets what after hearings on specific agency requests; 9) The Congress as a whole - Congress as a whole must approve taxes and appropriations; 10) The General Accounting Office (GAO) - works as Congress' eyes and ears after the budget is passed, monitoring and evaluating what agencies are doing with their budget allocations.

B. The President's Budget

In 1921 Congress passed the Budget and Accounting Act, requiring presidents to propose an executive budget to Congress and creating the Bureau of the Budget to help them. President Nixon reorganized the Bureau of the Budget and renamed it the Office of Management (OMB). The OMB, whose director is a presidential appointee requiring Senate approval, now supervises preparation of the federal budget and advises the president on budgetary matters.
It takes a long time to prepare a presidential budget. Almost a year before the president submits a budget in January, the OMB begins sounding out agency requests and issuing guidelines. In the summer the president decides on overall priorities and these are communicated to the agencies. During the fall the agencies submit formal, detailed estimates for their budgets, pushing their needs with the OMB. Budget analysts at OMB pare requests back within overall guidelines. Finally, last minute compromises are worked out and the budget is printed and sent to the Congress.

C. Congress and the Budget

According to the Constitution, all federal appropriations must be authorized by Congress. By law, Congress must decide between January, when the president submits the proposed budget, and October 1, when the fiscal year begins, how to spend more than a trillion dollars.

1. Reforming the Process.   For years Congress budgeted in a piecemeal fashion with each agency request handled by different appropriations subcommittees. The total budget was not known until all the independent appropriations were totalled up.   The CONGRESSIONAL BUDGET AND IMPOUNDMENT CONTROL ACT OF 1974 was designed to reform this process.   Reformers hoped it would make Congress less dependent on the president's budget and more able to set its own budget goals.   The act established the following: 1) a fixed budget calendar - an established completion date for each step in the process; 2) a Budget Committee in each house - that recommend target figures for the total budget size; 3) a CONGRESSIONAL BUDGET OFFICE (CBO) - which advises Congress on the likely consequences of its budget decisions and acts as a counterweight to the president's OMB.

An important part of the process of establishing a budget is to set limits on expenditures based on revenue projections, a step that is supposed to be done through a BUDGET RESOLUTION. In April each year Congress is supposed to pass a budget resolution that limits all federal spending for all programs.

The congressional budget resolution assumes that certain changes will be made in law, primarily to achieve savings incorporated into the spending totals and thus meet the budget resolution.   One way such changes are legislated is a budget RECONCILIATION bill, which revises program authorizations to achieve required savings. It usually also includes tax or other revenue adjustments. Reconciliation usually comes near the end of the budget process. A second way laws are changed to meet the budget resolution is through an AUTHORIZATION BILL, which establishes a discretionary government program or an entitlement, or that continues or changes such programs.   They are narrowly drawn and may be for one year, or they may run for a specified or indefinite number of years.

An additional measure, termed an APPROPRIATIONS BILL, must be passed to actually fund programs established by authorization bills.   The appropriations bills usually cover one year and cannot exceed the amount of money authorized for a program, but they may appropriate less than was authorized.

2. The Success of the 1974 Reforms. The reforms have not brought spending into line with revenues.   In fact, not only has Congress not balanced the budget, but budgets have become more imbalanced. Congress has also often missed its own budgetary timetable.   It has sometimes had to resort to CONTINUING RESOLUTIONS, laws that allow agencies to spend at the previous year's level in order to keep the government running.

On the other hand, the 1974 reforms have helped Congress view the entire budget early in the process. The problems are less with the procedure as with disagreement over how scarce resources should be spent.

3. More Reforms.   In response to growing frustration at its

inability to substantially reduce annual budget deficits, Congress enacted the GRAMM-RUDMAN-HOLLINGS Act. This legislation mandates maximum allowable deficit levels for each year until 1993, when the budget is to be in balance. If congress fails to meet the deficit goals, automatic across-the-board spending cuts must be ordered by the president. No one likes the arbitrary nature of the automatic budget cuts, half of which come form defense and half from domestic programs. In the absence of consensus on spending priorities, Congress felt it had no other way to force itself to reduce the deficit.

IV. The Budget: Where It Comes From And Where It Goes (522-536)

Most of the political struggles you read about in the newspapers are focused on determining policies about revenues and expenditures.

A. Where It Comes From

The three major sources of federal revenues are the personal and corporate income tax, social insurance taxes, and borrowing and deficit spending.

1. Income Tax: The Government's Golden Egg? INCOME TAXES take a share of money earned. An income tax had been declared unconstitutional in 1895, and did not become possible until the passage of the SIXTEENTH AMENDMENT (1915) which explicitly permits Congress to levy such a tax. The INTERNAL REVENUE SERVICE was established to collect it. Corporations, like individuals, pay income taxes. Today corporate taxes yield about eleven cents of every federal revenue dollar, compared with forty-three cents coming from individual income taxes.

2. Social Insurance Taxes. Social Security taxes come from both employers and employees in matching amounts. These funds are earmarked for the Social Security Fund, to pay benefits to the old, the disabled, and the widowed. Because of the demographic demands on the Social Security System, they have been and are likely to remain the fastest growing tax.

3. Borrowing. When the federal government wants to borrow money, the Treasury Department sells bonds, guaranteeing to pay interest to the bondholder. Today, the FEDERAL DEBT - all of the money borrowed over the years and still outstanding - exceeds $3.1 trillion. During the 1980s it more than tripled increasing from 34 to 56 percent of the GNP. The interest on the debt has become a major budget item - $176 billion in 1990 alone.

Borrowing shifts the burden of yesterday's consumption on to tomorrow's taxpayers, who must service the debt. Borrowing also crowds out individual and business private borrowers from the credit market. The magnitude of recent borrowing has also forced the government to become dependent on foreign investors.

Despite these considerations, not everyone is concerned about the federal debt. It is argued that concern should be tempered by the fact that as a percentage of GNP the federal debt has been much higher - 120 percent - after World War II. Also, taking inflation into account often turns deficit years into surplus years. Finally, if government counted debt by balancing assets against liabilities, as businesses do, it would be in pretty good shape.

Most observers are concerned about the national debt. The perceived perils of gigantic deficits have led to calls for a BALANCED BUDGET AMENDMENT. The proposed amendment would require Congress to balance peacetime federal budgets.

B. Taxes and Public Policy

In addition to raising revenues to finance its services, the government can use taxes to make citizens' incomes more or less equal, to encourage or discourage growth in the economy, and to promote specific interests.

1. Tax Loopholes. A tax loophole is some tax break or tax benefit. The IRS code has exemptions, deductions, and special cases that provide loopholes. Tax writing is done by the House Ways and Means Committee and the Senate Finance Committee. These committees are the focus of intense lobbying for special loopholes. Though they may offend our sense of fair play, they cost the government very little.

2. Tax Expenditures. What does cost the federal budget a substantial sum is the system of TAX EXPENDITURES - revenue losses attributable to provisions of the federal tax laws which allow a special exemption, exclusion, or deduction. Tax expenditures amount to subsidies for some activity. On the whole, these relatively obscure features of the budgetary system benefit the middle and upper-middle income taxpayers and corporations. To some, tax expenditures are loopholes. To others, they are public policy choices supporting a social activity worth subsidizing.

3. The Never-ending Quest for Tax Reduction. Taxes aren't popular and calls for reduction are frequent. The most recent major reform came in the wake of the election of Ronald Reagan. Reagan proposed a massive tax-cut bill which passed in 1981. It cut the federal tax bill 25 percent over three years. Intended to promote increased saving and investment, most of the cut went to those earning more than the median income.

4. The Never-ending Quest for Tax Reform. Tax reform plans are common. Any reform is likely to take away some group's tax benefits, however, and thus will be actively opposed. The tax reform effort of 1986 was not derailed despite protest from interest groups determined to hold on to their benefits. The Tax Reform Act of 1986 was one of the most sweeping alterations in federal tax

policy in history. It eliminated or reduced the value of many tax deductions and changed the system of fifteen separate tax brackets to just two generally lower rates.

C. Where It Goes: Federal Expenditures

Two points can be made about spending trends: 1) what the government spends money on changes; 2) expenditures keep rising.

1. The Big Change: Declining Defense Budgets and Growing Social Budgets. In the 1950s and early 1960s the Department of Defense got the majority of federal dollars. From the mid-1960s to the early 1980s, defense expenditures crept downward in real dollars while social welfare expenditures more than doubled. The Reagan Administration reversed this trend in the 1980s.

The biggest slice of the budget pie now belongs to income security expenditures, a bundle of policies extending direct and indirect aid to the old, the poor, and the needy.

2. Incrementalism. INCREMENTALISM means simply that the best predictor of this year's budget is last year's budget plus a little bit more (an increment). This is because most of each budget is a product of previous decisions. In any one year, little attention is given to the budgetary base. Instead, attention is focused on the proposed increment. With a few exceptions, incrementalism is a good general description of the budgetary process. Incrementalism makes budget cutting difficult.

There have been efforts to reform this irrational incrementalism. One was Program Planning-Budgeting Systems (PPBS) during the Johnson Administration. PPBS required agencies to budget by programs and show explicitly the goals being achieved. Jimmy Carter advocated zero-based budgeting (ZBB), which requires agencies to assume that their base is zero and justify their entire allocation, not just the increment. The federal budget is just too big to review from scratch each year, however.

3. The Allowance Theory and Uncontrollable Expenditures.

Vast expenditures are determined not by how much Congress appropriates to an agency (like an allowance) but by how many eligible beneficiaries there are for some particular program. Such expenditures are termed "uncontrollable." UNCONTROLLABLE EXPENDITURES result from policies that make some group automatically eligible for some benefit. They are not provided on a first come first served basis until the money runs out. Instead, Congress has obligated itself to pay X level of benefits to Y number of recipients based on eligibility standards. Social Security is the largest such program. Such policies are called ENTITLEMENTS. Congress could cut benefits or change eligibility requirements to save money on such programs, but as has been the case with such efforts regarding Social Security, there are often high political costs involved.

V. Understanding Budgeting (536-539)

A. Democracy and Budgeting

One explanation for the growth of government in democracies is that politicians spend money to "buy" votes. They spend money on things that voters will like - and will remember on election day. If so, it may be the equality of the vote that drives such growth. Everyone has a vote and parties must appeal to a majority of voters. Majorities necessarily involve the inclusion of many poorer voters, who use their voting power to support public policies that redistribute benefits from the rich to the poor.
While this helps to explain many entitlement programs, the rich also support big government that offers contracts, subsidies, and other benefits.   Both poor and rich have incentives to vote for politicians who promise the benefits.   Government grows by responding to groups and their demands.

Some politicians compete for votes by promising not to spend money. When Americans express this sentiment, they are thinking about their taxes not their benefits, however. They may want spending cuts, but they want the cuts to come from someone else's programs. They want the budget balanced, but they want to spend for their own programs and not pay taxes. Being a democracy, that is exactly what the government gives them. Debt is the result.

B. The Budget and the Size of Government

In many ways the budget indicates the size of government. The bigger the budget, the bigger the government. The budgetary process can limit government. Budgetary politics are the politics of scarcity - the scarcity of funds. The budget can thus be a force for reining in the government.

There is presently little money to back up President Bush's desires to expand the government's effort on the war on drugs, education, space exploration, and aid to emerging democracies in Western Europe, for example. America's large budget deficit is as much a constraint on government as it is evidence of a burgeoning public sector.

DOING RESEARCH ON THE POLITICS OF TAXING AND SPENDING

Nothing has generated more controversy in recent years than the national budget. The gigantic budget deficits of the 1980s have led to calls for a "balanced budget amendment," for example. The arguments for and against this controversial suggestion would make an interesting and researchable project.

On another front has been Congress' efforts to reform the budget process to provide greater control. An investigation of the several reforms and how they have, and have not, been successful would deepen your understanding of this vital political process.

Controversy also arises over how serious the budget deficit really is. Your paper might explore the rise of the current deficit, compare its dimensions to budgetary situations of the past, and review the arguments that it is or is not a serious threat to the nation's economic health. You may be able to clarify the nature of the dangers that the deficit poses, and understand better why it may pose fewer problems than its sheer size might imply.

REVIEW TEST

Read through the Chapter Overview and review the "Reading for Content" questions if you haven't already done so. If you feel like you have achieved the learning objectives listed at the beginning of the chapter, you should be ready for the Review Test. Again, take the test as if you were taking it in class. Remember, you are not only learning the answers, you are learning how to better take tests.

1. Today, the total national debt is over _____ dollars.
    (a) ten trillion
    (b) three trillion
    (c) 500 billion
    (d) 50 billion
Page 505

2. The main reason why budgets are so large is because:
    (a) Congress and the president never reach a consensus of opinion.
    (b) to make sure there is never another depression.
    (c) the Constitution demands it.
    (d) it takes a big budget to pay for a big government.
Page 505

3. The national budget is currently about $ _____ a year.
    (a) 1.2 trillion
    (b) 575 billion
    (c) 100 billion
    (d) 75 billion
Page 505

4. The Social Security Act was passed during the Great Depression during the administration of President:
    (a) Harry S Truman.
    (b) Herbert Hoover.
    (c) Lyndon Johnson.
    (d) Franklin D. Roosevelt.

Page 507

5. In 1965, _____ was added to the social security system, which provided hospital and physician coverage to retirees and some poor persons.
    (a) Medicare
    (b) Optifast
    (c) all purpose insurance
    (d) the elasticity clause
Page 507

6. It was President _____ who coined the phrase military industrial complex to characterize the close correspondence between the military and corporations that supply their hardware needs.
    (a) F.D. Roosevelt
    (b) Harry Truman
    (c) Dwight Eisenhower
    (d) John F. Kennedy
Page 510

7. By the year 2035, when today's college students will be getting their Social Security checks, fewer than _____ workers will be supporting each beneficiary.
    (a) seven
    (b) five
    (c) three
    (d) two
Page 508

8. In 1990, the Social Security system was financed by a _____ percent tax on payrolls.
    (a) 5
    (b) 7
    (c) 12
    (d) 15
Page 508

9. Since World War II, the _____ with the Soviet Union has resulted in a permanent military establishment and expensive military technology.
    (a) detente
    (b) cold war
    (c) INF treaty
    (d) SALT treaty
Page 510

10. Today, the budget of the Department of Defense constitutes about _____ of all federal expenditures.
    (a) three-fourths
    (b) one half
    (c) one fourth
    (d) two-thirds

Page 510

11. President _____ defended the padding of budget requests by saying that "if some superfluidity not be given to Congress to lop off, they will cut into the very flesh of the public necessities."
     (a) John Adams
     (b) Abraham Lincoln
     (c) Franklin D. Roosevelt
     (d) Ronald Reagan
Page 514

12. A smart agency head will be sure to involve _____, one of his most important weapons, in defending the agency's budget request.
     (a) interest groups
     (b) bureaucrats
     (c) tax committees from the department
     (d) legal affidavits
Page 514

13. The Senate committee responsible for writing the tax code, or tax codes, is the:
     (a) Senate Finance Committee.
     (b) Senate Ways and Means Committee.
     (c) Senate Budget Committee.
     (d) Senate Appropriations Committee.
Page 515

14. The _____ its parent committees set the parameters of the congressional budget process through examining revenues and expenditures in the aggregate and proposing resolutions to bind Congress within certain limits.
     (a) House Budget Office
     (b) Senate Budget Office
     (c) Congressional Budget Office
     (d) Policy Review Office
Page 515

15. All of the following have major roles in the budget process EXCEPT:
     (a) agencies seeking appropriations
     (b) subject-matter committees in Congress
     (c) the Tariff Commission
     (d) the president
Page 515

16. The Constitution requires that _____ approve taxes and appropriations.
     (a) The president
     (b) the Congress as a whole
     (c) the House of Representatives
     (d) the Senate

Page 516

17. All of the following are major players in the budgeting process
    EXCEPT:
    (a) the Congress as a whole.
    (b) both houses' Appropriations Committees.
    (c) the General Accounting Office.
    (d) the vice-president's office.
Page 516

18. Until 1921, the various agencies of the executive branch sent
    their budget requests to the Secretary of the Treasury, who in
    turn forwarded them to:
    (a) Congress.
    (b) the president.
    (c) the Senate.
    (d) the House of Representatives.
Page 516

19. In the 1970's, President _____ reorganized the Bureau of the
    Budget and gave it a new name -- the Office of Management and
    Budget.
    (a) Richard Nixon
    (b) Gerald Ford
    (c) Jimmy Carter
    (d) Ronald Reagan
Page 516

20. By law, the president must submit a budget on the fifteenth day
    of the new congressional session in:
    (a) November.
    (b) December.
    (c) January.
    (d) February.
Page 516

21. By law, Congress must decide between January, when the
    president submits the proposed budget, and _____, when the
    fiscal year begins, how to spend more than a trillion dollars.
    (a) February 1
    (b) April 15
    (c) June 1
    (d) October 1
Page 518

22. The _____ Act of 1974 was designed to reform the budgetary
    process.
    (a) Congressional Budget and Impoundment Control
    (b) Congressional Election Reform
    (c) Pendleton
    (d) Hatch
Page 518

23. The Budget Committees in each house are supposed to recommend to Congress target figures for the total budget size by _____ of each year.
   (a) January 1
   (b) April 1
   (c) June 1
   (d) October 1
Page 518

24. By April 15, Congress agrees on the total size of the budget, which guides the _____ committee(s) in juggling figures for individual agencies.
   (a) House Ways and Means
   (b) Budget
   (c) Senate Finance
   (d) Appropriations
Page 518

25. In _____ of each year, both houses of Congress are expected to agree upon a budget resolution.
   (a) January
   (b) April
   (c) September
   (d) October
Page 518

26. In 1981, _____ proposed a complex reconciliation bill to reduce the budget by approximately forty billion dollars.
   (a) President Reagan
   (b) James Baker III
   (c) Don Regan
   (d) David Stockman
Page 519

27. A(n) _____ must be passed to actually fund programs established by authorization bills.
   (a) reconciliation bill
   (b) appropriations bill
   (c) budget reconciliation
   (d) revenue adjustment
Page 520

28. Congressional budgets have been in the "red" _____ year(s) since the 1974 amendments.
   (a) five out of fifteen
   (b) ten out of fifteen
   (c) every
   (d) one out of fifteen
Page 520

29. The _____ Act of 1985 mandates a balanced budget by 1993.
    (a) Congressional Budget and Impoundment
    (b) Gramm-Rudman-Hollings
    (c) Pendleton
    (d) Rico
Page 520

30. Oliver Wendell Holmes said that "_____ are what we pay for civilization."
    (a) taxes
    (b) voting privileges
    (c) budgets
    (d) governments
Page 523

31. The first peacetime income tax in the United States was in:
    (a) 1864.
    (b) 1894.
    (c) 1914.
    (d) 1934.
Page 524

32. In 1915, the _____ Amendment was added to the Constitution, explicitly permitting Congress to levy an income tax.
    (a) Twenty-second
    (b) Twentieth
    (c) Nineteenth
    (d) Sixteenth
Page 523

33. _____ taxes have grown faster than any other source of federal revenue and are expected to grow even more.
    (a) Personal income
    (b) Social Security
    (c) Corporate
    (d) State and local
Page 523

34. Today, the federal debt, which is all the money borrowed over the years and still outstanding, exceeds $_____.
    (a) 500 billion
    (b) 900 billion
    (c) 1 trillion
    (d) 3.1 trillion
Page 525

35. When the federal government borrows money, the _____ sells bonds, guaranteeing to pay interest to the bondholder.
    (a) General Accounting Office
    (b) Treasury Department
    (c) Office of Management and Budget
    (d) Congressional Budget Office
Page 525

36. Gigantic deficits have led to calls for a _____ amendment.
    (a) revenue sharing
    (b) balanced budget
    (c) revenue enhancement
    (d) budget reconciliation
Page 525

37. During the Carter administration, the _____ bill set to cut federal income taxes in stages.
    (a) Gramm-Rudman-Hollings
    (b) Kemp-Roth
    (c) Laffer curve
    (d) Gingrich-Simpson
Page 529

38. All of the following men were largely responsible for the passage and success of the 1986 Tax Reform Act EXCEPT:
    (a) Senator Bill Bradley.
    (b) President Reagan.
    (c) Congressman Dan Rostenkowski.
    (d) Congressman Newt Gingrich.
Page 531-532

39. _____ expenditures result from policies that make some group automatically eligible for some benefit, or if it is "mandated under current law or by previous obligation."
    (a) Obligatory
    (b) Eligible
    (c) Mandated
    (d) Uncontrollable
Page 535

40. Economists have argued that government grows in a democracy because of:
    (a) the federal debt increases.
    (b) the expansion of land and properties.
    (c) the equality of suffrage.
    (d) the growth of business and industrialization.
Page 536

BEFORE GOING ON

Use the answer key below to "grade" your exam and see how you did. Go back and reread the relevant passages on the indicated page for any you have missed. Knowing why you missed what you missed will help you to remember the correct information.

Review Test Answers:

1:	b	11:	a	21:	d	31:	b
2:	d	12:	a	22:	a	32:	d
3:	a	13:	a	23:	b	33:	b
4:	d	14:	c	24:	d	34:	d
5:	a	15:	c	25:	b	35:	b
6:	c	16:	b	26:	a	36:	b
7:	d	17:	d	27:	b	37:	b
8:	d	18:	a	28:	c	38:	d
9:	b	19:	a	29:	b	39:	d
10:	c	20:	c	30:	a	40:	c

The complicated process of making a budget generates a lot of Key Terms (page 540) for you to worry about. So worry about them. When you are sure of all of them you can quit worrying. I recommend for your more general use the term "incrementalism." This phenomenon that characterizes the decision-making process in budgeting is present in many decision processes on important matters. Watch for incremental thinking in your own daily life!

CHAPTER 15

THE BUREAUCRACIES

CHAPTER LEARNING OBJECTIVES

After reading Chapter 15, you should be able to:

1. Discuss common myths concerning bureaucracy.
2. Describe the characteristics of bureaucrats.
3. Describe the characteristics of the civil service system.
4. Discuss the three prominent theories of bureaucracy.
5. Describe the four basic types of agencies.
6. Discuss the common reasons that policy implementation can breakdown.
7. Explain why the Voting Rights Act of 1965 illustrates effective implementation.
8. Discuss the growth and character of regulation in America.
9. Assess the extent of regulation, the alternative forms of regulation and the alternatives to regulation.
10. Discuss the means of democratic control of bureaucracy.
11. Discuss the difficulties of bureaucratic control and the role of iron triangles and issue networks.
12. Describe the relationship of bureaucracy to government size.

PRETEST QUESTIONS

The pretest below will give you an idea of the state of your knowledge about bureaucracies. The questions should also help you learn what to look for while studying the text. Take the whole pretest, then check your answers against the key that follows (don't peek!). As you read the chapter, watch for where these questions are addressed (indicated after each question) so that you may learn why the answer is what it is.

1. _____, the former Alabama governor and presidential candidate, warmed up his crowds while campaigning with a line about "pointy-headed bureaucrats who can't even park their bicycles straight."
    (a) Howell Heflin
    (b) Jimmy Carter
    (c) George Wallace
    (d) Lester Maddox

Page 545

2. The following is (are) true about bureaucracies, that:
    (a) the number of government employees has been expanding.
    (b) the number of federal employees has been shrinking.
    (c) almost all growth in the number of public employees has occurred in state and local governments.
    (d) all answers are correct
Page 546

3. The Department of Defense employs about _____ percent of federal civilian workers in addition to the 2.2 million men and women in uniform.
    (a) 11
    (b) 21
    (c) 36
    (d) 46
Page 548

4. An example of a typical bureaucrat would be a(n):
    (a) census analyst.
    (b) accountant.
    (c) truck driver.
    (d) all answers are correct
Page 549

5. After the assassination of President Garfield, _____ became president and did much to end the federal "spoils system." (a) Chester A. Arthur
    (b) Benjamin Harrison
    (c) Theodore Roosevelt
    (d) Andrew Johnson
Page 551

6. _____ percent of federal employees are exempt from the Civil Service.
    (a) 3
    (b) 10
    (c) 15
    (d) 23
Page 551

7. Office of Personnel Management members are appointed by:
    (a) the director of the OMP.
    (b) the president.
    (c) the Senate Finance Committee chairman.
    (d) the Secretary of the Interior.
Page 551

8. As a rule all federal employees:
    (a) are easy to fire or remove.
    (b) are unionized.
    (c) are forbidden by law to strike.
    (d) have no recourse if they are fired.
Page 551

9. The Supreme Court, in Arnett v. Kennedy, held that federal employees could not be fired without "due process of law," a protection provided in the _____ Amendment.
    (a) Sixteenth
    (b) Seventh
    (c) Ninth
    (d) Fifth
Page 552

10. Weber's bureaucratic structure includes all of the following EXCEPT:
    (a) a hierarchical authority structure.
    (b) a "spoils system."
    (c) task specialization.
    (d) extensive rules.
Page 554

11. It is more likely than not that most organizations and bureaucracies operate by:
    (a) trial and error.
    (b) acquisition.
    (c) monopolistic practices.
    (d) incoherent structure.
Page 556

12. The real work of a department (in Washington) is done in the:
    (a) bureaus.
    (b) under-secretary's office.
    (c) secretary's office.
    (d) White House.
Page 558

13. In Washington, the cabinet department known as the most unwieldy government agency is the Department of:
    (a) Defense.
    (b) State.
    (c) Justice.
    (d) Health and Human Services.
Page 558

14. All of the following are examples of an independent regulatory agency EXCEPT:
    (a) the Interstate Commerce Commission (ICC).
    (b) the Federal Reserve Board (FRB).
    (c) the Internal Revenue Service (IRS).
    (d) the National Labor Relations Board (NRLB).
Page 559

15. The _____ is charged with licensing radio and TV stations and regulating their programming in the public interest. It also regulates interstate long-distance telephone rates.
    (a) Interstate Commerce Commission
    (b) National Labor Relations Board
    (c) Federal Communications Commission
    (d) Federal Trade Commission
Page 558

16. The _____ was created to police the stock market. (a) Securities and Exchange Commission
    (b) Interstate Commerce Commission
    (c) Federal Reserve Board
    (d) Federal Trade Commission
Page 558

17. All of the following are examples of independent executive agencies EXCEPT:
    (a) the General Services Administration (GSA).
    (b) the National Labor Relations Board (NLRB).
    (c) the National Science Foundation (NSF).
    (d) the National Aeronautics and Space Administration (NASA).
Page 561

18. At a minimum, policy implementation includes all of the elements listed below EXCEPT:
    (a) creation of a new agency or assignment of responsibility to an old one.
    (b) translation of policy goals into operational rules of thumb.
    (c) coordination of resources and personnel to achieve the intended goals.
    (d) the disintegration of a non-functioning agency.
Page 562

19. Some describe the existing system of regulation as a _____ policy: the government tells business how to reach certain goals, checks that these commands are followed and punishes offenders.
    (a) "traffic cop"
    (b) seek and find
    (c) substandard
    (d) command and control
Page 574

20. It has been pointed out that the system of subgovernments is now overlaid with an amorphous system of:
    (a) issue networks.
    (b) policy review.
    (c) policy mandates.
    (d) issue relays.
Page 580

Pretest Answers:

1: c		11: a
2: d		12: a
3: c		13: d
4: d		14: c
5: a		15: c
6: c		16: a
7: b		17: b
8: c		18: d
9: d		19: d
10: b		20: a

READING FOR CONTENT

Listed below are sets of questions associated with the content of each major section of Chapter 15. Carefully review the questions associated with each section of the text before reading the section. Have the questions in mind as you read the section and, when you reach the end of each section, stop and see if you can answer the questions well. If not, reread the relevant paragraphs until you are sure of your response to each of the questions.

I.   The Bureaucrats

What are common bureaucratic myths that differ from reality?
What are the common characteristics of bureaucrats?
What is the basic purpose of the civil service system?
What laws and principles underpin the American civil service?
How is the civil service system administered?
What is the purpose of the "plum book?"
What function do non-merit "political" appointments serve?
What are the basic tenets of the three prominent theories of
    bureaucracy?

II.   How Bureaucracies are Organized

What are the four basic types of agencies?
How are the functions of each of the four types distinct?

III. Bureaucracies as Implementors

What does implementation mean?
What problems cause the breakdown of effective
    implementation?
Why does the Voting Rights Act of 1965 exemplify effective
    program implementation?

IV.   Bureaucracies and Regulators

What is government regulation?
How extensive is government regulation in the U.S?

How does government regulation work?
How can government regulation be argued to be too extensive?
What are the arguments for and against incentive systems as
    an alternative to the present regulatory practice?
What are the arguments for and against deregulation?

V.   Understanding Bureaucracies

How can presidents control the bureaucracy?
How can Congress act to control the bureaucracy?
What is the difference between iron triangles and issue
    networks?
Why do iron triangles and issue networks make policy control
    more difficult for the president and Congress?
Do iron triangles and issue networks make the system more or
    less democratic?
How can it be argued that bureaucracy is too small?

CHAPTER OVERVIEW

I.   Introduction (544-545)

Nothing better illustrates the complexity of modern government than
its massive bureaucracies. Each bureaucratic agency is created by
Congress, which sets its budget and writes the policies it
administers. Most agencies are responsible to the president.

II. The Bureaucrats (545-556)

Much less visible than the president or members of Congress,
Americans usually know little about bureaucrats.

A. Some Bureaucratic Myths and Realities

Any object as unpopular as bureaucracy will spawn plenty of myths.
Among the most prevalent are: 1) Americans dislike bureaucrats (most
are satisfied with bureaucratic contacts); 2) Most federal
bureaucrats work in Washington, D.C. (only 11 percent do); 3)
Bureaucracies are growing bigger each year (not at the federal
level); 4) Bureaucracies are ineffective, inefficient, and always
mired in red tape (no better form of organization has been found).

Despite all the carping about bureaucracies, the majority of tasks
carried out by governments at all levels are noncontroversial and
performed by ordinary folks likely to be your neighbors. Most
federal bureaucrats work for the Department of Defense (36 percent
of federal civilian workers) and the Postal Service (25 percent).

B. Who They Are and How They Got There

With 3 million bureaucrats (17 million counting state and local public employees), their make-up is broadly representative of the general public. Like other institutions, they have been required to make special efforts to recruit and promote previously disadvantaged groups. Women and nonwhites still cluster at the lower ranks, however. Not only the people, but the sorts of jobs that make up the public sector are diverse as well.

1. Civil Service: From Patronage to Protection. Until about one hundred years ago, a person got a job with the government through the patronage system. PATRONAGE is a hiring and promotion system based on knowing the right people - those who win public office. The PENDLETON ACT (1883) began to put an end to this practice by creating the Civil Service. The rationale for CIVIL SERVICE systems rests on the idea of merit and the desire to create a nonpartisan government service. The MERIT PRINCIPLE - using entrance exams and promotion ratings - is intended to produce administration by people with talent and skill. The HATCH ACT (1940) helped remove partisan influences by prohibiting employees from active participation in partisan politics.

The OFFICE OF PERSONNEL MANAGEMENT (OPM) is in charge of hiring for most agencies of the federal government. Once hired, a person is assigned a GS (GENERAL SCHEDULE) RATING, ranging from GS 1 to GS 18. Salaries are keyed to rating and experience. At the top of the civil service system are the members of the Senior Executive Service. These executives earn high salaries and may be moved from one agency to another as leadership needs change.

Once hired, and after a probationary period, civil servants are protected by the Civil Service System. Ensuring a nonpartisan Civil Service requires that workers have protection from dismissals that are politically motivated. This protection also makes firing incompetents difficult. The rise of public service unions has also made it more difficult to remove some federal employees. President Jimmy Carter tried to make it easier to fire nonperformers. It remains a complicated process, however, and courts have been protective of the right to keep a federal job.

2. The Other Route to Federal Jobs: Recruiting from the Plum Book. As a new administration comes to power, Congress publishes the PLUM BOOK, which lists top federal jobs ("plums") available for direct presidential appointment, often with Senate confirmation. There are about three hundred of these top policy-making posts. The president seeks individuals for them who combine executive talent, political skills, and sympathy for the president's policy positions. Once in office their most prominent trait is their transience. The average assistant secretary or undersecretary lasts about twenty-two months. As a result, the senior civil servants know more, have been there longer, and will outlast them. Thus the influence of top political appointees is less than it appears. The security of the civil servants' jobs combined with the transience (and ignorance) of their superiors also contribute to the bureaucracy's resistance to change.
C. What They Do: Some Theories of Bureaucracy

1. The Weberian Model. The classic conception of bureaucracy was advanced by the German sociologist Max Weber, who stressed that the bureaucracy was a "rational" way for a modern society to conduct its business. To Weber, a BUREAUCRACY depends on certain elements: it has a hierarchical authority structure; it uses task specialization; and it develops extensive rules. Bureaucracies work on the merit principle for entrance and promotion, and behave with impersonality to ensure that all clients are treated equally.

2. The Acquisitive, Monopolistic Bureaucracy. Bureaucracies can also be seen as essentially "acquisitive," busily maximizing their budgets and expanding their powers. Private bureaucracies seek to maximize profits, while public bureaucracies seek to maximize their budgets. Bureaucracies can also be monopolistic. In the public sector they are often monopolies - the only practicable source of their service. Thus, no matter how the bureaucracies behave, they will not lose their clients and there is no competitive pressure to force them to improve service. Critics of bureaucracy have favored privatizing some bureaucratic services to cut back on their monolithic and monopolistic power.

3. Garbage Cans and Bureaucracies. Both the Weberian model and the acquisitive, monopolistic model make bureaucracies sound calculating and purposeful. Another view, though, makes them sound ambling and groping, affected by chance. This view sees the typical organization as a loose collection of ideas, rather than a coherent structure. They operate by trial and error, pulling ideas from the "garbage can" of ideas and latching on to them. Organizations are not necessarily trying to find solutions to problems; just as often, solutions are in search of problems.

III. How Bureaucracies Are Organized (556-561)

The agencies of the federal executive branch can be grouped into four basic types: cabinet departments, regulatory agencies, government corporations, and independent agencies.

A. The Cabinet Departments

Each of the fourteen cabinet departments is headed by a secretary (except the Department of Justice, headed by the attorney general) chosen by the president and approved by the Senate. Each has a different mission and is organized somewhat differently, but the real work of each is done in the bureaus.

B. The Regulatory Agencies

Each INDEPENDENT REGULATORY AGENCY has responsibility for some sector of the economy, making and enforcing rules designed to protect the public interest. These agencies also judge disputes over these rules. They include the Interstate Commerce Commission (ICC), the Federal Reserve Board (FRB), and the Federal Communications Commission (FCC) among many others. Each is governed by a small commission, usually with five to ten members appointed by the president and confirmed by the Senate. Unlike cabinet members, however, they cannot be fired by the president.

Interest groups consider the rule making by independent regulatory agencies very important. So interested are interest groups in regulatory bodies that critics often contend that the regulators are "captured" by the interests. In fact, members of commissions are commonly drawn from the ranks of the interests regulated.

C. The Government Corporations

The federal government also has a handful of GOVERNMENT CORPORATIONS. They are like private corporations and different from the rest of government in two ways. First, they provide a service that could be handled by the private sector. Second, they typically charge for their services, though at lower rates than would be the case with a private provider. Examples include the Tennessee Valley Authority (TVA) providing electricity, the Post Office, and Amtrak, the railroad passenger service.

D. The Independent Executive Agencies

The INDEPENDENT EXECUTIVE AGENCIES are essentially all the rest of the government. Their administrators typically are appointed by the president and serve at his pleasure. The scores of such bureaus are listed in the United States Government Manual. They include the General Services Administration (GSA), the National Science Foundation (NSF), and the National Aeronautics and Space Administration (NASA).

IV. Bureaucracies As Implementors (561-570)

Bureaucracies are essentially implementors of policy. They also manage the routines of government, from delivering mail to collecting taxes to training troops.

A. What Implementation Means

Policy IMPLEMENTATION is the stage of policy-making between the establishment of a policy (such as the passage of a legislative act, the issuing of an executive order, the handing down of a judicial decision, or the promulgation of a regulatory rule) and the consequences of the policy for the people whom it affects. At minimum, implementation includes; 1) Creation of a new agency or assignment of new responsibility to an old one; 2) Translation of policy goals into operational rules of thumb; 3) Coordination of agency resources and personnel to achieve the intended goals.

B. Why the Best-Laid Plans Sometimes Flunk the Implementation Test

1. Program Design. It is impossible to implement a faulty policy

program well. If for example, an agency is assigned a theoretically impossible task, it will ultimately fail regardless of what it does or how much money it spends. This is not as odd or unusual as it sounds, public bureaucracies are sometimes given impossible tasks - like the elimination of poverty, for example.

2. Lack of Clarity. Congress is fond of stating a broad policy goal in legislation and then leaving implementation up to the bureaucracies. Congress thus escapes messy details and the blame for the (often controversial) implementation decisions can be placed elsewhere. Congress and the courts adopted the laudable policy of integration, for example, but implementation involves the less popular process of "busing."

3. Lack of Resources. As big as a bureaucracy may seem in the aggregate, it frequently lacks the staff, along with the necessary training, funding, supplies, and equipment, to carry out the tasks it has been assigned to do. Recently, for example, a shortage of staff was blamed for delays in testing of new drugs to combat AIDS and drug runners had more and faster ships and planes for smuggling drugs than government agents had for stopping them.

4. Administrative Routine. For most bureaucrats, most of the time, administration is a routine matter. They follow STANDARD OPERATING PROCEDURES to help them make numerous everyday decisions. Such rules save time and bring uniformity to complex organization. Justice is better served if rules are applied uniformly. Uniformity also makes personnel interchangeable.

Routines are thus essential to bureaucracy. They can also introduce rigidity, however, and become obstacles to action and innovation. Routine is thus the source of some of the most common pathologies of bureaucracy.

5. Administrator's Dispositions. ADMINISTRATIVE DISCRETION is the authority of administrative actors to select among various responses to a given problem. Some administrators exercise more discretion than others. Michael Lipsky coined the phrase STREET- LEVEL BUREAUCRATS to refer to those who are in constant contact with the public and have considerable discretion over what policy means in individual cases - such as police officers, welfare workers, and lower court judges.

How bureaucrats use discretion depends on their dispositions toward the policies and rules they administer. When policy is in conflict with their views and values, slippage and delay are likely to occur. Controlling the exercise of discretion is a difficult task. It is not easy to fire civil servants, and removing appointed officials may be politically embarrassing.

6. Fragmentation. Sometimes responsibility for a policy area is dispersed among several units within the bureaucracy. In the field of welfare, for example, more than one hundred federal human

services programs are administered by ten different departments and agencies. This diffusion of responsibility makes the coordination of policies both time-consuming and difficult. It may even make compliance difficult if there are contradictory signals from different agencies.

Reorganization and consolidation is politically difficult because it would alter jurisdictions of congressional committees. Neither the committees nor the interest groups that have developed close relationships with them want to have their power relationships with agencies changed. Agencies themselves don't want to be submerged within a broader bureaucratic unit. All this opposition is difficult to overcome.

C. A Case Study: The Voting Rights Act of 1965

While there are many pitfalls in policy implementation, even a controversial policy can be effective if goals are clear and means to achieve the goals are unambiguous. The Voting Rights Act was, by any reasonable standard, a successful case of implementation. It was successful because its goal was clear (to register large numbers of black voters); its implementation was straightforward (sending out people to register them); and the authority of the implementors was plain and concentrated in the Justice Department.

V.   Bureaucracies As Regulators (570-576)

Government REGULATION is the use of governmental authority to control or change some practice in the private sector. This is the most controversial role of bureaucracies, yet Congress gives them broad mandates to regulate a wide range of activities.

A. Regulation in the Economy and in Everyday Life

The scope of government regulation is sweeping and touches everyone's everyday life. Almost all agencies - not just independent regulatory agencies - are in the regulatory business.

B. Regulation: How It Grew, How It Works

From the beginnings of the American republic until 1887, the federal government made almost no regulatory policies. In 1887 Congress, reacting to farmers angry with alleged overcharging by railroads, created the first regulatory agency, the Interstate Commerce Commission (ICC), and charged it with regulating the railroads, their prices, and their services to farmers. The ICC thus set the precedent for regulatory policy-making.

As regulators, bureaucratic agencies typically operate with a large grant of power from Congress, which may set goals to be achieved but permits the agencies to detail the regulatory means. Whatever strategy Congress permits a regulating agency to use, all regulation contains these elements: 1) a grant of power and set of directions from Congress; 2) a set of rules and guidelines by the regulatory agency itself; and 3) some means of enforcing compliance with congressional goals and agency regulations.

1. Is There Too Much Regulation? Almost every regulatory policy was created to achieve some desirable social goal. Still, regulations are unpopular with the regulated. Critics are fond of stressing that Americans rarely evaluate the costs of regulation in relation to its benefits. Critics also point out that regulation is often confusing, contradictory, and inefficient.

2. Is There a Better Way? Some critics describe the existing regulatory system as COMMAND AND CONTROL POLICY: the government tells business how to reach certain goals, checks that these commands are followed, and punishes offenders. They argue for an INCENTIVE SYSTEM instead. Rather than trying to develop standards for 62,000 pollution sources, as the EPA does now, it would be easier and more effective to levy a high tax on those who cause pollution, for example. The government could even provide incentives in the form of rewards for such socially valuable behavior as developing technology to reduce pollution.

Not everyone sees incentives as an answer, however. Defenders of the present command and control system of regulation compare it to preventive medicine. It is designed to minimize pollution or workplace accidents before they become severe problems. The incentive systems' penalties would come only after the damage had been done. Such penalties might also simply be passed on to the consumer in the form of higher prices.

3. Toward Deregulation. The idea behind deregulation is that the number and reach of regulatory policies have made regulation too complex and burdensome. To critics, the problem with regulation is that it raises prices, distorts market forces, and does not work. Deregulation was supported broadly by conservatives and even found more limited support among liberals during the 1980s.

VI. Understanding Bureaucracies (576-582)

In implementing and regulating bureaucracies are making public policy - not just administering someone else's decisions. The fact that bureaucrats are not elected yet compose most of the government raises fundamental questions for democratic governance.
A. Bureaucracy and Democracy

Bureaucracies are one of America's two unelected policy-making institutions (with courts). In democratic theory, popular control of government depends on elections. The fact that bureaucrats are unelected does not mean that bureaucracies cannot respond to and represent the public's interests. The matter turns on whether bureaucracies are effectively controlled by people citizens do elect - the president and Congress.

1. Presidents Try to Control the Bureaucracy. Methods of controlling the bureaucracy for the president include: 1) Appoint the right people to head the agency - loyal and competent; 2) Issue Orders - presidents can issue EXECUTIVE ORDERS to agencies; 3) Tinker with an agency's budget - the OMB's threats to cut here or add there will usually get an agency's attention; 4) Reorganize an agency - this is hard to do if the agency is large, and not worth the effort if it is small.

2. Congress Tries to Control the Bureaucracy. Congress often finds a big bureaucracy congenial. Big government provides services to constituents and has answers to many policy problems. On the other hand, Congress finds it hard to control the government it helped to create. Among the measures Congress can take to oversee the bureaucracy are: 1) Influence the appointment of agency heads; 2) Tinker with an agency's budget - the power of the purse is a mighty weapon for controlling bureaucratic behavior; 3) Hold hearings - as part of their oversight function; 4) Rewrite the legislation or make it more detailed - to limit bureaucratic discretion.

3. Iron Triangles and Issue Networks. Bureaucracies are also hard to control because they have strong ties to interest groups on the one hand and to congressional committees and subcommittees on the other. When agencies, groups, and committees all depend on one another and are in close, frequent contact, they form what are sometimes called iron triangles or subgovernments. These triads have advantages on all sides (see Figure 15.5 in your textbook).

This system of subgovernments is now overlaid with an amorphous system of issue networks. There is now more widespread participation in bureaucratic policy-making, and many of the participants have technical policy expertise and emotional rather than material interests. They challenge formerly closed subgovernments. This opening of the policy process complicates political calculations and decreases policy predictability for those involved in subgovernments.

B. Bureaucracy and the Size of Government

Much of the political rhetoric against bureaucracy sees it as acquisitive, and thus contributing to government growth. The federal bureaucracy has not grown, however, over the past two decades. Its long term growth reflects the fact the government is now expected to play an active role in dealing with social and economic problems. Given its assignment, it may actually be too small. The question of what and how much the federal government should do - and thus how big the bureaucracy - is answered primarily at the polls and in Congress, the White House, and the courts - not by "faceless bureaucrats" themselves.

DOING RESEARCH ON BUREAUCRACY

Believe it or not there are a couple of interesting and potentially controversial matters you may want to research that concern bureaucracy. One concerns the whole question of regulation. The controversy over the role and impact of regulation itself could be explored, including the many arguments for and against it. On a more specific level, the impact of deregulation on some industries could be reviewed and assessed. What has been the effect on the airline industry, for example? What are the lessons that can be learned from this experiences? If you are brave you might want to explore the role of deregulation in the nation's Savings and Loan fiasco. What happened, how did deregulation contribute to what happened, and what lessons can be learned from it?

Again, most of the information on this would be found in recent periodical resources. Congressional Quarterly's <u>Federal Regulatory Directory</u> is also a good general source on the regulatory process and current issues in regulation. Your text also provides a number of good sources to start with in its For Further Reading section. Books by Martha Derthick and Paul Quirk, E.S. Savas, Susan and Martin Tolchin, and James Q. Wilson are particularly relevant.

Alternatively, you might want to take a look at how a particular department or agency is organized and functions to implement policy. An in depth look at the role of a bureaucracy can provide new appreciation for its complexity and the importance of its mission. Select an agency that you have an interest in and use <u>The United States Government Manual</u> as well as the <u>Federal Regulatory Directory</u> to help you focus on the specifics of the organization. The <u>U.S. Government Manual</u> has organization charts (in the back) as well as detailed descriptions of the purposes and roles of the agencies of government. A good understanding of even a narrow slice of the massive federal bureaucracy will make you an expert in comparison to the average citizen.

REVIEW TEST

Again, take the test as if you were taking it in class. Keep going over the Review Tests until you know them all - and know why the answers are correct. They are good preparation for exams.

1. Most bureaucratic agencies are responsible to _____, whose constitutional responsibility is to "take care that the laws shall be faithfully executed."
   (a) Congress
   (b) the president
   (c) the director of the OMB
   (d) the Secretary of the Treasury
Page 544-545

2. All of the following are prevalent myths about bureaucracies
    EXCEPT:
    (a) most bureaucrats work in Washington, D.C.
    (b) bureaucracies are large, confused and mired in red tape.
    (c) bureaucracies are growing larger all the time.
    (d) despite their faults, Americans generally like bureaucrats.
    Page 546

3. About _____ percent of three million federal civilian
    employees work in Washington, D.C.
    (a) 3
    (b) 11
    (c) 27
    (d) 52
    Page 546

4. _____ leads the nation in employing federal bureaucrats,
    with 325,000.
    (a) Washington, D.C.
    (b) New York
    (c) California
    (d) Texas
    Page 546

5. Federal government employment now amounts to about _____
    percent of all civilian jobs.
    (a) 3
    (b) 11
    (c) 24
    (d) 47
    Page 546

6. The Department of Defense employs well 3 million employees,
    making up about _____ percent of the federal bureaucracy.
    (a) 13
    (b) 24
    (c) 43
    (d) 60
    Page 548

7. An example of a typical bureaucrat would be a(n):
    (a) judge.
    (b) all answers are correct
    (c) zoologist.
    (d) kitchen worker.
    Page 549

8. There are about _____ bureaucrats, if you add state and
    local employees to the count.
    (a) 1 million

    (b)   3 million
    (c)   17 million
    (d)   37 million
Page 549

9. Until roughly one hundred years ago, a person got a job with the government through the _____ system.
    (a)   seniority
    (b)   patronage
    (c)   merit
    (d)   honor
Page 550

10. _____ helped end the "spoils system" of federal appointments when he shot and killed President Garfield because the president would not give him a job.
    (a)   Charles Guiteau
    (b)   Jonathan Czogz
    (c)   John Wilkes Booth
    (d)   Charles Whitmore
Page 550

11. President Arthur, who had previously held patronage-rich posts, surprised his critics by pushing for passage of the _____ Act, which created the federal Civil Service.
    (a)   Pendleton
    (b)   Hatch
    (c)   Civil Service
    (d)   Budget Impoundment
Page 551

12. At first, only about _____ percent of federal employees were covered by Civil Service when President Arthur created it in 1883.
    (a)   3
    (b)   10
    (c)   23
    (d)   30
Page 551

13. The _____ principle -- using entrance exams and promotion ratings -- is intended to produce administration by people with talent and skill.
    (a)   merit
    (b)   spoils system
    (c)   patronage
    (d)   elitist
Page 551

14. The _____ Act, passed in 1940, prohibits government

employees from active participation in partisan politics.
(a)   Pendleton
(b)   Kemp-Roth
(c)   Hatch
(d)   Gramm-Rudman-Hollings
Page 551

15.   After a person is hired in civil service, he or she is assigned
      a _____ rating from GS 1 to GS 18.
(a)   GS (General Schedule)
(b)   GAO (General Accounting office)
(c)   seniority
(d)   skills
Page 551

16.   The rise of public service unions has made it more difficult
      to:
(a)   remove or fire federal employees.
(b)   hire federal employees.
(c)   hire minorities and women for civil service jobs.
(d)   accomplish anything in the bureaucracy.
Page 551

17.   After the Professional Air Traffic Controllers Organization
      went on strike, which was in violation of federal law,
      President _____ responded after two days by firing all
      controllers that did not report to work.
(a)   Ronald Reagan
(b)   Jimmy Carter
(c)   Gerald Ford
(d)   Richard Nixon
Page 552

18.   President _____ tried to make it easier to fire
      nonperformers in the bureaucracy by pushing through legislation
      that reformed the firing system.
(a)   Ronald Reagan
(b)   Jimmy Carter
(c)   Gerald Ford
(d)   Richard Nixon
Page 552

19.   After a new administration takes over, Congress publishes the
      _____, which lists top federal jobs available for direct
      presidential appointment, often with Senate confirmation.
(a)   plum book
(b)   "spoils" catalog
(c)   Federal Directory
(d)   Executive List
Page 552

20.   Perhaps the oldest bureaucracy is the governance of the:

(a)   U.S. government.
(b)   Roman Catholic Church.
(c)   Greek Senate.
(d)   British Parliament.
Page 554

21.   The Weberian Model includes all of the following EXCEPT:
(a)   a hierarchical authority structure.
(b)   impersonality in hiring practices.
(c)   loosely structured rules.
(d)   a merit principle.
Page 554

22.   The least-staffed executive department is the Department of:
(a)   Education.
(b)   Justice.
(c)   Agriculture.
(d)   Transportation.
Page 548

23.   Critics charge that bureaucracies can be _____ in their practices.
(a)   acquisitive
(b)   partisan
(c)   monopolistic
(d)   both acquisitive and monopolistic
Page 555

24.   There are currently _____ cabinet departments, each headed by a secretary (except for the attorney general).
(a)   seven
(b)   ten
(c)   fourteen
(d)   seventeen
Page 556

25.   Until the 1970's the largest cabinet department was the Department of:
(a)   State.
(b)   Defense.
(c)   Health and Human Services.
(d)   Housing and Urban Development.
Page 558

26.   Each _____ agency has responsibility for some sector of the economy, making and enforcing rules designed to protect the public interest.
(a)   independent regulatory
(b)   appropriations
(c)   economic advisory
(d)   line-item
Page 558

27.   The oldest of the independent regulatory agencies is the

_____, founded in 1887 to regulate railroads.
(a)   Interstate Commerce Commission
(b)   Federal Trade Commission
(c)   the Securities and Exchange Commission
(d)   the National Labor Relations Board
Page 558

28.   The federal government also has a handful of _____,
that provide services that could be handled by the private
sector and they generally charge for their services, albeit at
low rates.
(a)   private corporations
(b)   public corporations
(c)   government corporations
(d)   independent regulatory agencies
Page 560

29.   The "granddaddy" of the government corporations is the
_____, which, until recently, provided inexpensive
electricity to millons of Americans in the South.
(a)   Tennessee Valley Authority (TVA)
(b)   Federal Trade Commission (FTC)
(c)   National Science Foundation (NSF)
(d)   Department of Housing and Urban Development (HUD)
Page 561

30.   One of the government corporations, the U.S. Postal Service was
originally a cabinet department.   The first head of this
department was:
(a)   Alexander Hamilton.
(b)   John Jay.
(c)   Benjamin Franklin.
(d)   James Monroe.
Page 561

31.   Policy _____ is the stage of policy-making between the
establishment of a policy and the consequences of a policy for
the people whom it affects.
(a)   incrementalism
(b)   review
(c)   implementation
(d)   subsidizing
Page 562

32.   _____ is the authority of administrative actors to
select among various responses to a given problem.
(a)   Executive privilege
(b)   Policy review
(c)   Administrative discretion
(d)   Executive mandate
Page 565

33.   The phrase _____ bureaucrats refer to those bureaucrats who
directly contact the public and have considerable discretion.

      (a)   street-level
      (b)   red tape
      (c)   discretionary
      (d)   entry level

Page 566

34. In 1965, Congress, responding to discrimination against prospective black voters in the South, passed the:
    (a)   Civil Rights Act.
    (b)   Food Stamps Act.
    (c)   Voting Rights Act.
    (d)   Registrar Act

Page 569

35. Administrative regulations contain all of the following elements EXCEPT:
    (a)   a grant of power and set of directions from Congress.
    (b)   a set of rules and guidelines by the regulatory agency itself.
    (c)   power granted under the Justice Department to enforce heavy sanctions, including abolishing the offending agency or company.
    (d)   a means of enforcing compliance with congressional goals and agency regulations.

Page 572

36. The idea behind _____ is that the number and complexity of regulatory policies have made regulation too complex and burdensome.
    (a)   bureaucratic entropy
    (b)   bureaucratic meltdown
    (c)   deregulation
    (d)   beefed up regulation

Page 576

37. Congress has all of the following weapons at its command to try and control the bureaucracy EXCEPT:
    (a)   influencing the appointment of agency heads.
    (b)   tinkering with an agency's budget.
    (c)   firing agency heads.
    (d)   rewriting legislation or making it more detailed so it will affect the agency.

Page 578

38. All of the following are part of "iron triangles" EXCEPT:
    (a)   bureaucratic agencies.
    (b)   the media.
    (c)   interest groups.
    (d)   congressional committees.

Page 580

39. _____, former Secretary of Housing and Urban Development during the Reagan administration, was accused of using his office to fund certain housing projects because of the

influence used on him by high paying lobbyists.
    (a)   Samuel Pierce
    (b)   James Watt
    (c)   Anne Gorsuch
    (d)   Edwin Meese
Page 567

40.   President Reagan appointed the controversial _____ as the head of the Environmental Protection Agency. The uproar caused by many of her decisions led to her resignation.
    (a)   Elizabeth Dole
    (b)   Carla Hills
    (c)   Anne Gorsuch
    (d)   Jeanne Kirkpatrick
Page 577

BEFORE GOING ON

Use the answer key below to "grade" your exam and see how you did. Be sure to, go back and reread the relevant passages on the indicated page for any you have missed. If you were sort of "asleep" when you read that passage, there may be something else you missed there as well.

Review Test Answers:

1: b	11: a	21: c	31: c
2: d	12: b	22: a	32: c
3: b	13: a	23: d	33: a
4: c	14: c	24: c	34: c
5: a	15: a	25: b	35: c
6: d	16: a	26: a	36: c
7: b	17: a	27: a	37: c
8: c	18: b	28: c	38: b
9: b	19: a	29: a	39: a
10: a	20: b	30: c	40: c

There are a bunch of Key Terms to check on (page 583) before going on. Be sure all of them sound real familiar. Though "street-level bureaucrats" is not the term for the week, I'd like to put in a word for them. In doing their job they have some "administrative discretion" but in most instances must follow "standard operating procedures" in order to do their job. Remember that the next time some government bureaucrat - whether a police officer or a clerk - has to implement policy you don't care for. Though it is they you come in contact with, it isn't the street-level bureaucrat that is the proper target of your ire. Aim it higher.

The term for the week is "plum book." It fits the criteria of our "college word" best. It is an insider's term (sort of) and is a deliciously (pardon the pun) graphic characterization of the concept it labels. It is also generalizable - one can refer to the jobs in the book as "plums," for example, and the notion can be applied to other sorts of rewards that may be distributed in your work or school environment. It you have gotten no plums lately you may wish to consider why.

CHAPTER 16

THE COURTS

CHAPTER LEARNING OBJECTIVES

After reading Chapter 16, you should be able to:

1. Distinguish criminal and civil law cases.
2. Identify the participants in the legal system and their roles.
3. Distinguish between original and appellate jurisdiction.
4. Explain the role of senatorial courtesy in the process of judicial appointment to the lower courts.
5. Describe the process and the roles of major players in the process of appointment to the Supreme Court.
6. Describe the backgrounds of appointees to the federal court system.
7. Describe the structure of the federal judicial system and the role of the various elements of the system.
8. Explain the role of the courts as policy-makers in accepting and deciding cases.
9. Describe the participants in implementing court decisions.
10. Discuss the implications of the implementation process for the impact of court decisions.
11. Describe the development of judicial review.
12. Discuss how the courts can be viewed as contributing to democracy, and as a not very a democratic institution.
13. Explain the difference between judicial restraint and activism.
14. Discuss the factors that limit and make more acceptable an active policy-making role for the courts.

PRETEST QUESTIONS

The pretest below will give you an idea of the state of your knowledge about the courts. The questions should also help you learn what to look for while studying the text. Take the whole pretest, then check your answers against the key that follows (don't peek!). As you read the chapter, watch for where these questions are addressed (indicated after each question) so that you may learn why the answer is what it is.

Chapter 16

1.   In many, but not all cases, a _____, or a group of citizens
      (usually twelve), is responsible for the determination of
      guilt.
      (a)   tribunal
      (b)   jury
      (c)   troika
      (d)   posse
Page 588

2.   More than _____ percent of court cases begin and end in the
      court of original jurisdiction.
      (a)   10
      (b)   35
      (c)   60
      (d)   90
Page 588

3.   Not everyone can challenge a law. Litigants must have what is
      called:
      (a)   a writ of habeas corpus
      (b)   a writ of certiorari.
      (c)   a standing to sue.
      (d)   a right to trial.
Page 590

4.   The NAACP counsel who argued the Brown v. the Board of
      Education case in the Supreme Court was _____, who,
      ironically, later became a Supreme Court justice.
      (a)   Earl Warren.
      (b)   William Brennan.
      (c)   Thurgood Marshall.
      (d)   Warren Burger.
Page 591

5.   Federal judges can only be removed by conviction of impeachment
      and this has happened _____ times in the two centuries under
      the Constitution.
      (a)   2
      (b)   5
      (c)   7
      (d)   11
Page 592

6.   Under the practice of senatorial courtesy, a nominee for a
      state-level federal judicial position is not confirmed when:
      (a)   opposed by a senator from the state in which the nominee
            is to serve.
      (b)   opposed by the president.
      (c)   opposed by the Senate Judiciary Committee.
      (d)   opposed by a two-thirds Senate vote.
Page 592

7. Usually presidents look outside the Supreme Court to find a new Chief Justice, but President Reagan elevated a sitting associate justice, _____, in 1986.
   (a) Earl Warren
   (b) Warren Burger
   (c) Abe Fortas
   (d) William Rehnquist
   Page 594

8. After Justice Lewis Powell announced his retirement from the Supreme Court, President Reagan named _____ to the seat. He was not confirmed by the Senate.
   (a) Antonin Scalia
   (b) William Rehnquist
   (c) Robert Bork
   (d) David Souter
   Page 595

9. The main argument for the nomination of Robert Bork to the Supreme Court was that he would adhere to _____ - the way cases had been handled in the past.
   (a) restraints
   (b) precedents
   (c) commitments
   (d) standings
   Page 595

10. In 1968, Chief Justice _____ submitted his resignation to President Johnson, who he felt would select an acceptable successor.
    (a) Earl Warren
    (b) Hugo Black
    (c) Warren Burger
    (d) William Brennan
    Page 600

11. After Earl Warren's resignation as Chief Justice and Abe Fortas' rejection as the new chief justice by the Senate, President Nixon named _____ to the job. He was confirmed and took his seat.
    (a) Warren Burger
    (b) William Brennan
    (c) William Rehnquist
    (d) Clement Haynsworth
    Page 600

12. Courts such as the Court of Military Appeals, the Court of Claims and the Tax Court are all examples of _____ courts.
    (a) unconstitutional
    (b) constitutional
    (c) legislative
    (d) district
    Page 601

13. The jurisdiction of the district courts extends to all of the following EXCEPT:
    (a) civil suits between citizens of different states where the amount exceeds $50,000.
    (b) appeals.
    (c) admiralty and maritime law cases.
    (d) supervision of the naturalization of aliens.
Page 602

14. The _____ is composed of twelve judges and was established by Congress in 1982 to hear appeals in specialized cases.
    (a) U.S. Court of International Trade
    (b) U.S. Court of Appeals for the Federal Circuit
    (c) U.S. Court for Tax Laws
    (d) U.S. Copyright Court
Page 604

15. _____ opinions are written by justices opposed to all or part of the majority's decision.
    (a) Concurring
    (b) Abstaining
    (c) Dissenting
    (d) Commentary
Page 610

16. Judicial _____ refers to how and whether court decisions are translated into actual policy, affecting the behavior of others.
    (a) review
    (b) restraint
    (c) implementation
    (d) incrementalism
Page 613

17. When President Jefferson refused to grant him (and sixteen others) his judicial seat, William Marbury asked the Supreme Court to issue a writ of _____ ordering James Madison to give them their commissions.
    (a) certiorari
    (b) mandamus
    (c) habeas corpus
    (d) amicus curiae
Page 616

18. Before the Civil War, the Supreme Court held the Missouri Compromise unconstitutional because it restricted slavery in the territories. The chief justice in the Dred Scott case was:
    (a) John Marshall
    (b) Roger Taney
    (c) Salmon Chase
    (d) Morrison Waite
Page 617

19. The man who was chief justice of the Supreme Court when

President Roosevelt railed against the "nine old men," was:
(a)   Oliver Wendell Holmes.
(b)   William Howard Taft.
(c)   Edward D. White.
(d)   Charles Evans Hughes.
Page 618

20.   Ironically, the chief justice of the Supreme Court that ruled
      President Nixon had to hand over the White House tapes to
      Congress was _____, a Nixon appointee.
(a)   Earl Warren
(b)   William Rehnquist
(c)   Clement Haynsworth
(d)   Warren Burger
Page 619

Pretest Answers:

1: b		11: a	
2: d		12: c	
3: c		13: b	
4: c		14: b	
5: c		15: c	
6: a		16: c	
7: d		17: b	
8: c		18: b	
9: b		19: d	
20: a		20: d	

READING FOR CONTENT

Listed below are sets of questions associated with the content of
each major section of Chapter 16. Carefully review the questions
associated with each section of the text before reading the section.
Have the questions in mind as you read the section and, when you
reach the end of each section, stop and see if you can answer the
questions well. If not, reread the relevant paragraphs until you
are sure of your response to each of the questions.

I.   The Nature of the Judicial System

      Who are the major players in the courts at work?
      What is the difference between criminal law and civil law?
      What is the distinction between original and appellate
         jurisdiction?
      Who are the major participants in the judicial system?

II.   The Politics of Judicial Selection

      How does senatorial courtesy affect judicial appointments to
         lower courts?
      How does the process of appointment for the Supreme Court

work and who plays significant roles?

III. The Backgrounds of Judges and Justices

How are the backgrounds of judges and justices similar?
How have the backgrounds of judges and justices varied?

IV. The Structure of the Federal Judicial System

What is the difference between constitutional and legislative
   courts?
What are some examples of legislative courts?
What is the role and jurisdiction of district courts?
What is the role and jurisdiction of courts of appeal?
What is the role and jurisdiction of the Supreme Court?

V.   The Courts as Policymakers

What is the process by which the Supreme Court accepts cases
   for review?
What is the role of the solicitor general?
What is the process by which the Supreme Court decides cases?
What types of opinions are issued by members of the Court?
What sorts of considerations guide judicial decision-making?
What actors are involved in the implementation of a court
   decision?
How does the nature of the implementation process affect the
impact of court decisions?
How does the case of the abortion decision illustrate the
   difficulties of implementation of judicial decisions?

VI. The Courts and the Policy Agenda

How was judicial review established?
What are major controversies involving judicial review in
   this century?
How have various Courts dealt in distinct ways with the major
   controversies of this century?

VII. Understanding the Courts

How can it be argued that powerful courts are undemocratic?
How can it be argued that the courts contribute to democracy?
What is the distinction between judicial restraint and
   judicial activism?
What considerations limit the policy-making role of the
   courts?
What factors increase the acceptability of activist courts?

CHAPTER OVERVIEW

I. Introduction (587-587)

The American court system is complex with both state and federal court systems. It is in the lower courts that the great bulk of American legal business is done. The Supreme Court hears only a small percentage of all cases brought to court. They include, however, some key issues that will shape people's lives.

II. The Nature Of The Judicial System (587-592)

The judicial system in the United States is an adversarial one in which the courts provide an arena for two parties to bring their conflict before an impartial arbiter (a judge). Federal judges are restricted by the Constitution to deciding "cases or controversies," that is, actual disputes rather than hypothetical ones. Thus the judiciary is essentially passive, dependent on others to take the initiative and bring cases to it. Another constraint on the courts is that they may decide only JUSTICIABLE DISPUTES - those capable of being settled by legal methods.

A. The Courts At Work

The task of judges is to apply and interpret the law in a particular CASE. Every case is a dispute between a PLAINTIFF and a DEFENDANT, the former bringing some charge against the latter. The judge applies the law to the case, determining whether the plaintiff or the defendant is legally correct. In many (but not all) cases, a JURY, a group of citizens (usually twelve), is responsible for the determination of guilt. In CRIMINAL LAW cases an individual is charged with violating a specific law. The offense is harmful and warrants punishment, such as imprisonment or a fine. CIVIL LAW involves no charge of criminality or that a law has been violated. It concerns a dispute between two parties and defines relationships between them.

The vast majority of all civil and criminal cases involve state law and are tried in state courts. Civil cases such as divorce and criminal cases such as burglary normally begin and end in the state, not the federal, courts.

Another important distinction among American courts involves jurisdiction. Courts with ORIGINAL JURISDICTION are those in which a case is heard first, usually in a trial. These courts determine the facts of a case. More than 90 percent of court cases begin and end in the court of original jurisdiction. Courts with APPELLATE JURISDICTION hear cases brought to them on appeal from a lower court. Appellate courts do not review the factual record, only the legal issues involved.

B. Participants in the Judicial System

Only a small part of the action takes place in the courtroom, and only a few persons participate: the judge; the LITIGANTS (the plaintiff and the defendant), the lawyers; and sometimes a jury.

Litigants must have STANDING TO SUE. This means they must have a serious interest in a case - they must have sustained or be in immediate danger of sustaining a direct and substantial injury from another party or an action of government. In recent years there has been some broadening of the concept of standing to sue. CLASS ACTION SUITS permit a small number of people to sue on behalf of all other people similarly situated. These suits have been useful to civil rights groups seeking to end discriminatory practices against a class of people, and environmental protection groups suing polluters on behalf of all affected by the pollution.

The central participants in the judicial system are the judges. They draw upon their backgrounds and beliefs to guide their decision-making, and thus are not neutral automatons who methodically and literally interpret the law. Who they are thus makes a difference in how they decide.

III. The Politics Of Judicial Selection (592-596)

Appointing a federal judge or a Supreme Court justice is a president's chance to leave an enduring mark on the legal system. Once confirmed by the Senate federal judges serve "during good behavior," removable only through impeachment. To further protect them from political pressures it is provided that their salaries cannot be reduced.

A. The Lower Courts

The customary manner in which the Senate disposes of state-level federal judicial nominations is through SENATORIAL COURTESY. Under this unwritten tradition, nominations for these positions are not confirmed when opposed by a senator from the state in which the nominee is to serve. In the case of courts of appeal judges, nominees are not confirmed if opposed by a senator from the state of the nominee's residence, if the senator is of the same party as the president. Because of the strength of this informal practice, presidents usually check with the relevant senator or senators ahead of time to avoid making a nomination that will fail to be confirmed. Typically, the senators of the president's party from the state where the judge will serve suggest names to the attorney general and the president.

The Department of Justice and the Federal Bureau of Investigation then conduct competency and background checks on these persons. If the person recommended clears the hurdles of professional standing and integrity, it is difficult for the president to reject the senators' recommendation. Thus the Constitution is turned on its head, and the Senate ends up making nominations, which the president then approves.

The president usually has more influence in the selection of judges to the federal courts of appeal than to federal district courts. Individual senators are in a weaker position to determine who the nominee will be because the jurisdiction of appeals courts encompass several states. However, senators from the state in which the candidate resides may be able to veto a nomination.

B. The Supreme Court

The president is vitally interested in the Supreme Court and will generally be intimately involved in the recruitment process. Nominations to the Supreme Court may be a president's most important legacy to the nation. On average there has been an opening on the Supreme Court every two years, but there is a substantial variance around this mean and some presidents few or no opportunities to appoint. When the chief justice's position is vacant, the president may nominate either someone already on the Court or someone from outside it to fill the position.

The president operates under fewer constraints in nominating members to the Supreme Court than to the lower courts. Nonetheless, presidents have failed 20 percent of the time to appoint the nominees of their choice to the Court, a percentage much higher than that for any other federal position. This is largely due to the aggressive involvement of the Senate. Though individual senators have little influence, the Judiciary Committee may probe a nominee's judicial philosophy in great detail.

Nominations are most likely to run into trouble when the president's party is in the minority in the Senate or when a nomination is near the end of a term. Also, if a candidate's competence or ethics can be questioned they are greatly weakened. Ideological opposition alone is not enough to defeat a candidate.

IV. The Backgrounds Of Judges And Justices (596-601)

The Constitution sets no special requirements for judges. In practice, they are all lawyers and they are overwhelmingly white males. Federal judges have typically held office as a judge or prosecutor, and often have been involved in partisan politics.

Supreme Court justices have all been lawyers, and all but two have been white males. Most have been in their fifties and sixties when they took office, from the upper-middle to upper class, and Protestant. Geography was once a prominent criterion for selection to the Supreme Court, but it is no longer very important. Typically justices have held high administrative or judicial positions before moving to the Supreme Court. Most have had some experience as a judge, often at the appellate level, and many have worked for the Department of Justice.

Partisanship is an important influence on the selection of judges and justices. Only 13 of 104 members of the Supreme Court have been nominated by presidents of a different party. Usually more than 90 percent of presidents' judicial nominations to lower courts are of members of their own parties.

Ideology is as important as party. Presidents want to appoint to the federal bench people who share their views. They want more than "justice," they want policies with which they agree. Members of the federal bench also play the game of politics, of course, and many try to time their retirements so that a president with compatible views will choose their successor. Presidents are typically pleased with the policy orientations of their choices for the Supreme Court. Nevertheless, it is not always easy to predict the policy inclinations of candidates, and presidents have been disappointed in their nominees about a fourth of the time.

Do policy differences occur when presidents nominate persons with different backgrounds to the bench? The impact of women and minorities is still too recent to assess. Partisan differences are clearer, however. Republican judges in general are somewhat more conservative than Democratic judges. Former prosecutors have been less sympathetic toward defendants' rights. Yet, on many issues party affiliation and other characteristics bring no more predictability to the courts than they do to Congress.

V. The Structure Of The Federal Judicial System (601-606)

Aside form specifying that there will be a Supreme court, the Constitution left it to Congress' discretion to establish lower federal courts of general jurisdiction. In the Judiciary Act of 1789, Congress saw fit to create these "constitutional courts." The current organization of the federal court system is displayed in Figure 16.1 in your textbook.

Congress has also established "legislative courts" for specialized purposes. These include the Court of Military Appeals, the Court of Claims, the Court of International Trade, and the Tax Court. They are staffed by judges who have fixed terms and also lack the protections against removal and salary reductions of those on the constitutional courts.

A. District Courts

The entry point for most litigation in the federal courts is one of the ninety-one DISTRICT COURTS. The district courts are courts of original jurisdiction and hear the following kinds of cases: federal crimes, civil suits under federal law, civil suits between citizens of different states where the amount exceeds fifty thousand dollars, supervision of bankruptcy proceedings, review of the actions of some federal administrative agencies, admiralty and maritime law cases, and supervision of naturalization of aliens.

District judges are assisted by an elaborate supporting cast. In addition to clerks, bailiffs, law clerks, stenographers, court reporters, and probation officers, they have U.S. marshals assigned to each district to protect the judicial process and serve the writs they issue. Another important player is the U.S. attorney. These attorneys and their staffs prosecute violations of federal law and represent the U.S. government in civil cases.

B. Courts of Appeal

The U.S. COURTS OF APPEAL are appellate courts empowered to review all final decisions of district courts except in the few instances that allow direct review by the Supreme Court. The United States is divided into twelve appellate judicial circuits. The focus of cases in the courts of appeal is on correcting errors of procedure and law that occurred in the original proceedings. The courts of appeal hold no trials and hear no testimony. Their decisions set precedent for the courts and agencies within their jurisdictions.

C. The Supreme Court

The Supreme Court does much more for the American political system than deciding discrete cases. Among its most important functions are resolving conflicts among the states and maintaining national supremacy in the law. It also plays an important role in ensuring uniformity in the interpretation of national laws.

There are nine justices on the Supreme Court: eight associates and one chief justice. The Constitution does not require nine - and Congress has set the number at as few as six and as many as ten justices. All nine sit together to hear cases and make decisions. The first decision is which cases to decide. Unlike other federal courts, the Supreme Court controls its own agenda. For a case to be accepted it must involve a "substantial federal question."

VI. The Courts As Policymakers (606-616)

A. Accepting Cases

Deciding what to decide about is the first step in all policy-making. In the Supreme Court the justices have two conferences a week to consider two important matters. The first is the agenda: the justices decide which cases they want to discuss. If four justices agree to take a case, it can be scheduled for oral argument or decided on the basis of the written record already on file with the Court. The most common way for the court to put a case on its docket is by issuing to a lower federal or state court a WRIT OF CERTIORARI, a formal document that calls up a case. The court exercises broad discretion over hearing cases, favoring those involving civil liberties, conflict between different lower courts on the interpretation of federal law, or disagreement between a majority of the Supreme Court and lower court decisions.
Another important influence on the Supreme Court is the SOLICITOR

GENERAL. A presidential appointee and the third-ranking official in the Department of Justice, the solicitor general is in charge of the appellate court litigation of the federal government. The solicitor general and staff decide whether or not to appeal cases the government has lost in lower courts, review and modify the briefs presented in government appeals, and represent the government before the Supreme Court.

B. Making Decisions

The second task of weekly conferences is to discuss the cases accepted and argued before the Court. The Court hears oral arguments in two-week cycles - two weeks of courtroom arguments followed by two weeks of writing opinions about them. Before the justices hear the arguments they receive elaborately prepared written briefs from each party, and from other parties interested in the case who file AMICUS CURIAE (friend of the court) BRIEFS. Amicus curiae briefs may raise additional points of view and information. They are also a way for the government, under the direction of the solicitor general, to seek to influence a case in which it has an interest but is not a party. Attorneys for each side have only a half-hour to address the Court, summarize their argument and respond to questions from the Court.

In conference, the chief justice, who presides, raises a particular case and invites discussion, turning first to the senior associate justice. Once a tentative vote is reached it is necessary to write an OPINION, a statement of the legal reasoning behind the decision. The content of an opinion may be as important as the decision itself. Broad opinions may have far- reaching implications for future cases, while narrowly-drawn opinions may have little impact beyond the specific case decided. If in the majority, the chief justice will either write the opinion or assign it to another justice. If the chief justice is not in the majority, the senior associate justice has this power.

Justices are free to write their own opinions detailing their own views on a case. "Dissenting opinions" are those written by justices opposed to all or part of the majority's decision. "Concurring decisions" are those written to support a majority decision stressing a different constitutional or legal basis for the judgment.

The vast majority of cases reaching the courts are settled on the principle of STARE DECISIS, meaning an earlier decision should hold for the case being considered. All courts rely heavily on precedent - the way similar cases were handled in the past - and lower courts are expected to follow the precedents of higher courts. The Supreme Court is in a position to overrule its own precedents, and it has done so frequently. When precedents are unclear, the ideological and philosophical biases of the members of the Court become more important in guiding their decisions.

C. Implementing Court Decisions

Court decisions carry legal, even moral, authority, but courts do not possess a staff of police to enforce their decisions. They must rely on other units of government to carry out their enforcement. JUDICIAL IMPLEMENTATION refers to how and whether court decisions are translated into actual policy. Resistance by lawyers, other judges, police, government agencies, and the population at large can greatly delay the implementation of judicial decisions.

D. Implementing a Court Decision: The Case of Abortion

The Court's Roe v. Wade (1973) decision protecting a woman's right to obtain an abortion during the first trimester of pregnancy has generated great debate and resistance. This case illustrates that the implementation of any court decision involves many actors besides the justices, and the justices have no way of ensuring that their decisions and policies will be implemented.

VII.   The Courts And The Policy Agenda (616-620)

A. A Historical Review

Until the Civil War, the dominant questions before the court regarded the strength and legitimacy of the federal government and slavery. These issues of nation-building were resolved in favor of the supremacy of the national government. From the Civil War until 1937, questions of the relationship between the federal government and the economy predominated. During this period the Court restricted the power of the federal government to regulate the economy. From 1938 to the present, the paramount issues before the Court have concerned personal liberty and social and political equality. In this era the Court has enlarged the scope of personal freedom and civil rights and has removed many of the constitutional restraints on the regulation of the economy.

1. John Marshall and the Growth of Judicial Review. In the case of MARBURY V. MADISON Chief Justice John Marshall faced a dilemma. When incoming president Thomas Jefferson and his secretary of state James Madison refused to deliver some commissions of the previous administration for minor judicial posts, one of those whose commission was undelivered, William Marbury, sued Madison, asking the Supreme Court to issue a WRIT OF MANDAMUS ordering Madison to give them their commissions. Marshall, also recently appointed by the outgoing administration to the Court, knew that if the court ordered Madison to deliver the commissions, he was likely to ignore it. If the Court denied Marbury's claim it would concede the issue and give the appearance of retreat, reducing the power of the Court. Instead, Marshall shrewdly decided the case by finding the Judiciary Act of 1789, under which Marbury had brought the case, unconstitutional. Thus, he sacrificed a small issue, the commissions, while asserting for the courts the very large power to

determine what is and is not constitutional. The case established the power of JUDICIAL REVIEW, the power to declare acts of Congress and the executive in violation of the Constitution. This is the courts' most controversial power.

2. The "Nine Old Men." The Court was never so controversial as when it was finding unconstitutional key legislation of Franklin Roosevelt's New Deal program. The aging conservative justices so frustrated Roosevelt that he dubbed them the "nine old men" and called on Congress to expand the size of the Court so that he could appoint members more sympathetic to the New Deal's effort to combat the Great Depression. Roosevelt's "court packing" plan became irrelevant when two justices, began to vote in favor of New Deal legislation.

3. The Warren Court. Few eras of the Supreme Court have been as active in shaping public policy as that of the Warren Court. In 1954 it held that laws requiring segregation of the public schools were unconstitutional and later it expanded the rights of criminal defendants and ordered the reapportionment of state legislatures according to the principle of "one man, one vote."

4. The Burger Court. The Burger court was more conservative than the Warren Court, narrowing defendants' rights in some ways. It did a number of "liberal" things, however, producing the Roe v. Wade decision on abortion, requiring busing to eliminate segregation and upholding affirmative action. It also unanimously ordered President Richard Nixon to turn over tapes to Congress in UNITED STATES V. NIXON (1974), hastening his resignation.

5. The Rehnquist Court. By the late 1980s the Court had a clear conservative majority. It has been slowly chipping away at liberal precedents concerning defendant's rights, abortion, and affirmative action.

VIII. Understanding The Courts (620-625)

The power of judges in the United States raises important questions about the compatibility of unelected courts with a democracy.

A. The Courts and Democracy

Federal judges are not elected and are almost impossible to remove. If democracy requires that key policymakers always be elected or be continually responsible to those who are, then the courts diverge from the requirements of democracy. The Constitution's framers wanted it that way, however. The courts were intended to be relatively immune from popular opinion.

The courts are not entirely independent of popular preferences, however. One political scientist found that the Court is normally in line with popular majorities. When it is out of step, it eventually swings around, as it did with the New Deal. Members of the Court are not isolated - they receive mail and read the newspapers. It is unlikely that members cave in to interest group pressures, but they are aware of the public's concern about issues and this becomes part of their consciousness as they decide cases.

Courts can also promote pluralism. Groups have found the courts to be another avenue through which to pursue their interests when others are unsuccessful. The early civil rights successes came largely in the courts rather than in the broader legislative or political process.

B. What courts Should Do: The Issue of Judicial Power

There are strong disagreements concerning the appropriateness of allowing the courts to have a policy-making role. Many scholars and judges favor a policy of JUDICIAL RESTRAINT, in which judges play minimal policy-making roles, leaving policy decisions strictly to the legislatures. Advocates of judicial restraint believe that decisions such as those on abortion and school prayer go well beyond the "referee" role they feel is appropriate for courts in a democracy. On the other side are proponents of JUDICIAL ACTIVISM, in which judges make bolder policy decisions, even charting new constitutional ground with a particular decision. It is important to note that judicial activists can be either liberals or conservatives.

The federal courts have developed a doctrine of POLITICAL QUESTIONS as a means to avoid deciding some cases, principally those regarding conflicts between the president and Congress. Similarly, judges typically exercise discretion to attempt, whenever possible, to avoid deciding a case on the basis of the Constitution, preferring less contentious "technical" grounds. They also employ issues of jurisdiction, mootness, standing, ripeness, and other conditions to avoid adjudication of some politically charged cases.

Court activism can also be checked by the other branches. The president and Senate determine who sits on the federal bench. Congress can begin the process of amending the Constitution to overcome a constitutional decision of the Supreme Court. Congress can also alter the appellate jurisdiction of the Supreme Court, its size, and the structure of lower courts. Finally, if the issue is one of STATUTORY CONSTRUCTION, in which a court interprets an act of Congress, the legislature routinely passes legislation that clarifies existing laws and, in effect, overturns the courts. Thus the description of the judiciary as the "ultimate arbiter of the Constitution" is overstated, all the branches of government help define and shape the Constitution.

DOING RESEARCH ON THE COURTS

Nearly every really controversial issue sooner or later winds up in the courts. The Supreme Court must finally resolve the most difficult of these. The issues the Supreme Court has been called upon to resolve thus provide an excellent source of ideas for research papers. Doing and investigation into the issue and the Court's decision on it will not only educated you on the issue, but also give you a better appreciation for the role of the courts in policy making and interpretation of the Constitution and statutory law. The importance of a relatively politically isolated body to make decisions concerning such issues will also be made clear in many cases. Abortion, school prayer, flag-burning, the teaching of "creationism" along with evolution, the death penalty, affirmative action, obscenity, etc., are examples that just begin to scratch the surface of the potential issues from which you can select.

If you are sold on the idea you are probably thinking, "Ok, but where do I get the information I need." Well, we are here to help and we aim to please. A very useful starting point for researching Supreme Court decisions is Nancy Guenther's <u>United States Supreme Court Decisions</u>. It lists Court decisions and, importantly, includes a bibliography of works on each case. The cases are indexed by subject as well as case name, so you will not necessarily need to know the formal case name to find what you are interested in. Once you find a case, however, record the name and the identifying numbers listed with it. These numbers indicate where the full official version of the opinion is to be found in <u>U.S. Reports</u>, published by the U.S. Government Printing Office. The first number being the volume number, while the number following the US indicates the page. You may find you wish to see the full opinion in some cases.

If you are more interested in researching the Supreme Court itself as an institution, a good place to begin is with <u>Congressional Quarterly's Guide to the U.S. Supreme Court</u>. This reviews the development of the Court from its origins, analyses the role of the Court, and its major decisions. It also provides brief biographies of every justice to ever have sat on the Court, if your research is focusing on a particular individual and their impact.

REVIEW TEST

Read through the Chapter Overview and review the "Reading for Content" questions if you haven't already done so. If you feel like you have achieved the learning objectives listed at the beginning of the chapter, you should be ready for the Review Test. Again, take the test as if you were taking it in class. Keep going over the Review Tests until you know them all - and know why the answers are correct. They are good preparation for exams.

1. In addition to the Supreme Court, there are _____ federal courts of appeal.
   (a) nine

(b) twelve
(c) twenty-two
(d) ninety-one
Page 587

2. The great bulk of American legal business is transacted in:
    (a) the thousands of state and local courts.
    (b) the ninety one federal district courts.
    (c) the twelve federal courts of appeal.
    (d) the Supreme Court.
Page 587

3. A constraint upon courts is that they can only decide _____
    disputes, or conflicts capable of being decided by legal
    methods.
    (a) certiorari
    (b) fiduciary
    (c) congressional
    (d) justiciable
Page 588

4. In _____ law cases, an individual is charged with violating
    a specific law and may warrant punishment.
    (a) civil
    (b) federal
    (c) criminal
    (d) jurisdiction
Page 588

5. More than 90 percent of court cases begin and end in the court
    of:
    (a) appeals.
    (b) original jurisdiction.
    (c) a jury.
    (d) municipals.
Page 589-590

6. At the state level, the appellate process normally ends with:
    (a) cases going back to the municipal level.
    (b) a dismissal.
    (c) the U.S. Supreme Court.
    (d) the state Supreme Court.
Page 590

7. Another name for a plaintiff or a defendant is a _____.
    (a) judiciary.
    (b) litigant.
    (c) jurist.
    (d) para-legal.
Page 590

8. One of the most famous class action suits resulted in the

347

landmark _____ case that desegregated public schools.
   (a)   Brown v. the Board of Education.
   (b)   Miller v. California
   (c)   Bakke v. the Board of Regents
   (d)   Roe v. Wade
Page 590-591

9.   The United States counted about _____ lawyers in 1990.
   (a)   25,000
   (b)   100,000
   (c)   500,000
   (d)   700,000
Page 591

10.   No Supreme Court justice has ever been removed from office, although one, _____, was tried but not convicted by the Senate in 1805.
   (a)   Samuel Chase
   (b)   John Jay
   (c)   John Marshall
   (d)   John Rutledge
Page 592

11.   The _____ nominates persons to fill judicial slots on the federal level, including the Supreme Court.
   (a)   Congress
   (b)   individual senators from each state.
   (c)   House of Representatives
   (d)   president
Page 592

12.   The customary manner in which the Senate disposes of state-level federal judicial nominations is through:
   (a)   presidential nominations.
   (b)   the Senate judiciary committee.
   (c)   the House of Representatives.
   (d)   senatorial courtesy.
Page 592

13.   Before a person is nominated by the president for a federal court position, his background and competency are closely examined by:
   (a)   sitting justices.
   (b)   the Department of Justice.
   (c)   the Federal Bureau of Investigation.
   (d)   all answers are correct.
Page 593

14. The president generally takes a greater interest and has more personal influence in the appointment of _____ judges.
    (a) federal appellate
    (b) federal district
    (c) municipal
    (d) state
Page 593

15. Presidents have failed _____ percent of the time to appoint the nominee of their choice to the Supreme Court.
    (a) 3
    (b) 10
    (c) 20
    (d) 35
Page 594

16. Future Supreme Court nominee, but not justice, _____ was in the Justice Department and had the responsibility of firing special Watergate prosecutor Archibald Cox.
    (a) Abe Fortas
    (b) Robert Bork
    (c) William Rehnquist
    (d) Antonin Scalia
Page 595

17. Six days after the defeat of Robert Bork's nomination, President Reagan nominated _____ for the Supreme Court seat. The judge withdrew his nomination after revealing that he had smoked marijuana while a professor at Harvard.
    (a) Anthony Kennedy
    (b) Douglas Souter
    (c) John Paul Stevens
    (d) Douglas Ginsburg
Page 595

18. The first African-American to serve on the Supreme Court was _____, appointed by President Lyndon Johnson in 1967.
    (a) Thurgood Marshall
    (b) Ralph David Abernathy
    (c) Carl Stokes
    (d) Stokeley Charmichael
Page 598

19. Former president and chief justice _____ remained at his post until his death because he feared that President Hoover, more moderate than he, would not nominate a suitable successor.
    (a) Earl Warren
    (b) Roger Taney
    (c) Theodore Roosevelt
    (d) William Howard Taft
Page 600

20. After Chief Justice Warren resigned in 1968, President Johnson named his old friend _____ to the post. He failed to win confirmation by the Senate.
    (a) Warren Burger
    (b) Abe Fortas
    (c) William Brennan
    (d) Hugo Black
Page 600

21. The Supreme Court nominations of President _____ did much to turn the court into a basically conservative direction.
    (a) Woodrow Wilson
    (b) Franklin Roosevelt
    (c) Lyndon Johnson
    (d) Richard Nixon
Page 600

22. In the Judiciary Act of 1789, Congress saw fit to create _____ courts and America has never been without them.
    (a) supreme
    (b) constitutional
    (c) state
    (d) municipal
Page 601

23. The _____ courts are courts of original jurisdiction and hear no appeals.
    (a) state Supreme
    (b) appellate
    (c) legislative
    (d) district
Page 602

24. The only federal courts in which trials are held and juries may be empaneled are in _____ courts.
    (a) appellate
    (b) district
    (c) state Supreme
    (d) legislative
Page 602

25. About _____ percent of criminal cases decided in the federal district courts in 1988 were disposed of without trial.
    (a) 15
    (b) 37
    (c) 52
    (d) 83
Page 602

26. The United States is divided into _____ judicial circuits, including one for the District of Columbia.

(a)   12
(b)   25
(c)   51
(d)   156
Page 602

27.   There are _____ justices on the Supreme Court.
(a)   six
(b)   nine
(c)   ten
(d)   twelve
Page 605

28.   The most common way for the Court to put a case on its docket
is by issuing to a lower federal or state court a _____
that calls up a case.
(a)   writ of certiorari
(b)   writ of habeas corpus
(c)   fiduciary
(d)   mandate
Page 607

29.   The _____ is in charge of the appellate court litigation of
the federal government.
(a)   Chief Justice
(b)   senior associate Supreme Court Justice
(c)   solicitor general
(d)   attorney general
Page 608

30.   _____ briefs attempt to influence the Court by raising
additional points of view and presenting information not
contained in attorney's briefs.
(a)   Amicus curiae
(b)   Writ of certiorari
(c)   Writ of habeas corpus
(d)   Per curiam
Page 609

31.   At least _____ justices must participate in a case and
decisions are made by majority vote.
(a)   nine
(b)   eight
(c)   seven
(d)   six
Page 610

32.   If the Supreme Court rules in favor of abortion under certain
conditions, it has established a _____ and lower courts

351

are expected to follow it.
(a)   mandate
(b)   precedent
(c)   law
(d)   stare decisis
Page 610

33.   The decision of _____ held that a woman has a right to an abortion in the first trimester of her pregnancy.
(a)   Texas v. Johnson
(b)   Webster v. Reproductive Health Services
(c)   Near v. Minnesota
(d)   Roe v. Wade
Page 614

34.   Few have played a more important role in making the Supreme Court a significant national agenda setter than _____, chief justice from 1801 to 1835.
(a)   John Jay
(b)   John Marshall
(c)   Oliver Ellsworth
(d)   John Rutledge
Page 616

35.   After the presidential victory by Thomas Jefferson, _____ caused a controversy when he appointed several people to judicial posts at the last minute, including William Marbury to a minor post.
(a)   President John Adams
(b)   Secretary of State John Marshall
(c)   Secretary of Treasury Alexander Hamilton
(d)   Chief Justice John Jay
Page 616

36.   In the case of Marbury v. Madison, the Supreme Court established the power of _____, the power of the courts to hold acts of Congress in violation of the Constitution.
(a)   judicial review
(b)   policy review
(c)   congressional review
(d)   mandamus
Page 617

37.   In 1937, _____ caused a controversy when he proposed that Congress expand the size of the Supreme Court, which would allow the president to appoint additional justices sympathetic to the New Deal.
(a)   Vice-President Garner
(b)   Chief Justice Charles Evans Hughes
(c)   President Franklin Roosevelt
(d)   Wendell Wilkie
Page 618

38. Few eras of the Supreme Court have been as active in shaping public policy as that of the 1953-1969 court presided over by Chief Justice:
    (a) Earl Warren.
    (b) Abe Fortas.
    (c) Fred Vinson.
    (d) Charles Evans Hughes.
Page 618

39. Many scholars and judges favor a policy of judicial _____, in which judges play a minimal role in policy making, leaving policy decisions strictly to the legislatures.
    (a) activism
    (b) restraint
    (c) review
    (d) parity
Page 623

40. The federal courts have developed a doctrine of _____ as a means to avoid deciding some cases, principally those regarding conflicts between the president and Congress.
    (a) judicial review
    (b) judicial activism
    (c) judicial restraint
    (d) political questions
Page 623

BEFORE GOING ON

Use the answer key below to "grade" your exam and see how you did. Be sure to go back and reread the relevant passages on the indicated page for any you have missed. If you were sort of "asleep" when you read that passage, there may be something else you missed there as well.

Review Test Answers:

1: b	11: d	21: d	31: d
2: a	12: d	22: b	32: b
3: d	13: d	23: d	33: d
4: c	14: a	24: b	34: b
5: b	15: c	25: d	35: a
6: d	16: b	26: a	36: a
7: b	17: d	27: b	37: c
8: a	18: a	28: a	38: a

| 9: d | 19: d | 29: c | 39: b |
| 10: a | 20: b | 30: a | 40: d |

Of course, a chapter on the courts generates an impressive list of Key Terms. Look at those three long columns on page 626! Not only are there a lot of them, but there are a lot of impressive sounding ones too - lots of Latin! Be sure you have a good grasp of all that because it is in matters like the courts that terms reach there maximum importance for the purposes of exams. It is hard not to choose one of those Latin terms for the word of the week - but there are so many juicy ones to choose from. I think the most useful one is "per curiam decision." It is useful because we often have need of making them ourselves. My father issued a lot of per curiam decisions as I remember, though he didn't have the fancy term for them. As I get older I appreciate the need for them ever more thoroughly. If challenged on a course of behavior or choice, you can simply say your decision is a "per curiam" decision, and while they are looking it up you can make your escape. Incidently, if you want to read some juicy stuff on some pretentious guys in black robes, pick up a copy of Woodward and Armstrong's The Brethren (listed in your For Further Reading). Oh the stories those clerks can tell!

CHAPTER 17

ECONOMIC POLICY-MAKING

CHAPTER LEARNING OBJECTIVES

After reading Chapter 17, you should be able to:

1. Describe how the government measures unemployment and inflation.
2. Discuss how economic conditions are related to voting behavior and the policy positions of political parties.
3. Describe how monetary policy is made.
4. Define fiscal policy.
5. Describe Keynesian and supply-side economic theories.
6. Discuss factors limiting the government's ability to control the economy.
7. Discuss the major government policies in each arena of economic policy-making.
8. Discuss the nature of "democratic" economic policy.

PRETEST QUESTIONS

The pretest below will give you an idea of the state of your knowledge about economic policy-making. Take the whole pretest, then check your answers against the key that follows. As you read the chapter, watch for where these questions are addressed so that you may learn why the answer is what it is.

1. All of the following have been effects of even slight increase in unemployment EXCEPT:
    (a) a decrease in the suicide rate.
    (b) an increase in the homicide rate.
    (c) an increase in admissions to state hospitals.
    (d) a slight increase in deaths from cirrhosis of the liver.
    Page 638

2. _____ administrations are more willing to tolerate recessions and high unemployment.
    (a) neither Republican nor Democratic
    (b) both Republican and Democratic
    (c) Republican
    (d) Democratic
    Page 641

3. All of the following are members of the Republican coalition are
    most interested in keeping inflation down EXCEPT:
    (a) business owners.
    (b) business managers.
    (c) professional workers.
    (d) labor unions.
    Page 642

4. When the stock market crashed in 1929, President _____ clung
    to the laissez-faire principle that government should not meddle
    with the economy.
    (a) Franklin Roosevelt
    (b) Calvin Coolidge
    (c) Woodrow Wilson
    (d) Herbert Hoover
    Page 642

5. One way the government can control the economy is through _____
    policy, or the manipulation of the supply of money.
    (a) monetary
    (b) fiscal
    (c) laissez-faire
    (d) liberal
    Page 642

6. The Board of Governors of the Federal Reserve is called:
    (a) the BOG.
    (b) the "Fed."
    (c) the GOB.
    (d) SNAFU.
    Page 642

7. All of the following are affected either directly or indirectly
    by the financial dealings of the "Fed" EXCEPT:
    (a) the amount of money available.
    (b) interest rates.
    (c) availability of jobs.
    (d) the price of oil and gas.
    Page 643

8. The central issue in economic policy-making has been if
    _____ government best ensures a strong economy.
    (a) laissez-faire
    (b) classical liberal
    (c) populist
    (d) bigger or smaller
    Page 644-645

9. John Maynard Keynes argued that America could find its way out of the Depression by stimulating the economy through:
   (a) raising interest rates.
   (b) decreasing the money supply.
   (c) spending.
   (d) raising taxes.
Page 645

10. Edward Tufte concluded that, between World War II and 1976, real disposable income (after taxes and inflation) tended to _____ more at election time than other times.
   (a) increase
   (b) decrease
   (c) stay the same
   (d) spiral downward rapidly
Page 646

11. Fiscal policy is hindered by:
   (a) constant international interference.
   (b) the budgetary process.
   (c) Social Security.
   (d) the cost of living.
Page 647

12. President Reagan's controversial budget director was:
   (a) James A. Baker III.
   (b) Paul Volker.
   (c) David Stockman.
   (d) James Watt.
Page 647

13. From 1970 to the late 1980's the American farm population dropped:
   (a) a third.
   (b) a fourth.
   (c) a half.
   (d) three-quarters.
Page 648

14. Corporate mergers amounted to a whopping $_____ billion in 1986 compared to just $30 billion six years earlier.
   (a) 60
   (b) 120
   (c) 200
   (d) 560
Page 651

15. The first anti-trust act in the United States was the _____
    Act of 1890.
    (a) Hatch
    (b) Pendleton
    (c) Taft-Hartley
    (d) Sherman
Page 653

16. The Food and Drug Administration has come under fire recently
    for its inability to quickly approve experimental drugs for the
    treatment of:
    (a) cancer.
    (b) leukemia.
    (c) AIDS.
    (d) alzheimer's disease.
Page 656

17. The federal government was busier busting unions than trusts
    until the _____ Act of 1914 exempted unions from
    antitrust laws.
    (a) Clayton antitrust
    (b) Sherman
    (c) Taft-Hartley
    (d) Pendleton
Page 658

18. The _____ Act of 1947 continued to guarantee unions the
    right of collective bargaining but prohibited various unfair
    practices by unions as well.
    (a) Taft-Hartley
    (b) Clayton Antitrust
    (c) Sherman
    (d) Wagner
Page 658

19. More recently, President _____ approved a measure that will
    raise the minimum wage to $4.25 by 1991 and establish a lower
    "training wage" for teenage employees.
    (a) Nixon
    (b) Carter
    (c) Bush
    (d) Reagan
Page 660

20. In terms of assets, and according to Fortune magazine, the top
    industrial corporation in America in 1989-90 is:
    (a) RJR Nabisco.
    (b) General Motors.
    (c) IBM.
    (d) Texaco.
Page 650

Pretest Answers:

1: a		11: b	
2: c		12: c	
3: d		13: a	
4: d		14: c	
5: a		15: d	
6: b		16: c	
7: d		17: a	
8: d		18: a	
9: c		19: c	
10: a		20: b	

READING FOR CONTENT

Listed below are sets of questions associated with the content of each major section of Chapter 17. Carefully review the questions associated with each section of the text before reading the section. Have the questions in mind as you read the section and, when you reach the end of each section, stop and see if you can answer the questions well. If not, reread the relevant paragraphs until you are sure of your response to each of the questions.

I. Politics and Economics

   How is the unemployment rate measured?
   What impact does increasing unemployment have on society?
   How is the inflation rate measured?
   What is the consequence of rising inflation?
   How do economic conditions affect voting behavior?
   What are the differences in the major parties on economic
      policy direction?

II. Government's Instruments for Controlling the Economy

   What is monetary policy?
   How is monetary policy made?
   What is fiscal policy?
   What are the central tenets of Keynesian economic theory?
   What are the central tenets of supply-side economics?

III. Obstacles to Controlling the Economy

   What are the major obstacles limiting government's ability to
      control the economy?

IV. Arenas of Economic Policy-Making

   What are the major policies in the agricultural arena?
   What are the major policies in the business arena?
   What are the major policies in the consumer arena?
   What are the major policies in the labor arena?

Chapter 17

V.   Democracy and Economic Policy-Making

     How has the democratic policy-making process affected
        economic policy?

CHAPTER OVERVIEW

I.   Introduction   (636-636)

Few policy issues evoke stronger disagreement than those about the
economy. Voters often judge officeholders by how well the economy
performs. Economists do not agree about the causes and cures of
economic problems, complicating the job of policy-makers.

II. Politics And Economics (636-642)

The view that politics and economics are closely linked is neither
new or unique.   Both James Madison, the architect of the
Constitution, and Karl Marx, the founder of communist theory, argued
that economic conflict was at the root of politics.

A. Government and the Economy

Unemployment and inflation create social problems. As a result,
they have an impact on voting behavior. Unemployment is measured by
the Bureau of Labor Statistics (BLS) in the Department of Labor.
The BLS conducts a massive fifty thousand person survey to determine
the UNEMPLOYMENT RATE - the proportion of the labor force actively
seeking work but unable to find a job. Increased unemployment is
associated with increases in such social problems as alcoholism,
suicide, mental health, and homicide.

The problem of inflation is the other half of policy-makers' regular
economic concern. The key measure of inflation is the CONSUMER
PRICE INDEX (CPI). Unlike unemployment, inflation hurts some but
actually benefits others. Some groups are especially hard hit, such
as those on fixed incomes. People whose salary increases with the
CPI but whose mortgage payments are fixed find inflation actually
increases their buying power. There are few who want the economic
uncertainty of high inflation, however.

B. Elections and the Economy

Ample evidence indicates that voters pay attention to economic
trends in making up their minds on election day, those of the nation
as well as their personal situation. Voters who experience
unemployment in their family and even those who just feel that
unemployment is a serious problem lean toward the Democrats. On the
other hand, most of the time people are not sufficiently affected by
inflation for it to influence their vote.

C. Political Parties and the Economy

All over the world it has been found that parties adopt economic policies broadly in accordance with the objective economic interest and subjective preferences of their core political constituencies. The Democratic coalition is made up of groups who worry about unemployment - union members, minorities, and the poor. The Republican coalition rests more heavily on people who are most concerned abut steady prices for their goods and services -business owners, managers, and professional people.

III. Government's Instruments For Controlling The Economy (642-646)

If it ever existed, the time when government could assume that the private marketplace could handle economic problems ended with the Great Depression. In the face of soaring unemployment in the wake of the 1929 stock market crash, President Herbert Hoover clung to the LAISSEZ-FAIRE principle that government should not meddle with the economy. In 1932 Hoover was handed a crushing defeat by Franklin D. Roosevelt, whose New Deal experimented with dozens of new federal policies to put the economy back on track. Since the New Deal policy-makers have routinely used monetary and fiscal policy to seek to control the economy.

A. Monetary Policy and the Fed

MONETARY POLICY is the manipulation of the supply of money in private hands. An economic theory called MONETARISM holds that the supply of money is the key to the nation's economic health. Having too much cash and credit available generates inflation, monetarists argue, so growth in the money supply should be held to the growth in the real gross national product (GNP).

The main agency for making monetary policy is "the Fed," whose formal title is the Board of Governors of the Federal Reserve System. Created in 1913 by Congress to regulate the lending practices of banks and thus the money supply, the FEDERAL RESERVE SYSTEM was intended to be beyond the control of the president and Congress - thus able to make monetary policy without regard to partisan politics.

The Fed has three basic instruments for controlling the money supply. First, the Fed sets "discount rates" for the money that banks borrow from the Federal Reserve banks. If they raise this rate, the increase will be passed on to banks' customers. Fewer people will want to take out loans and thus less money will be in circulation. Second, the Fed sets "reserve requirements" that determine the amount of money that banks must keep in reserve at all times. Increases in the requirement mean less money to lend out. Third, the Fed can create more money to sell to the banks. Whereas raising the costs of borrowing money increases the risk of unemployment and recession, making more money available to borrow increases the risk of inflation.

With so much riding on its decisions, presidents naturally try to persuade the Fed to pursue policies in line with their plan for the economy. There is some evidence that the Fed is generally responsive to the White House, though not to the extent of trying to influence election results.

B. Fiscal Policy: Bigger versus Smaller Government

FISCAL POLICY describes the impact of the federal budget - taxing, spending, borrowing - on the economy. Unlike monetary policy, fiscal policy is shaped mostly by the Congress and the president. Whether bigger government (more active in fiscal policy) or smaller government best ensures a strong economy has become the central issue in economic policy-making.

On the side of big government is KEYNESIAN ECONOMIC THEORY, based on the work of English economist John Maynard Keynes. The dominant economic philosophy of America in the late 1930s, this theory emphasized that government spending could help the economy weather its normal ups and downs. Keynes argued, for example, that government could end the Depression by stimulating the economy through spending. The government's job was to increase the demand when necessary - the supply would take care of itself.

Until the Reagan administration, both Democrats and Republicans adhered to the basic tenets of Keynesianism. Reagan's economic advisors proposed a radically different theory based on the premise that the key task for government economic policy is to stimulate supply of goods, not their demand. Thus, this theory has been labeled SUPPLY-SIDE ECONOMICS. To supply-siders, by taxing too heavily, spending too freely, and regulating too tightly, government curtailed economic growth. They argued that incentives to invest, work harder, and save could be increased by cutting back on the scope of government - especially tax rates.

When the Reagan administration was faced with the worst downturn since the 1930's, it responded with massive tax cuts, mostly for the well-to-do, rather than public works programs to stimulate demand. The tax cuts were consistent with the supply-siders' desire to stimulate supply and reduce the size of government.

Whichever fiscal approach politicians favor, one formerly controversial issue is now agreed upon - it is the government's responsibility to use fiscal policy to try to control the economy.

IV. Obstacles To Controlling The Economy (646-647)

If politicians could control the economy they would always ensure that all was well at election time. But all the instruments for controlling the economy have one aspect in common: they are difficult to use. First, politicians do not understand the workings of the economy well enough to always choose the correct adjustments. Many spending programs, like Social Security, are indexed - meaning they go up automatically with the cost of living - reducing control by politicians. Also, as we have seen, budget decisions are made far in advance of their impact on the economy.

The American capitalist system presents an additional restraint on controlling the economy. The private sector is much larger than the public, and dominates the economy. A rise in oil prices, for example, can offset all government policies to control inflation. Fiscal policy is also hindered by the budget process. Most of the budget expenditures are "uncontrollable," and coordinating economic policy in a highly decentralized system is difficult.

V.   Arenas Of Economic Policy-Making (647-660)

Liberals tend to favor active government involvement in the economy in order to smooth out the unavoidable inequalities of a capitalist system. Conservatives maintain that a more productive economy will be realized if government exercises a hands-off policy of minimal regulation. Liberal or conservative, most interest groups seek benefits, protection from unemployment, or safeguards against harmful business practices from government.

A. Agriculture and Public Policy: The Bitter Harvest

Ever since the Agricultural Adjustment Act of 1933, passed in response to the ravages of the Depression, the government has subsidized farmers. Through "price supports" the government guarantees the prices of certain commodities in order to ensure stability in agricultural production. The argument is that the short-run costs of keeping prices up are less than the long-run costs that might result from falling prices. If low prices forced many farmers out of business, America's food supply might be threatened. Critics see farm subsidies as nothing more than a huge welfare program. Despite government subsidies for agriculture small many family farms have been squeezed out of business. High costs of technology and falling prices of farm property led to many resulted in bankruptcies in the 1980s rivaling Depression-era rates.

B. Business and Public Policy: Subsidies amidst Regulations

The corporation has long stood at the center of the American economy. The largest corporations represent "monopoly capital," a concentration of wealth sufficient to shape both America's and the world's economy. Concentration of wealth has been increasing since the 1950s and has internationalized as well. Some MULTINATIONAL CORPORATIONS are bigger than most governments.
1. The Changing Face of Corporate Capitalism. Providing innovative new products or better service not only leads to a good profit, it also to contributes to economic growth. In the 1980s, however, a

new form of entrepreneurship flourished - conglomerates buying up and buying out other companies. Indeed, millions can be made merely by threatening to buy another company. This highly risky business has been labeled "paper entrepreneurialism" by Robert Reich. He and others criticize it as producing no products and no new jobs - nothing of tangible use. Business leaders argue, however, that fear of corporate takeovers keeps management constantly on its toes, providing better services and products.

Another popular argument in favor of the increased concentration of corporate assets is that it strengthens the American economy against competition from giant Japanese and European firms. An increasing number of Americans believe that the greatest threat to national security comes not from communist military power, but from the economic power of Japan and other capitalist competitors. It is important to keep in mind, however, that while foreign investment in the United States is growing, it still remains below that of most other economic powers. The United States remains the world's leading exporter of merchandise, twice as much as Japan.

2. Regulating Business. Government regulation of business is at least as old as the Sherman Act of 1890. The purpose of ANTITRUST POLICY is to ensure competition and prevent monopoly (control of a market by one company). Such legislation permits the Justice Department to sue in federal court to break up companies controlling too large a share of the market. It also generally prevents restraints on trade or limitations on competition. Antitrust is not the only way business is regulated (see Chapter 15). Business owners complain constantly about regulation, but they also get many benefits from government.

3. Benefiting Business. When a crucial industry has hard times, it usually looks to the government for help in the form of subsidies, tax breaks, or loan guarantees. The Department of Commerce serves as a storehouse of aids for business. It collects data on products and markets, helps businesses export, and protects inventions. The Small Business Administration is the government's counselor and loan maker to small businesses. In fact, the federal government is the principal source of research and development funding in the United States. Support is more prevalent during Republican administrations, but this sort of aid is available all the time.

C. Consumer Policy: The Rise of the Consumer Lobby

The first major consumer protection policy in the United States was the Food and Drug Act of 1906, which prohibited the interstate transportation of dangerous or impure food and drugs. Today the FOOD AND DRUG ADMINISTRATION (FDA) has broad regulatory powers over the content, marketing, and labeling of food and drugs.
Consumerism was a sleeping political giant until the 1960s, when it was awakened by consumer activists such as Ralph Nader. They found unsafe products and called for government to be a watchdog on behalf of the public. A flood of consumer protection legislation followed.

The Consumer Product Safety commission (CPSC) has broad powers to ban hazardous products from the market. The FEDERAL TRADE COMMISSION (FTC), traditionally responsible for regulating trade practices, also jumped into the business of consumer protection, becoming a defender of consumer interests in truth in advertising and lending practices.

D. Labor and Government

The biggest change in economic policy-making has been the 180 degree turn in public policy toward labor unions over the past century. Throughout the nineteenth century and into the twentieth, the federal government joined with business to squelch labor unions. The major turnabout in government policy toward labor took place during the New Deal. In 1935 Congress passed the NATIONAL LABOR RELATIONS ACT (Wagner Act), which guaranteed workers the right of COLLECTIVE BARGAINING - the right to have representatives of their unions negotiate with management to determine working conditions.

The TAFT-HARTLEY ACT of 1947 continued to guarantee unions the right of collective bargaining, but protected management by prohibiting various unfair practices by unions as well. Most importantly, this law permitted states to adopt what union opponents call RIGHT-TO-WORK LAWS. Such laws forbid requirements in labor contracts that workers must join a union to hold their jobs. Right-to-work laws subject unions to the free-rider problem (see Chapter 10). Later public policies, such as the Landrum- Griffin Act, focused on union corruption.

Unions have had two notable policy successes. One is the establishment of government unemployment compensation (paid for by workers and employers) to cushion the blows of unemployment. The second is the guaranteed minimum wage.

VI. Democracy And Economic Policy-Making (660-661)

The minimum wage and unemployment compensation are just two of many economic policies that contradict Karl Marx's assumptions of how a capitalist system inevitably exploits ordinary workers. These policies reflect how solutions to many of the problems of a free enterprise economy were achieved through the democratic process. As the voting power of the ordinary worker grew, so did the potential for government regulation of the worst ravages of the capitalist system. Through the ballot box, Americans essentially decided to give up certain economic freedoms for the good of society as a whole.

It would be an exaggeration to say that democracy regularly facilitates an economic policy that looks after general rather than specific interests. The decentralized American political system often works against efficiency in government. Groups that may be adversely affected by an economic policy have many avenues through which they can block it. One of the consequences of democracy for economic policy-making is thus that it is difficult to make decisions that hurt particular groups or that involve short-term pain for long-term gain.

DOING RESEARCH ON ECONOMIC POLICY

Papers on economic policy might focus on the processes and controversies surrounding either monetary or fiscal policy, on the question of business regulation and subsidies, on the general theories or approaches to economic policy, or on economic policy and the nation's international trade position. Monetary policy is a mystery to most students, and the importance of its impact is a surprise. If you are interested in looking at the process and impact of monetary policy a good place to begin is by reading an article in the New York Times on the resignation of Paul Volker as Chairman of the Federal Reserve Board on June 3, 1987. The article provides an interesting insight on the tools and impact of the Fed.

The major controversy surrounding fiscal policy involves the massive deficit spending policies of the 1980s. Papers could focus on the sources of the sudden jump in the size of the deficits in the early 1980s, the possible impact of the huge national debt that has been built up, or possible reforms that might bring the deficit under control. The impact of the Gramm-Rudman-Hollings Act or the viability of a balanced budget amendment are related topics that you might wish to explore.

The question of business regulation and subsidies is always a source of great controversy. The implications of business regulation for competition, prices, profitability, quality of service and/or safety can be addressed in a paper. The conflict of such laudable values can be explored in the context of regulation of the airline, trucking, or savings and loan industries, for example.

You may wish to delve more deeply into each of the economic theoretical approaches introduced in your text. The role of government in each and their likely political ramifications (who gets what) by policies guided by each theory can provide interesting discussions. In addition, to Keynesianism and supply-side theories you may also wish to include an approach that is not discussed in your text called "industrial policy" in your analysis. You may even wish to focus your attention on this approach. A good starting point for gaining a perspective on the industrial policy approach is the works of Robert Reich. I would recommend starting with his The Next American Frontier.

REVIEW TEST

Read through the Chapter Overview and review the "Reading for Content" questions if you haven't already done so. If you feel like you have achieved the learning objectives listed at the beginning of the chapter, you should be ready for the Review Test. Again, take

the test as if you were taking it in class. Keep going over the
Review Tests until you know them all - and know why the answers are
correct. They are good preparation for exams.

1. Both James Madison, the architect of the Constitution, and Karl
    Marx, founder of communist theory, argued that _____ was
    at the root of politics.
    (a) economic conflict
    (b) personality
    (c) compromise
    (d) economic consensus
Page 637

2. Measuring how many and what types of workers are unemployed is
    one of the major jobs of the:
    (a) White House Staff
    (b) Bureau of Labor Statistics (BLS)
    (c) Department of the Interior
    (d) Department of Treasury
Page 637

3. It seems to be a general rule that _____ administrations are
    more willing to tolerate high inflation rates.
    (a) Republican
    (b) Democratic
    (c) Republican and Democratic
    (d) neither Republican nor Democratic
Page 641

4. It has been noted that when inflation is high:
    (a) incumbents in Congress are lose their offices.
    (b) Democrats generally win presidential elections.
    (c) Republicans generally win presidential elections.
    (d) people don't care enough or are not sufficiently affected
         by inflation to let it influence their vote.
Page 641

5. All of the following are members of the Democratic coalition
    that would worry the most about unemployment EXCEPT:
    (a) union members.
    (b) minorities.
    (c) corporate presidents.
    (d) the poor.
Page 641

6. Government has been actively steering the economy ever since:
    (a) the Vietnam War.
    (b) World War II.
    (c) the Great Depression.
    (d) World War I.
Page 642

7. In the next presidential election after the Great Crash of 1929, President _____ experimented with dozens of new federal policies to put the economy back on track.
    (a) Herbert Hoover
    (b) Franklin Roosevelt
    (c) Calvin Coolidge
    (d) Theodore Roosevelt
Page 642

8. When _____ was campaigning against Ronald Reagan in 1980, he called Reagan's economic policy "voodoo economics."
    (a) Jimmy Carter
    (b) Edward M. Kennedy
    (c) George Bush
    (d) Walter Mondale
Page 642

9. The main agency for making monetary policy is:
    (a) the president.
    (b) the Congress.
    (c) the Secretary of the Treasury.
    (d) the Board of Governors of the Federal Reserve System.
Page 642

10. The three main instruments the "Fed" has for controlling the money supply are all of the following EXCEPT:
    (a) setting discount rates for the money banks borrow from the Federal Reserve banks.
    (b) selling the gold reserve supply to foreign nationals.
    (c) setting reserve requirements and determining how much money banks must keep in reserve at all times.
    (d) creating more money to sell to the banks.
Page 643

11. The Fed can set _____ rates for the money that banks borrow from the Federal Reserve banks.
    (a) reserve
    (b) discount
    (c) interest
    (d) capital income
Page 643

12. When the Fed, under the leadership of _____, decided to tighten the money supply in late 1979 in order to control inflation, interest rates soared.
    (a) Paul Volker
    (b) David Stockman
    (c) Bert Lance
    (d) William Greider
Page 643

13. Fiscal policy is shaped mostly by:
    (a) the Federal Reserve Board.
    (b) the Senate Appropriations Committee.
    (c) the Treasury Department.
    (d) Congress and the president.
Page 644

14. The landmark 1936 book The General Theory of Employment, Interest and Money was written by famed economist _____ and had a profound influence on economic theory in America.
    (a) John Maynard Keynes
    (b) Karl Marx
    (c) John Kenneth Galbraith
    (d) Henry Hazlitt
Page 645

15. So dominant was Keynesian thinking in government policy- making that Democrats and Republicans alike adhered to its basic tenets -- that is, until the _____ administration.
    (a) Roosevelt
    (b) Truman
    (c) Kennedy
    (d) Reagan
Page 645

16. The economic gurus of President _____ believed that the key task for government economic policy was to stimulate the supply of goods, not their demand.
    (a) Franklin Roosevelt
    (b) Ronald Reagan
    (c) John Kennedy
    (d) Richard Nixon
Page 645

17. Economist _____ proposed a curve suggesting that the more government taxed, the less people worked, and thus the smaller the government's tax revenues.
    (a) John Kenneth Galbraith
    (b) Lester Thurow
    (c) Arthur Laffer
    (d) John Maynard Keynes
Page 645

18. Benefits like Social Security are now _____ meaning that they go up automatically as the cost of living increases.
    (a) indexed
    (b) fixed
    (c) reserved
    (d) tapped
Page 646

19. As with the rest of policy making in the United States, the

369

power to make economic policy is:
(a)   paralyzed.
(b)   centralized.
(c)   one of consensus.
(d)   decentralized.
Page 647

20.   Government now spends _____ of America's gross national product and regulates much of the rest.
(a)   one-third
(b)   one-half
(c)   two-thirds
(d)   three-fourths
Page 647

21.   _____ maintain that the most productive economy is one in which the government exercises a hands-off policy of minimal regulation.
(a)   Conservatives
(b)   Liberals
(c)   Libertarians
(d)   Both conservatives and libertarians
Page 647

22.   Ever since the Agricultural Adjustment Act of ____, government has subsidized farmers.
(a)   1922
(b)   1929
(c)   1933
(d)   1953
Page 648

23.   The price to taxpayers to help subsidize the agriculture industry was _____ dollars in fiscal year 1989.
(a)   20 million
(b)   122 million
(c)   3 billion
(d)   22 billion
Page 648

24.   In the decade between 1960 and 1970, the American farm population dropped by about:
(a)   a tenth.
(b)   a third.
(c)   a half.
(d)   three-quarters.
Page 648

25.   From 1981 to 1987, the price of an average acre of farm

property:
(a)   rose by 45 percent.
(b)   rose by 15 percent.
(c)   fell by 3 percent.
(d)   fell by 34 percent.
Page 649

26.   Every year, _____ magazine publishes a listing of the five
      hundred largest industrial corporations in the United States.
      (a)   Fortune
      (b)   Rolling Stone
      (d)   Forbes
      (c)   Business Week
Page 649

27.   Some _____ -- large businesses with vast holdings in many
      countries -- are bigger than most governments.
      (a)   unilateral business interests
      (b)   multinational corporations
      (c)   industrial enterprises
      (d)   uninational incorporations
Page 650

28.   Foreign products now account for about a _____ of all
      American consumption.
      (a)   tenth
      (b)   fifth
      (c)   third
      (d)   half
Page 652

29.   Antitrust legislation permits the _____ to sue in federal
      court to break up companies with too large a market share.
      (a)   president
      (b)   Justice Department
      (c)   Congress
      (d)   Supreme Court
Page 653

30.   When a crucial industry falls on hard times, it usually looks
      to the government for help in all of these areas EXCEPT:
      (a)   subsidies.
      (b)   loan guarantees.
      (c)   buyouts.
      (d)   capital gains tax increases for a specific corporation.
Page 655

31.   When _____ said that "the business of America is

371

business," he seemed to be speaking for all Republican administrations.
(a) Theodore Roosevelt
(b) Herbert Hoover
(c) Calvin Coolidge
(d) Ronald Reagan
Page 656

32. _____ are a relatively new entry onto the economic policy stage.
(a) Corporate buyouts
(b) Small businesses
(c) Business lobbying groups
(d) Consumer groups
Page 656

33. _____ was the first consumer advocate to really generate results in the 1960's and 1970's.
(a) T. Boone Pickens
(b) Donald Trump
(c) Ron Nessen
(d) Ralph Nader
Page 657

34. The major turnabout in government policy toward labor took place during:
(a) the period from 1901 to 1910.
(b) World War I.
(c) the New Deal.
(d) World War II.
Page 658

35. In 1935, Congress passed the National Labor Relations Act, often called the _____ Act. This guaranteed the workers the right of collective bargaining.
(a) Sherman
(b) Wagner
(c) Taft-Hartley
(d) Hatch
Page 658

36. Section 14B of the Taft-Hartley Act permitted states to adopt _____ laws, which forbid requirements in union contracts that workers must join a union to hold their jobs.
(a) scab labor
(b) collective bargaining
(c) right to work
(d) open labor
Page 658-659

37. The effect of right-to-work laws is to subject unions to the
_____ problem; workers can enjoy the benefits of union
negotiations without contributing dues to support the union.
    (a) collective bargaining
    (b) association
    (c) trust buster
    (d) free-rider
Page 659

38. During the _____ Administration and ever since then,
the government has guaranteed a minimum wage, setting a floor
on the hourly wages earned by employees.
    (a) F.D. Roosevelt
    (b) Eisenhower
    (c) Carter
    (d) Reagan
Page 659

39. According to the Office of Management and Budget, U.S. citizens
save about _____ percent of their income.
    (a) 4.2
    (b) 9.9
    (c) 10.8
    (d) 20.3
Page 636

40. The current chairman of the Federal Reserve Board,
_____, believes that secrecy makes it possible for the
"Fed" to take unpopular stands, such as raising interest rates
when necessary.
    (a) Paul Volker
    (b) Allan Greenspan
    (c) David Stockman
    (d) Richard Darman
Page 644

BEFORE GOING ON

Use the answer key below to "grade" your exam and see how you did.
Be sure to go back and reread the relevant passages on the indicated
page for any you have missed. If you were sort of "asleep" when you
read that passage, there may be something else you missed there as
well.
Review Test Answers:

1: a	11: b	21: d	31: c
2: b	12: a	22: c	32: d
3: b	13: d	23: d	33: d
4: d	14: a	24: b	34: c
5: c	15: d	25: d	35: b
6: c	16: b	26: a	36: c
7: b	17: c	27: b	37: d

8: c	18: a	28: b	38: a
9: d	19: d	29: b	39: a
10: b	20: a	30: d	40: b

Recheck the Key Terms on page 662 - this time I'm sure there are some that the exercises above have missed! One of those that I didn't give much attention to above is "laissez-faire" - our term for the week. It is always good to have a little French to go with one's little Latin. Using this one isn't likely to impress a lot of people, but if you can spell it you'll be way ahead of most. It is more impressive if you can pronounce it just as the French would. See if you can get a French major - or professor - to give you some lessons. It is a useful term no matter how you pronounce it. It can be used to refer to any "let it be" attitude or policy. If you tend to approach the world with an "if it ain't broke, don't fix it" philosophy, you should have plenty of use for "laissez-faire."

CHAPTER 18

SOCIAL WELFARE POLICY-MAKING

CHAPTER LEARNING OBJECTIVES

After reading Chapter 18, you should be able to:

1. Describe the income distribution in the U.S. and compare it to other nations.
2. Distinguish relative deprivation from absolute income and wealth.
3. Describe the demographic make-up of the poor.
4. Discuss the meaning and importance of the notion of a culture of poverty.
5. Describe how differing forms of taxation affect income and income distribution.
6. Discuss government transfer payment programs and how they affect income.
7. Distinguish between the types of social welfare programs.
8. Describe how social welfare has developed in the U.S.
9. Discuss how social welfare is related to democracy.
10. Discuss how social welfare has contributed to the growth of government.

PRETEST QUESTIONS

The pretest below will give you an idea of the state of your knowledge about social welfare policy-making. The questions should also help you know what to look for while studying the text. Take the whole pretest, then check your answers against the key that follows (don't peek!). As you read the chapter, watch for where these questions are addressed (indicated after each question) so that you may learn why the answer is what it is.

1. In 1987, Americans' median family income was $_____.
    (a) 15,238
    (b) 22,592
    (c) 30,853
    (d) 50,971
Page 668

2. Beginning in 1978 and continuing through the 1980's, the trend

in the distribution of income in the U.S. has been:
(a)   a gradual deterioration of the upper-class wealth.
(b)   the rich getting richer and the poor getting poorer.
(c)   one of less and less people being poor.
(d)   a burgeoning middle-class.
Page 668

3.   Between 1979 and 1986, the poorest one-fifth of Americans saw their incomes:
(a)   rise from $8,761 to $12,890.
(b)   fall from $8,761 to $8,033.
(c)   rise from $12,890 to $15,672.
(d)   fall from $16,534 to $12,890.
Page 668-669

4.   Since 1978, the number of poor has:
(a)   risen to around 30 million in 1987.
(b)   remained constant through 1987.
(c)   dropped about fifteen percent through 1987.
(d)   risen slightly through 1987.
Page 670

5.   The culture of poverty argument regarding the poor contains all of the following elements EXCEPT:
(a)   strong family structures and relationships.
(b)   possession of poor work habits.
(c)   being present-oriented.
(d)   lacking of self-control.
Page 672

6.   According to studies, nearly three of every ten AFDC families had received welfare benefits for:
(a)   over ten years.
(b)   less than a year.
(c)   more than four years.
(d)   over fifteen years.
Page 672

7.   Fewer than 8 percent of all AFDC families had received assistance without interruption for more than _____ years.
(a)   ten
(b)   five
(c)   four
(d)   two
Page 672

8.   _____ said "nothing is certain in life but death and taxes."
(a)   H.L. Mencken
(b)   Benjamin Franklin
(c)   Fredrich Nietchze
(d)   Woody Allen
Page 673
9.   In general, there are three types of taxes, which include all

of the following EXCEPT:
(a)   a progressive tax.
(b)   a relative tax.
(c)   a proportional tax.
(d)   a regressive tax.
Page 674

10.   State sales taxes tend to make taxes _____ in effect.
(a)   relative
(b)   regressive
(c)   progressive
(d)   proportional
Page 674

11.   It is true that at the national level, the _____ are paying a good deal of the income taxes used to support many government policies, including welfare programs.
(a)   wealthy
(b)   middle-class
(c)   poor
(d)   lower middle-class
Page 675

12.   In 1986, taxpayers making under $11,000 made up 32 percent of taxpayers and paid about _____ percent of total income taxes that year.
(a)   35
(b)   22
(c)   18
(d)   2
Page 675

13.   In 1990, payments for Medicare amounted to almost $_____.
(a)   50 million
(b)   900 million
(c)   3 billion
(d)   100 billion
Page 676

14.   Thanks to Social Security and Medicare, about _____ percent of America's elderly families are below the poverty line.
(a)   50
(b)   35
(c)   25
(d)   15
Page 676

15.   After the onset of _____ in 1929, many nations, including the

United States, began to think that governments must do more to protect their citizens against such events.
(a)   World War I
(b)   the Great Depression
(c)   the German Recession
(d)   World War II
Page 679

16.   In 1953, when the Social Security bill was still small (because benefits were limited and retirees were fewer), the average family paid just _____ percent of its income in federal income and payroll taxes.
(a)   8.7
(b)   14.9
(c)   16.2
(d)   25.4
Page 680

17.   The most important element for the success of entitlement and poverty programs in the Great Society was:
(a)   the need for such programs.
(b)   the availability of funds, despite the Vietnam War.
(c)   strong congressional support.
(d)   strong presidential leadership by President Johnson.
Page 683

18.   Ellwood and Summers found that all of the following were results of the Great Society programs EXCEPT:
(a)   increased foreign economic competition.
(b)   expansion of the labor force when the baby boomers entered the job market.
(c)   easing shocks to the American economic and social system caused by international oil crises.
(d)   reducing poverty by a whopping 34.9 percent throughout the U.S.
Page 686

19.   In 1990, there are more than 38 million Social Security beneficiaries receiving over $_____ billion.
(a)   11.3
(b)   50
(c)   99
(d)   200
Page 688

20.   By the mid-1980's, _____ percent of black children were living below the poverty line.
(a)   12
(b)   27
(c)   46
(d)   59
Page 674
Pretest Answers:

1: c	11: a
2: b	12: d
3: b	13: d
4: a	14: d
5: a	15: b
6: b	16: a
7: a	17: d
8: b	18: d
9: b	19: d
10: b	20: c

READING FOR CONTENT

Listed below are sets of questions associated with the content of each major section of Chapter 18. Carefully review the questions associated with each section of the text before reading the section. Have the questions in mind as you read the section and, when you reach the end of each section, stop and see if you can answer the questions well. If not, reread the relevant paragraphs until you are sure of your response to each of the questions.

I. Income, Poverty, and Public Policy

How does income distribution in the U.S. compare to that of other nations?
What is relative deprivation?
Why is the distinction between relative deprivation and absolute income and wealth important?
Who are the poor?
How is the poverty line determined?

II. The Nature of Wealth and Poverty

What is meant by the notion of a "culture of poverty?"
What are the policy implications of the "culture of poverty" thesis?
What evidence exists for and against the existence of a "culture of poverty?"
What are the different types of taxes?
How do the differing types of taxes each affect the distribution of income?
What has been the impact of government transfer payments?

III. Social Welfare Programs

What is the difference between entitlement and poverty programs?
Why does the U.S. rank below most other nations in social welfare spending effort?

IV. The Evolution of America's Social Welfare Programs

How does the notion of intergenerational equity relate to the
   development of Social Security?
How did the Great Society expand social welfare policy in the
   United States?
What has been the impact of the Reagan Administration on
   social welfare policy?
What are the arguments for and against the present approach
   to social welfare policy as an aid to the poor?

V.   Understanding Social Welfare Policy

How is democracy related to social welfare policy?
How has social welfare policy contributed to government
   growth?

CHAPTER OVERVIEW

I.   Introduction   (666-668)

The United States has a great variety of citizens and population
groups, that have achieved different levels of material success.
These differences raise important political questions. The answers
to these questions determine the nation's approach to SOCIAL WELFARE
POLICIES.   Social welfare policies are attempts to provide
assistance to specific groups in society. Who gets these benefits,
how they are provided, and what level of support is provided are
issues that must be resolved by the political system.

II. Income, Poverty, And Public Policy

A. Who's Getting What?

The distribution of income across segments of the American
population is quite uneven.   The concept of INCOME DISTRIBUTION
describes the share of national income earned by various groups in
the United States. Since 1978 the rich have gotten richer and the
poor poorer in the United States.

One group believing it is doing less well in relation to another
reference group is called RELATIVE DEPRIVATION.   Some researchers
argue that relative deprivation is increasing as the wealthiest have
seen their incomes grow and the poorest have seen their incomes
actually fall (adjusting for inflation in both cases).

Although the words income and wealth might seem similar, they are
not the same thing. INCOME is the amount of money collected between
any two points in time; WEALTH is the amount already owned including
stocks, bonds, bank accounts, cars, houses, and so forth. Wealth
has been much less evenly distributed than income.
The poor are losing ground in absolute terms in wealth as well.

B. Who's at the Bottom? Poverty in America

Counting the poor requires a definition of poverty. The U.S. Bureau of the census has established the POVERTY LINE, which takes into account what a families of various sizes would need for an "austere" standard of living. Americans living below the poverty line dropped from 22.2 percent in 1960 to 11.4 percent in 1978, but the poverty rate has increased again to 13.5 percent in 1987. Around 13 million are children under the age of eighteen. Poverty may also be more extensive than the poverty line suggests. Almost a third of families were under the poverty line at least once during the decade, suggesting that 70 million Americans live close enough to poverty that a crisis can push them below the line. Poverty is more common among African Americans, the young female-headed families, and rural residents (see Table 18.1).

III. The Nature Of Wealth And Poverty (671-676)

Citizen's views on who are poor and why they are poor affect their approaches to solving the problems of poverty. If most Americans think people are poor because of weaknesses within themselves, they will support very different kinds of government actions than if they believe that poverty is more the result of environmental or situational factors. People's understanding of the causes of poverty will direct and limit what they believe government can and should do about it. No consensus on the causes of poverty exists.

A. Is There a Culture of Poverty?

Conservatives and liberals in America disagree on the reasons why some are rich and some are poor. In general, conservatives tend to believe that differences are due to individual characteristics, attitudes, and values. The poor, many conservatives argue, possess a CULTURE OF POVERTY. The poor are present-oriented, lack self-control, possess poor work habits, and have weak family structures that condemn them to lower levels of accomplishment.

Liberals argue that some people face more hostile environments than others. These environments include legal restrictions, social and cultural customs, educational limits, discrimination, and stereotypical attitudes toward the poor. Thus people are poor because they face external barriers to their success.

If conservatives are right, social scientists should find long- term welfare status among America's poor, and should also see evidence of a distinct set of values and attitudes developing among America's poor. The facts do not support either of these conditions supporting the culture of poverty thesis, however. A majority of welfare families receive aid for less than four years, and most researchers can find no distinctive set of attitudes distinguishing the poor from others. More commonly some crisis or opportunity - losing a job, getting a divorce, working longer hours - accounts for movement into or out of poverty.

Chapter 18

B. How Public Policy Affects Income

The government spends one out of every three dollars in the American economy thus having a major impact on its citizens' wealth and income. There are two principal ways in which government can affect a person's income: 1) government can manipulate incomes through its taxing powers, and 2) government can affect income through its expenditure policies.

1. Taxation.   In general, there are three types of taxes: each affects citizens' income in a different way. First, if a tax takes a bigger bite from higher incomes than lower, it is a PROGRESSIVE TAX. Second, if the a tax takes the same shares from everyone, rich and poor alike, it is a PROPORTIONAL TAX. Third, if the government establishes a REGRESSIVE TAX, the poor pay a greater share of their income in taxes than do the rich.

Rarely are taxes overtly regressive. Some are regressive in effect, however. State sales taxes, which charge all the same rate on their purchases, are regressive in effect because the poor spend a larger proportion of their income on items subject to the tax. As a result, poor families pay a higher percentage of their incomes in sales taxes than well-to-do families.

Taxes can have an impact on the distribution of income in three ways: 1) progressive taxes can make the poor richer and the rich poorer, 2) proportional taxes can have no net effect on income distribution; and 3) regressive taxes can make the rich richer and the poor poorer.   The best evidence is that, overall, taxes in America are proportional. Progressive income taxes being offset by regressive Social Security and state and local taxes.

2. Government Expenditures. One way government affects the income of citizens is by writing literally billions of checks every year, mostly to Social Security beneficiaries and retired government employees. Government can also give an "in-kind payment," something with cash value that is not cash itself (everything from food stamps to low-interest student loans).   All these benefits are called TRANSFER PAYMENTS. Transfer payments have made their recipients (especially the elderly, who are far less poor than twenty-five years ago) better off. Transfer payments raise half those in poverty above the official poverty line. Nonetheless, transfer payments have not substantially redistributed income in America. Policies of income redistribution aimed at reducing this inequality have never been generally accepted public policy in America. Americans favor equal opportunity over equal outcomes and reject redistributional policies that would work to achieve an end to income inequality by government action.

IV. Social Welfare Programs (676-679)

Social welfare programs have not ended poverty or substantially reduced income inequality in America. Many would argue that they were not intended to accomplish such goals. It is true, however, that these programs have produced substantial improvements in the day-to-day living conditions of many Americans.

A. Entitlement and Poverty Programs

Programs like Social Security and Medicare have substantially improved older Americans' quality of life. These are entitlement programs that do not require a means test for eligibility and are the largest and most expensive social welfare programs in America. These programs have had a substantial positive impact on the health and impact of the elderly in America.

Programs like Medicaid, Food Stamps, and housing and family assistance programs require a certain level of poverty for eligibility. They are funded at much lower levels than entitlement programs for the elderly. Nonetheless, they have raised many of the poor above the official poverty line.

B. Social Welfare Policy Elsewhere

Most industrial nations provide such benefits at more generous levels than those in the United States. Americans tend to see poverty and social welfare needs as individual rather than governmental concerns, while European nations tend to support greater governmental responsibility for these problems.

Nations also differ in how universal or selective they make their social welfare programs. Some focus on selective benefits targeted on specific groups, others favor universal benefits that go to large categories of citizens as entitlements. America has both types: Social Security and Medicare programs are universal, while poverty programs are selective.

Greater taxes commensurate with the greater benefits of social policy are commonplace in Western European nations, often reaching more than 40 percent of personal income. In the United States taxes are about 33 percent of personal income and support a much larger defense budget than in Europe. Japan spends proportionally less on social services than the United States, because of the role of family in its culture, and the more extensive pensions and benefits provided by Japanese corporations.

V. The Evolution Of America's Social Welfare Programs (679-686)

For centuries societies considered family welfare a private, not a public concern. Children were nurtured by their parents and, in turn, nurtured them in their old age. After the turn of the century, American and other industrialized societies recognized the breakdown in these family-based support networks. Large cities and the requirements of the urban work force, made the old ways of thinking about the problems of the elderly and the poor seem inadequate. Changes in policy were incremental, key innovations coming at times of particular societal need or crisis. A major change in how Americans viewed government's role in providing social welfare support came during the Great Depression.

A. The New Deal and the Elderly

With the Great Depression many people began to think that governments must do more to protect citizens against events like depressions. Such events were beyond the means of families to deal with, and beyond their control or responsibility as well. This lead to the passage of the Social Security Act in 1935 which brought government into the equation of one generation's obligations to another. Social Security and later Medicare were government benefits that provided a crucial cushion at a time when money was needed for other things.

The costs, of course, were shifted but not reduced; what citizens had once paid out of their pocket they now paid for in taxes. This tax burden continues to grow as medical costs escalate and the elderly become a larger and larger proportion of the population. In the 1980s, for the first time, the United States spent more of its public dollars on the aged than the young. A higher proportion of young people now live in poverty than the elderly. Nationally, there has been a redistribution of government benefits from younger people to older people.

As a result, intergenerational equality issues are becoming more important. Social Security taxes have gone from 3 percent of earnings in 1944 to more than 15 percent. In 1949 the average thirty year old could by a house on 14 percent of his or her income; by 1985 that figure has risen to 44 percent. Thus younger people increasingly feel relatively deprived. Interest groups have now been formed by the middle generation, and where interest groups form, an issue will arise on the governmental agenda. The issue posed by problems of INTERGENERATIONAL EQUITY is: Who should get what share of public policy benefits and at what cost?

B. President Johnson and the Great Society

During the presidency of Lyndon B. Johnson in the 1960s America experienced an outpouring of federal programs to help the poor and the elderly, to create economic opportunities for those at the lower rungs of the economic ladder, and to reduce discrimination against minorities. We have already learned that these programs were of two types - entitlement and poverty (means tested) programs. The entitlement programs, aimed primarily at the elderly, had strong political support. Advocates of greater spending for poverty programs had a more difficult time. Poverty was closely tied to race issues in the minds of many people, and the poor and their supporters had less ability to form strong constituency groups from which to demand government programs.

Perhaps the most important element for the success of both program types was strong presidential leadership. This was provided by President Johnson. The role of political leadership, particularly presidential leadership, cannot be overestimated in building the public and political coalitions needed to support new program initiatives in the area of social welfare policy.

C. President Reagan and Limits to the Great Society

Public support for some welfare programs was eroding by 1980, and it was possible for Republicans to make some headway into the Democratic party's constituency by taking a more restrictive stand on social welfare programs. In addition, the growing demands of defense spending and elderly entitlements threatened to raise taxes and stifle economic growth. When looking for areas to cut, the traditional weaknesses of the poor as an interest group made their programs vulnerable.

Again, the major actor was the president. In this case, President Reagan chose to target poverty programs as the major way to cut government spending. The president set the tone, rallied public opinion, and worked to create congressional coalitions to support these efforts. Democratic leaders in the Congress worked to limit these cuts. Although many cuts were made - program growth rates were reduced, benefits were reduced, and many previously eligible recipients were removed from the roles - the basic outlines of the original programs have persisted.

D. The Future of Social Welfare Policy

The major point of disagreement is over the extent to which social welfare policies work. Discussion is over whether these programs help or hurt the poor; whether they ameliorate or exacerbate poverty; whether they provide a much needed safety net for the truly needy, or encourage dependence and failure.

Many came to believe that the programs of the Great Society contributed to the problems of growing inflation, burgeoning budget deficits, increased unemployment and crime that arose during the 1970s. It was argued that not only did the social programs of the Great Society fail to curb the advance of poverty, they actually made the situation worse - discouraging the poor from solving their problems and providing them with an incentive to remain poor. Such arguments supported the Reagan administration's often successful efforts to limit these programs.

Many scholars have strongly criticized these arguments, however, and the program cuts that were based on them. They argue that programs begun in the Great Society contributed much to easing the shocks to the American economic and social system caused by international oil crises, deindustrialization, increased foreign economic competition, and the vast expansion of the labor force when baby boomers entered the job market. With all this going on, these analysts believe that the position of the poor would have been much worse but for the safety net provided by the Great Society.

The evidence on social welfare programs is mixed. Although the preponderance of evidence does seem to support the notion that the programs were helpful in general, more might have been done with other programs or other approaches.

VI.   Understanding Social Welfare Policy

Americans struggle to balance individual merit and the rewards of initiative with the reality of systemic environmental inequalities and the need to provide support to many. In short, Americans seek to retain a commitment to both competition and compassion.

A. Democracy and Social Welfare

As with other issue areas in a democracy, competing demands concerning social welfare policy are resolved by government decision makers in response to various groups in society. In the social welfare policy arena, the competing groups are often quite uneven in the resources they bring to the struggle. The elderly are relatively well organized and have the resources needed to wield influence. They are thus usually successful in protecting and expanding their programs.

For the poor, influencing political decisions is more difficult. They vote less, lack strong, focused organizations and money, and face powerful, well organized opposition. Thus they are often unsuccessful in the competitive political game.

Once benefits are given to citizens, the nature of democratic politics makes it difficult to withdraw them. Once in place they develop supporters in Congress, the bureaucracy, interest groups and the public that give them a life of their own.

B. Social Welfare Policy and the Size of Government

Americans' social welfare policy choices have resulted in hundreds of billions of dollars in taxes and expenditures. Large government programs, be they in the area of national defense or social welfare, require large organizations to administer them. The appropriate way to evaluate these administrative systems is not to focus on their size or expense alone, but to weigh their size and expense against the goals and accomplishments of their programs, and the extent to which private, non-governmental entities could realistically be depended on to help.

DOING RESEARCH ON SOCIAL WELFARE POLICY

Your text raises a couple of interesting questions about social welfare policy that you may wish to investigate further. One such question is the matter of intergenerational equity. By the year 2000, about 17 percent of the population will be over 65. That percentage will continue to climb through the first few decades of the 21st century. Life expectancy will lengthen as well, and with these changes the cost of Social Security will continue to climb as well, a growing burden for the younger work force. Can we continue to be as generous to the elderly as we are today? Given the political clout of this age group will we have any choice? A paper can report on expert opinion on such questions, and draw some conclusions of its own. Research on the Social Security system itself may suggested reforms that might help the system survive the challenge of the 21st century.

Your book also points out that while Social Security has succeeded in bringing the income of elderly Americans up to levels comparable to the rest of society, AFDC and other programs aimed at the poor have not been successful in significantly reducing poverty. A paper could investigate the reasons for this difference in programmatic outcomes. The reasons explored could cover everything from administrative details to explanations rooted in general cultural biases. Your findings might also lead you to suggestions for reforming poverty programs, and to an appreciation of the limits of such reforms. An interesting and challenging topic, however.

REVIEW TEST

Read through the Chapter Overview and review the "Reading for Content" questions if you haven't already done so. If you feel like you have achieved the learning objectives listed at the beginning of the chapter, you should be ready for the Review Test.

1. An example of a social welfare policy would include all of the following EXCEPT:
    (a) food stamp payments.
    (b) Blue Shield insurance payments.
    (c) Social Security payments.
    (d) Medicare benefits.
Page 667

2. In very general terms, the distribution of income in the United States has been one of:
    (a) very little change.
    (b) extreme shifts in power.
    (c) a gradual drain of upper-class wealth.
    (d) deterioration.
Page 668

3. Between 1979 and 1986, the wealthiest one-fifth of Americans saw their incomes grow from:
    (a) $70,260 to $76,300.
    (b) $62,980 to $65,722.
    (c) $49,654 to $53,713.
    (d) $12,315 to $15,679.
Page 668

4.   _____ is the amount of money a person already owns before
        making money (including stocks, bonds, bank account, cars,
        houses, etc.).
        (a)   Revenue
        (b)   A sub
        (c)   Income
        (d)   Wealth
Page 669

5.   Throughout the last generation, the top _____ percent of
        wealth-holders in the United States possessed about 25 percent
        of all American wealth.
        (a)   1
        (b)   7
        (c)   12
        (d)   20
Page 669

6.   To count the poor, the U.S. Bureau of the Census has
        established the _____, which takes establishes a minimum
        standard of living for a family's size.
        (a)   wealth threshold
        (b)   income measure
        (c)   poverty line
        (d)   welfare circle
Page 670

7.   What is most disconcerting is that many of the poor in the
        U.S., about _____, are children under the age of eighteen.
        (a)   50,000
        (b)   100,500
        (c)   1 million
        (d)   13 million
Page 670

8.   Recent studies show that about _____ Americans live close
        enough to the poverty line that some crisis can push them into
        poverty.
        (a)   5 million
        (b)   25 million
        (c)   70 million
        (d)   150 million
Page 671

9.   The poor, conservatives argue, possess a _____, negative
        attitudes and values toward work, family and success.
        (a)   nihilism factor
        (b)   benign neglect
        (c)   culture of poverty
        (d)   gene factor
Page 672

10.   The _____ argument holds that the poor lack self-

388

control, possess poor work habits and have weak family structures and relationships.

(a) relative deprivation
(b) culture of poverty
(c) benign neglect
(d) poverty line

Page 672

11. _____ argue that the poor face negative environments that include legal restrictions, social and cultural customs, educational limits and discrimination.

(a) Conservatives
(b) Populists
(c) Libertarians
(d) Liberals

Page 672

12. Examination of welfare roles over time indicates that most beneficiaries are:

(a) not long time recipients.
(b) recipients of no less than ten years and running.
(c) recipients of no less than fifteen years and running.
(d) recipients of no less than twenty years and running.

Page 672

13. About _____ percent of all AFDC welfare families had received assistance without interruption for more than ten years.

(a) 24
(b) 18
(c) 12
(d) 8

Page 672

14. The more common reasons for moving into the poverty class include all of the following EXCEPT:

(a) losing a job.
(b) getting a divorce.
(c) laziness.
(d) a new mouth to feed.

Page 672-673

15. The urban underclass is threatened by all of the following EXCEPT:

(a) homelessness.
(b) alcoholism.
(c) unwanted pregnancies.
(d) all answers are correct.

Page 673

16. The government spends one out of every _____ dollars in the American economy and has a large impact on its citizens' wealth

and income.
(a) three
(b) seven
(c) ten
(d) fifteen
Page 673

17. A _____ tax is when the government charges the same rate for everyone, rich and poor alike.
(a) regressive
(b) progressive
(c) relative
(d) proportional
Page 674

18. Federal taxes are generally more _____ in effect.
(a) relative
(b) regressive
(c) progressive
(d) proportional
Page 674-675

19. Your text states that the overall incidence of taxes in America is:
(a) relative.
(b) regressive.
(c) progressive.
(d) proportional.
Page 675

20. In 1986, taxpayers making under $11,000 made up _____ percent of taxpayers and paid less than 2 percent of total income taxes that year.
(a) 12
(b) 21
(c) 32
(d) 45
Page 675

21. In 1986, taxpayers making over $100,000, about _____ percent of taxpayers, paid about 30 percent of total income taxes.
(a) 1.5
(b) 6
(c) 15
(d) 20
Page 675

22. All the following are examples of transfer payments EXCEPT: food stamps.

(b)   low-interest loans for college students.
(c)   Social Security payments.
(d)   Blue Cross insurance payments.
Page 675

23.   There is _____ evidence to suggest that transfer programs
      have significantly redistributed income in America and created
      greater income equality.
      (a)   scattered
      (b)   little
      (c)   substantial
      (d)   overwhelming
Page 675

24.   Programs that do not require an income or means test for
      eligibility are called _____ programs.
      (a)   welfare
      (b)   proportional
      (c)   entitlement
      (d)   transfer
Page 676

25.   In 1962, nearly _____ percent of America's elderly families
      were below the poverty line.
      (a)   50
      (b)   35
      (c)   25
      (d)   15
Page 676

26.   In 1982, cash and in-kind transfers lifted _____ percent of
      the pretransfer poor out of poverty.
      (a)   89.2
      (b)   63.3
      (c)   44.2
      (d)   32.8
Page 677

27.   Other countries offer social welfare benefits to their
      citizens. _____ offers comprehensive medical services
      through the National Health Service.
      (a)   Canada
      (b)   Mexico
      (c)   Great Britain
      (d)   Peru
Page 678

28.   _____ is the only nation with a developed economy that

spends a smaller proportion of its gross national product on social policies than does the United States.
(a) Great Britain
(b) Japan
(c) The Soviet Union
(d) Argentina
Page 679

29. In 1965, adults were freed from paying for their own parents' expenses when the federal government adopted:
(a) Social Security.
(b) Medicare.
(c) Food Stamps.
(d) day care centers.
Page 680

30. Americans spend _____ percent of their nation's gross national product on medical care.
(a) 5
(b) 12
(c) 24
(d) 42
Page 680

31. In the 1960's, America experienced a great burst of federal programs to help the poor and the elderly. Many of these programs were established during the presidency of _____, whose administration coined the term "The Great Society."
(a) Dwight D. Eisenhower
(b) John F. Kennedy
(c) Lyndon B. Johnson
(d) Richard M. Nixon
Page 681

32. The _____ programs of the Great Society had strong political support partly because they were aimed primarily at the elderly, a rapidly expanding political constituency important to both parties.
(a) poverty
(b) distribution
(c) entitlement
(d) welfare
Page 682

33. Advocates of greater spending for _____ programs in the Great Society had a much more difficult time -- politically.
(a) entitlement
(b) medical
(c) job training
(d) poverty
Page 683

34. The Omnibus Budget Reconciliation Act of 1981 resulted in:
(a) an increase in Medicare funding by 8 percent.

(b)   an increase in AFDC welfare budgeting by 14 percent.
(c)   a decrease in military expenditures by about 7 percent.
(d)   a decrease in AFDC welfare budgeting by 14 percent.
Page 684

35.   A major study underwritten by the Manhattan Institute put
      forth that the social programs of the Great Society:
      (a)   discouraged the poor from solving their own problems.
      (b)   helped eradicate poverty from hundreds of major cities.
      (c)   helped eradicate poverty in rural, but not urban areas.
      (d)   only helped ease poverty levels, not eradicate them.
Page 684

36.   In 1960, there were 14.2 million Social Security beneficiaries
      receiving $_____.
      (a)   2.4 billion
      (b)   11.3 billion
      (c)   50.4 billion
      (d)   200 billion
Page 688

37.   In 1959, ____ percent of black births were to single mothers.
      (a)   15
      (b)   25
      (c)   34
      (d)   57
Page 674

38.   The proportion of black men who are employed _____ in 1930 to
      56 percent in 1983.
      (a)   rose from 32 percent
      (b)   rose from 43 percent
      (c)   dropped from 63 percent
      (d)   dropped from 80 percent
Page 674

39.   In _____, social security benefits take up 14 percent of
      the national income.
      (a)   the United States
      (b)   Japan
      (c)   Sweden
      (d)   Germany
Page 678

40.   American levels of spending on social security benefits are
      substantially less than that of every other nation except:
      (a)   Japan.
      (b)   Sweden.
      (c)   Germany.
      (d)   France.
Page 678

BEFORE GOING ON

Chapter 18

Use the answer key below to "grade" your exam and see how you did. Be sure to go back and reread the relevant passages on the indicated page for any you have missed. If you were sort of "asleep" when you read that passage, there may be something else you missed there as well.

Review Test Answers:

1: b	11: d	21: a	31: c
2: a	12: a	22: d	32: c
3: a	13: d	23: b	33: d
4: d	14: c	24: c	34: d
5: a	15: d	25: a	35: a
6: c	16: a	26: b	36: b
7: d	17: d	27: c	37: a
8: c	18: c	28: b	38: d
9: c	19: d	29: b	39: b
10: b	20: c	30: b	40: a

Well, this time the relevant page is 691 for that check of Key Terms. I know it is getting (getting?) to be a grind, but - look at it this way: there are only two more chapters after this one. Also, there are only a dozen terms there and not a foreign word in the lot! There is not a real good candidate for our word of the week either, but I guess if I have to pick one it has to be "intergenerational equity." If for no other reason it qualifies on the grounds of having ten, count 'em, ten syllables - seven in "intergenerational" alone. Got to learn to handle these long words if you are going to be a college grad. If you are looking for a way to work this term into a conversation, you might find a "baby-boomer" of your acquaintance and point out that this generation first made an issue of the "generation gap" and now, as they approach retirement in the first part of the 21st century, they raise the issue of "intergenerational equity." They fought with their parents over the beatles, beads and bellbottoms, now they may fight with their kids over bucks.

POLICY-MAKING FOR HEALTH, ENERGY AND THE ENVIRONMENT

CHAPTER LEARNING OBJECTIVES

After reading Chapter 19, you should be able to:

1. Describe the state of health care in America.
2. Explain why Americans spend more but get less health care on average.
3. Discuss the extensiveness and character of government's role in health care provision in America.
4. Discuss the effects of a disaggregated health care policy process involving government, private insurance, and consumer payments.
5. Describe America's energy use profile.
6. Discuss the players and policy problems in energy policy-making.
7. Discuss the conflict between economic growth and the environment and the players and policy problems with environmental policy.
8. Describe the provisions of the major environmental protection legislation.
9. Discuss the dilemma technology presents for democracy.
10. Discuss the role technological issues play in government growth.

PRETEST QUESTIONS

The pretest below will give you an idea of the state of your knowledge about health, energy and environmental policy-making. Take the whole pretest, then check your answers against the key that follows (don't peek!). As you read the chapter, watch for where these questions are addressed (indicated after each question) so that you may learn why the answer is what it is.

1. Overall, about _____ percent of the GNP goes to the health industry.
    (a) 4
    (b) 12
    (c) 25
    (d) 46

Page 695

2.   In 1983, _____ million Americans went without health
     insurance for all or part of the year.
     (a)   5
     (b)   11
     (c)   22
     (d)   34
Page 698-699

3.   In 1988, whites had an average life expectancy of _____ years.
     (a)   65.7
     (b)   75.5
     (c)   82.3
     (d)   89
Page 699

4.   The average health bill payments by the government in most
     industrialized nations is about _____ percent.
     (a)   35
     (b)   56
     (c)   77
     (d)   89
Page 700

5.   Private insurance companies cover _____ percent of all
     health care payments.
     (a)   41
     (b)   32
     (c)   25
     (d)   13
Page 701

6.   The Medicare program primarily benefits to _____ Americans.
     (a)   African-American
     (b)   Hispanic
     (c)   poor
     (d)   elderly
Page 701

7.   In the U.S., the health policy emphasis is placed mainly on:
     (a)   equality of care.
     (b)   high-tech, expensive medical solutions.
     (c)   containment of costs.
     (d)   quality medicine.
Page 702

8.   Oil and coal are examples of _____ resources, or sources of
     energy that are finite.
     (a)   renewable
     (b)   nonrenewable
     (c)   recycled
     (d)   regurgitated
Page 704
9.   America imports ___ percent of its annual consumption of oil?

(a)   15
(b)   32
(c)   40
(d)   54
Page 704

10.   All of the following countries must import almost all of
      its oil from foreign countries EXCEPT:
      (a)   Japan.
      (b)   France.
      (c)   Italy.
      (d)   the United States.
Page 704

11.   In 1990, the United States imported about _____ percent of its
      oil from foreign countries.
      (a)   22
      (b)   33
      (c)   42
      (d)   54
Page 704

12.   The United States generates about _____ percent of its
      electricity by burning coal.
      (a)   14
      (b)   44
      (c)   72
      (d)   98
Page 706

13.   In the U.S., solar, wind, wood, and geothermal energy all
      provide about _____ percent of electricity generated.
      (a)   .5
      (b)   10
      (c)   25
      (d)   59
Page 706

14.   In the spring of 1990, polls found _____ of all Americans
      saying that "we must protect the environment, even if it means
      increased government spending and higher taxes."
      (a)   25%
      (b)   50%
      (c)   75%
      (d)   98%
Page 709-710

15.   The "centerpiece" of federal environmental policy is the _____

Act passed in 1969.
(a)   Clean Air
(b)   National Environmental Policy
(c)   Water Pollution Control
(d)   Environmental Protection
Page 710

16.   Legitimate questions regarding cleaning up the environment arise in all of the following areas EXCEPT concerns about:
(a)   foreign trade.
(b)   economic growth.
(c)   jobs.
(d)   tax breaks for production.
Page 715

17.   Within six months of its founding in August 1970, Common Cause had _____ members.
(a)   6,000
(b)   20,000
(c)   50,000
(d)   100,000
Page 716

18.   Governmental activities in the fields of providing funds to the elderly, regulating the health industry and ensuring environmental quality are expected to _____ in the coming years.
(a)   increase greatly
(b)   decrease slightly
(c)   decrease greatly
(d)   stay the same
Page 719

19.   In 1983, over _____ percent of France's electricity came from nuclear power.
(a)   60
(b)   42
(c)   33
(d)   21
Page 708

20.   Most countries face a choice between conventional sources of electricity (essentially coal or oil) and nuclear power. In the United States over _____ percent of the country's electricity comes from conventional sources.
(a)   70
(b)   80
(c)   85
(d)   90
Page 708

Pretest Answers:

1: b	11: d
2: d	12: b
3: b	13: a
4: c	14: c
5: b	15: b
6: d	16: d
7: b	17: d
8: b	18: a
9: d	19: a
10: d	20: d

READING FOR CONTENT

Listed below are sets of questions associated with the content of each major section of Chapter 19. Carefully review the questions associated with each section of the text before reading the section. Have the questions in mind as you read the section and, when you reach the end of each section, stop and see if you can answer the questions well. If not, reread the relevant paragraphs until you are sure of your response to each of the questions.

I.   Health

Why do Americans not have the highest standard of average
    health, despite spending more on health care than other
    nations?
What is the role of government in the delivery of health
    care in America?
What is the effect of dependence on private health
    insurance?
Who are the interests involved in health care policy-making
    and what do they want?

II. Energy

What is America's use and supply energy profile?
Who are the interests involved in energy policy-making and
    what do they want?

III. The Environment

What is the nature of the conflict between economic
    development and the environment?
What are the major environmental protection acts?
What are the key provisions of the major environmental
    protection legislation?
Who are the interests involved in environmental policy and
    what do they want?

IV. Understanding Technology and Policy

What are the problems high technology presents for
democratic policy-making?
How does high technology contribute to the growth of
government?

CHAPTER OVERVIEW

I. Introduction (695-695)

The increasing speed of technological advance creates special
problems for government. New issues must be dealt with, posing both
practical and moral problems for the political system. Expensive new
medical technologies create new public policy problems. The rapid
growth of the American economy has brought energy and pollution
problems to the forefront of politics. Not only does technological
change affect how Americans live, but also changes what they expect
the government to do.

II. Health (695-704)

Three important questions can be asked about health care and public
policy in the United States: What is the quality of health care in
America? How is health care policy organized? Who influences
health care policy in the United States?

A. Health Care in America

America is one of the wealthiest countries and it spends a higher
proportion of its wealth on health care than any other country.
Still, Americans are not the healthiest people in the world. In
terms of infant mortality rate - the proportion of babies who do not
survive their first year of life, a common indicator of a nation's
health - the United States is only eighteenth among the world's
nations.

Much of the money that Americans pay for health care goes to
expensive services like organ transplants, kidney dialysis, and
other treatments that are not widely available elsewhere. The
high-tech services available to Americans are far superior to those
available in most other Western countries. They also cost a lot.
America spends 12 percent of its GNP on health, more than double the
percentage of a generation ago. The reasons for this increase are
many. American health providers have overbuilt medical care
facilities, and doctors and hospitals have few incentives to be more
efficient. In addition, the threat of malpractice suits leads to
the practice of "defensive medicine," doctors ordering extra tests,
no matter how expensive, to ensure that they cannot be sued.

One explanation for the fact that Americans are not the world's
healthiest people despite paying more for health care is the way the
American health care industry organizes itself.

B. Health Care Policy

1. Access. Access to health care and health insurance is unequal in the American system. These inequalities are related to income and race. Access to health insurance is not universal in the United States, as it is in many countries, and access to health care for those without it is difficult. Most Americans, 90 percent, have some form of health insurance. Getting and keeping health insurance is often linked to having a job, thus many go without health insurance for short periods when unemployed.

Even among those with insurance, coverage is often incomplete. For those with low-paying jobs, health insurance may not cover all their health needs. Seven percent of Americans reported foregoing needed medical care because of financial concerns in a recent poll, while the figure in Canada and Britain (countries with systems of universal coverage) was less than one percent.

Patterns for life expectancy and infant mortality rates mirror those apparent for health insurance (see Table 19.1 in your text). Inequalities are again related to income and race. Infant mortality rates for those with good insurance and a family doctor are low, but are quite high for the poor and those without insurance. Clearly the prenatal care so vital to health in the first year of life is not available to all.

The simple availability of family doctors and routine hospital services are more important in determining the general quality of health care than high-tech medical equipment and research.

2. The Role of Government. Compared to other countries, American governments play a relatively small role in health care. About 41 percent of the country's total health bill is paid for by government sources, while the average for industrialized countries is 77 percent. The total of 41 percent of health care costs paid by government includes Medicare, Medicaid, and other payments, such as those for veterans. Also much medical research is funded through the NATIONAL INSTITUTES OF HEALTH (HIH) and conducted in hospitals connected to public universities. Private insurance companies cover 32 percent of health care costs and Americans pay full 25 percent out of their own pockets. Ours is the most private medical care system in the developed world, a fact which helps to explain why access to quality health care is unequal, and why Americans spend more for the health care they receive.
Harry S Truman was the first president to call for NATIONAL HEALTH INSURANCE, a compulsory insurance program to finance all Americans' medical care. Opposed strongly by the American Medical Association, it has never been adopted. Congress has recognized the special medical needs of the elderly with MEDICARE and the poor with MEDICAID. With the number of elderly (and medical costs) growing rapidly, funding Medicare is one of the country's most pressing public policy issues. Medicaid is a means-tested program, going only to those whose incomes fall below a set level.

C. Policy-making for Health Care

One of the reasons for American's emphasis on expensive and high-tech solutions to health problems may be that there has never been a single institution paying medical bills. With a mixture of government funds, private insurance, and out-of-pocket payments, no one actor has responsibility for all costs. In countries with national health care systems, government policy-makers have focused more on ensuring equality of care and keeping costs down. In the United States equality of care and cost containment have taken a back seat to technological advances for those who could afford them. Thus Americans have high-tech, expensive, and unequal care.

One reason for uneven government and private health care policies has to do with the representation of interests. Powerful lobbying organizations representing hospitals, doctors, and the elderly want Medicare to pay for the latest techniques. Groups whose health needs are not well represented may not be met. The elderly, for example, are one of the most powerful groups. Health care policy which favors the elderly is one of the results. For workers in jobs that do not include health insurance, or for those who are unemployed and cannot afford private health insurance, no organization exists capable of strongly influencing government.

Insurance rates and medical fees will be an important public policy problem for some time to come. There are likely to be increasing calls for more government regulation over fees, and some attempt to help those who fall through the cracks of the American health care and health insurance systems.

III. Energy (704-707)

Producing the amounts of energy necessary to retain Americans' standard of living is increasingly difficult. Government is involved in battles concerning what forms, what sources, and how much energy the country should be producing. Government shapes energy policies in dozens of ways and it owns much of the land from which energy comes. Energy politics is fragmented. Whereas some energy sources (nuclear power) are tightly regulated by the government, others (coal) are left mostly to the free market.

A. America's Energy Profile

Today 95 percent of the nation's energy comes from coal, oil, and natural gas. America searches for new and more efficient sources of energy, both to increase supplies and to reduce pollution. Much of the research on new energy sources and efficiencies comes from the government in Washington.

Oil, accounting for half the energy Americans use, is one of nature's NONRENEWABLE RESOURCES. Wind or solar energy are renewable - using them once does not reduce the supply left for the future.

All of America's major sources of energy are nonrenewable. Moreover, half of the world's recoverable reserves of oil lie in the Middle East. America imports just over 50 percent of its annual consumption of oil, mostly from the Middle East. The United States is less dependent on foreign sources of oil than most European countries or Japan, however.

Coal, not oil, is America's most abundant fuel. While it accounts for 90 percent of the nation's energy resources, it accounts for just 20 percent of the energy used. One of the reasons is that it is the dirtiest energy source. It is dirty to mine, produces air-pollution when burned, and is linked to acid rain.

The most controversial energy source is nuclear power, which accounts for about 14 percent of America's energy profile. Environmentalists dislike nuclear power both because of the possibility of a radiation leak at a plant and because of the enormous difficulty of nuclear waste disposal. It is not as hard on the environment as coal, however, a fact pointed out by its advocates. With greater concerns about global warming and acid rain, and with new, safer designs for nuclear power plants, a resurgence of interest in this alternative may come in the future.

Finally, the contribution of renewable sources, solar energy, windmills, geothermal power, etc. - is likely to remain negligible until the nonrenewable sources become much more expensive.

B. Policy-making for Energy Issues

Energy issues present thorny problems for policy-makers to resolve. For example, there are a number of ways to generate electricity, but each creates problems. Coal, used for 44 percent of the nation's electricity, is abundant but dirty. Natural gas and petroleum, 29 percent of production, contribute to depletion of the ozone and petroleum is associated with oil spills. Nuclear power, 14 percent of production, produces radioactive waste. Hydroelectric power, 13 percent of production, requires flooding of large tracts of land. Policy-makers must decide the proper mix of sources of energy to use, balancing Americans' desire to have the lights come on and their concern for the environment.

IV. The Environment (707-716)

Politics infuses itself into even measures as popular in the abstract as protecting the environment. Pollution control has impacts on business, economic growth, and jobs, and thus activates interests that attempt to influence political choices.
A. Economic Growth and the Environment

Environmental controls figure prominently in the debate about local and state economic development. The federal system puts the states in competition for economic advantage. Business elites can often argue that stringent pollution control laws will drive businesses away by raising their costs. On the other hand, lax pollution control may make citizens unhappy and businesses may find it difficult to bring workers into the state to live. If tougher pollution controls will drive off business and industry is one of the questions policy-makers face. Easing this tension is the fact than many new high-tech and service industries create little pollution and desire clean environments.

B. Public concern about the Environment

Politicians know that pollution regulations can impact economic development, they also know that public sentiment is strongly in favor of cleaning up the environment. The strong public support for the environment is probably a greater influence on politicians than a state's interest in attracting business.

Americans are now much more concerned about the environment than they were ten years ago. In the spring of 1990 polls found three-quarters of all Americans saying that "we must protect the environment, even if it means increased government spending and higher taxes." Since the 1950s environmental groups have grown dramatically and have won important victories. Many of their goals are now part of the political mainstream.

C. Environmental Policies in America

The centerpiece of federal environmental policy is the NATIONAL ENVIRONMENTAL POLICY ACT (NEPA) passed in 1969. It requires ENVIRONMENTAL IMPACT STATEMENTS (EIS). Every time a government agency proposes to undertake a policy potentially disruptive to the natural environment, if must file an EIS with the Environmental Protection Agency, specifying what effects the policy could have. The filing of impact statements alerts environmentalists to proposed projects. Time and again, agencies have abandoned proposed projects to avoid prolonged court battles with environmental action groups.

The environmental movement has had other policy successes. Automotive pollution has gotten attention in the form of the CLEAN AIR ACT OF 1970. The WATER POLLUTION CONTROL ACT OF 1972 was intended to clean up the nation's lakes and rivers. And an agency, the ENVIRONMENTAL PROTECTION AGENCY (EPA), was created in 1970 to enforce all this environmental regulation.

The EPA also enforces the government's efforts to control and clean up toxic wastes. In response to increased pressure for dealing with toxins, Congress established a $1.6 billion SUPERFUND, funded by taxing chemical products. Renewed in the 1980s, the Superfund has a long way to go. The damage is often so serious that the sites may never be satisfactorily cleaned-up. Not only are they more difficult than previously thought to clean, there are many more of them than imagined.

D. Making Environmental Policy

Nobody is against a clean environment. It is a political question only because environmental concerns conflict with equally legitimate concerns about foreign trade, economic growth, and jobs. Policy-making concerning the environment essentially concerns two groups: those that pollute, and those who complain about the pollution. Those who pollute do so in the process of producing energy, jobs, wealth, and consumer products that Americans take for granted. Pollution was once seen as an inevitable product of economic growth - since Americans wanted jobs, they accepted the pollution that accompanied the businesses.
Environmental groups have become larger and more active in recent years, pressing for government action. With their entry into the policy process the nature of environmental policy-making changed. Issues that were once considered only from the point of view of jobs and economic growth are now much more controversial.

VI. Understanding Technology And Policy (716-717)

Technologically complex issues are difficult to understand for non-experts. They are so important, however, that most Americans do not want to leave them to "experts" to decide. Thus they pose special problems for a democracy.

A. Democracy and Technology

High-tech issues, more than any others, strain the limits of public participation in a democracy. Often groups of specialists are the only ones who seem qualified to make decisions. This has made the role of public interest groups even more vital. As with the environment, democratic policy-making for technological issues seems to rely heavily on group representation. Individual citizens are unlikely to have the information or the resources to participate meaningfully, because of the complexity of the debates. Well informed interest groups - associations of professionals and citizens - play an active role in making the complicated decisions which effect all citizens.

B. Technology Issues and the Size of Government

Americans have not been hesitant to call for government to play a greater role in high-technology issues. Citizens expect all levels of the government to become more active in protecting the environment, providing energy, and in other areas of high-technology. The aging of America's population means that health issues are going to gain in importance. Social Security enjoys broad public support and increasing demands. The FOOD AND DRUG ADMINISTRATION (FDA) also faces a rapidly increasing work load, as the health industry explores new horizons in genetics.

Americans want toxic wastes and oil spills cleaned up, nuclear plants inspected, and new energy sources explored. All these demands means a more active government role. Future growth, not decline, in the size of government is expected in all these areas.

DOING RESEARCH ON HIGH-TECH ISSUES

The emphasis given to the matters raised in this chapter is what makes your textbook unique among American government texts. It also is what makes it especially valuable, for these are the issues that are most likely to dominate the political agenda as your generation takes its turn at the helm of the nation. This makes these topics particularly valuable and appropriate for your research.

Perhaps nothing is more certain than that something will have to be done about the nation's health care delivery system. The pressures that the future will bring to bear will likely make it impossible to continue to tolerate its inefficiencies and gaps. Your research could investigate the alternative forms of national health policy that might be adopted, and the advantages and disadvantages of each. Alternatively, you might wish to explore the horizons of biomedical and genetic research, and discuss the technical and ethical dilemmas that these new frontiers pose for the policy process. How can we handle the questions of technologically extended life and the right to die, the questions raised by the expanding ability to extend fetal viability back toward the moment of conception, and the complications attendant with technologically assisted methods of conception itself? What are the possibilities and dangers of genetically altered bacteria, plants, and animals to the economy, the international security, even the make-up of the species? Lots of questions to answer.

The issue of the relative scarcity of energy aren't about to go away either. It is not certain when the day will actually come, but it seems certain that we must someday find a cheap renewable source of energy - or return to the lifestyle of our ancestors. You might wish to study the problems and possibilities of any one of the renewable sources of energy we have been experimenting with. They include everything from harnessing the wind or the earth's heat, to capturing (or recreating through fusion) the energy of the sun. More immediately, you may wish to discuss the problems associated with our present sources of energy and ways to handle them. We have lots of coal, but how can we make use of it without dirtying the air? How can we develop a dependable supply of oil that can be delivered without threat to the seas, the shores, and the life that they support? Can nuclear power plants be made adequately safe? If so, how can we deal with the wastes produced by such plants? Again, lots of research questions here.

The environment also poses vital questions worthy of your inquiry. What are the dimensions of the toxic waste problem and how can it be handled? What are the implications of acid raid, deforestation, global warming, or the depletion of the ozone layer - and is government capable of addressing such problems. If not, what are the implications? Is it because pluralistic democracy is an inappropriate decision making structure for saving the environment? Is it because we can no longer afford nation-states in an interdependent world? Assuming we can even draw the distinction, should we only worry about the quality of the environment that man directly experiences and is dependent on, or do all of nature's creatures have a right to have their habitat protected? What are the economic costs to man's economy and lifestyle of protecting all of mother nature's creatures? Are such costs worth the benefits?

Once again, your text provides some good jumping off places to look into this multitude of questions in its footnotes and "For Further Reading" section (pages 720-721.) Particularly thought provoking is William Ophuls' Ecology and the Politics of Scarcity which raises the question of whether our basic governmental form is appropriate to circumstances of scarcity and capable of being farsighted enough to prevent environmental catastrophe.

REVIEW TEST

Read through the Chapter Overview and review the "Reading for Content" questions if you haven't already done so. If you feel like you have achieved the learning objectives listed at the beginning of the chapter, you should be ready for the Review Test. Keep going over the Review Tests until you know them all - they are good preparation for exams.

1. The health care industry now consumes about _____ of the nation's gross national product.
    (a) 12 percent
    (b) 25 percent
    (c) 33 percent
    (d) 50 percent
Page 695

2. The average American has a life expectancy of _____ years.
    (a) 60
    (b) 65
    (c) 75
    (d) 85
Page 696

3. In terms of infant mortality rate -- the proportion of babies who do not survive their first year of life -- the United States is _____ among the world's nations.
    (a) eighteenth
    (b) tenth
    (c) fifth
    (d) first
Page 696

4. About _____ percent of the American population does have some form of health insurance.
   (a) 50
   (b) 65
   (c) 90
   (d) 98
Page 698

5. In 1986 and 1987, the Census Bureau reported that over a period of twenty eight months, _____ million Americans went without health insurance coverage part of the time.
   (a) 63
   (b) 34
   (c) 28
   (d) 11
Page 699

6. _____ percent of Americans polled said that the health care system was in need of fundamental change.
   (a) Fifty-two
   (b) Sixty-seven
   (c) Seventy-three
   (d) Eighty-nine
Page 699

7. In 1988, life expectancy for black males was _____ years.
   (a) 72.4
   (b) 69.9
   (c) 65.1
   (d) 59.3
Page 699

8. Just over _____ percent of the United States' total health bill is paid for by government sources.
   (a) 20
   (b) 40
   (c) 60
   (d) 80
Page 700

9. The U.S. government provides payments for about 41 percent of all health care. This includes all of the following EXCEPT:
   (a) Blue Cross Insurance.
   (b) Medicare.
   (c) veterans benefits.
   (d) Medicaid.
Page 701

10. Americans pay _____ percent of their health care costs

out of their own pocket.
    (a)   41
    (b)   32
    (c)   25
    (d)   14
Page 701

11. Truman was the first president to ask for _____, a compulsory insurance program to finance all Americans' medical care.
    (a)   national health insurance
    (b)   mandatory health welfare
    (c)   Medicare
    (d)   Medicaid
Page 701

12. The Medicaid program chiefly benefits _____ Americans.
    (a)   elderly
    (b)   poor
    (c)   wealthy
    (a)   all
Page 702

13. _____ percent of all Americans die either in hospitals or in nursing homes, most funded and regulated by the government.
    (a)   50
    (b)   60
    (c)   75
    (d)   90
Page 702

14. More than 80 thousand patients with problems due to kidney failure or end stage renal disease cost Medicare _____.
    (a)   two billion dollars annually
    (b)   90 million dollars annually
    (c)   10 million dollars annually
    (d)   3 million dollars annually
Page 703

15. In 1989, the government saved $ _____ dollars by forcing patients to exhaust their private insurance before allowing government programs to begin making payments.
    (a)   10 million
    (b)   90 million
    (c)   1.3 billion
    (d)   50 billion
Page 703

16. Today _____ percent of the nation's energy comes from coal, oil and natural gas.
    (a) 95
    (b) 75
    (c) 50
    (d) 40
Page 704

17. An example of a renewable resource, one that can be replenished by nature, would be all of the following EXCEPT:
    (a) water.
    (b) the wind.
    (c) oil.
    (d) solar energy.
Page 704

18. _____ alone controls much of the world's reserves of oil.
    (a) Saudi Arabia
    (b) Ethiopia
    (c) South Africa
    (d) Egypt
Page 704

19. America's dependence on foreign oil increased from less than _____ percent of demand in 1985 to _____ percent in 1990.
    (a) 22; 85
    (b) 33; 54
    (c) 46; 62
    (d) 54; 95
Page 704

20. An estimated _____ percent of the country's energy resources are in coal deposits, enough to last for hundreds of years.
    (a) 25
    (b) 50
    (c) 75
    (d) 90
Page 705

21. The most controversial energy source in America is nuclear power, which accounts for about _____ percent of America's energy profile.
    (a) 2
    (b) 9
    (c) 14
    (d) 22
Page 705

posts and employs _____ people.
   (a)   8,000
   (b)   16,000
   (c)   24,000
   (d)   160,000
Page 728

11. Jimmy Carter relied more on his national security advisor,
     _____, than he did his secretary of state.
   (a)   Hodding Carter III
   (b)   Edmund S. Muskie
   (c)   Bert Lance
   (d)   Zbigniew Brezinski
Page 729

12. Under President Reagan Secretary of State _____ became a
     major player in foreign policy.
   (a)   George Schultz
   (b)   Alexander M. Haig
   (c)   Oliver North
   (d)   Edwin Meese
Page 729

13. The Department of Defense was created after:
   (a)   the Spanish American War in 1898.
   (b)   World War I in 1918.
   (c)   World War II in 1946.
   (d)   the Korean War in 1953.
Page 729

14. The commanding officers of each of the armed services, plus a
     chair, constitute the:
   (a)   Joint Chiefs of Staff.
   (b)   National Security team.
   (c)   Pentagon.
   (d)   Department of Defense.
Page 730

15. Which of the following people were convicted of felony charges
     related to the diversion of funds and misleading Congress about
     the Iran/Contra scandal in 1986-87:
   (a)   Oliver North.
   (b)   Robert Bork.
   (c)   David Kennedy.
   (d)   William Casey.
Page 731

16. The _____ was created after World War II to coordinate American intelligence activities abroad.
   (a) National Security Council
   (b) Central Intelligence Agency
   (c) Office of Strategic Services (OSS)
   (d) MI-6
Page 731

17. _____ has sole authority to declare war, to raise and organize the armed forces and to appropriate funds for national security activities.
   (a) The president
   (b) Congress
   (c) The House of Representatives
   (d) The National Security Staff
Page 731

18. The famous _____ Doctrine reaffirmed America's inattention to Europe's problems and warned European nations to stay out of Latin America.
   (a) Monroe
   (b) Truman
   (c) Nixon
   (d) Reagan
Page 732

19. After World War II, _____ was unquestionably the dominant world power, both economically and militarily.
   (a) Great Britain
   (b) the Soviet Union
   (c) Germany
   (d) the United States
Page 732

20. Writing in Foreign Affairs in 1947, foreign policy strategist _____ proposed a policy of "containment" towards the Soviet Union.
   (a) MacGeorge Bundy
   (b) Dean Acheson
   (c) George F. Kennan
   (d) Chip Bohlen
Page 733

21. All of the following incidents led to the fueling of American fears of communist aggression EXCEPT:
   (a) the Marshall Plan.
   (b) Mao Tse-Tung's takeover of China.
   (c) the Soviet Union's successful testing of an atomic bomb.
   (d) the invasion of South Korea by communist North Korea
Page734

22. _____, secretary of state under President Einsenhower,

proclaimed a policy of "brinksmanship," in which the United States was to be prepared to use nuclear weapon to influence the actions of China and the Soviet Union.
- (a) Dean Acheson
- (b) Dean Rusk
- (c) James R. Byrnes
- (d) John Foster Dulles

Page 734

23. Senator _____ used evidence (real and manufactured) to accuse scores of prominent Americans of being Communists.
- (a) Robert A. Taft
- (b) Joseph R. McCarthy
- (c) Richard M. Nixon
- (c) Barry M. Goldwater

Page 734

24. The phrase 'military industrial complex' was coined by _____ to illustrate the interests shared by the armed services and defense contractors.
- (a) Norman Thomas
- (b) Henry A. Wallace
- (c) John F. Kennedy
- (d) Dwight D. Eisenhower

Page 734

25. Economist Seymour Melman wrote about _____, linking the military's drive to expand with the profit motives of private industry.
- (a) pentagon capitalism
- (b) iron triangles
- (c) multi-national corporations
- (d) zero-sum solutions

Page 734

26. In the 1950's, President _____ decided to aid the French effort to retain France's colonial possessions in Southeast Asia -- including Vietnam.
- (a) Truman
- (b) Eisenhower
- (c) Kennedy
- (d) Johnson

Page 735

27. In 1954, the French were defeated by the Viet Minh, led by _____, in a battle at Dien Bien Phu.
- (a) Dgo Diem
- (b) Ho Chi Minh
- (c) Chiang Kai-Shek
- (d) Mao Tse-Tung

Page 735

28. South Vietnam's capital, Saigon, finally fell to the North

433

Vietnamese Army in:
(a)   1968.
(b)   1973.
(c)   1975.
(d)   1979.
Page 736

29.   The term detente was popularized by Nixon's national security
      advisor, later secretary of state, _____.
      (a)   William Rogers
      (b)   Dr. Henry Kissinger
      (c)   Cyrus Vance
      (d)   Dr. Vilheim Strangelove
Page 736

30.   The first SALT treaty was signed in 1972 by _____ and
      was followed by negotiations for a second SALT treaty.
      (a)   Henry Kissinger
      (b)   Richard Nixon
      (c)   Gerald Ford
      (d)   Jimmy Carter
Page 736-737

31.   _____ was an implacable foe of "Red" China when he was
      a U.S. senator. But, he became the first U.S. president to
      visit the People's Republic of China and opened relations
      between the two countries.
      (a)   John F. Kennedy
      (b)   Lyndon B. Johnson
      (c)   Richard M. Nixon
      (d)   Gerald R. Ford
Page 737

32.   President Reagan proposed the largest peacetime defense
      spending increase in American history -- a five year defense
      buildup to cost:
      (a) $100 billion.
      (b) $750 billion.
      (c) $990 billion.
      (d) $1.5 trillion.
Page 737

33.   Forces of change in the late 1980's sparked by Soviet leader
      _____ led to a staggering wave of upheaval ending Communist
      regimes and barriers between Eastern and Western Europe.
      (a)   Leonid Brezhnev
      (b)   Mikhail Gorbachev
      (c)   Vasili Chernenko
      (d)   Yuri Andropov
Page 738-739

34. The reform movement in _____ suffered a serious setback
     when government forces crushed a demonstration by pro-democracy
     students in 1989.
     (a) China
     (b) Romania
     (c) East Germany
     (d) Poland
Page 739

35. _____ fight deep cuts in defense spending, pointing out that
     the Soviet Union retains a potent military capability and that
     America needs to maintain its readiness.
     (a) Liberals
     (b) Conservatives
     (c) Libertarians
     (d) Socialists
Page 742

36. To deter attack, the U.S. presently relies on a triad of
     nuclear weapons that include all of the following EXCEPT:
     (a) intercontinental ballistic missiles (ICBMs).
     (b) submarine-launched ballistic missiles (SLBMs).
     (c) strategic bombers.
     (d) the Strategic Defense Initiative (SDI), or "Star Wars."
Page 742

37. President Reagan's Secretary of Defense _____ was a major
     negotiator when persuading Congress to fund the MX missile. It
     was to be used as a bargaining tool with the Soviet Union.
     (a) Henry Kissinger
     (b) Caspar Weinberger
     (c) Michael Deaver
     (d) James Baker III
Page 745-746

38. Secretary of Defense Caspar Weinberger urged Congress to fund
     the MX missile in 1984. He stressed its importance as a
     bargaining chip so the Reagan administration could begin
     _____ with the Soviet Union.
     (a) Strategic Arms Limitation Talks (SALT)
     (b) Strategic Defense Initiatives
     (c) Strategic Arms Reduction Talks (START)
     (d) detente
Page 746

39. In 1948, the United Nations created the state of _____,
     intended as a homeland for Jews surviving World War II.
     (a) Palestine
     (b) Israel
     (c) Syria
     (d) Libya
Page 749

40. Following an oil glut, prices sank as supplies increased and

435

nations and businesses depending on oil income suffered a
severe recession. The recession encompassed all of the
following states, which are oil-producers, EXCEPT:
(a) Texas
(b) Oklahoma
(c) Louisiana
(d) Iowa
Page 758

BEFORE GOING ON

Ok - now your can use the answer key below to "grade" your very last
Review Test and see how you did. Go back and reread the relevant
passages on the indicated page for any you have missed just this one
last time. That's right -- there's a good student.

Answers:

1: a	11: d	21: a	31: c
2: c	12: a	22: d	32: d
3: b	13: c	23: b	33: b
4: c	24: a	24: d	34: a
5: d	15: a	25: a	35: b
6: a	16: b	26: a	36: d
7: b	17: b	27: b	37: b
8: b	18: a	28: c	38: c
9: c	19: d	29: b	39: b
10: c	20: c	30: b	40: d

Just one more thing to do. There they are on page 762 (a lot of
pages, huh?). Nail down those terms. Got them? Then you deserve
a treat. Reward yourself with your favorite sweet indulgence (don't
worry about the calories just this once), kick back and rest secure
in the knowledge that you are now "educated" on American government.
Puff up a little, few are. In fact, you are now of such status that
it would be inappropriate and presumptuous of me to suggest any more
"college words." You can pick your own!
Good luck with all the courses to come ..... click.